Good Queen Anne

*Appraising the Life and Reign
of the Last Stuart Monarch*

JUDITH LISSAUER CROMWELL

McFarland & Company, Inc., Publishers
Jefferson, North Carolina

ALSO BY JUDITH LISSAUER CROMWELL

Florence Nightingale, Feminist (McFarland, 2013)

*Dorothea Lieven: A Russian Princess in London
and Paris, 1785–1857* (McFarland, 2007)

Frontispiece: The House of Stuart

Names: Cromwell, Judith Lissauer, 1935– author.
Title: Good Queen Anne : appraising the life and reign of the
last Stuart monarch / Judith Lissauer Cromwell.
Description: Jefferson, North Carolina : McFarland & Company,
[2019] | Includes bibliographical references and index.
Identifiers: LCCN 2019000307 | ISBN 9781476676814
(softcover : acid free paper) ∞
Subjects: LCSH: Anne, Queen of Great Britain, 1665–1714. |
Queens—Great Britain—Biography. | Great Britain—History—
Anne, 1702–1714.
Classification: LCC DA495 .C76 2019 | DDC 941.06/9092 [B] —dc23
LC record available at https://lccn.loc.gov/2019000307

ISBN (print) 978-1-4766-7681-4
ISBN (ebook) 978-1-4766-3582-8

The front cover portrait of Queen Anne is by Michael Dahl, circa
1702, oil on canvas (© National Portrait Gallery, London)

Printed in the United States of America

*McFarland & Company, Inc., Publishers
Box 611, Jefferson, North Carolina 28640
www.mcfarlandpub.com*

Good Queen Anne

House of Stuart

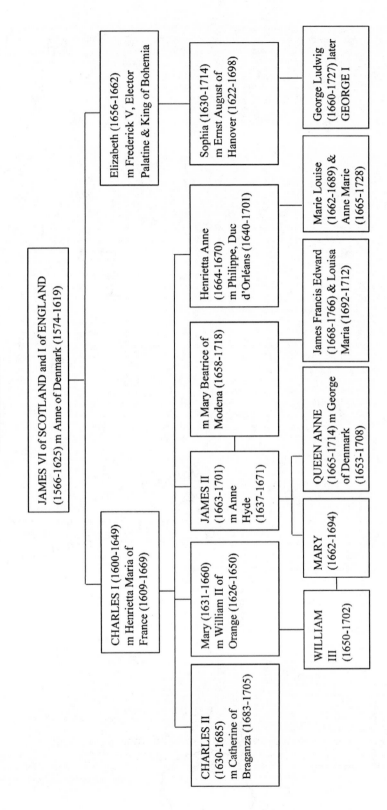

JAMES VI of SCOTLAND and I of ENGLAND (1566-1625) m Anne of Denmark (1574-1619)

Elizabeth (1656-1662) m Frederick V, Elector Palatine & King of Bohemia

Sophia (1630-1714) m Ernst August of Hanover (1622-1698)

George Ludwig (1660-1727) later GEORGE I

CHARLES I (1600-1649) m Henrietta Maria of France (1609-1669)

Henrietta Anne (1664-1670) m Philippe, Duc d'Orléans (1640-1701)

Marie Louise (1662-1689) & Anne Marie (1665-1728)

m Mary Beatrice of Modena (1658-1718)

James Francis Edward (1668-1766) & Louisa Maria (1692-1712)

Mary (1631-1660) m William II of Orange (1626-1650)

JAMES II (1663-1701) m Anne Hyde (1637-1671)

QUEEN ANNE (1665-1714) m George of Denmark (1653-1708)

MARY (1662-1694)

CHARLES II (1630-1685) m Catherine of Braganza (1683-1705)

WILLIAM III (1650-1702)

To my father, John Lissauer, MD

Table of Contents

Preface   1

ONE. "Something of majesty"   3

TWO. My Father the King   21

THREE. Revolution   30

FOUR. "Utmost respect for king and queen"   40

FIVE. "I will be obeyed"   52

SIX. "Nursing mother"   66

SEVEN. "A lady of intelligence and ambition"   79

EIGHT. "So glorious a victory"   90

NINE. Moderation   102

TEN. Queen Anne's War   112

ELEVEN. Great Britain   124

TWELVE. "A disagreeable noise"   135

THIRTEEN. "That good man"   148

FOURTEEN. Murdering Malplaquet   159

FIFTEEN. "We four must never part"   172

SIXTEEN. "I cannot change my resolution"   188

SEVENTEEN. Peace   202

EIGHTEEN. "The kindest of queens"   212

NINETEEN. The Last Stuart   220

Afterword: The Age of Anne   233

Appendix   237

Chapter Notes   241

Bibliography   253

Index   259

Preface

Of the few women who ruled England in their own right, Queen Anne is least known and most underrated. Yet, her brief reign (1702–1714) marked a glorious period in her country's history, a period in which Anne Stuart played a key part.

Her small island nation off the coast of continental Europe rose from the chaos of regicide, civil war, and revolution to the cusp of global supremacy, an advance mainly due to the men Anne chose to lead her army and government.

Queen Anne inherited the throne of a Protestant nation already committed to combat the hegemony of Europe's superpower, Catholic France. With their country on the verge of a momentous war, many of the new queen's subjects feared for their nation, now to be led by an unproven ruler, and a woman, no less. But this ailing female who, after seventeen pregnancies had failed in her most important duty—to provide her country with an heir, a female, moreover, without any formal training in statecraft, would prove the skeptics wrong.

In early youth, Anne did not anticipate becoming queen. Her uncle, King Charles II, as well as his brother and heir, Anne's father James, could still sire sons; besides, Anne had an older sister. At best, and because Anne's status as a royal princess meant her marriage must be subject to state concerns, she could expect compatibility and the joys of motherhood. But as a young woman, the prospect of becoming queen arose, especially when Princess Anne decided to preserve her Protestantism despite her Catholic father King James II's attempts to convert her, as well as the country.

"When she thinks herself in the right, she needs no advice to help her to be very firm and positive."[1] Anne had neither education in, nor experience of, government. But she grew up in a court notorious for depravity and deceit, a court where adders dangled from the trees, and alligators slithered underfoot. That taught the kind-hearted princess valuable lessons about life and the human psyche. She evolved into an astute head of state, deftly navigating the shoals of power politics and party polarity to steer a middle course between combative political parties.

The queen favored Tories over Whigs. But in order to keep the crown independent, and function as a unifying force, she preferred a mixed ministry, one made up of moderates from both the Whig and Tory parties. Anne thus acted as a brake on the ambitious men around her.

Despite her limitations, not the least of which consisted of the contemporary notion that females were inferior to men, Anne turned out to be an effective ruler. Pragmatism and a strong sense of duty resulted in sound decisions, even brave ones—after her predecessor King William III's death, Anne could easily have withdrawn from the Grand Alliance

1

against France; instead, she steadily supported her handpicked captain general, John Churchill, Duke of Marlborough, against the advice of several senior ministers.

A peace-loving woman, Anne backed the long, costly War of the Spanish Succession until she judged the time right to end it. The Peace of Utrecht, signed a year before the queen's death, gave Great Britain the means to create an empire that would give the world its language and its form of government.

An eruption of patriotism and approval greeted Anne's advent to the throne, and lasted throughout her reign. Anne's subjects knew that, like them, Their Queen had no foreign blood, like them she adhered to the Church of England; and that their welfare and her love of country would guide Anne's decisions.

Patriotism, piety, and a happy home life sustained Anne Stuart. Her marriage to Prince George of Denmark had its genesis in geopolitics. But Anne's "greatest blessing, on earth [consisted of the] entire union of affections and inclinations, between her and her royal consort; [they were a] perfect pattern of conjugal love."[2] George's death robbed Anne of "all that is dear to her, the only comfort of her life."[3]

Bereft, at an early age, of close female relatives, surrounded by sycophants, or, worse, spies, Anne yearned for a friend. She found one in Sarah Churchill, Duchess of Marlborough.

Both ambitious, the two young women were close, absorbed in domesticity but concerned about the future. Until fate made one of them queen.

That doomed the friendship. Consequently, Sarah concentrated her multiple memoirs on justifying herself and disparaging Anne. And since Sarah's papers constitute the most complete account of her long relationship with the queen, Sarah's pen left posterity a picture of Anne as a dim-witted, religious hypocrite constitutionally incapable of independent thought, a puppet in the hands of others.

My re-examination of archives, as well as the welter of often contradictory contemporary and later evidence, reveals a different story. Although some recent biographies have given Queen Anne the respect she deserves, their focus on political intricacies tends to overshadow everything else about the queen. My book differs because, for the first time, it tells Anne's Stuart's story from a nuanced perspective. Succinct, yet comprehensive and meticulously researched, *Good Queen Anne* paints a rounded portrait of a popular and sensible head of state, a loving and beloved wife, a woman who indulged in her passion for music, delighted in her gardens, enjoyed hunting and horse-racing; above all, a resolute female who succeeded in resolving the central conflict in her life: Anne Stuart overcame personal tragedy and physical frailty to become a revered and effective queen.

Good Queen Anne owes a debt of thanks to many. The British Library manuscript reading room librarians; Columbia University research librarians; and the facilities of the New York Public Library. My gratitude for permission to quote from their manuscripts to the British Library Board, the Morgan Library & Museum; for permission to use their images as illustrations to the British Museum Board, the National Portrait Gallery London, and the Royal Collection Trust. My appreciation, as always, for their support and forbearance, to my family and friends.

One

"Something of majesty"

I am very glad to hear that your indisposition of health is turned into a great belly. I hope you will have better luck with it than the duchess here had, who was brought to bed … of a girl."[1]—King Charles II to his favorite sister Henriette-Anne, Duchess of Orléans.

A bright April sun beamed from clear blue skies in the second year of the eighteenth century as Anne Stuart rode to Westminster Abbey in grand procession through London streets jammed with jubilant crowds, to take her coronation oath as Queen of England, Ireland, Scotland, and Wales. Aged thirty-seven, scarred emotionally and debilitated physically, Anne's "strong, but regular [featured] ruddy"[2] face and grey eyes held a serious expression. Wearing a dress of gold tissue encrusted with gems, over it a crimson velvet cloak lined with ermine and trimmed with gold galloon, her petticoat of gold tissue showed gold and silver lace between rows of diamonds. They also glittered in Anne's thick, shining, dark chestnut hair; large diamonds clustered over her crown. Anne's middle-sized figure still attractive, she looked every inch a queen.

After the ceremony, Anne "walked to the door of the Abbey with obliging looks and bows to all that saluted her and were spectators, which were prodigious numbers in scaffolds built in the Abbey"[3] and lining London streets. "The day concluded with bonfires, illuminations, ringing of bells, and other demonstrations of general satisfaction and joy."[4]

—∿—

Five years before Anne's birth a crucial event occurred in her country's history. Almost twenty years of civil war, regicide, and political chaos[5] ended with the return (1660) of Anne's uncle, Charles Stuart, from indigent exile to the full, rich glory of his crown.

King Charles II sired fourteen bastards[6] by seven different mothers, but his marriage proved barren. Since kings and queens determined the destiny of nations, the children of Charles's heir, his brother James, Duke of York and Albany, assumed importance.

Anne Stuart's father experienced the trauma of his country's revolution and his father King Charles I's execution early in life. James and the king, both prisoners of parliament, were often together. Charles impressed on his teen-age son the importance of loyalty and obedience to his older brother Charles; devotion to the Church of England; and the need to escape.

James did escape—dressed as a girl—to join his elder brother and his mother, Catholic Queen Henrietta Maria, living in exile at her nephew French King Louis XIV's court in Paris. The French court liked the "charming young prince, very handsome, very well made, and of fair complexion. [He] spoke French with admirable fluency [and his remarks] were much to the point."[7]

Over his strong-minded mother's objections, James volunteered to serve in the French army. He showed "undaunted courage, an inviolable attachment for his word, great economy in his affairs, hauteur, application, arrogance, each in their turn. [Scrupulously observing] the rules of duty and the laws of justice, [Anne Stuart's father also proved to be] a faithful friend and an implacable enemy."[8]

—⚬⚬—

Anne Stuart's mother, Anne Hyde, came from a cultured, but not noble, family. Her maternal grandfather, a prominent civil servant and mathematician, surrounded himself with scholars, and his daughter brought this refined ambiance to the home she created on marrying Edward Hyde. Their first child, Anne—her father's favorite and mother's mainstay—grew into a considerate and pious girl of "infinite character,"[9] with a stable, astute mind. Unusually well-read for a female of her time, witty[10] and attractive, Anne had a good figure and the slender, white hands that contemporaries considered integral to beauty.

Oxford educated lawyer Edward Hyde, scion of ancient minor nobility, rose to be senior advisor to King Charles I. That beleaguered monarch entrusted Hyde with escorting the young Prince of Wales (future King Charles II) into exile. Hence, like many Royalist families, the Hydes left England. They settled at Breda, (in the Dutch Republic) occupying a house Mary, Princess Royal of England (eldest daughter of Charles I) and widowed Princess of Orange (Princes of Orange were de facto heads of the Dutch government) provided rent free.

Taking a liking to Anne, the princess invited the seventeen-year-old to join her household as a maid of honor.[11] Hyde demurred. Despising the plotting, jealousies, and petty warfare that typified court life, he shrank from having his beloved daughter exposed to them; besides, Anne kept her mother company during Hyde's frequent absences from home in the course of his duties as young King Charles II's chancellor and chief advisor. So, since the king had little money to remunerate Hyde, Anne's father told the princess that exile had left him too poor to provide Anne with the funds necessary to sustain life at court. Princess Mary promised to assume the expense.

"I should be the worst of children if I were not very sensible of leaving so good a mother and leaving her so much alone, [Anne wrote her father. But] since you think it fit for me.... I shall very cheerfully submit to a life which I have not much desired."[12]

Beguiling and lively Anne Hyde became Princess Mary's favorite. As a result, when the princess decided to visit her mother, Dowager Queen Henrietta Maria, she took Anne to Paris in her entourage.

During this visit eighteen-year-old Anne Hyde and twenty-three-year-old James Stuart met, and fell in love. But unlike other females, she refused to enter his bed without marriage.

"In the height of his passion"[13] James subsequently visited his sister Princess Mary at her home in The Hague. There, via a secret, signed document, he promised Anne marriage. Their clandestine nuptials took place at Breda.

James told his brother. Aghast, Charles questioned what possible political benefit such a union could bring; moreover, with his restoration imminent and Charles still single, James's choice of a wife became significant for the succession. In tears, on his knees, James threatened to remain in exile unless Charles gave his blessing. Anne's pregnancy brought matters to a head. Charles made a virtue of necessity; he grudgingly accepted the marriage of Anne Stuart's parents.

—⚏—

"The Duke of York lately matched to my lord chancellor's [the king kept Hyde as chancellor and created him Earl of Clarendon] daughter which does not please many."[14] An understatement.

Fuming at her favorite son's mésalliance, Queen Mother Henrietta Maria hastened to England to stop an official re-marriage; James could do better for himself. Furious at her favorite maid of honor for marrying her brother, and in secret no less, Princess Mary followed her mother. Livid at his dearest child's deceit, Lord Clarendon swore to have Anne incarcerated in the Tower of London, the nation's leading state prison; and he vowed to petition parliament to have her executed for treason. (Anne's father also feared his enemies would accuse him of purposely insinuating his daughter into the royal family, then use this supposed audacity to engineer his fall.)

Eventually Clarendon's choler subsided, but not before adjuring his wife to confine Anne to her bedroom. Facing the street in front, Clarendon's grand London house backed onto a shady garden slanting gently down to the River Thames, the city's busiest and best-liked thoroughfare, bustling with every kind of craft from the royal barge, gaudy with gilding and gorgeous silk hangings to small single passenger boats, large vessels providing travelers with musical entertainment, and loaded barges moving laboriously to the open sea.

In the dulcet darkness of a summer night James, Duke of York, stealthily took a light rowboat downriver to Clarendon's imposing new house. Having tied up his craft at the ornate ironwork dock flanked by tall pillars, James mounted the stone steps where Anne's maid waited. Quickly and quietly she led him up the silent garden to Anne's room.

Hoping, meanwhile, to ingratiate themselves with the queen mother, princess royal, and king, four resourceful young members of the intrigue-ridden, dissolute restoration court concocted a plan. One

> boldly declared that he had had the honor of being upon the most intimate of terms with [Anne Hyde.] Of a sprightly and witty humor, [talented in] telling a story in the most entertaining manner, by the graceful and natural turn he could give it: he affirmed that he had found the critical minute in a certain closet built over the water, for a purpose very different from that of giving ease to the pains of love: that three or four swains had been witness to his happiness, and might perhaps have [witnessed] the happiness of many others, as the lady [often went] to that place, and was particularly delighted with it.[15]

Yes, James paid attention to his mother and sister; yes, he did waver in devotion to Anne, but James "found this last accusation greatly out of bounds, being convinced he himself had sufficient proofs to the contrary."[16]

At the same time King Charles asked a panel of bishops and judges to examine James and Anne's secret marriage contract. They agreed that according to the Gospel and English laws, the couple had married legally. This, Anne's pregnancy, and the king's wish to spare Clarendon the humiliation of having his daughter rejected, caused Charles to tell his brother, he "must drink as he brewed, and live with her whom he had made his wife."[17]

To halt any hint of irregularity, an Anglican chaplain married Anne Stuart's parents for the second time, and before witnesses. On this occasion James swore he had married Anne at Breda on November 24, 1659 and lived with her, in secrecy, as his wife.

Anne Hyde's labor began while the king and his council were meeting in her father's house. As a sign of respect for Anne's new royal status, Charles instantly ordered senior court ladies "of known honor and fidelity to the crown" to hurry to Anne's side. In between her "greatest pangs, and sometimes" during them, a high cleric asked Anne

> such questions as were thought fit for the occasion: 'whose the child was of which she was in labor,' whom she averred, with all protestation to be the duke's: 'Whether she had ever known any other man'; which she renounced with all vehemence, saying she was confident that the duke did not think she had; and being asked whether she was married to the duke she answered she was and there were witnesses enough. [This] abundantly satisfied the ladies who were present of her innocence from the reproach; and they were not reserved in their declaration of it.[18]

Anne Stuart's oldest brother, her parents' firstborn, soon died. Six more children would follow. Only two daughters survived childhood.

—⚬—

The new Duchess of York took up her royal duties with a natural air of majesty. Clever, polite, urbane and sensible, a kind and faithful friend to those she liked, but not gentle, Anne Hyde earned respect rather than love. Wit, fluency in French, patronage of painters, and a gift for attracting interesting people made her court the center of youth and beauty, amusement, polish and fashion; besides, it proved decorous and dignified in contrast to King Charles's informal, lively, generous yet corrupt court, seething with political and romantic plots, never mind sexual and other excesses (e.g., courtiers relieved themselves in any handy corner, and the king let his spaniels jump onto the dinner table to demolish leftover meat).

Anne Hyde, 1637–1671, Duchess of York, and James Stuart, 1633–1701, Duke of York, later King James II. Queen Anne's parents. Anne lost her mother at age six and later had to choose between loyalty to her father or to her religion. Artist: Sir Peter Lely. © National Portrait Gallery, London.

But no rivalry existed between the king's court held at Whitehall Palace and the Duke and Duchess of York's court held at their St. James's Palace residence; for the courts took place on different days of the week.

Besides, king and duchess soon became friends. For although Charles's paramours were all beauties, he valued wit and welcomed those who could amuse him; as well, the king liked to dance with his graceful sister-in-law. Charles's favor facilitated the duchess's acceptance.

"The Duke of York, in all things but his codpiece, [a cloth covering the genitals] is led by the nose by his wife."[19] James liked women. He indulged himself to the full. Mortified, Anne became jealous.

"The Duke of York is smitten in love with my Lady Chesterfield ... and so much, that the Duchess of York has complained to the king and her father." Consequently, while attending a play some weeks later, James and Anne showed "impertinent ... dalliances before the whole world, such as kissing of hands and leaning upon one another."[20]

Her husband's succession of lovers handed Anne Hyde a hold over him. Wiser, better-read, and more resolute than James, his duchess attended James's council meetings. She managed household expenses efficiently, giving herself a liberal allowance, much of which Anne spent on jewelry. And besides compensating for her husband's infidelities with gems, Anne overate. But obesity failed to weaken her poise or strength of character.

Suddenly, after a large meal, Anne died. She had reached age thirty-three. "Honored in power, [she had] much wit, much money, much esteem: she was full of unspeakable torture, in doubt of her religion, without the sacrament, or divine by her, like a poor wretch; none remembered her after one week, none sorry for her; she was tossed and flung about, and everyone did what they wanted with that stately carcass."[21]

Raised a strict Protestant, Anne Hyde had devoted her last year of life to rigorous contemplation and reading before converting to Roman Catholicism. Her body at death grossly fat and in an advanced state of decay, she apparently died of metastatic breast cancer.

Anne Hyde's favorite daughter and namesake, Princess Anne, had recently celebrated her sixth birthday.

—⟐—

"The best natured and best humored child in the world"[22] entered it on one of the coldest days in memory, February 6, 1665.

Baby Anne joined her three-year-old sister Mary and a brother in the royal nursery. The new arrival's immediate entourage included her wet nurse, a dresser, seamstress, necessary woman, footman, and three rockers. Surrounded by servants, many of them sycophants, or intent on their own gain, the little princess soon learned the difference between flatterers, and those who really had her interests at heart.

Like most aristocrats, Anne's parents did not involve themselves in the daily upbringing of their children. But James, Duke of York, doted on his pretty firstborn daughter; he played with Mary "like an ordinary private father."[23] The Duchess of York favored her namesake and look-alike. Anne Hyde enjoyed having her small daughter Anne's company at supper; they shared a new delicacy—hot chocolate—which King Charles's Portuguese wife had brought to England from her native country's Brazilian colony.

It soon became apparent that Princess Anne suffered from defluxion of the eyes, what contemporaries called watery eyes.[24]

English oculists in particular, hyped themselves into notoriety during this age of complete and unchecked quackery, not to mention primitive medical knowledge. Europe's finest physicians were at the Sorbonne's renowned faculty of medicine. Hence, a few months after Anne's third birthday, the royal yacht carried the shy, chubby, rosy-cheeked princess and her small household to Dieppe. From there a cavalcade of carriages conveyed Anne and her entourage to the home of her paternal grandmother, Dowager Queen Henrietta Maria, now living in a suburb of Paris. Daily, a Sorbonne eye specialist came to treat the princess.

Upon the dowager queen's sudden death, Anne's aunt, her father's youngest sister Henriette-Anne, Duchess of Orléans, welcomed the somewhat solemn little girl into her household. The "wittiest woman in France,"[25] her word a "caress for all those who approached her,"[26] charming, warmhearted Henriette-Anne lavished affection on her little niece; and Anne basked in the loving ambience of her cousins' nursery. But before Anne's caring aunt could bring her bashful niece out of her shell, she died. "One lost with her all the joy, all the amicability, and all the pleasures of the court."[27] Reluctant to leave his daughter in France without direct family supervision, James ordered five-year-old Anne, now fluent in French, but not necessarily cured of her eye affliction, to come home.

—⁑—

In her absence, Anne's parents had taken a critical step. They converted to Roman Catholicism. Despite his father's directive to stay loyal to the Church of England, James had been attracted to his mother's religion since his exile in France; as well, Henrietta Maria had urged her favorite son to convert. James, Duke of York openly practiced Catholicism. Anne Hyde's deathbed refusal to accept the sacrament from any Anglican prelate made her conversion public knowledge.

Roman Catholicism had precise meaning in England. Most people were Protestant.

They considered Catholicism a foreign concept headed by a foreign Papacy and buttressed by foreign despots (especially French King Louis XIV). The English public equated Protestantism with patriotism and English liberties. Every English Protestant, regardless of faction, saw Catholicism as an oppressive political system rather than as a religion per se.

As part of the restoration settlement, Charles had promised parliament to secure the Protestant succession. Sensitive, besides, to popular dread of a Catholic ruler, childless King Charles believed England would be more likely to tolerate Catholic James as its king if assured of Protestant queens to follow. But James, now a widower, might well raise Anne and her sister Mary as Catholics.

The king thus declared his nieces Children of State. As such, Charles could order Mary and Anne moved from James's care to their own household. At Richmond Palace, located outside London in a gentle valley created by the meandering Thames, the

Princess Anne at age three, with her spaniel. Painted in France during Anne's stay (1668–1670) with her paternal grandmother, then with her aunt, at Paris, to receive treatment for her eyes. Artist: unknown. Royal Collection Trust/©Her Majesty Queen Elizabeth II 2018.

girls, under the kindly but firm Protestant eye of their governess Lady Frances Villiers, and their religious instructor Bishop Compton, enjoyed the palace's large park, fruit-laden orchard, and cages of turtle doves.

Although the Duke of York knew his brother's failure to sire legitimate children enhanced Anne and Mary's importance, James hardly welcomed having his daughters reared in the Church of England. But he could not cavil because his open Catholicism brought about the king's action. Indeed, James had no choice. His father had drummed into him the need to obey his older brother Charles. Furthermore, James had other interests.

"Perpetually in one amour or another, without being very nice in his choice," James, according to his brother Charles, had his "mistresses given him by his priests for a penance."[28] Besides women, James's naval duties occupied him. The king had appointed his brother to be lord high admiral, an important position since their island nation not only relied on her navy for defense, but also, England's wealth depended on overseas trade carried in her merchant ships, and those vessels must be safeguarded. Princess Anne's father had known next to nothing about naval matters, but soon grew to understand all "concerns of the sea very particularly."[29]

—⁂—

The royal ménage at Richmond included six Villiers daughters, plus a few other well born girls who shared the princess's lessons and amusements. Anne especially liked plain, witty and elegant Barbara Villiers; gentle, cultured and lovely Frances Apsley; (eleven years her senior) and a vivacious, blue-eyed, golden-haired beauty, Sarah Jennings.

Five years older than Anne, Sarah's quick laugh, often shocking manners, and confident mien attracted and amused the shy six-year-old who had recently lost her mother, whose father paid her scant attention, and whose older sister preferred the company of her best friend. Anne saw Sarah as someone to admire, to want for a friend; Sarah's frankness, her refusal to flatter, made a welcome change from the sycophants who had always surrounded Anne, who made her aware of the need to cloak her feelings, to look askance on toadies. And Sarah, youngest of a large family, liked the role of older sister. "We used to play together when she was a child," Sarah later wrote. Even then, Anne expressed "particular fondness" for Sarah, an "inclination" that increased as the girls grew older. The princess "always distinguished me by the pleasure she took to honor me, preferably to others, with her conversation and confidence."[30]

Since Anne's sister Mary disliked Sarah's incisive, forthright attitude, Anne faced no competition for Sarah's affections from a prettier, livelier sibling who had always been their father's favorite, and because older and thus more accomplished, roused more admiration. Mary proved better than Anne at lessons, (except for French) danced more gracefully, played piano more melodiously, surpassed in painting and singing, and, because as firstborn Mary held precedence in succession to the throne, got more attention. True, the sisters were close, as sisters who are constant companions are apt to be, but sibling rivalry interfered with any deeper intimacy.

—⁂—

In Anne Stuart's day men occupied a higher plane than women; current wisdom considered males to have better minds, superior ability in conducting politics and business. A female's purpose in life consisted of marriage and motherhood. That concept determined Anne and Mary's education. Like other aristocratic girls, the princesses had no formal lessons in the classics, mathematics, geography, or history. But court life taught the girls about foreign wars and English politics; court protocol made them aware of their place in the succession to the throne; and every girl exposed to the restoration court knew of its depravity—Anne's father and uncle openly kept mistresses, Anne heard chitchat about maids of honor and their lovers.

The princesses had formal lessons in French and English composition; got a good grounding in English literature; were taught enough about contemporary culture to allow them to converse easily in society; learned sufficient arithmetic to allow management of their household accounts; and acquired feminine skills like drawing and needlework. Recurring defluxion of her eyes hampered Anne's ability to read by candlelight, which embarrassed her; blushing added to Anne's discomfiture.

She and Mary learned the courtly arts (dancing, singing, playing musical instruments, and acting). Regular participation in plays prepared the princesses for a time when they would always be on stage. At age ten, Anne made her first public appearance—in a play presented at court.

The "natural sweetness" of Princess Anne's voice so pleased her uncle Charles that the king ordered a famous actress to teach her elocution, "which she did with such success" that one heard Anne speak with "real pleasure." But the princess had a "bashfulness that made it very uneasy to herself to say much in public."[31]

Since his younger daughter "had an excellent ear, which qualified her for a true dancer, and gave her a great relish for music," the Duke of York hired music teachers—specialists in singing, harpsichord, guitar, and theory—for Anne. At age twelve she studied with a famous Italian virtuoso guitarist. The princess earned a reputation as "one of the best performers on the guitar."[32]

Anne developed a lifelong interest in music, both sacred and secular. But her favorite pastime consisted of accompanying her father in hunting the stag and fox at Richmond park or Windsor forest.

Religion took precedence in Anne and Mary's education. Their tutor, London's Bishop Henry Compton, had excellent anti–Catholic credentials, if less than stellar erudition. He gave the girls thorough training in the Protestant religion, impressing on them that the Church of England constituted Christ's only true church; Roman Catholicism represented the world's most evil influence.

Anne truly believed in Anglicanism; it, in turn, solaced and supported her. The princess clung to her religion as an anchor in a childhood and adolescence that featured few.

—⚉—

Despite a lack of formal lessons in statecraft, Anne learned practicalities. She knew why her parents had spent their youth in exile. Like all her compatriots, the princess observed the anniversary of her grandfather Charles I's execution as a day of national mourning which, at the same time, illustrated the result of a ruler impeding popular will. And life at a court where snakes hung from the trees and crocodiles slunk under foot, taught Anne the value of discretion and bred in her a realistic outlook on the human psyche.

Of course, she heard chatter about the need for her father to remarry. With King Charles still childless, his brother and heir, James, Duke of York, must fulfill his duty and produce a legitimate son to perpetuate the Stuart line.

I have "provided a playfellow for"[33] you, James told his eleven-year-old daughter Mary. Having scoured continental courts to find the Duke of York an appropriate (Catholic) bride, England's envoy, ably abetted by Europe's leading lay Catholic, the French king, settled on fourteen-year-old Mary Beatrice d'Este, sister to the ruler of Modena, one of Italy's independent duchies. Intelligent and witty, educated by nuns in Latin and French, believing she had a vocation and planning to enter a convent, Mary Beatrice agreed to marry a stranger three times her age only at the Pope's urging—she must be a beacon for Roman Catholicism in England.

Their father's remarriage signaled Anne and Mary's return from Richmond to St. James's Palace, traditional residence of the heir to the throne. There, willowy, attractive Mary Beatrice, with her fair complexion, jet black hair, and lovely, large, dark eyes created a lively young court. Anne and her sister joined in games like hide-and-seek, pelted each other and their step-mother with snow balls; walked in St. James's park which King Charles had stocked with animals from all over the world, besides turning three stagnant ponds into one long lake where the king bred a large variety of ducks; and, on fine summer evenings, joined their uncle and his court at playing bowls in the garden beneath the palace windows.

The new Duchess of York liked playing with her step-daughters. But the young woman's ardent Catholicism, plus her potential as a mother of sons who would precede Mary and Anne in succession to the throne, thwarted development of a close relationship.

—m—

Politics now invaded Anne's adolescence. To polish his Protestant credentials in the eyes of his subjects, who, not without reason suspected their king of Catholic leanings, to further allay public fears by distancing himself from France, Charles overrode his brother James's strenuous objections. The king agreed that Anne's fifteen-year-old sister Mary marry her first cousin, Protestant Prince William of Orange, son of Charles and James's late sister Princess Mary. Stadtholder (ruler) of Holland,[34] locked in a lifelong struggle against French violation of Dutch territory, William, currently visiting the English court, wanted the match.

Tall, slender, vivacious Mary, with her large, almond-shaped eyes and glowing white skin greeted the news of her abrupt betrothal to short, austere and ugly, twenty-seven-year-old William by shedding copious tears. And James's obvious dislike of William did nothing to ease Mary's reaction. Her tears continued to fall during the hastily arranged marriage ceremony, immediately after which William took his weeping wife home to The Hague.

Anne could not attend her sister's wedding. Like many at the palace, she had small-pox. Lying on her big four poster bed, auburn curls clustering damply about her flushed face, Anne suffered fever, dizziness, and delirium. "Her highness requested me [her tutor-chaplain] not to leave her but come often."[35] James visited daily and, so as not to upset Mary further, or Anne at all, "commanded that her sister's departure should be concealed from her; wherefore there was a feigned message sent every morning from the princess [Mary] to her highness to know how she did."[36]

"Perfectly recovered" after two weeks, with no scars to spoil her smooth complexion, Anne asked her chaplain "to give God thanks in her chamber for safe recovery; at which time she gave two guineas to bestow on the poor."[37]

James personally broke the news of Mary's departure, which Anne "appeared to bear very patiently."[38] "I can never express myself in words,"[39] Anne would later admit.

The smallpox outbreak killed Anne's caring governess, Lady Villiers. The princess had already lost mother, grandmother, and aunt. Her sister Mary had moved to a foreign country. Anne's step-mother Mary Beatrice did not fill the void. Indeed, the princess and Mary Beatrice were never intimate. The lovely, spirited Duchess of York condescended to Anne as the daughter of a commoner, and overshadowed the shy, tongue-tied teenager. Nonetheless, they never quarreled; for, "good nature predominated in her [Anne's] temper."[40]

—⁂—

Shortly after Anne and her stepmother returned from a lightning descent on The Hague (Mary Beatrice wanted to see one of Europe's finest cities, Anne wanted to see her sister Mary), a defrocked Anglican priest (Titus Oates) concocted the existence of a Popish Plot—to murder King Charles so that James, Duke of York could lead Catholic French and Irish armies into England to erase Protestantism. The Plot had enough verifiable detail to drive London's volatile mob into anti–Catholic frenzy, let alone fan national fears of Jesuit plots, especially after the murder of an investigating judge, and information that James's secretary and Louis XIV's Jesuit confessor were corresponding. Public dislike of James escalated; plus, his young Catholic wife did James no good because if Mary Beatrice had a son, the boy would precede Protestant princesses Mary and Anne in the succession.

Parliament seemed ready to exclude James from the throne. The Exclusionists, and those suspicious of king, Catholics, and France, were called Whigs. The parliamentary Whig party drew its main strength from landed magnates and city merchants. Those loyal to king and Church, nicknamed Tories, generally consisted of lesser aristocracy and country squires.

To escape any such draconian measure as parliament excluding James from succeeding him, Charles ordered his brother to leave the country for a time. James planned to take Anne with him to Brussels, capital of the Catholic Spanish Netherlands. But since the king feared Anne's religion might be compromised, he ordered her to stay in England.

The princess had a "good heart, thank God, or else it would have been down long ago."[41] Although disconsolate, she knew state interests came first. Protestantism must be protected at the expense of personal preference.

After a year at Brussels, James convinced Charles to let Anne join him. The York family—James, Mary Beatrice, Anne, and her little half-sister Isabella—lived in harmony. James and Mary Beatrice refrained from trying to convert Anne, not only because Anglican chaplains accompanied her, but also because she proved firm in her Protestant faith.

"All the fine churches & monasteries you know I must not see so can give you no good account of them," fourteen-year-old Anne wrote her friend Frances Apsley. "But those things which I must needs see, [such as] their images which are in every shop & corner of the street the more I hear of that religion, the more I dislike it."[42]

Anne judged Brussels a "great and fine town," and although the streets were not as clean as in Holland, they were not "so dirty as ours" even if they did have "odd kinds of smells." The "very pretty" park did not measure up to London's St. James park. Anne's hotel proved better than expected, people were extremely polite, and she had gone, incognito, to the court see a ball that "I liked very well." As for the fireworks, dancing, and celebrations in honor of the Spanish king's marriage to Anne's cousin and childhood play-mate, the Princess of Orléans, they far surpassed expectations. And at another ball Anne judged the "lemonade, cinnamon water and chocolate sweetmeats all very good."[43]

—⁂—

Her uncle Charles, meanwhile, agreed to let James move to his kingdom of Scot-land.[44] But Charles ordered Anne and Isabella back to London. Anne had reached the marriageable age of fifteen. State considerations would now dictate the most important decision of her life.

Marriage discussions took place with Sophia, Electress of Hanover (James I's grand-daughter; Charles and James's first cousin) for the hand of her son Electoral Prince George, who had recently visited London as part of his Grand Tour. George met Anne briefly. She liked him. But while the Exclusion (of James from the throne) Crisis persisted, Charles and James agreed on the wisdom of postponing the choice of a husband for Anne.

King Charles, meanwhile, had refused to convene parliament because he feared the lower (elected) house of England's bicameral legislature, the house of commons, would pass an Exclusion bill. Financial straits then forced the king to summon the legislature. (Only the house of commons had the power to levy and collect taxes.) The Commons promptly confirmed the king's fear. But the upper (hereditary) house of lords, which had the power to veto bills passed by the Commons, rejected the Exclusion bill.

To complicate matters, the death Anne's small half-sister Isabella fortified the belief that James and Mary Beatrice could not produce healthy children. Hence, various schemes for resolving the succession of Catholic James circulated. Charles floated the idea of mak-ing Protestant Mary and her husband William of Orange regents for James's lifetime; the parliamentary Whig party supported the Protestant Duke of Monmouth, Charles's eldest bastard; others wanted James and Mary (both with foreign spouses) set aside in Anne's favor. All this came to nothing except to make teenaged Anne aware of the chance that one day she might be queen.

King Charles's subjects dreaded a return to civil war. They rallied to the crown, including the vilified James, Duke of York. Hence, Charles heeded his brother's plea to let Anne join him in Scotland.

—⁂—

Brooding over the Scottish capital, battlemented Edinburgh Castle offered Princess Anne a life similar to that of London's St. James's Palace. "I ride every day & then I was often with the duchess [Mary Beatrice] & then I took a little time in my closet when I could catch it.... I do assure you I do love you dearly & not with that kind of love that I love all others who proffer themselves to be my friends," the princess assured her special friend Frances Apsley. "Love me as well as ever be as free with me as ever write me all the news you know send me the Gazette & other printed papers that are good & forgive [for not writing at length and often] & believe your"[45] Anne.

To her disappointment the terrain around Edinburgh precluded one of the princess's preferred pastimes—hunting with her father. But James and Mary Beatrice gave balls and card parties; indeed, basset provided Anne with daily diversion because, like her contemporaries of all classes and both sexes, she thought card-playing most entertaining and, like everyone else, gambled at various games.

Anne also enjoyed attending plays and acting in private theatricals, not to mention dancing country dances. And the princess learned to like tea, a novel and costly luxury introduced by Mary Beatrice.

Yet, Anne felt ill at ease. Although her father functioned as King Charles's deputy in Scotland, James knew he must secure his own eventual succession to the Scottish crown. This the duke accomplished via a compliant Scots parliament. James must then suppress anti–Stuart activity. That he achieved by persecuting Presbyterians who refused to accept the Anglicized Episcopal Church of Scotland. James condoned, even attended, barbaric tortures that horrified English Protestants regardless of their aversion to Presbyterianism. Living at the center of Edinburgh's court, Anne, to her dismay, saw religious zeal turn her kind, decent father into an instrument of oppression.

—m—

Life at Edinburgh, as at Brussels, gave the adolescent princess ample opportunity to refresh her childhood friendship with Sarah Jennings, now married and a member of Mary Beatrice's household. Indeed, Anne's sister Mary, when visiting her family at Brussels, had been jealous of Anne's growing preference for Sarah's company.

Youngest daughter of an old country gentry family, outspoken and self-assured, Sarah had never learned to curb her hot temper. At age thirteen she entered court as a maid of honor to Anne's step-mother. Long, heavy strawberry blond hair that her maid washed daily in honey-water to keep its shine, framed Sarah's face with its large, luminous blue eyes under perfectly shaped brows, "bee-stung" mouth, clear pink complexion, rounded chin, and straight, slightly tip-tilted nose.

Shrewder, maybe more moral than her fellow maids of honor, Sarah held herself aloof from the court's sexual dissipations. Hence, when she fell in love with a handsome, penniless young guardsman, Sarah treated John Churchill's attentions with caution; but, she did follow the prevailing custom by letting him tie her black velvet garters. "There is nothing so dainty as the English woman's chaussure, [noted the French ambassador.] Their shoes fit them with great nicety; their skirts are short, and their stockings very clean and tidy. English ladies do not mind showing a great deal of their legs, which are perfect pictures. Green stockings are most in vogue, with ... garters fashioned above the knees by diamond buckles."[46]

In the year that Princess Anne entered the world, John Churchill, scion of a long line of barristers and minor landowners, entered the Duke of York's household as a page through the good offices of his sister Arabella, James's longtime mistress. While reviewing elite troops at a military parade, James asked his adolescent page which profession John preferred. To join one of the regiments on display, John eagerly replied. Reminded of his own youthful enthusiasm for the army, James granted the request.

Posted overseas, John distinguished himself, soon becoming a colonel and senior liaison officer, his duties part military, part diplomatic. He returned to court as a gentleman of the bedchamber, a promotion his mistress bought for him.

A man of "noble and graceful appearance, [with] solid and clear understanding, [and] constant presence of mind, [John Churchill] knew the arts of living in a court beyond [any other man. He] "caressed all people with a soft and obliging deportment, [and stood] always ready to do good offices."[47]

Sarah's family opposed her marrying an impecunious soldier. Had she not been brought to court to marry a rich peer? One, to John's consternation, already paid Sarah marked attention. Concomitantly, the Churchills were pressuring their promising, ambitious son to marry a rich heiress. Hence, John offered Sarah love without marriage. But like Anne Hyde, mother of her friend Princess Anne, Sarah insisted on wedlock.

John wooed her for two years. Sarah then forced the issue by refusing to see him without a promise of marriage.

—◊◊◊—

Rosy-cheeked, seventeen-year-old Anne, meanwhile, with her large grey eyes, full-lipped sensual mouth, smooth complexion, and profusion of auburn highlighted brown curls, her beautiful voice, lovely white arms and slender hands, attracted some questionable attention at her uncle Charles's rumor-ridden court.

Husbands quaked when handsome Lord Mulgrave's roving eye alit on their wives. Twice Anne's age, this dashing, worldly rake took marked notice of the attractive princess whose father he admired. So much so that when politics forced James into exile at Brussels, Mulgrave felt "a strange impulse, a strong desire, (for what vain thoughts will not a muse inspire) to sing on lofty subjects, and to raise my own fame, by writing *James's* praise." The many versed paean concluded, "in those black times, when faction raging high, valor and innocence were forced to fly; with [the Duke of] *York* they fled."[48]

Anne's vigilant guardians prevented a harmless flirtation (rides in Windsor park, Mulgrave's poems, and sentimental letters) from developing further. Still, the attentions of a debonair, engaging, older man flattered the princess.

King Charles soon ended Mulgrave's activities by expelling him from court. But Mulgrave's conduct exposed Anne to potential disaster. The lax morals of the restoration court did not apply to females. Any lapse from the strict rules girdling them could mean ruin, especially for an unmarried princess; because any hint of scandal could compromise her virtue and thus, her value in the marriage market.

Anne invited criticism even by taking notice of Mulgrave's attentions. "I never knew what it was to be so vexed & troubled as I am at it, not but that I believe my sister very innocent however I am so nice upon the point of reputation that it makes me mad she should be exposed to such reports, & now what will not this insolent man say being provoked."[49] Exceedingly concerned she "should ever live to see the only sister I have in the world, the sister I love like my own life thus abused and wronged," Mary wrote in the exaggeratedly emotional style young women typically used when describing their feelings to a close female friend. She felt deserving of "some pity as well as my poor sister for all her afflictions I reckon as my own."[50]

Besides removing Mulgrave from Anne's orbit, the king dismissed her favorite lady-in-waiting, Katherine Cornwallis, for acting as go-between. (Charles also feared Catholic Cornwallis might rock the princess's Protestantism.) Consequently, Anne felt bereft. At the same time, maturity lessened the impact of the five-year age difference between her and Sarah Churchill.

Much together during childhood and adolescence when bashful, inarticulate Anne admired magnetic, beautiful Sarah's vivacity, self-assurance, and flow of amusing talk, while Sarah liked agreeable, easygoing Anne with her pleasant face and figure, beautiful voice, and fine hands, their friendship now blossomed with the blessing of Sarah's husband. John Churchill perceived potential value in the favor of a Protestant princess.

Anne's father and uncle, meanwhile, decided that regardless of rumor's hyperbole over the Mulgrave business, they must accelerate negotiations for the princess's marriage.

—⟨⟨⟨—

In the late seventeenth century reigning families embodied their nations; a marriageable daughter thus constituted a valuable pawn in the great international chess game, for alliances were often based on the union of a country's prince or a princess. Anne's older sister, Princess Mary, wife of Holland's Prince of Orange, had, after two miscarriages, failed to conceive; Anne's step-mother Mary Beatrice had, among several infant deaths, produced one daughter, now dead. Princess Anne's marriage, therefore, assumed significance.

English public opinion, plus King Charles's wish to dispel the stir caused by his suspected inclination towards Catholicism, not to mention James's open avowal of that religion, precluded Anne marrying a Catholic prince. But she must marry a prince agreeable to French King Louis XIV whose subsidy to Charles let him, for the most part, live without having to request funds from parliament.

Despite his aversion to another Protestant son-in-law, James submitted to "the king's

Prince George of Denmark, 1653–1708. Anne's favorite portrait of her husband, "the best of men who led the best of lives, the best of husbands to the best of wives." Anne and George were a "perfect pattern of conjugal love." His death robbed her of "the only comfort of her life." Artist: after John Riley, based on a 1687 work. © National Portrait Gallery, London.

pleasure in marrying his second daughter to a Protestant prince too, tho the late comportment of the Prince of Orange was no great encouragement to try what another son-in-law might prove of the same religion."[51] (William of Orange had intrigued in England and on the Continent to have his wife and himself supplant James in the succession.)

King Charles favored Prince George of Denmark, the Danish king's brother. Besides being Protestant, "having no dominions of his own to gratify, he would have nothing else in view, but the interest of England."[52]

Marriage negotiations began under the aegis of Louis XIV who wanted the navies of England and pro–French Denmark to curb Dutch sea power, source of his arch-rival Holland's wealth. Dutch William of Orange tried to stop the match. Aside from the French aspect, Prince George could become leader of England's Protestant party, thus vying with William (a prospect James welcomed). Then there were galling personal factors: as son and brother of a king, George would precede William at court; Charles and James gave Anne a substantial allowance but made no effort either to get Louis to restore to

William the wealthy Principality of Orange, or augment Mary's meager dowry to make up for her husband's loss. The royal brothers, in effect, penalized Mary, a compliant spouse, for her strong-willed husband's machinations.

Anne's uncle, hot-tempered but able Laurence Hyde, Earl of Rochester, her mother's brother, led the English marriage negotiations team. George and Anne must live in England; his household must have only English servants. If so, said the Danes, Anne and George should precede Mary and William in the succession. No. Charles and James refused to change what they deemed a divinely ordered sequence; but, George would be considered as an English prince of the blood royal.

The king then ordered a promising member of his court, to say nothing of his favorite tennis partner, to Denmark. Urbane Colonel John Churchill would escort Prince George, in state, to his new home.

—m—

This day ... the Prince of Denmark arrived at Whitehall." He "is a very comely person, fair hair, few pock holes in his visage, but of very decent and graceful behavior. The king and the duke are very much pleased with him."[53]

Anne accepted the news of her engagement without any outward sign of emotion. "I have not, [she owned] maybe, so good a way of expressing myself as some people have."[54] The shy, quiet princess had learned early in life to hide her thoughts. Still, Anne had reason to be pleased with her Danish prince.

When a princess married a foreign prince, she usually moved to her husband's court where she would be expected to assume his nationality in fact as well as in name. But since the Danish king already had a son, which assured his country's succession, Anne, unlike her sister Mary, need not acclimate to a strange land on her marriage. As well, Prince George could accede to Charles and James's demand that he live in England.

Aside from this salient fact, Anne and George had much in common. Both had lost parents early—Anne, her mother at age six; George, his father at seventeen. Both had older siblings of the same sex—pretty, lively, clever Mary had overshadowed Anne; his older brother the crown prince had overshadowed George. Both had grown up at court; both had traveled—Anne to the Netherlands and Scotland; George on the Grand Tour. Distantly related through Anne's great-grandmother (Princess Anne of Denmark, wife of James I) Anne and George shared a practical view of life. Both were good-natured, both were committed Protestants. (Lutheran George had refused the crown of Catholic Poland.)

As befitted the son of a king, George had an excellent education. It emphasized the military, as well as the naval concerns so crucial for a seafaring nation like Denmark.

The prince "showed himself brave"[55] on the battlefield. Engaged in war against Sweden, George's brother, King Christian, commanded the Danish army. The Swedes captured him. Prince George rallied the outnumbered, discouraged Danish cavalry, cut his way through Swedish troops, and rescued his brother.

George possessed a "mild and gentle [temper. He had made] "significant progress in mathematics, [had traveled throughout] France, Italy, and Germany. [As well, the prince] knew much more [than he could easily] express, for he spoke acquired languages ill and ungracefully."[56]

Certainly, a strong Danish accent that George never lost, (scarcely surprising since he married Anne at age thirty) encumbered his English. That and reticence caused some to think the prince stupid. Not so. When discussing state affairs in German or Danish, George showed knowledge, lucidity, and common sense.

Unlike her sister, Anne got to know her fiancé before they married. George visited Anne daily from "dinner to prayers" during their brief engagement, and after prayers until "half past four." Unless the princess expected company to play cards, she went to Whitehall at six to see Mary Beatrice, so that hour and a half constituted the only time she had to herself, for which Anne felt "glad." Afterwards, George "either comes to me or I go to him."[57]

—w—

Anne's marriage meant enlargement of her household. Several courtiers jockeyed for places. Since the salary for lady of the bedchamber[58] to Princess Anne exceeded that for maid of honor to Mary Beatrice, Duchess of York, and since Anne's favor would offer opportunities, Sarah and John Churchill agreed that Sarah suggest she transfer from Mary Beatrice's household to Anne's, so that the princess and Sarah could continue to enjoy their friendship on a daily basis.

The powerful Hyde family, however, sought to place one of theirs high in Anne's household. Her mother's brother Laurence Hyde, Lord Rochester, convinced James to appoint Anne's aunt, (wife of her mother's brother Henry Hyde, Lord Clarendon) first lady of the bedchamber.

> Let me beg you [again, Anne wrote Sarah, not to believe] I am at fault though I must confess you may have some reason to believe it because I gave you my word so often.... I have said all was possible for one to say, the only reason that kept me from telling it to you was because I was yet in hopes that I might prevail with the duke [James] & I will try once more, be he never so angry; but oh do not let this take away your kindness from me, for I assure you tis the greatest trouble in the world to me & I am sure you have not a faithfuller friend on earth nor that loves you better than I do, my eyes are full, I cannot say a word more. The trouble I am in is not to be expressed.[59]

Anne did prevail over appointing Sarah as her second lady of the bedchamber. James thought himself a generous father, "made no difficulties, but has promised me that I shall have you, which I assure you is a great joy to me: I should say a great deal for your kindness in offering it, but I am not good at compliments."[60]

The princess cloaked her dislike of Lady Clarendon, whose "discourse and manner, [Sarah noted, could not] possibly recommend her to so young a mistress, for she looked like a madwoman and talked like a scholar."[61] Hence, when Anne's uncle Clarendon decamped for the governorship of Ireland, the princess, heaving a sigh of relief, promptly appointed Sarah to Lady Clarendon's vacated position as first lady of the bedchamber.

When, initially, she "became this high favorite, [Sarah insisted that] flattery [would betray her] trust and gratitude to my greatest friend; [felt undeserving of] so much favor [unless she could risk its loss by] speaking the truth, [by putting Anne's] real interest [ahead of the princess's whims.] From this rule [Sarah] never swerved [although her] temper and notions in most things [differed] widely [from those of Anne. Nevertheless, the princess insisted on Sarah always] openly"[62] speaking her mind.

Since Anne understood and respected true friendship, she held frank communication between friends in high esteem, especially in the sycophantic climate of a court. The princess's liking for Sarah grew.

—w—

On a golden late July afternoon George and Anne went to the theatre. They emerged into the remains of a lovely summer sunset. The sky continued to glow as their coach conveyed the royal couple to St. James's Palace through cobbled streets filled with crowds cheering the imminent marriage of their princess to her attractive Protestant prince.

By ten pm, an extremely select company of richly and colorfully clad court nobles packed into the small, brightly lit Tudor chapel at St. James's Palace to witness the marriage. Claiming his royal prerogative, Anne's uncle, King Charles, gave the bride away. Clad in a splendid gown of French silk drawn in at the bodice by a gauzy silk scarf festooned with pearls and diamonds, full sleeves draped at the elbow showed the bride's elegant white forearms and hands to advantage. In "person and appearance very graceful, something of majesty in her look,"[63] the princess and her prince, "a universal gentleman ... whatever a good prince ought to be,"[64] exchanged their marriage vows.

The company then sat down to an elegant feast—pigeon pottage, hot pig and hot larded capons, sirloin of beef, cabbage pudding, periwinkles, partridges, ragout of sweetbreads, vegetables including Anne's favorite fresh green peas, sweets—cheese cakes and sugar cakes, French macaroons, orange pudding in puff pastry, Naples biscuits, and syllabubs, (sweetened milk or cream and egg white beaten to a froth and flavored with vanilla) all washed down with the finest French wines. As this repast drew to a close, Prince George, sitting next to his bride at one end of the table, rose to present her with a gold box containing a valuable pearl necklace, diamonds, and pendant earrings.

Entertainment followed; it included a paean to bride and groom, written especially for the occasion and set to music by the young, upcoming English composer Henry Purcell. Dancing concluded the festivities. Outside the palace, church bells pealed, bonfires crackled, and crowds reveled in royalty's provision of free wine and entertainments to mark Princess Anne's nuptials.

—◊◊◊—

Besides the liberal allowance King Charles settled on Anne, he bought her a spacious residence. Part of the Whitehall Palace complex, the Cockpit[65] had luxurious Tudor apartments overlooking St. James's park.

The princess employed a composer and band of private musicians for her entertainment, danced at court balls and masquerades, attended public concerts, operas, and theatres. She and her husband often indulged in their love of hunting, went riding together, dined in grand style, gambled at cards, and exchanged calls with friends. Still, Anne and George valued their privacy; neither could converse wittily but they talked easily together and with their close friends.

These, known as the Cockpit Circle, included Colonel John Berkeley (head of the princess's dragoon troupe) and his wife Barbara Villiers, one of Anne's childhood favorites; Sir Benjamin Bathurst (controller of Anne's household) and his wife Frances Apsley, another of the princess's old friends. And the Churchills.

Colonel John Churchill got on exceedingly well with Prince George, particularly as the prince showed keen interest in military matters. And John developed "a tenderness"[66] for Anne, who liked Sarah's husband, and grew to value his advice. "Of all the men that I ever knew in my life (and I knew him extremely well)," [John Churchill had the] graces [charisma] in the highest degree, not to say engrossed them; and, indeed, he got the most by them ... his manner was irresistible, by either man or woman."[67]

The Churchills introduced a close friend into the Cockpit Circle. Intimate with John Churchill since their teen years as pages at court, grave and taciturn Sidney Godolphin had risen to a senior treasury position; had already acquired a reputation as one of the most able men in government. The short and awkward widower (his wife had been maid of honor to Anne Hyde) with the long face hated sycophants, which instantly endeared Godolphin to the princess.

The newlyweds kept "very good hours," Anne wrote her sister Mary. They usually finished dinner by a quarter past one; from then until four, the prince stayed with his wife, unless he prepared to go riding at four. If Anne had no company, she went to chapel; if she had company, they played cards. After everybody left, she went to "prayers before supper & I have supped every night by nine o'clock. [Eleven] at latest & sometimes before [found the princess] abed."[68]

—⚶—

The Prince and Princess of Denmark's companionable lifestyle contrasted sharply with the quasi-separate routine of most upper-class couples. An easygoing husband, affable and kind, George lived so happily with his loving and attentive wife that, unlike many, if not most, royals, he never strayed from the bedroom he and Anne shared throughout their marriage. Anne's "greatest blessing, on earth [consisted of the] entire union of affections and inclinations, between her and her royal consort; [it] made them a perfect pattern of conjugal love."[69]

Fully conscious of her duty to produce a Protestant heir, let alone eager to experience the joys of motherhood, Anne felt elated to find herself pregnant. Extreme disappointment ensued with the birth of a dead daughter.

In the middle of her next pregnancy and on the princess's twentieth birthday, her uncle Charles, affectionately nicknamed The Merry Monarch, suddenly cast his country into misery. A massive stroke killed King Charles II. Up, down, and across the land, in town squares and on village greens, heralds, having hastily buttoned themselves into their royal blue liveries, raised their trumpets to proclaim the accession of King James II.

Two

My Father the King

"If he so persist (as I am confident he will)" in his "industry, sedulity, gravity, and great understanding & experience of affairs ... there could be nothing more desired, to accomplish our prosperity, but that he were of the national religion."[1]—Diarist John Evelyn

"I ... am resolved to undergo anything rather than change my religion. Nay, if it should come to such extremities, I will choose to live on alms rather than change."[2]—Princess Anne

Leafless trees dripped cold rain drops as sharp winds tossed their branches to and fro under a streaming sky when Princess Anne's father ascended the throne. (February 6, 1685) Anne now stood next in line to reign after her sister Mary. And since Mary had no children, hopes for perpetuation of the Stuart line rested with pregnant Anne, the senior Protestant royal residing in England.

To her gratification, King James II appointed Prince George to the privy council (formal advisory body) and cabinet council on foreign affairs. But mindful of his son-in-law Prince William of Orange's intrigues to advance his claim to the throne, James excluded George from his inner council. Still, even symbolic recognition of George's importance ignited William's envy, already fanned into flame because George, son and brother of hereditary Danish kings, ranked above William, a mere Dutch Stadtholder.

"It cannot be denied that the king was a very kind parent to Princess Anne: he inquired into her debts at the Christmas after his accession and took care to clear her of every one."[3] Since the princess and her husband both kept large households, and George's Danish income came slowly, if at all, Anne, who, like all court ladies, liked gambling at cards, again incurred debt despite careful household management. "I am sorry you have so ill luck at dice, yesterday, [the princess commiserated with her favorite lady-in-waiting Sarah Churchill,] "I won three hundred pounds but have lost almost half of it again this morning."[4]

The princess appealed to her uncle Laurence Hyde, Earl Rochester, now lord treasurer, to intercede with the king. Wary of rousing James's wrath, testy Rochester refused. The princess thus turned to one of her Cockpit Circle cronies, solemn Sidney Godolphin, recently promoted lord chamberlain to Queen Mary Beatrice. Sidney convinced James to pay "all she owed, without a word of reproach."[5] Her father also gave Princess Anne a liberal, (£32,000) annual allowance.[6]

Daughter of efficient household manager Anne Hyde and frugal James II, the princess handled her income so as to live in the style appropriate for a king's daughter.

She drove in Hyde Park; walked in the flower-scented Spring Garden, an enclosed park full of thickets and songbirds with, at its center, a small restaurant serving jam tarts, meats, and wine; enjoyed visits to opera and theatre plus, like all Londoners, liked water parties on the wide, sun-dappled Thames river. But as Protestant princess in a Catholic court, Anne kept "her court as private as could be consistent with her station."[7]

—ɯ—

Focused on domestic matters, particularly child-bearing, the paramount duty of a princess, Anne felt additional pressure to produce an heir because her sister and step-mother were childless. Without a mother, or any female relative she liked and trusted, Anne craved a friend.

The princess preferred to be alone with Sarah Churchill, which caused Sarah some conflict for she wanted time to supervise her children. They lived at the Churchill country property, Holywell House, St. Albans. Hence, Anne spent much time writing letters.

"I wondered a little that you did not come this afternoon having promised me you would & indeed it is but charity to come for I have a very melancholy time of it all alone but I will now say no more for the least kind word from my dear Lady Churchill[8] banishes all my anger & one kind look will make full amends for the ill fortune I have had in not seeing you all this day."[9]

Although an exacting mistress, Anne recognized Sarah's wish to be with her children, and gave her ample time to do so. Yet, impatient, impulsive Sarah chafed at the demanding, often tedious, lot of a lady-in-waiting, and protested about too much work. A sharp exchange ensued, ending with Anne's admission of "error," and promise not to "expect anything from you but what one friend may from another." She shouldered the expense of engaging an extra lady of the bedchamber "that you may have more ease and have no just cause to grow weary of me."[10]

Feeling affection for, and a sense of duty towards, Anne, Sarah assured the princess she reciprocated such sentiments of Anne's as—"I hope that next to Lord Churchill I may claim the first place in your heart."[11] Yet, proof is elusive. The princess obeyed Sarah's command to destroy her letters although Anne, later, declared that Sarah addressed her in the same exaggerated emotional style that young, aristocratic females like Anne used towards Sarah.

The princess and her contemporaries saw no harm in a close friendship between two women, for such friendships were considered platonic. In fact, both women and men admired, even idealized, passionate platonic love between two of the same sex, a concept the French philosopher Michel de Montaigne had popularized in his influential essay *On Friendship*, which praised an intimacy that possesses the soul.

Women often addressed each other in hyperbolic style. Anne described Sarah's absences "in appearance a sort of death."[12] All the princess wanted "*at any time* is to have as much of your company as I can without any inconvenience to yourself & I am sure knowing the kindness I have for you you cannot blame me."[13]

From infancy surrounded by toadies and self-seekers, the princess had developed a sound understanding of human nature. She valued loyalty and especially, friendship, which Anne saw as an extremely loving, sexually free, and emotionally close relationship. She begged Sarah not to "call me your highness at every word. [Sarah must be as] free with me" as friends should be with each other. The greatest proof of Sarah's friendship would consist of "telling me your mind freely in all things," which the princess begged her friend to do. And if Anne ever had the power to serve Sarah, "nobody would be more ready than myself."[14]

Montaigne's concept of friendship appealed to the princess. She recognized its duties and sought to abide by its laws. Resolved that her status should not stand in the way of reaching the personal satisfaction friendship could provide, Anne wanted even the "equality [she thought] belonged to it," Sarah tells us. The princess became uneasy when Sarah applied the "form and ceremony" due her rank; nor could Anne bear her friend using words that implied "distance or superiority."[15]

—⁓—

The Prince and Princess of Denmark's first child, a frail daughter christened Mary in the Protestant faith, greeted the world shortly after her grandfather King James II's coronation. Almost at once Anne fell ill with "the vapors [hysterics] which sometimes trouble women in her condition, [James wrote his son-in-law William.] This frighted us at first, but now, God be thanked, our fears are over. She took some remedies and has slept after them most of this afternoon and evening, and is in a very good way."[16]

Because she gave birth to a daughter, and a delicate one at that, Anne felt impelled to improve her fertility. So, putting her duty to perpetuate the Stuart line ahead of worry over her fragile baby, the princess betook herself to England's most fashionable spa, Tunbridge Wells, not too far from London.

Anne and her contemporaries trusted in the curative quality of spas, which, considering the abysmal state of medical science, not to mention the repulsive treatments physicians inflicted on their hapless patients, can readily be understood. So, while Sarah kept a vigilant eye on Anne's nursery, the princess slept "in quiet which else I should not have done," despite good news about the infant's welfare from her governess. "I rely more upon your goodness and sincerity to me than I could ever do upon her, [since] without any compliment I don't believe there is so much truth in anybody as there is in you and this I am sure ... there is none I have so great a value or kindness [for. Anne hoped] a little corner of your heart my Lord Churchill has left empty is mine."[17]

Tunbridge Wells developed into a spa on discovery of the healing effect of its chalybeate waters, best drunk straight from the spring since the water's mineral contents (salts of iron and manganese) evaporated if carried any distance. Several fine buildings thus surrounded the spacious wells where water bubbled out of the ground. The princess sipped the waters, visited smart drawing-rooms, and sauntered on the famous promenade with its tall trees, variety of small shops, and coffee houses also serving tea and Anne's favorite—hot chocolate.

In the middle of this pleasant regimen, her cousin and sometimes dancing partner at court balls, the handsome Protestant Duke of Monmouth, (King Charles II's eldest illegitimate son) returned to England from self-imposed exile claiming to be the true king. Monmouth accused his uncle James of poisoning Charles to gain the throne and make England Catholic.

Having landed in western England, Monmouth amassed enough of a volunteer army to give James cause to double the size of his. With John Churchill in de facto command, the king's army then proceeded to defeat Monmouth.[18]

King James decreed that for committing treason, his nephew Monmouth must be executed—a sentence that proved especially gruesome because the executioner failed five times to sever Monmouth's head with one stroke before finally succeeding. The king then wreaked revenge on the West Country. Chief Justice Jeffreys, infamous for his Bloody Assizes, sentenced hundreds of men who had joined Monmouth (many of them ignorant, unemployed farm workers) to be hung, drawn, and quartered, their corpses left to dangle by the roadside as a grisly example; other rebels were sent to West Indies plantations for a decade of forced, unpaid labor.

The king's conduct shocked his subjects, to say nothing of his daughter Anne. But she hid her views because the court bristled with distrust and anxiety. Spies abounded; some reported to William of Orange, seeking an opening to assert his claim to the English throne; others spied for James. Most courtiers plotted with both, for all feared the future. A spy living in Anne's household corresponded with one of Mary's entourage at The Hague, so she and William knew everything occurring in the Cockpit.

Anne's second child arrived a year after her first. Immediately before infant Anne Sophia's christening, King James went to visit his daughter "and the priest with him, who no sooner the princess saw but she fell a crying, the king seeing it, told her he came only as a fatherly visit and sent the priest away. Her chapel at Whitehall is taken away to have mass said there, and all the chaplains discharged."[19]

—⁂—

Over a hundred years before Anne's father became king, England broke with the Roman Catholic Church in order to be free of foreign fetters. The Church of England, therefore, stood for the nation's independence, the nation's very identity. And anti-popery constituted the strongest, most pervasive, and steadfast creed in English life and thought. Moreover, religion served national self-interest because commerce, vital to the nation's economy and naval power, affected everyone; but Catholic Spain restricted trade with the Americas and Indies, as did Catholic France with Europe and North America.

Despite Catholic James's shaky popularity while Duke of York, he ascended the throne peacefully because the public shrank from civil war. People believed James's first speech to parliament promising to rule by law and preserve the Church of England. Further, his subjects felt they could afford to be patient. At age fifty-four, (considered old at that time) James surely could not reign for long; his wife had no living children and James's successors were young Protestant princesses married to Protestant princes. Yet, within a year of his accession King James II made clear his intent to return his country to Catholicism.

James had been raised an Anglican. His adored father had adjured him to be faithful to the Church of England. The king justified his pro–Catholic policies by proclaiming the Anglican Church "so little removed from the Catholic that it should not be difficult to bring the majority of them [English citizens] to declare themselves openly … they are Roman Catholics without knowing it."[20] In expressing this sentiment James conveniently ignored a salient aspect of English Protestantism—his subjects equated it with their country's freedom from foreign influence.

Despite having crushed the Monmouth rebellion, James kept his large army. That violated peacetime policy. And alarmed Protestants. They feared the army might be used to repress them; for, had not Catholic King Louis XIV used his army to harass French (Protestant) Huguenots? But parliament let James keep his army, which he then expanded.

Parliament and the army's loyalty, Monmouth's speedy defeat and the revenge taken on his cohorts, gave the king enough security to embark on a course close to his heart. Britain must not only become Catholic, but James would turn himself into an absolute monarch like his French cousin.

King Louis dominated the Continent. He revoked the Edict of Nantes, which for the past hundred years had given Huguenots religious and civil liberties. Louis's action caused every English Protestant to dread Catholic dictatorship—a dread hardly eased by the flood of Huguenot émigrés seeking asylum in England. But because James's subjects believed a Protestant queen would surely soon succeed him, most continued to tolerate their king's alarming policies.

"When the designs of that bigoted unhappy prince came to be barefaced, [Princess Anne's bosom friend Sarah Churchill tells us] no wonder there were attempts made to draw his daughter into the measures of that court. [But all James's] endeavors were in vain."[21]

—∽∾—

Believing universal religious freedom would give Catholicism a chance to appeal, and to increase its power, James asked parliament to repeal the Test Acts, which barred Catholics from holding military or administrative positions. Parliament refused. The king resolved to de-fang the Acts. Having purged the judiciary, he had a test case brought before the high court: could the king grant an exemption excusing an individual, before he took office, from swearing, on oath, his denial of Catholicism's doctrine of transubstantiation? Yes.

James instantly appointed Catholics to senior government positions. Princess Anne expressed great surprise at hearing of four new privy councilors; she felt "very sorry [about their appointment because] it will give great countenance to those sort of people," the princess confided to Sarah. Whatever changes might be ahead, Anne hoped Sarah would "never forsake me, and I shall be happy."[22]

To make the crown financially independent, let alone facilitate the passage of laws promoting absolutism, the king next initiated a vigorous campaign to pack parliament. Although ultimately futile, James's attempt roused his subjects' fear of losing their liberties.

The king then attacked the Anglican Church. First, he barred prelates from preaching controversial sermons. This, several prominent churchmen chose to ignore. As official head of the Church of England, James created a special ecclesiastical commission empowered to dismiss recalcitrant clerics. It did.

Princess Anne fought back. She attended London churches when the most admired Protestant, or anti–Catholic, clerics preached. Aware of the practical political effect of royal ritual, Anne, as the sole royal attending Anglican services within the palace, (king and queen worshipped in their Catholic chapel) wore full royal regalia for her formal daily worship at the chapel royal, and insisted on receiving full royal honors. Further, since her father's Catholic chapel had its own musical establishment consisting mostly of foreigners, the princess commissioned popular English composer Henry Purcell to compose, for the Protestant service, symphony anthems featuring stringed instruments, soloists, and choir.

—∽∾—

Across the choppy slate-blue Channel, Princess Anne's brother-in-law, Prince William of Orange, worriedly watched developments in England; for if James killed faith in the crown, Mary—and William's—chance of ruling would end. To keep hope for Protestant rule alive, William thus urged his submissive wife to make sure her younger sister Anne, nominal head of the Protestant cause in England, stayed steadfast in her religion.

Already "on my guard [against James's conversion efforts, which were] more likely [to come via] fair means rather than force, [Anne fully expected to] be tormented"[23] if her father failed to harbor at least a little hope that eventually he would convert one of his daughters. Mary proved to be a difficult and less tempting target; for, she lived abroad and had no children. Anne lived close at hand, had two daughters, and could still produce a son. As well, Louis XIV and the Pope, to say nothing of James's Catholic wife Mary Beatrice, put constant pressure on the king to have Anne, her husband George, and their children converted to Catholicism.

According to Sarah, James used "no harshness" with his daughter. He merely gave Anne her mother's papers stating the reasons for her conversion, as well as some books, which, the king hoped, might make the princess change her religion. Had Anne been so inclined, Sarah remarked, her chaplains "were such [as could have said] but little in defense of their own religion, or to secure her against the pretenses of Popery."[24]

Sarah gave Anne scant support in her challenging role as Protestant princess in a Catholic court, for aside from seeing Protestantism as an integral part of being English, Sarah scorned organized religion, and mocked its ritual. But sensible, pious, committed Protestant Prince George did fortify his wife's loyalty to her faith.

Anne hoped her sister Mary believed "I will ever be firm to my religion whatever happens. [The princess hated the] principles of the Church of Rome [and accorded maximum possible value to Church of England doctrine. The] greatest reason in the world [justified Anne's faith for] wicked and dangerous [Church of Rome doctrine] directly [violated the Scriptures; Catholic ceremonies were] plain, downright idolatry. [Anne and Mary,] God be thanked, [belonged to] a pious and sincere [church that conformed in] all its principles to the Scriptures. [Their church taught only doctrine that qualified as] just, holy, and good, or … profitable to salvation." Certainly, Anne assured her sister, the Church of England constituted the "only true Church."[25]

James now outraged his Protestant subjects with an action that had been illegal for one hundred years—officially recognizing papal officials. Declaring himself above the law, the king formally received a papal nuncio (the Holy See's diplomatic representative) at court. The wealthy and powerful Protestant Duke of Somerset refused to attend this ceremony. When James took him to task, the duke replied, 'I am not above the law.' James banned him from court, and dismissed Somerset from all his offices.

The king then dissolved his uncooperative parliament.

Anne thought her father's actions "very much to be feared," because James's wish to revoke the Test Act and all other laws against Catholics, cloaked his intent "to bring in popery." The princess felt compelled, even obliged, to be frank with Mary "in all things … both as a friend and as a sister."[26]

—⁂—

On a steel grey, sleet-flooded winter's day, Anne suffered another miscarriage (her ladies blamed it on severe jolting in her coach, but the princess faulted a new French dance involving much jumping). Hardly had she recovered when illness threatened Prince George's life. Catholic hopes soared. George's death would free Anne to re-marry.

She nursed her husband devotedly, but no sooner had his doctors pronounced the prince out of danger when the Denmarks' younger (and healthier) daughter began to ail. "I am so worried about my poor child [that] I can hardly write half of what I want to tell you, for I must return at once to my poor child, as I am too nervous when away from [her, Anne wrote Mary.] I greatly fear the king's strong support of the Papists.… All we can do is pray that God will open the king's eyes."[27]

Raindrops crawled down the Cockpit's window-panes and a vicious wind whipped the Thames on Anne's twenty-second birthday, the day her two little girls died within hours of each other. "Both the children were opened; the eldest was all-consumed, [with smallpox] but the youngest very sound, and likely to live."[28]

"The good princess has taken her chastisement heavily; the first relief of that sorrow proceeded from the threatening of a greater, the prince being ill. I never heard any relation more moving than that of seeing them together. Sometimes they wept, sometimes they mourned; in a word, then sat silent, hand in hand; he sick in his bed, and she the carefullest nurse to him that can be imagined."[29]

—⁂—

By the end of cold, capricious April, George felt well enough to brave the long and rough sea passage to Denmark. He requested permission to leave England for a visit to his brother King Christian while the newly pregnant princess, unwilling to hazard a voyage to Denmark, proposed the brief Channel crossing to see her sister. Since James saw Anne as politically harmless, he gave consent. But Mary Beatrice and the king's Catholic counselors disagreed—the two Protestant princesses must not be allowed to discuss matters too delicate to commit to correspondence; William might well contrive to keep Anne in Holland; and her reunion with Mary would embolden England's Protestant party to urge the princesses jointly and officially to deplore the king's Catholic policy.

James changed his mind. Her father's refusal offended Anne. She resented the curb on her freedom as an Englishwoman; as well, the princess felt insulted in her status as royal.

During George's absence, Anne used her pregnancy (the fifth in under four years of marriage) as a pretext to retire from her father's court in London, where the city's thousands of domestic fires, as well as industrial furnaces, belched out clouds of enveloping, choking, coal smoke. The princess's move to the pure country air at Richmond also served to avoid James's conversion attempts, for with her prudent, good-natured, steadfastly Protestant husband away, Anne expected her father to talk to her about religion because he would "find me more alone"[30] than before.

Nonetheless, Anne could not entirely escape royal duties. The new papal nuncio must formally be presented to her. Refusal would mean an open break with James. The princess procrastinated as long as possible. She then made known that her reception of the nuncio represented a token of respect and submission to the king. Regardless, Catholics hoped the princess might convert; and if she had a son, he could be baptized a Catholic and the succession changed to bar barren Princess Mary of Orange.

—⁂—

Thus far, Anne wrote Mary from Richmond, their father had said nothing to her about religion. If he remained reticent on the subject until Prince George returned, Anne would start to hope "he will not do it at all."[31] Still, dread of James's proselytizing failed to prevent the princess from giving her father his due. She blamed his zeal on his Catholic cronies, especially Earl Sunderland.

A recent convert to Catholicism, Sunderland served as James's chief advisor. Working "with all his might to bring in popery … perpetually with the priests," Sunderland roused the king to excesses that, Anne judged, he would not undertake on his own. Matters had gone so far that if they persisted much longer, the princess believed soon, "no Protestant will be able to live here." James had refrained from confronting his daughter about religion, but she expected he would "every minute, and am resolved to undergo anything rather than change my religion."[32]

Mary must, Anne entreated, show her letters only to William. "For it is all treason that I have spoke." Besides, Sunderland watched her so closely "that I am afraid."[33]

Prince George marked his return from Denmark by bringing his wife to court to pay formal resects. Correct, efficient James had restored the royal court to fiscal solvency and a degree of decorum. But frequent balls, plays, and other entertainments failed to compensate for the Catholic king's unpopular policies, which estranged both Protestants and Royalists. Indeed, the Denmarks lost no time in retiring to Windsor for, Anne averred, country air suited her husband's weak lungs better than London smog. Actually, she wanted to avoid Catholic Sunderland's spying, never mind parental pressure to convert.

—⁓—

Mulling over whether to invade England, meanwhile, Prince William of Orange prepared his army and navy. Further, William dispatched his confidential advisor to London as special envoy; Everard Dijkvelt also served to convey correspondence between the royal sisters for every country's secret service opened letters sent through the regular post. Anne had "never ventured to speak [to Dijkvelt, she wrote Mary, not being] used to speak to people about business."[34]

Hence, the princess asked her friend Sarah's husband, John Churchill, someone Anne assured Mary she could trust, a "very honest man and good Protestant" besides, to talk to Dijkvelt for her, to ascertain what he had to say to her. The princess promised a reply at her earliest opportunity for she dared not "write anything by the post."[35]

William and Mary looked askance at Anne's intimates, questioned their suitability to surround the titular head of the Protestant interest in England. Since childhood Mary had disliked Sarah Churchill for her frankness; later, Mary deplored Sarah's open scorn for organized religion, doubted her faith; and when the York family lived in Brussels, with Sarah serving as Mary Beatrice's lady-in-waiting, Mary, on a visit to her relatives, watched Anne's partiality for Sarah with envious eyes. The princess now assured her sister that:

John Churchill, 1650–1722, later first Duke of Marlborough. The charismatic soldier-statesman had "a tenderness" for Anne, whom he could "not but love, and endeavor to serve, as long as I have life." Their friendship and mutual esteem made him her longest serving and most trusted counselor. Artist: possibly John Closterman, after a 1685–1690 painting by John Riley. © National Portrait Gallery, London.

nobody in the world has better notions of religion. [True, Sarah did not show herself to be as] strict as some are, nor does not keep such a bustle with religion [but] one sees so many saints mere devils that if one be a good Christian, the less show one makes, it is the better in my opinion.... As for moral principles, it is impossible to have better; and without that, all the lifting up of hands and eyes, and going often to church, will prove but a very lame devotion. [Further, Sarah hated] all the principles of the Church of Rome; so that as to this particular ... she will never change.[36]

John Churchill certainly showed himself "a very faithful servant to the king, [and James] very kind to him." But although John stood ready to obey the king in everything consistent with his religion, the princess thought "rather than change that, [Churchill would] lose all his places, and all that he has."[37]

"Under my own hand," John wrote William, that "my places and the king's favor I felt as naught, in comparison of the being true to my religion. In all things but this the king may command me." And since Anne had ordered John to speak with Dijkvelt, and "let him know her resolutions, so that he might let your highness and the princess, her sister, know that she was resolved, by the assistance of God, to suffer all extremities, even to death itself, rather than be brought to change her religion ... it may be a great ease to your highness and the princess to be satisfied that the Princess of Denmark is safe in the trusting of me."[38]

—⚍—

Anne went into labor during the eighth month of her fifth pregnancy only to be delivered of a stillborn son. Her first two miscarriages had been blamed on external causes like energetic dancing, but since Anne carried this baby almost to term, the loss assumed a worrisome, not to mention exceedingly distressing, aspect.

The princess failed to find comfort in her father and stepmother's sympathy. Mary Beatrice professed "a great deal of kindness [for Anne, who thought it] not real [because she never saw] proofs of it but rather the contrary." Still, the princess refused to complain, for so long as her stepmother did not "make the king unkind to me, I don't care what she is. [Anne] resolved always" to be very respectful to her father's wife, so as not to give Mary Beatrice "any just cause against me."[39]

The two women were never close. Mary Beatrice disdained Anne as the daughter of a commoner, "had repelled her by her pride, and spoke ill of her."[40]

The princess resented her step-mother's elevated rank. "The queen sent me a watch with her picture on it set with diamonds for which present I must return her most thankful acknowledgments, [Anne told Sarah,] but among friends I think I may say without being vain that the goddess may have showered down her favors on her poor vassals with more liberality."[41]

Denial of permission to visit her sister at The Hague earlier in the year had scarcely endeared Mary Beatrice to the princess; nor had the queen's attempts to convert her step-daughter to Catholicism. Besides, "everybody [believed the queen] pressed the king to be more violent than he would be of himself; which is not unlikely, for she is a very great bigot in her way, and one may see by her that she hates all Protestants."[42]

Antipathy and resentment combined with distress over her miscarriages, stillbirth, and the death of her two little daughters to breed in Anne a great dread. Her young stepmother might yet bear a healthy child.

At this juncture, astounding news consumed the court. Queen Mary Beatrice had become pregnant.

Three

Revolution

"No words can express the [Princess of Denmark's] rage at the queen's condition, she can dissimulate it to no one; and seeing ... the Catholic religion has a prospect of advancement, she affects more than ever, both in public and in private to show herself hostile to it."[1]—Tuscan envoy.

Anxious about at her father King James II's Catholicism at first, rather than alarmed, Princess Anne, like her compatriots, felt she could afford to be patient. But by the third year of James's reign (1688) what Anne saw as Queen Mary Beatrice's insidious foreign influence and firm Catholic hand behind James, frightened her. If the queen give birth to a boy, he would not only supersede his half-sisters in the succession, but also make Mary Beatrice mother of a Catholic Prince of Wales who could be counted on to perpetuate his father's Catholic policies. The queen's power, her sway over the king, would grow, and if James died during his son's minority, Mary Beatrice would be regent.

Equal dismay gripped the English public. Their Protestant princesses had no progeny; their king's pro–Catholic policies were extremely troubling. Protestants greeted the official confirmation of the queen's pregnancy with skepticism.

Mary Beatrice had, for the past several years, been in such an "ill state of health, that every winter brought her very near death. [Those surrounding the queen seemed sure that she,] who had buried all her children soon after they were born, and had now for several years ceased bearing, would have no more children."[2]

Every Protestant at court thought all matters concerning Mary Beatrice's "person were managed with mysterious secrecy; [only a] few Papists" were admitted. The queen failed to dress or undress with the usual ceremony. Princess Anne asked to feel her stomach for the baby's movement, "sometimes stayed by her even indecently long in the mornings, to see her rise,"[3] in order to give her stepmother her shift (undergarment). Indeed, Anne once dallied in Mary Beatrice's dressing room for so long that the queen threw a hairbrush at her.

Mary Beatrice never offered "any satisfaction ... by letter to the Princess of Orange, not to any of the ladies of quality ... whose word the world [would have believed. Were the queen really pregnant, she] "owned it to the king and herself, to the king's daughters, but most of all the infant she carried, to give such reasonable satisfaction, as might put an end to jealousy. [Mary Beatrice had opportunity to do] this every day. And her not doing it gave just grounds for suspicion."[4]

Catholic elation, not to mention confidence in the birth of a healthy male child, fanned the flames of rumor about a false pregnancy. Pamphlets[5] proliferated, many printed in Holland, home of Prince William of Orange and his wife, Anne's older sister Mary.

Ample reason existed to believe Mary Beatrice had a "false belly," Anne wrote her sister Mary. Were their stepmother truly with child, and especially in view of the many "stories and jests" about a false pregnancy, she should dispel all rumors by asking Anne, or some of her friends, to feel her stomach. Instead, whenever anybody mentioned Mary Beatrice being pregnant, she looked as if she "were afraid one should touch her"; if Anne happened to be present when Mary Beatrice changed her clothes, the latter went into the next room. This conduct caused the princess's suspicions. Anne believed that when her step-mother gave birth, no one would be "convinced it is her child, except it prove a daughter."[6]

Princess Anne had abundant motive for hoping Mary Beatrice's pregnancy would turn out to be a hoax. Not only would a hoax remove the possibility of a half-brother, and a Catholic to boot, but a hoax would relieve Anne of having to choose between loyalty to her father or fidelity to her faith. Hence, the princess could not "help thinking [Mary Beatrice's] great belly ... a little suspicious, [Anne wrote Mary.] Her being so positive it will be a son, and the principles of that religion being such that they will stick at nothing, be it never so wicked, if it will promote their interest, [made many fear] foul play [might be] intended."[7]

—⁓—

On a bleak morning in early March when the boughs of the bare brown trees glistened with rain, King James, buoyed by his queen's pregnancy and the chance of a son, issued his Declaration of Indulgence. It suspended the Test Act (avowal of Anglican faith so as to qualify for a government office or commission in the armed forces) and allowed public Catholic worship. Seven Anglican bishops formally protested the king's order and queried his right to disobey laws. James had them charged with seditious libel, then imprisoned in the Tower pending trial.

Anne's unease grew. "If the king invites you and the Prince of Orange to pay him a visit here, I think it would be better (if you can find an honest excuse) not to do it; for although I dare think the king could not have any evil intent against either one of you ... one cannot help being afraid.... I would be ecstatic to see you, but if you or the prince were to come, I would be terrified of some-thing bad happening to either one of you."[8]

—⁓—

On a bright but cold day with showers and a yellow sun sharing the sky, Princess Anne again miscarried. After a hiatus of some weeks her health, this time, failed to rebound, so Anne's doctors advised recuperation at a spa. The princess chose Bath, at its most beautiful, to say nothing of most fashionable, during an English May.

Situated in the pretty Avon river valley, on the southern edge of the scenic Cotswold hills, and about a hundred miles from London, Bath's bubbling geothermal hot springs had, since Roman times, benefited the sick from all over Europe. Besides being famous for furthering fertility, the Bath waters were also thought to cleanse and fortify the womb, as well as provide protection against miscarriage.

Over a six weeks course of treatment, women were advised to soak for long periods in the warm mineral waters, directed into comfortable bathing buildings via underground pipes; further, they should daily drink from one to three pints of hot water fresh from the pump. Anne planned to return to London in ample time to witness the birth of Mary Beatrice's baby, due in mid–July.

But before the princess could embark for home in her cumbersome carriage of black leather stretched over a wooden frame, embellished with big shining brass nails, the whole hung low between huge springs that made the vehicle sway with every jolt, (of which the badly rutted roads boasted many) let alone lumber along at five miles an hour despite the coachman having four swift horses at his command, Mary Beatrice gave birth to a healthy boy. (June 10, 1688)

—w—

Royal births involved the succession. Witnesses thus were essential. Most of those at the little prince's birth were Catholic. Key observers were absent. They included the Church of England's senior cleric; (imprisoned in the Tower for questioning the king's right to disobey laws) the Earls of Rochester and Clarendon; (privy councilors as well as uncles to Anne and Mary whose rights to the crown would be affected) the Dutch ambassador; (representing William of Orange) and, of course, Anne, still at Bath. She had not deliberately removed herself from London for the birth; Mary Beatrice either miscalculated her due date or gave birth prematurely. Regardless, the princess stood in the expedient position of being unable to confirm the birth's validity.

Anne "found herself much the better for the Bath"[9] although distressed at being "out of town during the queen's confinement, because now I cannot be sure the child is truly hers. Whether he is our brother, only God knows, for she has never taken the trouble to satisfy the world, nor given people any proof."[10]

Several courtiers swore that witnesses "stood at the end of the room" when Mary Beatrice went into labor. Lying on her richly carved, canopied four poster royal bed, which stood near a private staircase leading to an inner court, the bed's lavishly embroidered, crimson velvet curtains were "drawn close. [Only the midwife and an] underdresser … came within them. [To heat one side of the huge bed, a] warming pan was brought. But [no one opened it,] that it might be seen there was fire and nothing else in it." This, plus the bed's proximity to the staircase made many harbor "suspicion."[11]

Before the official bonfires celebrating the birth of a boy had burned out, Protestants believed he had been smuggled into the queen's bed in a warming pan for hot coals.

Anne agreed. And she thought it especially suspect that the queen had been brought to bed right after she heard of Anne's imminent return; besides, Mary Beatrice said the baby came at full term, when everybody knew "by her own reckoning, that she should have gone a month longer." Yes, the possibility of the baby being Mary Beatrice's did exist, Anne wrote Mary, "but where one believes it, a thousand do not. [Unless very plain proofs] *almost impossible now*, [were given, the princess vowed to be always among the] "unbelievers."[12]

—w—

To forestall another miscarriage should Anne again become pregnant, her doctors recommended she go "speedily to Tunbridge"[13] spa. The princess confessed relief at having to leave London where she felt uneasy at being with people that "every moment of one's life one must be dissembling with, [and the Catholics] so very insolent that it is insupportable to be living with them. [Besides, Anne disliked having to put on a] face of joy when one's heart has more cause to ache."[14]

But before Anne could go to England's most elegant spa, Mary gave her some work to do. The Princess of Orange had always doubted Mary Beatrice's pregnancy. A loyal and compliant wife, Mary did not covet the crown, but she knew her husband did; thus, his craving to be king would be thwarted if she proved less than assiduous in claiming her right to reign. Angry over her younger sister's absence when the queen gave birth, annoyed by Anne's hastily cobbled together account of the event, Mary now composed an exhaustive list of extremely explicit questions about the queen's labor and her son's birth.

Anne did her best to find out everything. Because she had not been present at the birth, the princess spoke with someone who had—a Protestant woman of the royal household who had witnessed both Mary and Anne's births and who would, besides, be "less likely to speak" about the princess's questioning her. Anne thought Mrs. Dawson could tell her as much as anybody could; asked Dawson every possible question; and took care to talk to Dawson "in such a manner" as not only to ascertain every detail, but also that "in case she should betray" Anne, the king and queen "might not be angry with me."[15]

Anne's replies to her sister's questions failed to present a compelling case against the Prince of Wales. (Please see Appendix.) But her letters during the queen's pregnancy gave William and Mary the pretext to believe what they wanted.

—◊◊◊—

Prince William made up his mind to move. Initially hesitant, William feared that his wife, with a better claim to the throne than his, might supplant him. But Mary convinced William that she would function solely in a submissive role. So, William told his Protestant backers in England that, if invited, he would come to their country to restore English liberty and protect the Protestant religion.

James, meanwhile, ignored his advisors; they pressed him to pardon the bishops he had imprisoned for challenging the Declaration of Indulgence (removing restraints on Catholics). Their trial acquitted the bishops. England reacted with more eruptions of spontaneous joy than had greeted the Prince of Wales's birth five days before.

Concomitantly, seven prominent Protestants (The Immortal Seven[16]) signed a letter inviting Prince William of Orange to England, with an army if needed, to reinstate English liberty, (rule of law under direction of a freely elected parliament) and uphold the Protestant religion. Ostensibly, therefore, William came to England to restore English freedoms; actually, he came for the crown.

Locked in a life-or-death struggle with France to protect Dutch territorial integrity and the commerce crucial to Holland's well-being, not to mention stop France's Catholic King Louis XIV from dominating Europe, William decided to assert Mary's birthright, while at the same time bring benefit to Holland. For William meant to add England's wealth and power to the anti–French coalition.

—◊◊◊—

As Princess Anne observed russet and gold leaves carpeting London parks, panic swept her country. The French, their hands gory with Huguenot blood, were coming, everyone said, so were the Irish. These Catholics would kill all Protestants, topple Church and parliament. Only Protestant William could save England.

Everybody expected William to set sail with the first favorable wind, so James's ministers urged the king to give formal proof of his son's legitimacy. "To satisfy the minds of my subjects, and to prevent this kingdom being engaged in blood and confusion,"[17] James summoned the queen dowager, (his brother Charles's widow) all peers and bishops, his entire privy council, (which included Anne's husband Prince George) plus London's mayor and aldermen to a special meeting to hear sworn testimony validating the Prince of Wales's birth.

James opened the meeting by announcing that "the princess would have been there; but being with child, and having been subject to miscarry, it was not safe for her to go out of the chamber."[18] Forty witnesses "of the highest rank, of the most unquestioned credit" then testified on oath to "the legitimacy of the prince."[19]

Since the king's meeting took place in mid–October, and Anne gave birth at the end of the following July, the princess could hardly have known she had conceived at this point. Anne feigned pregnancy as a ploy to avoid open conflict with her father. For the princess still persisted in refusing to state absolutely her belief in the legitimacy of her half-brother's birth—she had not witnessed it.

James ordered the privy council personally to present the evidence to his daughter. Anne told them their visit "was not necessary; for I have so much duty to the king, that his word must be more to me than these depositions."[20]

—⟋⟍⟋—

Princess Anne knew about William's plans well before the Prince of Wales's birth. She had expressed to Mary the hope that her sister would tell her friends what to "do if a change should occur, which it is to be feared it will, especially if Mansell [the royal sisters' code name for their father] has a son, as I conclude he will, there being reasons to fear this is a false pregnancy."[21]

The Denmarks had ample time to consider their options. Anne gained specific knowledge of William's intentions from speaking with his envoy to London, as well as with one of the chief conspirators—John Churchill, her close friend Sarah's husband and by now Anne's trusted advisor. Churchill coordinated Anne and George's moves with the main body of plotters. Sarah seconded her husband.

> Having on all occasions given you and my sister all imaginable assurances of the real friendship and kindness I have for you both, I hope it is not necessary for me to repeat anything of that kind, [Anne wrote William.]. I shall not trouble you with many compliments, only in short to assure you, that you have my wishes for your good success in this so just an undertaking; and I hope the prince will soon be with you, to let you see his readiness to join with you.[22]

"Having but little English, and being naturally modest," Prince George "made no considerable figure … in the reign of King James, till the increase of popery alarming the whole nation, he concurred with the rest of the Protestant nobility for the bringing over the Prince of Orange."[23]

—⟋⟍⟋—

Princess Anne confided to her "friendly and good-natured"[24] uncle Clarendon (Henry Hyde) that "she found the king much disordered about the preparations which were making in Holland."[25] William poured a steady stream of propaganda into England via his capable web of agents; many of his pamphlets cast doubt on Mary Beatrice's chastity and the Prince of Wales's legitimacy. As well, William quickly and efficiently organized and trained a large army, equipped his expanded navy for every eventuality.

King James had difficulty in accepting the truth of an impending attack. Rather than rallying his army in person and stirring English nationalism against the foreign invader, James confined himself to dismissing Catholics from prominent government and army posts, and appointing Protestants in their place. Most of these delighted their compatriots by declining to serve.

At the same time James's infant son took ill. Medical wisdom—if such one can call it—blamed breast milk. So, his doctors put the baby on a special diet; it consisted of a paste made of barley, flour, water, sugar, and a few currants. Of course, the little prince got worse. Try wine and emetic, said the medical specialists. The infant's illness persisted. In desperation, his doctors returned their patient to his wet nurse. He improved immediately; but, Protestants said the child had died and Catholics smuggled a healthy baby into his crib.

Prince George, meanwhile, received the new Danish envoy to London. He told the prince about the great invasion fleet gathering in Dutch ports, and the King of Denmark's contribution to both it and William's army. The envoy advised George that, as a former army officer, he should accept James's invitation to join him on the battlefield. Cognizant of military sentiment through his friendship with John Churchill, the prince replied that general hostility in the ranks precluded James relying on the army; hence, he, George, had decided to refuse formal command and join the army as a volunteer.

—⟋⟍⟋—

When news of Dutch embarkation arrived, Clarendon visited his niece.

ANNE: "The king seemed much disturbed, and very melancholy."
CLARENDON: It is a pity, no one will "take this opportunity of speaking freely and honestly to the king." But you could "say something to him, and ... beg him to confer with some of his old friends; who ... always served him faithfully."
ANNE: I never speak "to the king on business."
CLARENDON: The king "could not but take it well to see [your] royal highness so concerned for him."
ANNE: He has "no reason to doubt [my] concern."

Clarendon tried his utmost to persuade the princess to speak to her father—she might "possibly produce some good effect, and no ill could come of it." But Anne could not be convinced. The more Clarendon pressed, the "more reserved" she became, finally closing their conversation with a request to be excused to get dressed since it was "almost prayer time."[26]

Two days before William and his army landed in England, Anne's "obliging" uncle Clarendon, "most beloved of all the family,"[27] again tried to appeal to her filial feelings.

CLARENDON: Since the temporal and spiritual lords are going to address the king, "it would be seasonable to say something ... whereby he might see [your] concern for him."
ANNE: "The king did not love that [I] should meddle with anything, and ... the papists would let him do nothing."
CLARENDON: The king is your father and you know the duty owed him; you know "how very tender and kind he had been, [that] he had never given [you] any trouble about religion."
ANNE: "True."

She then "grew exceedingly uneasy,"[28] and excused herself to get dressed.

Princess Anne used evasions and silence to avoid open conflict with her uncle because she had already made her choice. "It was a great trouble to her to be forced to act such a part against"[29] her father. But Anne decided to put allegiance to religion and country, above loyalty and duty to parent.

—⁓—

William wanted to avoid direct military, or, indeed, any other, confrontation with James; rather, William sought to cast the king into such gloom that he would cede without a fight. James inadvertently cooperated. Instead of personally rallying his army, he dithered in London. That gave droves of prominent men who opposed the king, time to raise troops and join William.

When King James at last rode out of London to join the army, Prince George of Denmark and Major General John Churchill were in his entourage. Rumors instantly swept the court—Mary Beatrice, her son, and Anne were going to be conveyed to Portsmouth for easy passage to France; the princess would be forcibly taken to France as a hostage.

Churchill and several senior army officers lost little time in defecting to William. So, too, did Prince George—scarcely surprising for a man who had declined to be king of Catholic Poland, besides having recently resisted French and papal efforts to convert him.

> While the restless spirit of the enemies of the reformed religion, backed by the cruel zeal and prevailing power of France, justly alarm and unite all the Protestant Princes of Christendom and engage them in so vast an expense for the support of it, can I act so degenerate and mean a part as to deny my concurrence to such worthy endeavors?[30] The well-being of the Protestant religion [in England and all Europe] is that irrefutable and only cause that could come in competition with my duty and obligation to your majesty.[31]

Well aware that their husbands meant to join William, Anne and Sarah waited in London for confirmation, but did not intend to stay until James returned. Sarah "had reason enough to desire to get out of the way, since [her husband had] left the king, and gone over to [William. The princess] could not bear the thought of seeing her father."[32]

Late in the evening a foam-flecked horse with heaving flanks clattered into the palace courtyard. The breathless rider bore urgent instructions from the king: Mary Beatrice must have guards placed around the princess. Assuming her already asleep, the queen ordered a guard for Anne's rooms, but not her person. Further, James commanded Sarah Churchill's arrest. "Instead of proceeding instantly to the work by way of surprise, [the official responsible for carrying out this instruction] "suffered himself in complacence to be delayed by the princess for half an hour by her express desiring of it from him."[33]

James's orders confirmed Prince George and John Churchill's desertions. Hence, "without the least previous occasion for, or appearance of any discontent, [Princess Anne] went in her usual manner and time to bed,"[34] instructing her ladies not to call her until next morning.

Having dressed herself hastily, Anne, with Sarah and another trusted lady-in-waiting, crept along a passage, "as is concluded by the door being found but single locked that way, leading to the stool-room [toilet] down a pair of small back stairs, by which the necessary woman uses to go in and out for the cleaning of that room."[35] The three women then descended a wooden staircase Sarah had earlier ordered built at Anne's behest, connecting the princess's rooms to Sarah's because the latter had unguarded exit from the Cockpit.

The ladies now must walk a little way in the soft, windy darkness to where they knew Bishop Compton (Anne's former religious tutor and one of the Immortal Seven who had invited William to England) would be waiting with an unobtrusive hackney coach. An armed and mounted escort stood quietly in the nearby shadows.

Despite being Europe's largest, most populous, and splendid city, London's streets were filled with rotting trash, to say nothing of human excrement and urine dumped out of windows at night; by day the sheep, cattle, pigs and poultry led through the fetid streets to slaughter, contributed their droppings to the stinking mess. Hence, Anne and her ladies held their skirts high with one hand while with the other they deployed the delicate, perfumed, cotton handkerchiefs that wealthy Londoners habitually held over their noses and mouths when venturing outdoors.

One of Anne's fine, high-heeled satin shoes got stuck in the filth. Rather than soiling the perfumed gloves she, like all fastidious Londoners wore to ameliorate the city's malodorous streets, Anne laughingly left her shoe in the muck and hopped along on one foot. Fearing for his precious charge, a nobleman in her escort pulled off his embroidered, scented leather gauntlet and asked the princess's permission to draw it over her foot. Yes. Amidst much mirth from all, he did.

—m—

Next morning, Anne's bedchamber woman entered her room "to call her, and receiving no answer, [she opened the bed curtains to find] the princess gone, and the bed cold, with all her yesterday's clothes, even her stockings and shoes left behind."[36] Panic seized the palace and quickly swept through London—"papists had murdered"[37] the princess—or—kidnapped her with evil intent.

Two days later, newspapers printed the letter Anne left for Mary Beatrice. "Never was anyone in such an unhappy condition, so divided between duty and affection to a father and a husband [who remained faithful to his religion.] Therefore, I know not what I must do, but to follow one to preserve the other."[38]

The princess had left London, to "avoid the king's displeasure," which she felt unable to bear either against the prince or herself, Anne continued. She would go far enough away so as not to return before hearing the "happy news of a reconcilement." Confident Prince George did not leave James with any other purpose than to "use all possible means for his preservation," Anne hoped Mary Beatrice would believe her "incapable of following him for any other end."[39]

Having vindicated herself, Anne could not resist noting the general desertion "of nobility and gentry, *who own to have no other end, than to prevail with the king to secure their religion*; which they saw so much in danger by the violent counsels of the priests, who, to promote their own religion, did not care to what danger they exposed the king."[40]

He arrived in London to be met with the news of Anne's flight. James "burst into tears, and in a transport of nature cried out, 'God help me, my own children have forsaken me'"[41] That, plus the defection of men like Churchill, whom he trusted, decided the king to send his wife and son to safety in France. With his father's decapitation etched on his psyche, James promised to follow soon.

The king's friends warned him against fleeing, for in England James remained king in fact; once out of England he would be king only in law. "What would you have me do? My children abandoned me. My army deserted me, those that I raised from nothing [Churchill] have done the same, what can I expect from those I have done little or nothing for"?[42] Fearing for his life if he stayed, King James II, on a moonless and stormy night, left for France with a few friends while his Dutch guards looked the other way.[43]

—◊—

Princess Anne agreed with her compatriots that James had "followed such counsels as made the nation see they could not be safe in their religion and laws without coming to the extremities they did."[44] Nevertheless, to be driven into a choice against her father, even as the price of security for her country and religion, caused Anne immense soul-searching. But as a Protestant princess, she had a public role to play.

She, Sarah, and Compton decided to avoid the risk of troops loyal to James intercepting them if Anne tried to reach George and William in the west. Compton had reliable contacts at Nottingham. So, the princess's party traveled north.

Their small entourage left London on horseback to achieve maximum speed on England's potholed roads. Bishop Compton "who, in his youth, had been a cornet of dragoons … rode before her [Anne] with a drawn sword in his hand, and pistols on his saddle."[45] After the princess and her companions had refreshed themselves at an inn in a market town, Anne rode "pillion behind a guide."[46]

In the meantime, rumors reached Nottingham that two thousand of the king's dragoons were pursuing the princess. Hence, hastily mustered and armed volunteers rode out from the town to escort her; jubilant crowds lined the streets in welcome. Reports then reached Nottingham of nearby Catholic nobles massing an army to support James, so neighboring Protestant aristocrats gathered several thousand cavalry and called the county militia to protect Their Princess.

"I came to this place yesterday," Anne wrote her household controller, "& am very well but how long I shall stay here I cannot tell you: when I am settled I will be sure to send for you & the rest of my servants: in the meantime, I…desire you to give order that the back stairs at the Cockpit [used for Anne's flight] may be painted that they may be dry against when I come home but when next that may be God knows."[47]

William soon summoned Anne to Oxford where he and George awaited her. Enroute, swarms of people from all classes of society turned out to pay their respects. Arrayed in royal splendor, her mood ecstatic, the princess formally entered Oxford and, after an emotional and joyful reunion with George, sat down to the magnificent banquet the university gave for them. At the same time Anne learned of her father's flight to France.

—◊—

Anne's uncle Clarendon "took the liberty to tell her, that many good people were extremely troubled to find, she seemed no more concerned for her father's misfortune; that people … took notice, that, when the news came of the king's being gone, she seemed not at all moved, but called for cards, and was as merry as she used to be."[48]

People "did her wrong to make such reflections upon her actions, [Anne replied.] True, she did call for cards, because she used to play, and she never loved to do anything, that looked like an affected constraint."

Clarendon then said he felt sorry Anne thought "showing a trouble for the king her father's misfortunes should be interpreted by any as an affected constraint; that I was afraid, such behavior rendered her much less in the opinion of the world, even with her father's enemies, than she ought to be. At all this she seemed not one jot moved."[49] By her own admission, Anne had never been good at expressing her feelings.

She attended the magnificent court Prince William of Orange held at St. James's Palace on the evening of the day he officially entered London—in what should have been a triumph of popular acclaim. Delighting in royal pomp, sensing that William's advent marked an important moment, ordinary citizens filled the streets to welcome the savior of Protestantism and English liberties. William's future subjects waited for hours in the clammy December drizzle, only to hear that William, who hated display as much as he disregarded public acclamation, had driven unescorted, through the park, in a closed carriage, to the palace.

There the Princess of Denmark, arrayed in an elegant gown of figured orange silk, and matching manto[50] of pale grey satin embroidered with tiny orange flowers, orange satin shoes fashionably tapered to a square toe and with high Louis heels, proclaimed her loyalty to England's new ruler.

Anne had made her choice and would abide by it. She felt intensely Protestant, profoundly English. Her father's pro–Catholic policy disturbed Anne from a religious as well as a patriotic perspective; and her foreign stepmother's Catholicizing compounded Anne's concern. That underlay her doubting the truth of Mary Beatrice's pregnancy. For the princess not only feared losing a throne, she also feared for the future—of her country, her religion, and herself. The prospect of a succession of male Stuarts maintaining Catholic rule modeled on French absolutism and subject to Papal influence, appalled Princess Anne.

Four

"Utmost respect for king and queen"

"All hail to the Orange, my masters come on, I'll tell you what wonders he for us has done, He has pulled down the father, and thrust out the son, And put by the daughter, and filled up the throne With an Orange."[1]— Anonymous contemporary verse

Princess Anne and Prince William of Orange coalesced over the specter of a Catholic succession. Indeed, Anne and her husband Prince George of Denmark's backing did much to boost William's position during the Glorious Revolution of 1688. But harmony soon disintegrated into discord.

To settle the nation's affairs expeditiously, William convened the most recent freely elected (under Charles II) parliament, plus London's elected officials. They promptly agreed to assemble a special parliament.

Meeting early in the new year (1689) while a biting east wind blew, the convention parliament at once consolidated revolutionary gains by passing the Bill of Rights. It curbed the monarch's power. The Bill basically barred the ruler from suspending laws passed by parliament; levying taxes; interfering with parliamentary elections; punishing members of parliament for what they said during debates; keeping a standing army without parliamentary consent; denying Protestants the right to bear arms; arresting and detaining any subject (however poor) without legal process; requiring excessive bail; inflicting cruel or unusual punishment. And the Bill banned Catholics from the throne.

The convention parliament then considered the succession. Consensus favored James's eldest child, Protestant Mary Princess of Orange, as sole monarch in her own right. William opposed. A husband could not be secondary to his wife. Mary agreed. "Women should not meddle in government."[2]

William wanted the crown in his own right; that, after all, had been his main reason for invading England. To underscore his claim to the crown, William presented himself as closest male heir in the hereditary line, even if through his mother; as well, William pushed his claim as superior to Mary and Anne's because their mother had been a commoner. But in the eyes of the convention parliament, Mary's status as James's eldest child gave her husband's position legitimacy. And her refusal to reign alone, plus her full and unflagging support of the man she adored,[3] allowed William to insist on a joint monarchy with sole and complete exercise of royal power vested in him for life.

Mary's readiness to submit to William led him to expect the same from Anne. But the princess opposed William becoming king for life. She and her spouse Prince George, told Anne's caring uncle Lord Clarendon (a member of the convention parliament) that they could not agree to have the succession altered. Should Mary die before William, the Denmarks insisted that Anne succeed as queen, rather than William reigning alone and Anne ascending the throne after him.

Furious, William threatened to return to Holland forthwith if not made king for life. Since the convention parliament had already declared James's voluntary departure to connote abdication of his throne, the Convention would now back William whether the princess consented or not, John Churchill told his wife Sarah, Anne's best friend and first lady of the bedchamber. John's opinion carried weight with the Denmarks since he had been concerned in the Convention debates from the beginning; besides, Anne had come to trust Churchill's advice.

Both Churchills thought it would look bad for the princess to be seen as snatching at her father's crown, more especially as Mary refused to reign alone. So, Sarah enlisted the aid of the devout and apolitical dean of St. Paul's Cathedral, a cleric Anne respected, to help persuade the princess that, in her own interest, she should give in with "good grace."[4]

Princess Anne made a virtue of necessity. She sent a message to the convention parliament. Anne promised submission to whatever the Convention decided would be best for the country and the security of Protestantism.

The Convention agreed on William and Mary becoming joint sovereigns, with William having full and sole exercise of royal power. If they died childless, Anne would become queen after them. If Mary died before William and he remarried and had children, they would inherit the throne after Anne and her children.

The princess at once took care to scuttle any rumor of her dissatisfaction "with what was done, in reference to disposing the crown."[5] In fact, Anne assured everybody of her approval. She publicly supported the Convention's succession settlement, used her influence with clergy who refused to recognize the joint monarchs, and declined to receive her uncle Clarendon "since he does not see [refused to swear allegiance to] the king."[6]

Still, "most people seemed to wonder, that the Princess of Denmark could be pleased to be put by her right, and to see the course of the succession altered."[7]

Privately, Anne called this episode her Abdication.

—⁂—

King William III now judged the time right for his wife to leave Holland and come to England. "My heart is not made for a kingdom, [Mary confided to her diary] and my inclination leads me to a retired quiet life ... the prince being made king has lessened the pain, but not the trouble of what I am like to endure."[8]

Elegantly arrayed in blue satin with an orange cloak and scarf, her hair twisted with ropes of diamonds and pearls, and piled up under a high headdress, the extremely fashion-conscious Mary landed at Gravesend, on the Thames estuary. A barge then carried her upriver to Whitehall Stairs where Princess Anne, in high good humor at seeing her sister, and Prince George received Mary in state. King William awaited his wife at the palace.

Their coronation day dawned fair, with a brisk breeze sending white clouds scudding across the blue sky. But news disturbed this promising scene. James had landed in Catholic Ireland accompanied by an army, courtesy of his cousin French King Louis XIV. Louis and James sought to use conquest of Ireland as a stepping-stone to taking England.

Princess Anne and her compatriots agreed on the Irish—they "had a mind to be independent, if they could; but they should not."[9] Completely under English control, Ireland acknowledged England's king as its ruler. Ireland's majority Catholic population naturally looked on Catholic James as Ireland's legitimate king, welcomed his French Catholic forces as a possible means to national independence.

—⚭—

With timing as exquisite as his invasion of Ireland, James's letter reached Mary immediately before she left the palace to be crowned at Westminster Abbey. "Hitherto … willing to make excuses for [Mary's actions as caused by] obedience to her husband, and compliance with the nation, [Mary's coronation differed, for it lay within] her own power; and if she did it, while he and the Prince of Wales were living, the curses of an angry father would fall on her, as well as of a God, who commanded obedience to parents."[10]

Anne received a similar letter. It failed to deter her from participating in the coronation festivities. The pregnant princess then left the Cockpit for the clean, country air and manicured green lawns of Hampton court. There, on her sixth wedding anniversary, Anne gave birth to her fourth child and first son. The princess had been pregnant with him during all the "disorder we were in at the Revolution, though she did not know it herself"[11] when she fled from her father's court.

To thwart any charges of fraud, Queen Mary sat with her sister throughout the three-hour labor; King William and his senior officials also witnessed the "auspicious [birth. It] contributed much to dissipate … fears of a Popish successor"[12]; indeed, the new government presented the birth of a healthy, if not robust, boy as divine endorsement of the Glorious Revolution.

Anne and George's son cemented the Convention's succession settlement. England had a Protestant heir to rival the Catholic Prince of Wales. Named William after the King of England, one of his godfathers, (George's brother, King Christian of Denmark, acted as the child's other godfather by proxy) the infant received the title, Duke of Gloucester.

—⚭—

England's new rulers acknowledged the Denmarks' role in the Revolution, not to mention Anne's consent to the succession settlement. She and George got splendid apartments at Whitehall Palace. The prince remained a member of the privy council; became Duke of Cumberland and Earl of Kendal, which gave him a seat in the house of lords; by special law obtained British citizenship; and, due to his membership in the royal family, George received the ranking of first nobleman in the land. But the princess's friend Sarah Churchill aptly, if caustically, remarked that William judged Anne and her husband to have been of "more use to him than they were ever like to be again."[13]

The cold and unsociable king treated George with open contempt. William's compliant spouse acted frostily towards her good-natured brother-in-law. The joint monarchs' behavior insulted Anne politically and hurt her personally.

William made no secret of his scorn for Anne. In fact, he disliked female company (court ladies called him The Low Dutch Bear). Hating display as much as flattery, William felt most comfortable in the company of his male Dutch friends.

Late in the princess's pregnancy, the Denmarks dined with William and Mary. A plate of fresh green peas, the first to be seen that year, came to the table. Without offering any to Anne, the king "ate them every one up himself. [William could safely offer some to his wife, for he knew] she durst not touch them. [Pregnant Anne would have so much liked to eat some] peas, that she was afraid to look at them, and yet could hardly keep her eyes off them,"[14] she confessed to Sarah,

—⚏—

The princess had greeted her sister eagerly on Mary's arrival in England. Yet, the "great appearance of kindness between them"[15] soon changed.

An ebullient Mary entered her apartment in Whitehall Palace. She ran all through it, "looking into every closet and convenience, [turning up the bed quilts] as people do when they come into an inn, and with no other concern in her appearance, but such as they express." Mary promptly decided to move into her stepmother's newly redecorated private quarters. She used the bed Mary Beatrice had shared with James; and ignored her father's request to send him some personal items. The court, let alone Mary's sister, thought her conduct "very strange and unbecoming. For, whatever necessity there was of deposing King James, he was still her father, who had been so lately driven from that chamber, and that bed."[16]

After her son's birth Anne asked Mary and William for added space in the palace to accommodate him. King and queen gave the rooms Anne wanted to one of their cronies. The princess then requested use of Richmond Palace, where she had grown up. King and queen gave Richmond to another of their favorites.

Anne and George insisted on their precious baby having open air and daily outings. His nurses demurred. Hence, George bought a small open carriage, had it harnessed to a pair of tiny Shetland ponies, and hired a boy as driver. Well wrapped up and cozily ensconced in his little coach, the infant Duke of Gloucester, every morning, rode up and down in front of his mother's windows.

—⚏—

Apart, the Stuart sisters had been on good terms. Both loved their husbands, shared concern over their father's Catholicism, and were united in dislike of their stepmother. Now, Mary envied her sister's ability to bear children, as well as her happy marriage; for, William openly kept a mistress, and his intimacy with male favorites roused suspicion of homosexuality. Nevertheless, Mary pleaded with her husband to "love me and I can bear all things with ease."[17]

Proximity also aggravated the sisters' relationship by bringing personality differences into play. Mary grew "weary of anybody who would not talk a great deal; [Anne kept] "so silent that she rarely spoke more than was necessary to answer a question."[18]

Mary had always disliked Sarah, then envied her place in Anne's affections. As queen, Mary mistrusted both Churchills—they were too close to popular Anne for comfort, and they were too ambitious. William agreed. He valued John Churchill's military abilities, but doubted his loyalty. Yes, William rewarded Churchill for his role in the Revolution by conferring the Earldom of Marlborough on him, but a man who deserted his king in the field, as John had done vis-à-vis James, might well do so again. For William recognized the constant danger of Jacobitism, (return of James or his son) and realized his subjects did not love him.

After the euphoria of the Glorious Revolution ebbed, English people saw that, instead of a Catholic king, they had an austere Calvinist who scorned Anglican liturgy. Further, this foreigner put Holland's interests first, besides surrounding himself with Dutchmen. Antagonism rose as William spent months out of England returning only to ask parliament for ever more taxes to support ever larger armies to fight France. Public resentment against William made Anne the locus of discontent.

She showed extreme reluctance to assume the role of opposition leader. The princess "took care that no disturbance would be made by her pretended friends, the Jacobites; [in fact, those who favored James's return had pressed Anne] earnestly to form the opposition"[19] over the succession question. Bred in contemporary belief that opposition to the crown caused conflict, also that it constituted treason, the princess, further, feared a Jacobite restoration; for, it would imperil her and her son's succession to the throne.

— ɯ —

James's departure ended Anne's £30,000 annual allowance; William balked at continuing what he considered an excessively high revenue. To compensate, the princess thought she should have half of the property (with its immense income) her father had owned as a private person. William took control of James's estates; he gave the lucrative Irish lands to his mistress.

Prince George's Danish income came slowly. His sole asset consisted of land the Danish crown had seized from Sweden a century ago. To keep Sweden neutral in his war against France, William sought to mediate peace between Sweden and Denmark; but, in recompense, Sweden demanded return of that land now belonging to George. If he ceded the land, William promised personally to guarantee the prince full reimbursement. Good-natured George at once agreed. William failed to keep his promise.

Anne considered the king to have "neglected [her too much.] No propositions were made to her of a settlement, nor any advance of money."[20] Having done her duty over the succession, put the nation's welfare before her personal preference, Anne thought she deserved her own lifetime income, especially as parliament had voted William £600,000 a year from the civil list.[21]

Unwilling to confront king and queen openly, the princess thought a "settlement by act of parliament" would be best. On the other hand, the custom had always been for the royal family to depend on the king, that no member received an allowance except from his "favor and kindness. [But in this case, where Anne had agreed to be] put out of the succession, during the king's life, it seemed reasonable, that somewhat more than ordinary should be done in confirmation of that."[22]

Since Anne had never found it easy to live within her £30,000 annual income, her supporters proposed an additional £40,000[23] annually that parliament should guarantee via an official grant. True, such a direct grant to the heir presumptive, and outside the monarch's control, would break precedent; but the princess had broken precedent by consenting to defer the succession to William; "she had not forgot the importance of the concession she had made; nor William, perhaps, that he had been obliged to ask it."[24]

The king avoided speaking to Anne about money and told Mary to do likewise. But Mary could not refrain from scolding her younger sister in private.

Mary: "What [is] the meaning of these [parliamentary] proceedings"?
Anne: My friends have a mind to make me some settlement.
Mary: "Pray what friends have you but the king and me"?

Sarah recorded that she had never seen Anne express such extreme "resentment as she did at this usage … it was unjust in her sister not to allow her some decent provision without an entire dependence on the king."[25]

—⟋⟍—

A parliamentary committee resolved that "revenue of £40,000 a year should be settled on [Anne for life.] "Neither the king nor the queen, nor any of their ministers, had been consulted in this motion." William worked to defeat it. The house of commons voted to postpone a vote. William adjourned "parliament to prevent a settlement on the princess."[26]

The new Earl of Marlborough, John Churchill, ably abetted behind the scenes by his wife Sarah, led parliamentary action for Anne. Aside from his personal interest in her fortunes, Marlborough saw supporting the princess as his duty in the national interest, for with a foreigner on the throne, and a Catholic ex-king claimant, the English heir designate should be independent.

The joint monarchs concentrated their efforts on Sarah. She must convince Anne to drop her request for the additional allowance. As well, William and Mary threatened to remove John from his lucrative offices[27] should parliament accede to Anne's request. Regardless, Sarah refused to act for king and queen.

When the issue re-surfaced in the Commons, many, including the king's "firmest friends [made] excuses, that they could not in decency oppose the interest of the queen's sister."[28] Hence, the king decided to try compromise with Marlborough via his minister the Duke of Shrewsbury who, through his friendship with Marlborough, had become a member of the Denmarks' Cockpit Circle.

"Of great probity [and a] high sense of honor," one of the Immortal Seven who invited William to England, Shrewsbury had abundant "learning, a correct judgment, with a sweetness of temper that charmed all who knew him."[29]

Nick-named King of Hearts, Shrewsbury, on the king's behalf, proposed to Marlborough that if the princess dropped her request in parliament, William would grant her £50,000 for one year, plus pay her debts. Marlborough replied that he could do nothing; and Sarah would certainly refuse to listen to any such suggestion.

Shrewsbury then tackled Sarah, but since she had heard on good authority that William thought even £30,000 excessive as an annual income, Shrewsbury's appeal fell flat. He promised to resign if William failed to keep his side of the bargain. "That, my lord, may bind you, but what shall bind the king"?[30] retorted Sarah.

Anne herself told Shrewsbury that since the king had given her so little reassurance of his kindness for her, she could now expect none. In any case, the matter had already gone so far that she thought it reasonable to see what her friends could achieve.

On hearing this, Mary took her sister to task in no uncertain terms. The habitually tongue-tied princess, anxious, besides, to avoid giving more offense by explaining or justifying herself, remained silent. Mary took that to mean Anne "could tell me no one thing in which the king had not been kind to her, and would not own herself in the wrong for not speaking to either of us…. I told her she had shown as much want of kindnessto me as respect to the king and I both. Upon this we parted ill friends."[31]

—⟋⟍—

Anne and the Marlboroughs continued their campaign. Those dissatisfied with William—the public and the Tory party, one of the two major parties dominating English politics—backed the princess. Mostly made up of country squires, Tories were staunch upholders of the Anglican Church and the royal prerogative; Tories dominated the house of commons, lower chamber of England's bicameral legislature.

The other principal party in English politics mostly supported King William. Great landed aristocrats, commercial interests, and all dissenters from Anglican orthodoxy made up the Whig party. In general, Whigs wanted to curb royal power, (the law stood above the monarch) and promote parliamentary control of government. Whigs dominated the house of lords, parliament's upper chamber.

William's Whig advisors encouraged him to fight Anne and her supporters. "To give the princess a great revenue, and make her independent" of the king, his leading Whig counselor warned, could make the princess gratify "Tories and high church men [by becoming] "the head of a party against you."[32]

King William eventually "saw the advantage which the princess had over him and opposed a parliamentary settlement no longer."[33] To counter Anne's friends insisting on £70,000—which the Commons might well have granted—William convinced the princess's supporters to agree that parliament vote her £50,000 annually. Anne concurred with her backers that £50,000 annually, "securely settled, [presented a better option than] further struggle, considering the great power"[34] of the crown. Still, the Commons grant of a £50,000 annual allowance for the princess connoted open rebuff to king and queen, which hardly eased ill feeling between the royal sisters and, besides, buttressed Mary and William's misgiving about Anne's status.

The entire affair also aggravated the joint monarchs' "dissatisfaction" with the Marlboroughs. But Anne recognized John and Sarah's efforts on her behalf with as "deep a sense of kindness, as could be expressed, and in a manner generous in a very high degree."[35]

The princess offered to give Sarah a liberal annual pension. That made Queen Mary scowl. She lost no time in scolding her younger sister. How could Anne give that troublemaker, that cause of discord in the royal family, that wife of an unsafe man who annoyed the king, a £1,000 annuity out of her parliamentary grant. The princess should, rather, dismiss Sarah forthwith.

The inarticulate princess met Mary's verbal barrage with silence broken only by a few murmured negatives. Shouting, the queen threatened to make sure her (again) pregnant sister got only half her parliamentary grant; that, Anne muttered, lay outside Mary's power. An irate exchange ensued. To their courtiers' consternation, the sisters parted in anger.

—◆—

When azaleas and rhododendrons lent splashes of brilliant color to the landscape and filled the air with their scent, King James reinvigorated his push to conquer Catholic Ireland whose public backed him as a means to get rid of English control. Catholic absolutist French King Louis XIV funded James's army at the least to distract King William from fighting France on the Continent, at the most to gain a foothold for invading England. Fearing that a Catholic-Jacobite victory would allow James and Louis to attack England from two fronts (Ireland and France) parliament convinced William to postpone going to the Spanish Netherlands to lead the allied armies against France; he should, rather, concentrate on defending his kingdom of Ireland.

William appointed a council to help Mary rule in his absence. "I long to hear from you, and know in what we have failed, [her politically detailed letter concluded in typical fashion.] "For my own part, if I do in anything what you don't like, 'tis my misfortune, and not my fault; for I love you more than my life, and desire only to please you."[36]

The king did not invite Prince George to accompany him to Ireland, a gross insult because as husband of the heiress presumptive, and a former soldier besides, George had every right to be included. But William, an average general even if an astute politician, wanted no battlefield competition from a prince well known for his bravery in the Scandinavian wars.

Prince George wholeheartedly backed the Protestant rulers fighting French hegemony. Keen to serve, he went to Ireland at his own—considerable—expense. William tolerated his presence only to keep Anne loyal. But envy of George's status as a hereditary royal personage, let alone his wife's position, caused the king to exclude George from all councils of war. And William barely acknowledged the prince's participation in the Battle of the Boyne, (July 1690) even though the king, in the first hours of that great Protestant victory, "lay ... in the Prince of Denmark's coach, for the baggage was not come up."[37]

To make matters worse, William not only sent couriers to London without waiting for George's letters, which made it difficult for the prince to stay in touch with his pregnant wife, but also ignored George as if he "had been a page of the back stairs." William even denied George a seat in the royal coach, to which his status as Anne's husband entitled him, an insult never before delivered to a "person of that rank."[38] But because the sensible, good-humored prince had discerned the king's Achilles heel—jealousy—George, during the whole campaign, did not "fail in any part of duty or respect."[39]

By refusing to give the prince his rightful military role, to say nothing of publicly insulting him, William widened the rift between the royal sisters.

When leaves on the trees turned to auburn and gold, George arrived at home—in time for his wife's delivery of a premature daughter. But little Mary (named after her aunt the queen) died within hours, casting a long shadow over Anne's relief and joy at having her husband back beside her.

—⚬—

Early in the next year (1691) William betook himself to the Continent to command the allied army against France. Again, he failed to fulfill George's wish for a military role. Memories of the "extreme ill-usage he had met with, when at great expense, he had attended his majesty into Ireland, [plus George's aversion to stay at home while abroad] there was so much action"[40] caused him, like many wealthy aristocrats lacking naval combat experience, to decide on volunteering to serve at sea without command.

George broached the idea to William; the king embraced him. According to contemporary custom, embrace connoted consent. George arranged to join a ship.

Refusing to believe the prince sought only to serve, William and Mary suspected him and Anne of plotting to embarrass the government and, at the same time, court further popularity. (Thanks to her resisting James's conversion attempts, Anne enjoyed widespread approval, as evinced by the many mounted volunteers who rallied round her when she fled London during the Glorious Revolution.) The king thus decided to bar George from any active service, and before leaving for the Continent, told Mary to nip in the bud what he saw as a rival bid for status.

To make the prince's withdrawal from active naval service appear as his decision, Mary asked Sarah to persuade Anne to keep the prince at home, but not to tell the princess that her sister wished it. Sarah replied that she would raise the issue only if she had permission to use the queen's name, but in any case, Sarah doubted Anne could dissuade George from serving.

William's minister and Anne's uncle, Earl Rochester, then reiterated Mary's request. But news of the prince's naval arrangements had by now become so well known that George felt unable to reverse them suddenly without reason; for how could a brave and experienced soldier abruptly leave the naval campaign with no explanation? Hence, Mary issued official orders banning the prince from joining his ship, an awkward move, since George's gear, already stowed on board, had to be removed in full public view.

This episode stoked the flames of ill feeling between the royal sisters, to say nothing of arousing popular criticism. England resented the Dutchman's insults to the heir apparent.

—⁓—

Estranged from her sister, upset over yet another failed pregnancy, the princess drew closer to her favorite. Sarah had proved her loyalty—a quality Anne esteemed—by helping to have parliament grant Anne's annual income; besides, Sarah provided delightful and amusing company; and never flattered. To underline their friendship, the princess proposed that in their letters she and Sarah should address each other "by feigned names, such as would import nothing of distinction of rank." Like many aristocratic ladies, Anne liked sometimes to affect the customs of common people. So, she selected the names Morley and Freeman, and let Sarah choose. Her "frank, open temper naturally led [Sarah to pick] Freeman, & so the princess took the other; & from this time Mrs. Morley and Mrs. Freeman[41] began to converse as equals, made so by affection and friendship."[42]

Still, Sarah thought her favored position jeopardized not only her relations with the joint monarchs, but, more to the point, her husband's; far better for all concerned if the princess mended relations with her sister.

> You must give me leave to endeavor to clear myself of my behavior to the queen, [Anne wrote Sarah.] I see you think me to … blame. The queen and I are of very different humors; as she is my sister, if ever it were possible to lie in my power to serve her I should be readier to do it than anybody, as for respect I have always behaved myself towards her with as much as possible…
>
> I know I am morose & grave & therefore may not be so pleasing to her as other company but I have been with her as often and as long at a time as I could. I have never missed a day of dining with her whenever the king has been out of England, &…when the prince was in Ireland I used to stay [late except when] people came to speak to her or that she told me she had something to do…
>
> I told her…. I should be glad to stay with her if I knew when she was alone, to which she answered … she should be very glad of my company but yet when she had spoke with everybody she was every day obliged to do, she was glad she could get some time to herself … what I could do more than all this I cannot comprehend…
>
> I could not love her more than I do & I think it is very hard I may not have the liberty of following my inclinations & being very kind … to those I really dote on, as long as I do nothing extravagant, but if it will be any satisfaction to you I promise you I will never take any more notice of you before folks [than of others] for I would in all things make you easy.[43]

To make things easy for Sarah, Anne sought a favor for her husband. Marlborough had successfully reorganized the army, created and executed effective follow-up strategy to the Battle of the Boyne, and won a victory against France in the Spanish Netherlands. Nonetheless, William had failed to treat him well. Recently denied the powerful and lucrative master of the ordnance position, John now sought the Order of the Garter, England's most prestigious award.

The princess seconded Prince George's request that William "remember your promise of a Garter [for Marlborough. The king could not] bestow it upon anyone that has been more serviceable to you in the late revolution, nor that ventured their lives for you as he has done ever since your coming to the crown. [If all that failed to qualify John for the Garter, Anne could not believe anyone] will be so unreasonable [as to be] dissatisfied when 'tis known you are pleased to give it to him on the prince's account and mine. [The princess would] not trouble [her brother-in-law with] ceremony, because I know you don't care for it."[44]

William ignored Anne's appeal.

—⁂—

The king saw Marlborough as a military rival; besides, he stood too close to Anne, whom William persisted in seeing as a potential threat to his crown. And since William distrusted John for having deserted his patron, King James, William would not give him independent military command.

The king's cavalier conduct towards Marlborough, as well as other prominent Englishmen who had helped him onto the throne, caused many of them to contact James as insurance against reprisals should he return. That looked possible. William seemed indifferent to his growing unpopularity. French arms might well foist a Catholic restoration on England in the person of James's son, the little Prince of Wales; as well, the dual monarchs continued, despite his parents' refusal, to want to adopt the child and raise him a Protestant. John thus asked his erstwhile patron James, for pardon—but—did not promise to work for his return.

The Denmarks, meanwhile, had for months been trying to get payment for the Danish lands Prince George had ceded to Sweden at King William's behest and upon his pledge of full compensation, which the king had failed to honor. Driven by the need for funds, George now reluctantly accepted much less money from William than the lands were worth, but on condition of prompt restitution. It did not materialize. This and continued insults to her husband, fed Anne's disillusion with the dual monarchs.

Convinced their conduct absolved her of any loyalty, Anne sought to protect her family. Initially, she, like many of her compatriots, welcomed William's invasion as the means of making James respect English laws; once these were secured, Anne, like most English people, thought William would leave. She now sought insurance against William being forced off the throne, as well as protection against rumors that he planned to craft a peace with France that would give James's son the crown after William and Mary's death. Hence, the princess heeded John and Sarah's advice—to write to her father. No law barred corresponding with the exiled king, or easing guilt over conduct towards a parent.

She had sought "some safe opportunity, [Anne wrote, to make James a] sincere and humble offer [of] duty and submission, [to beg him to be assured of her being] both truly concerned for the misfortune of your condition and sensible, as I ought to be, of my own unhappiness. [Anne would have been extremely relieved to have earlier] found means to acquaint [James with her] repentant thoughts, [but now hoped he would prove] as indulgent and easy to receive [her] humble submissions as I am to make them in a free, disinterested acknowledgement of my fault, for no other end but to deserve and receive your pardon."[45]

Although Marlborough sent Anne's letter via a reliable courier, it reached James six months late. Regardless, the letter fooled no one at her father's court, least of all its addressee.

—⚹—

Thanks to his efficient intelligence service, King William knew most highly placed Englishmen kept some contact with James's court. William did not fear a Jacobite restoration. He feared the Anne-Marlborough combination; for, church and state respected Anne; the army respected John—the only capable English officer holding high command.

Marlborough's ability had caused the king to treat him leniently. But when John started to speak up for English officers excluded from the highest military positions in favor of Dutchmen, let alone criticized William's conduct of the war, the king saw a threat to his position as leader of the anti–French alliance. Because if William lost control of England's army, he would lose control of the allied armies. Marlborough's proposal of parliamentary measures to disallow employment of foreigners for state business proved the limit.

Especially as William, and even more so, Mary, suspected Anne of encouraging what the joint monarchs believed to be Marlborough's intrigues to transfer their joint crown to herself. To scuttle this supposed scheme, Mary resolved to rid her sister of Sarah, the woman she had never liked, never trusted, Anne's evil genius who had worked so effectively to get the princess her parliamentary grant.

January (1692) blew in at its most abysmal—frigid, damp, and bleak. The queen summoned her sister. Mary abruptly ordered Anne to dismiss Sarah. No. Mary threatened the princess "with the loss of her revenue."[46]

Next morning, without any official explanation, William ordered John at once to sell all his offices, (a severe financial blow) and banned him from court. That, the joint monarchs thought, would sever Anne's ties to the Marlboroughs, since she could hardly continue to employ the wife of a disgraced man.

Distraught at Marlborough's dismissal, Anne blamed herself—William had punished John for consistently backing her. To mark her condemnation of the king's conduct the princess stayed away from court for three weeks. When she returned, Anne brought Sarah, her senior lady-in-waiting, with her.

The princess's knowledge of court etiquette, to say nothing of her acute sense of the practical political implications of royal ritual, made her action a deliberate insult to king and queen. And a bravado gesture of support for Marlborough.

—⚹—

Unwilling to challenge her visibly pregnant sister in public, the queen said nothing. But next day her letter notified Anne that bringing Sarah to court

> was very unkind in a sister, would have been very uncivil in an equal … and I have more to claim, which, though my kindness would never make me exact, yet, when I see the use you would make of it, I must tell you I know what is due to me and expect to have it from you. [Therefore, to be plain] Lady Marlborough must not continue with you…
>
> This will be uneasy to you, and I am sorry for it, for I have all the real kindness imaginable for you … but the sight of Lady Marlborough [proves] how little you seem to consider what even in common civility you owe us, I have told you plainly, but withal assure you … my kindness is so great that I can pass over most things and live with you as becomes me.[47]
>
> I do not desire an answer presently because I would not have you give a rash one. I shall come to your drawing-room tomorrow; it shall never be my fault if we do not live kindly together.[48]

Mary judged her letter gentle and kind. Anne disagreed. Rising to what she took as a test, the princess replied at once. "This proceeding can be for no other intent than to give me a very sensible mortification. [Anne had every right to choose her servants. Therefore,] no misery" existed that she could not "readily resolve to suffer rather than the thoughts of parting with"[49] Sarah.

This retort enraged the joint monarchs. William ordered Sarah immediately to vacate her rooms at the Cockpit—which he had no right to do since Anne owned it. Still, pride and anger decided the princess against contesting William's command. If Sarah could not live with Anne at the Cockpit, Anne would leave the Cockpit with Sarah. Prince George supported his wife.

"I am very sorry to find that all I have said, [Anne told her sister] has not had effect enough to keep your majesty from persisting in a resolution, which you are satisfied must be so great a mortification to me, as, to avoid it, I shall be obliged to retire, and deprive myself of the satisfaction of living where I might have frequent opportunities of offering you of that duty and respect, which I always have been, and shall be desirous to pay you upon all occasions."[50]

Five

"I will be obeyed"

"Express orders" forbad "all honors being paid to her rank; nor were the mouths of the malicious stopped ... even her person was scarcely protected from insult: but all this she bore with fortitude and patience, without complaining of the indignity put upon her—for never did woman possess a sweeter disposition than this amiable princess."[1]—Jenkin Lewis, personal attendant to the Duke of Gloucester.

"Notwithstanding all the harsh things done to the prince and princess, they never failed in the least thing ... to show respect to the king and queen."[2]—Sarah Marlborough.

Princess Anne moved out of the Cockpit to preserve her autonomy. She thought that, like every English individual, she had the right to choose not only her servants, but also her friends. Yet, when "enemies of the government tried what could be made of this, to create distractions among us, [Anne did not give any] encouragement to them."[3] Indeed, in response to a Jacobite nobleman offering the Prince and Princess of Denmark his country house "by reason of the great parks and woods which would divert the prince, and the air most good ... they both received me with great attention and goodness, and the princess with many thanks told me that her affairs required her being near London."[4]

Anne wished to lease stately Syon House. The unused property abutting the Thames had vast and diverse gardens that bore mute witness to the care of a skilled gardener whose underlings would not dare to let a weed show itself, a border or hedge to become ragged. Syon had come into the Duke of Somerset's possession through his exceedingly wealthy wife. King William ordered Somerset to refuse the princess. He did. But the duchess, daughter of ancient and proud English nobility, would not let any upstart Dutchman dictate to her, especially about an English princess. The Duchess of Somerset offered to loan her house. William cancelled the Denmarks' military escort.

Hence, during an abnormally frigid February, (1692) as heavy grey clouds hung over the river, the very pregnant princess traveled from Cockpit to Syon without guard, in fact, without any decent escort, along rutted roads rimed with frost and infested with highwaymen. The public condemned King William and Queen Mary for endangering England's heiress presumptive.

"These things are so far from vexing either the prince or me,"[5] the princess confided to her bosom friend Sarah, Countess Marlborough. That day, Prince George had gone to London to attend the privy council, which he did consistently, as well as took his seat in parliament "regularly ... during all King William's reign. [The prince] never openly declared himself of any [political] party ... never entered the administration, [but came] often to court, [and] diverted himself with hunting."[6]

As Prince George approached the palace, "the guards in St. James park did not stand to their arms neither when the prince went nor came & I can't believe it was their Dutch breeding alone without Dutch orders that made them do it because they never omitted it before. [Still, Anne averred,] "nothing great or small can really trouble me as long as dear Mrs. Freeman's kindness continues."[7]

—⁂—

Determined to make Anne obey, the joint monarchs considered moves to curtail her allowance. But the king shrank from losing his lord treasurer. Despite Sidney Godolphin's friendship with the Marlboroughs and Denmarks, William had put glum, capable Godolphin in charge of the treasury. The king valued thoughtful, incorruptible men; besides, he knew Sidney could be relied on to raise funds sufficient for William to fight his continental wars. The king also knew Godolphin would surely resign rather than refuse to pay an annuity sanctioned by parliament.

Parliament refused to consider the matter. But rumors of a reduction in the princess's income plus isolation at Syon, (Queen Mary banned courtiers from visiting Anne) made several of George's gentlemen urge the prince to persuade his wife to dismiss Sarah. "He had so much tenderness for the princess, [George told them, that he did not want to] make her so uneasy. [Further, the prince thought] he had done a great deal [for the joint monarchs] and been very ill used."[8]

Troubled about the royal sisters' quarrel, Sarah might easily have resolved it by resigning; but, could not afford such a grand gesture. With her husband still in disgrace, and the joint monarchs childless, Sarah's connection to Anne, heiress apparent, had become crucial for the ambitious Marlboroughs. Further, Sarah's salary as senior lady-in-waiting made an important contribution to her family's finances, now severely depleted since John lost his offices. Nonetheless, Sarah made a token offer to resign.

Anne reacted predictably. She understood and respected the obligations implicit in friendship. She would stand by her friend—and expected the same of Sarah.

"You must not deprive me of one of the greatest comforts of my life; you must pardon me for saying this but seeing you vex & torment yourself at all the malicious things you hear, and knowing how base & ungrateful a world we live in.... I can't help begging my dear Mrs. Freeman again & again if she would never think of parting more but leave it only in death's power."[9]

Sarah urged Anne to make no definitive decision without consulting George. She did. The prince "strengthened [his wife in her resolve.] We both beg you would never mention so cruel a thing anymore. [Did Sarah think] either of us so wretched that for the sake of twenty thousand pound, [besides being] tormented from morning to night with flattering knaves and fools, we would forsake those we have such obligations to, [those, furthermore, the Denmarks were sure] are the occasion of their misfortune?"

Could Sarah believe Anne and George would

ever truckle to that monster [who, from the moment of his arrival, ill-treated them as] all the world can witness. [Even if Anne did submit, even if William could change his nature] so much as to use me with humanity ... all reasonable people [would despise her. How] would that Dutch abortive [laugh at her, be pleased at] having got the better. [And more.] "How would my conscience reproach me for having sacrificed it, my honor, reputation ... for transitory interest, which ... can never afford any real satisfaction. [Anne's] "dear Mrs. Freeman [must never believe her] faithful Mrs. Morley will ever submit. She can wait with patience for a sun-shine day, and if she does not live to see it, yet she hopes England will flourish again."[10]

—⁓—

Living quietly at Syon House, the Denmarks were "so far from repenting of what we have done that the more we think of it the better we are satisfied," Anne wrote Sarah after listening to her sister Mary's emissary—their choleric uncle Earl Rochester. He had come to convey the queen's command that Anne dismiss her friend forthwith. The princess felt "so mightily at ease here, [that should the] monsters grow good natured & indulge [her] in everything she could desire, [Anne] would be hardly persuaded to leave her retirement, but of these great changes I think there is no great danger."[11]

Happy wives and mothers, Anne and Sarah chatted about their nurseries and domestic arrangements as together they embroidered an elaborate quilt of ivory silk. The princess indulged her love of music by learning to play the lute and harpsichord, went to London to see opera and theater. But above all, banishment meant Anne had the leisure to spend unlimited time with her son.

The little Duke of Gloucester's periodic convulsions and severe fevers caused "the tenderest of mothers"[12] constant worry. When the boy developed a bloodshot eye, and a swollen lid obscured his vision, England's premier physician ordered a blister applied to the child's back. To no avail. The doctor prescribed a medicine that looked, smelled, and tasted disgusting. The boy balked, then, at last, swallowed the potion. His eye got worse; Gloucester could not bear any light. Desperate, Anne recalled having years ago consulted a physician famous for curing such complaints. She visited the doctor, returning with a small bottle of strange liquid which, according to instructions, the princess carefully applied to her son's eyelid with a fine camel's hair brush. Gloucester's eye returned to normal.

Anne saw him daily. Much as her own mother had enjoyed sharing hot chocolate with her favorite daughter at supper, the princess liked her son to "come to her dinners after his own, when he would behave himself very well."[13] And the child joined his parents on their daily morning walk along the graveled paths crisscrossing Syon's smooth green lawns.

—⁓—

The heady scent of spring flowers perfumed the ambient air when, during her seventh month, the princess went into premature labor. George immediately sent Mary a message: her sister's "accouchement was at hand; [Anne felt extremely ill,] much worse"[14] than usual. The queen took no notice. Anne's long, difficult labor yielded a boy who died within minutes.

That news galvanized Mary into ordering her carriage. Since the queen's sudden descent on Syon surprised the household, no one waited to escort her to Anne's bedroom. Mary betook herself up the back stairs to find her sister wan and exhausted, heartbroken besides, lying in her canopied four-poster bed, its royal blue velvet curtains lined with pale blue silk open to admit the waning daylight. Over her soft, scented, white linen shift lavishly trimmed at neck and cuffs with Flemish lace, Anne wore a white and red vertical striped silk nightgown, faced and sashed with matching horizontal material.

Mary wasted no time, never asked her sister "how she did, [never] expressed the least concern for her condition, [never] so much as took her by the hand."

> MARY: "I have made the first step by coming to you, and I now expect you should make the next by removing my Lady Marlborough."
>
> ANNE: "I have never in all my life disobeyed you ... except in that one particular, which I hope will, some time or other, appear as unreasonable to your majesty, as it does to me."

The queen instantly left the room, "repeating to the prince, as he led her to the coach, the same thing she had said to the princess."[15]

Anne had summoned the stamina to refuse her sister's diktat. But Mary's visit so distressed the weakened princess that she succumbed to a serious fever.

—⁂—

Although bitter cold delayed the arrival of crocuses and daffodils that year, when they yielded to gaily colored tulips and purple petaled pansies, exiled King James, backed by his cousin and patron, French Catholic King Louis XIV, prepared to invade his native land. Concomitantly, King William decamped for the Continent. He would lead the allied armies fighting against French incursion into the Spanish Netherlands. William left his wife in charge of the realm.

MARIA KONINGIN VAN ENGELAND
Schotland Vrankryk en Yrland.

Queen Mary II, 1662–1694. Anne's only sibling reigned jointly with her husband King William III. Mary insisted on her younger sister's compliance: "I am a queen and will be obeyed." Artist: unknown; drawn between 1689 and 1694. © National Portrait Gallery, London.

The princess heard from a reliable source that "as soon as the wind turns westerly" Queen Mary would order soldiers to guard her and George. If Sarah learned of any such measure, and if she could easily arrange to come to Syon from her country house at St. Albans, where Sarah nursed her ailing mother, "pray let me see you before the wind changes. [After, the princess did not know if] they will let one have opportunities for speaking to one another."[16]

With invasion imminent and her husband away, Queen Mary reacted to rampant rumors of a Jacobite plot to kill him on the Continent. Suspecting Marlborough of being a primary plotter, the queen had him arrested for high treason, and ordered him to be imprisoned in the Tower. Frantic about her husband, let alone the mortal illness of their younger son, Sarah again offered to resign in the best interests of all concerned.

Anne felt confident Sarah did "not doubt of my constancy; [but, knowing] how base and false all the world is, [the princess thought she could] never say enough to assure [Sarah that] they can never change me. [Further, Anne could suffer any] misery ... rather than the thought of parting from you. [She would] sooner be torn to pieces than alter this my resolution."[17]

Two women united in friendship, Anne and Sarah now worried about what the uncertain future might bring.

—⁂—

Late one night, a visitor surprised the princess. With good reason to fear William's resourceful spies, Anne dismissed all her attendants. The princess then beckoned Lady Ailesbury to a seat beside her bed and listened closely to the message she brought from her Jacobite husband. "He would be very sorry that you should be one of the last to know that the king your father, if wind permit, might very well be in twenty-four hours in the kingdom, and with an army to support him. [The princess must, Lady Ailesbury adjured,] take this into her serious consideration, [adding that] upwards of five thousand men well horsed, and good officers, would be ready to escort her."[18]

Her message duly delivered, Lady Ailesbury took it upon herself to add. "Your highness may please to consider that you exerted yourself to go in a manner against the king your father when in the kingdom; why may not you as well get on horseback for to restore him to what you assisted in taking away from him, and by which glorious action you will repair for what you did in time past."

Still weak from childbed fever and, so, hardly able to undertake a long and tiring ride, Anne sighed, and with "thoughtful and unhappy mien [gave her visitor a diplomatic reply.] Well, madam, tell your lord I am ready to do what he can advise me to."[19]

Shortly afterwards, an Anglo-Dutch flotilla routed the French invasion fleet at La Hogue. Lord Ailesbury at once called on "the princess, who had much ado to get rid of her ladies and women, most of them spies over her."

> AILESBURY: "The face of affairs has much altered since my wife had the honor to impart … a message from me."
>
> ANNE: with a sad face. "Yes, greatly."
>
> AILESBURY: "In this unhappy conjuncture for the king [your father,] nothing would comfort him more than a tender line from" you.
>
> ANNE: with "low voice and fetching sigh." "It is not a proper time for you and I to talk of that matter any farther."

The princess gave her visitor "a gracious look on parting." He admitted the matter of a missive to James "very nice [risky] and her handwriting might have been intercepted in spite of all care that would have been taken to have had it safely delivered."[20]

—⁂—

Once recovered from her fever, Anne took up her pen. She acknowledged the honor of Mary's visit, and asked if she might wait on her sister to mend fences. Mary had little to say in reply, for

> I never use compliments, so now they cannot [serve.] Tis none of my fault that we live at this distance, and I have endeavored to show my willingness to do otherwise; and I will do no more. Don't give yourself any unnecessary trouble, for be assured 'tis not words can make us live together as we ought. You know what I required of you; and now I tell you, if you doubted it before, that I cannot change my mind, but expect to be complied with, or you must not wonder that I doubt of your kindness.[21]

Anne than asked one of her ladies-in-waiting, who could "speak more freely to the queen than anybody else she could employ, [to convey to Mary that Anne had been] flattering herself she had mistaken her majesty's last words. [The princess would be] very ready to give her majesty any satisfaction [except dismissing Sarah. On hearing this, the queen] fell into a great passion and said her sister had not mistaken her, for she never would see her upon any other terms than parting [with Sarah,] not for a time but forever, adding [and repeating, that] she was a queen and would be obeyed."[22]

—⚬⚬—

Again pregnant, the princess decided on the precautionary measure of having a water treatment at Bath. Prince George would accompany her, and, as the Denmarks usually did when going away from home, they took their son with them. Since doting nurses surrounded him, and courtiers, public, and press fawned over him, Anne and George took an active part in Gloucester's upbringing to make sure their pleasant-tempered child developed a sense of proportion about his place in the world, saw himself as a servant of state, not master of it.

Municipal dignitaries received the Denmark family with full honors. On hearing of this, Queen Mary instructed her secretary of state officially to order Bath's mayor "not for the future to pay her highness any … respect of ceremony without leave from her majesty."[23]

"This is a thing to be laughed at, [Anne confided to Sarah.] If they imagine either to vex me or gain upon me by such sort of usage they will be mightily disappointed, & I hope these foolish things they do will every day show people more & more what they are."[24]

On their return from Bath, the Denmarks moved into London's elegant Berkeley House, on Piccadilly, but since visiting the princess still meant exclusion from court "no persons of the court and flatterers out of it durst go thither. [Nonetheless, Jacobite Lord Ailesbury] attended them often." So, too, did Marlborough's friend and Cockpit Circle member the urbane and congenial Duke of Shrewsbury, who, having already resigned as King William's secretary of state, "went there constantly. Some few generous spirited ladies, but very few in number, waited on [the Denmarks as well] but to play there was only us two, [Ailesbury and Shrewsbury] and the game was whist with honors, in vogue at that time."[25]

Sarah did not figure among the "few generous spirited ladies," for she had gone to her St. Albans country house to nurse her dying mother. "My dear Mrs. Freeman's letters are always very welcome to her faithful Morley but such kind ones as I now receive every day give me more real satisfaction than can be expressed and deserve more thanks than 'tis possible to return."[26] Anne warned her friend not to "expect any news from Berkeley House. As dull and despicable as some people may think it, I am so far from being weary of my way of living or repenting of the least of my action that, were the year to run over again, I would tread the same steps."[27]

—⚬⚬—

Rather than have her frail son live with her in London's foggy, coal-grimed air, the princess installed Gloucester and his household in handsome Campden House, a comfortable red-brick mansion with spacious gardens and shrubbery, set high above the hamlet of Kensington. Anne and George were often there, usually staying overnight in their suite of three large first floor rooms furnished with walls of red damask tapestry in a foliage design and handsome stucco ceilings.

Like his father interested in all matters military, the eager, energetic boy resented his nurses' vigilance, as well as his mother and her physicians' endless questions and examinations. Hence, Prince George, in his pleasant way, begged the ladies not to baby the boy. At age four he could hardly walk by himself, much less climb stairs. Anne took Gloucester aside to explain why he must walk on his own. The child still refused. George then took up a birch rod. He thrashed (a common contemporary practice) Gloucester so severely that pain made him run all round the room. From then on, the boy walked on his own everywhere.

Gloomy at again failing to provide Gloucester with a sibling, the princess, nonetheless, busied herself with getting a good portrait of her favorite—selecting an artist and persuading Sarah to sit for him—so that during her absences, Anne could derive solace from looking at Sarah's likeness. The princess disapproved of Swedish Michael Dahl's portrait despite Prince George being Dahl's patron in England, so she visited other studios to choose a worthy painter.

"I can't help asking if I may not come to St. Albans sometime next week, [Anne wrote after learning Sarah planned to stay in the country with her children.] Name any day then or when tis most convenient for you, & I will not fail in that, nor anything else for my dear, dear Mrs. Freeman, who's I am with all the passion and sincerity imaginable."[28]

Prince George's brother, the Danish king, meanwhile, urged George to make peace with William and Mary. The easygoing prince did. And tried to bring the sisters together by minimizing bad feeling between their respective households despite Mary having bribed some of her sister's servants into being spies, lured others to more lucrative employment, and had Anne's letters opened. But the princess remained resolute. Reiterating her promise to Sarah, Anne said she would never dismiss her.

—⁂—

The new year (1694) began inauspiciously for Princess Anne. She suffered another miscarriage. Shortly after, ague (persistent fever, chills, and sweating, which doctors treated by confining Anne to a hot, airless room, and dosing her with various potions today considered unsafe) made the princess extremely ill. And Gloucester's recurrent fever did little to ease his mother's sickness. Failure to provide her delicate son with a sibling increased Anne's concern about him,

Princess Anne and her son William Henry, Duke of Gloucester, 1689–1700. The longest-lived of Anne's children, his death took from "the best ... the tenderest of mothers ... what she held most dear, the last fond hopes for her family." Artist: after Sir Godfrey Kneller, based on a circa 1694 painting. © National Portrait Gallery, London.

not only as a mother, but because the boy secured her future; if he died without siblings, William and Mary might well adopt the Prince of Wales, have him converted to Protestantism, and raise him as their successor.

Aware, nevertheless, that as a Protestant prince, Gloucester fortified their position, the joint monarchs took great interest in him; besides, they felt genuinely fond of their bright little nephew. William and Mary made crystal clear that their quarrel with his mother did not include the boy. Mary "made a great show of kindness" towards Gloucester, gave him toys; and—made sure these gestures were always noted "in the *Gazette*."[29]

Whenever Gloucester fell ill, his aunt Mary sent a servant to ask about him. "But this compliment [came in a manner] so offensive [to Anne that Sarah] often wondered how any mortal could bear it with the patience she did." Because Mary's servant entered the room without the ceremony due Princess Anne, and taking "no more notice of her, than if she were a rocker, [walked directly up to Gloucester, and spoke to him or the] nurse, as he lay in her lap."[30]

Of course, Anne resented her sister's conduct. She thought "it often enough if" Gloucester went to see the king and queen on their birthdays. But Mary invited him at other times as well. "I have often told you it goes extremely against the grain, [Anne confided to Sarah, but] so much better judgments than mine [Marlborough,[31] Prince George] think it necessary he shall go."[32] Giving William and Mary easy access to engaging, promising Gloucester would discourage them from adopting the Prince of Wales as part of a peace treaty with France.

—⁂—

As the year waned, the once again pregnant princess focused on averting another tragic result. She followed medical advice to avoid exercise, stay one floor, and recline on her couch. But when Anne heard that dreaded smallpox had struck her sister, she instantly sent a note begging Mary to believe in her concern, and asking for permission to visit. "When one considered that the first meeting must be emotional, which would harm the queen, and also the pregnant princess, the queen's doctors advised her sister not to come; and when the princess insisted, William personally wrote to explain why she must stay away, but if God willed the queen's recovery, Anne could come whenever she wished."[33]

Royals died as they were born—in public. Courtiers and politicians crowded into the queen's overheated, stuffy bedroom, her crimson velvet bed-curtains drawn against any breath of air. Clergymen prayed close to the bedside. Physicians conferred in corners, then plagued their patient with bleeding, purging, blistering, and placing hot irons on her forehead all, naturally, in vain. At the end, Mary declared "that she had nothing in her heart against her sister and that she loved the Duke of Gloucester very much."[34]

Barely had Mary expired, when Anne's most trusted advisors, Marlborough and Godolphin, arrived at Berkeley House. (Wise in the ways of court politics, Godolphin had, on resigning his office as William's lord treasurer, complied with his close friend Marlborough's request that he counsel the princess on her problems with the court.) The royal rift must, the two men urged, swiftly be repaired.

Her grief in any case genuine, Anne wrote William a warm and conciliatory condolence letter. It expressed her grief as if the quarrel with Mary had never been, and asked to see her brother-in-law to assure him of her loyalty and sisterly affection.

The king felt averse to accepting Anne's letter as a peace offering. He still disliked her, still mistrusted her, envied her popularity. But William realized that his wife's death had weakened his position, for although parliament granted him the kingship for life, Mary, as King James's eldest child, gave her husband's crown legitimacy. Besides, the Duke of Shrewsbury, whom William respected for his disinterested counsel, convinced the king of the impossibility of continuing "open indifference [to Anne] without exposing himself to daily slights and a manifest disregard for his sovereign pleasure. [Because William could not expect England's nobility to be] hindered, [now that Mary had died,] from paying respect to a princess [parliament had made] next heir to him ... and who if title by blood had taken place, would have had the crown before him; [as well, William knew everyone] who had a mind to show they did not care for him would certainly do it by making their court to her."[35]

Dropping the demand for Sarah's dismissal, William agreed to receive Anne. Advanced pregnancy necessitated her having to be carried up to the king's official reception chamber in a chair. I am truly sorry for your loss, the princess whispered through her tears. I am much concerned for yours, William muttered shakily. The king then escorted his sister-in-law to his private parlor for a long talk; it concluded with William marking their reunion by bestowing Mary's jewels on Anne.

Public knowledge that the royal quarrel had ended, caused "crowds of people of all sorts [to flock to Berkeley House to pay their] respects to the prince and princess"[36] regardless of how much they had previously slighted the Denmarks. Yet, although William gave Anne the apartments in St. James's Palace habitually occupied by the heir apparent, and announced that she would keep court as if she were queen, the king excluded his successor from all state concerns.

"Not made acquainted with public affairs; [not encouraged to recommend anybody to] posts of trust or advantage; [no orders either that the ministry] inform her how matters went [or] oblige those around her, [the princess] lived in a due abstraction from business."[37] Nevertheless, Anne seemed "more satisfied with [William] though he had used her ill and usurped her right, than that her father, who had always cherished her beyond expression, should be restored."[38]

Princess Anne wanted to be queen as much to satisfy her ambition as to prevent a Catholic from becoming king.

—ɯ—

The windows of Anne's new residence in St. James's Palace overlooked a pretty, private garden; beyond its trellised walls were two long rows of tall trees enclosing the Mall, a fashionable promenade; Westminster Abbey's pointed Gothic towers rose beyond. But the princess had little time to admire the view.

"Those who enjoyed her confidence [judged Anne a] lady of intelligence and ambition."[39] But although well-versed in family history, (her grandfather's execution in the civil war, her uncle's restoration, revolution against her father) and experienced in the ways of courts, the princess had no formal education in statecraft. Like her father conscientious, like her mother sensible, the princess now consulted the royal librarian about starting a course of reading in history. And despite her inability, as a female, openly to participate in politics, Anne sought to understand current issues via Prince George, who represented her interests in government councils, and Marlborough, who served the same function in parliament. Further, to explain the legislature's inner workings, Anne summoned John's protégé, short and plump Robert Harley, whose ruddy face revealed his fancy for fine food and wine, whose matchless parliamentary management and expertise in constitutional history had resulted in his election as speaker of the house of commons.

—⋙—

The princess's disheartening cycle of pregnancy and miscarriages, not to mention an enforced sedentary lifestyle had, meanwhile, debilitated Anne and destroyed her once slender figure. (By all accounts she ate and drank in moderation.) But the princess still enjoyed stag hunting—until thirty-two-year-old Anne "endured cruel torture."[40] Gout[41] attacked "my knee as well as my foot, and at this time I am a perfect cripple.... I am indeed mightily sunk with this bad pain, and, let people say what they will, it is impossible to help having the spleen when one is in such misery."[42]

Of more concern to the princess than her own health were Gloucester's constant fevers. She "loved him to a great degree, [visiting almost every day] in her sedan chair and was carried upstairs."[43] Focus of her dynastic ambitions, Gloucester's importance grew as Anne seemed unlikely to have more children. Hence, the Denmarks succeeded, after much urging, in getting William to honor the boy. Amidst great pomp, Gloucester, on his seventh birthday, became a member of England's most exalted fraternity, the Order of the Garter. His parents marked the occasion with a formal dinner for one hundred guests.

Gloucester now merited a separate household and appropriate tutors. Parliament voted £50,000 annually for the purpose. William gave Anne £15,000 and kept the rest. Diplomatically swallowing her chagrin, the princess made up the difference.

Others disappointed in the king began to gravitate towards her. Sensing peril in conflict, the king again sought counsel from Shrewsbury. William must set aside personal feelings, Shrewsbury advised, and accept the man who had proved himself to be England's most talented soldier; Marlborough's position as trusted counselor to the heiress apparent should also weigh with William. Hence, the king placated the princess by reinstating John's army rank and appointing him to the important post of Gloucester's governor, which brought Marlborough a substantial salary.

William refused the Denmarks' choice for their son's principal tutor, but the king allowed Anne to appoint other members of Gloucester's household. William then changed his mind. That forced the princess into a humiliating position—she must rescind her promises. Advising Anne to be patient, Marlborough waited for a propitious moment to tell William that the princess had already awarded the places; besides, an upset might affect her pregnancy. Enraged, the king roared "she should not be queen before her time."[44]

—⋙—

William now moved to have parliament confirm his grants of King James's Irish estates to his Dutch friends and a former mistress. Anne thought the estates rightfully hers. Hence, the princess asked her household controller to write, "by the first opportunity, [to someone he knew in Ireland to request,] in your name, [that this acquaintance] send you a copy [of the Irish parliament's act giving the estate] settled upon the king my father ... to Lady Orkney." Anne warned her controller not to name her in the correspondence, not to tell "anybody whatsoever that you have sent any such thing."[45]

Armed with appropriate documentation, Anne wrote William: he might not know James had willed the Irish estates to his daughters, so, with all due respect, she requested that he drop parliamentary action. The king did not deign to reply.

He also ignored Anne's note of congratulation on his successful siege of Namur, one of William's rare victories in nine years of war. She had written on Marlborough's advice, although Sarah disagreed: the king's conduct towards the princess did not merit such notice. John re-sent the princess's note, writing tactfully that the original must have got lost in transit. William ignored that missive as well.

Tired of war, the combatants began peace talks. Anne worried that as part of a peace treaty, William would agree to Louis XIV's demand that James, or his son, be restored after William's death. But James insisted on instant restoration. Consequently, the Treaty of Ryswick (1697) turned out well for Anne; because although Louis failed to recognize William as King of England, Scotland, and Ireland in the treaty itself, the French king did accord William the honor in the preamble; and a formula binding Louis to deny any direct or indirect aid to William's enemies, confirmed him as king.

After Ryswick, Prince George asked King William to repay the debt he owed over the Danish land George had ceded to Sweden at William's behest shortly after the Revolution. William refused. With right on his side, George insisted. Prince and king traded harsh words.

Hence, in the waning days of the seventeenth century, Marlborough "bestirred himself [to bring] the state of the Prince of Denmark's debt"[46] before parliament. As a result, the new century brought "success."[47]

> I was once going to endeavor to thank your lord myself for what was done last night concerning the prince's business, it being wholly owing to your & his kindness, [Anne wrote Sarah.] But I durst not do it, for fear of not being able to express the true sense of my poor heart, & therefore must desire my dear Mrs. Freeman to say a great deal both for Mr. Morley and myself, & though we are poor in words, be so just as to believe we are truly sensible & most faithfully yours.[48]

After previously bearing a dead baby girl, Anne now miscarried male twins. Courtiers commented on her physical recovery; but no one could fathom the depth of her emotional agony. The princess's next pregnancy resulted in another miscarriage. Gout followed; severe pain in her right hand prevented Anne from writing—a particular blow because she could not communicate with Sarah. After three more miscarriages, the princess's seventeenth and final pregnancy ended with the stillbirth of a premature son that the doctors judged to have been dead in her womb for a month.[49]

Amidst this misery Anne experienced some joy in the engagement of her favorite Marlborough offspring (eldest daughter Henrietta) to Sidney Godolphin's only child. The princess expressed her liking for Henrietta, affection for Sarah, and general satisfaction with the nuptials, via the generous dowry she gave the bride.

> My dear Mrs. Freeman has no reason to be uneasy with the thoughts that she can never do enough to deserve my kindness, for she has done more than any other mortal did to merit another's friendship & it is very kind in setting so great a value upon so poor an expression as I have made of my truth, which upon my word I am not satisfied with, it coming far short of what my heart is inclined to do, but as long as I live, [Anne wrote in exaggerated contemporary style] I must be endeavoring to show that never anybody had a sincerer passion for another than I have for my dear dear Mrs. Freeman.[50]

Ten-year-old Gloucester, meanwhile, appeared to have outgrown his childhood ailments. Tall, upright, and active, the agile, intelligent boy had a large head, long oval face, good color and complexion, and his mother's glossy brown hair. Pride and pleasure in her son eased Anne's anguish over her failure to give Gloucester siblings.

The boy celebrated his eleventh birthday a few months after his mother's last stillbirth. Gloucester took an energetic part in each festivity, but by evening seemed tired, complained of chills and a sore throat. Anne stayed at her son's bedside, nursing him with "great tenderness [and a] grave composedness, that amazed all who saw it."[51] In her battle with death, Anne suffered with her son, soothed his burning brow through days of delirium, blinding headaches, and raging thirst as the boy threshed from side to side of his bed, endured the pointless blood-lettings and painful blistering mandated by contemporary medical—so-called—science.

The princess bore her son's death[52] with "a very singular … resignation and piety."[53] But the tragedy left a permanent bruise on her heart. Because it snatched from "the best of princesses, the best of mothers … what she held most dear, the last fond hopes of her family."[54]

During Anne's subsequent lingering fever, she and her husband mourned together alone, (admitting only the Marlboroughs, and then rarely) and read each other religious texts; for, although the princess's "grief was great, her resignation to the will of him, who is the wise disposer of all … things, was still greater. [Anne's piety] enabled her to bear the shock. [Observing] with silent astonishment, the pious fortitude of his beloved princess, [George became] reconciled to his own irreparable loss."[55]

Anne took some comfort in her strong sense of ceremonial. Gloucester must have full royal funerary honors. After the boy's body had lain in state for several days, a cavalcade conveyed the small casket to Westminster Abbey with all due pomp; burial followed after a solemn and dignified private service. The princess did not break her seclusion to attend; but did order that the day of Gloucester's death be kept as a day of mourning in her family.

And after this calamity the childless princess signed herself "poor unfortunate Morley" in letters to Sarah, who had recently married two of her four beautiful daughters to scions of England's oldest noble houses,[56] and had a handsome, promising son.

—⚹—

"I do not consider it necessary to use many words to tell you of the surprise and sorrow with which I learned of the death of the Duke of Gloucester, [King William wrote.] It is so great a loss for me and for all England that my heart is pierced with pain."[57]

Gloucester's death shook the succession. Who would ascend the throne after William and Anne? With a better hereditary claim than either, the Prince of Wales could still change his religion, and claim his patrimony.

William favored James I's granddaughter Sophia, Electress of Hanover. The king originally broached the idea to her during one of his annual summer holidays in Holland. Contact had been secret, and intensified after Mary's death, later Gloucester's. Since Hanover proved a reliable Protestant ally in the war against France, William then personally convinced Sophia to accept the British succession. In fact, William would have preferred that Sophia, not Anne, succeed him; after all, he and Sophia both claimed the British throne through their mothers.

Anne agreed that Sophia succeed her—better that Protestant Sophia and her son succeed than leave open a path for the Catholic Prince of Wales.

Parliament passed the Act of Settlement. It confirmed a Protestant succession in the Hanoverian line: Sophia and her Protestant heirs would succeed should Anne die childless; further, all future monarchs must belong to the Church of England. The Act also slapped at William by providing that the monarch could not leave the country without parliament's consent or involve the nation in war for Hanoverian interests; the privy council, not secret cabinets, must approve all state business; and only native Englishmen were eligible to hold crown offices.

William swallowed the Act's unprecedented, not to say offensive, curbs on royal prerogative because the European situation had become acute.

—ɯ—

The sudden death of childless King Carlos of Spain caused a conundrum. Carlos designated no heir but did leave a will. It gave the entire Spanish empire[58] to Carlos's teenaged nephew Philip, Duc d'Anjou, grandson of Louis XIV. The will further stipulated that if Louis failed to accept the whole empire on Philip's behalf, it must go, intact, to the Austrian claimant, the emperor's brother. Louis hesitated. Rejection meant his archenemy, the Hapsburg Emperor of Austria, would add Spanish domains to his vast continental holdings already stretching across eastern Europe from the Balkans to the Baltic. Acceptance meant such expansion of French power, that war would surely result. For creation of a French behemoth in western Europe would be anathema to Austria; and the major maritime nations, England and Holland, would never countenance the prospect of France and Spain united under one crown and ruling over a global empire that controlled a large portion of the world's commerce.

Yet, Louis had good cause for confidence. As Europe's most powerful state, France had an invincible army made up of disciplined French (not mercenary) troops equipped with superior firepower and backed by Europe's biggest and best militia.

Wasting little time in idle speculation, therefore, Louis accepted; and in declaring his grandson King Philip V of Spain, averred that since the boy would rule Spain and, eventually, France, the Pyrenees no longer existed—a prospect Britain's King William viewed with alarm. But his subjects believed Philip would be an independent ruler, thus assuring the continued flow of English commerce.

The French king immediately imposed high tariffs on English goods, excluded England and Holland from trade with Spanish possessions, and took over the *Asiento* (monopoly of the lucrative slave trade between Africa and the Americas). And to prove his point about the Pyrenees, Louis promptly marched an army, on behalf of his grandson Philip, into the Spanish Netherlands, thereby threatening the adjacent Dutch Republic in direct violation of the recently signed Treaty of Ryswick.

Since English wealth depended on commerce, parliament asked the king to re-form the Grand Alliance. (England, the Austrian Hapsburg Empire, the Dutch Republic, and several German states.) The Alliance had fought French power for nine years until Ryswick. Parliament further urged William to resurrect England's defensive treaty with Holland; and authorized the dispatch of ten thousand troops to the Dutch Republic.

Never physically strong, the now ailing king needed a man with superior diplomatic skills to accomplish the arduous task of rebuilding the Alliance as well as bringing into it Denmark, Sweden, Prussia and as many other independent German states as possible. In addition, this man must be an English general, for English troops would not follow a foreigner. Marlborough had the additional advantage of being confidential advisor to

Princess Anne, whom William had at last brought himself to admit, would soon succeed him. Hence, the king appointed Marlborough commander in chief of the British forces currently deployed in Holland, and ambassador extraordinary to its government.

—⁂—

Hardly had the signatories to the reconstituted Grand Alliance[59] put down their quill pens, when Princess Anne's father died. Shortly before his death, James asked his wife "to let you know that he forgave you, [Mary Beatrice wrote Anne] "from the bottom of his heart and prayed God to do so too; that he gave you his last blessing, and prayed to God to convert your heart, and confirm you in the resolution of repairing to his son the wrongs done to himself."[60]

Against this assault, Anne took refuge in her religion. She could not betray it, give up her crown to a Catholic, but would do her duty to the best of her ability. The princess at once ordered her entire household and her home in St. James's Palace into full royal mourning, which she and George would, of course, also observe. But William decided not to mourn James as a king; he would mark his predecessor's death like that of a private citizen—mourning clothes for himself and his personal servants only. Anne's action thus posed a problem.

For her own sake, for her country's sake, the princess must not so obviously oppose the king, said Marlborough. In Holland with William, John urged Godolphin to impress his advice on Anne. "Out of all patience [to think she] must do so monstrous a thing [as not put her home] in mourning for my father,"[61] Anne prudently complied.

French King Louis, meanwhile, lost no time in formally acknowledging the Prince of Wales as King James III. This blatant violation of the Treaty of Ryswick, (which recognized William as king) never mind brazen meddling in British business, outraged the nation as well as its princess—what right did a foreign ruler, and a Catholic to boot, have to cast doubt on the legitimacy of Anne's succession.

Not content with his moves thus far, Louis marked the new year (1702) by rejecting allied conditions as set forth in the Treaty of Grand Alliance. The French king thereby challenged Europe's two foremost naval powers, England and Holland, plus Austria's Hapsburg emperor and several German states, to accept French hegemony.

At about the same time that King Louis XIV's actions launched the War of the Spanish Succession, King William III went hunting in Windsor Forest. His horse stumbled on a molehill, sending the king sprawling on the ground with a broken collarbone, a painful albeit minor injury. The king seemed to recover, but his frail body, for years beset by chronic asthma, swollen legs, and gout, failed to sustain the effect of his fall, particularly when William caught a chill, became feverish, and could not eat.

Marlborough, Godolphin, and Harley began to meet privately with Anne to hammer out a smooth succession. She had resolved not to be a cipher. Despite her sex, Anne meant to perform all the duties expected of a sovereign.

Consistent to the end, the dying king refused her requests to visit him.

Six

"Nursing mother"

"A native queen in all her pomp appears to crown our hopes and dissipate our fears."[1]—Coronation hymn

Anne Stuart's ascent to the throne (March 8, 1702) "afforded a remarkable mixture of sorrow [at King William's death] and joy [at Anne's accession; but the] latter as it was more general, so it seemed to be justified by heaven itself. The sky having never been more serene, nor the sun shone more bright and glorious."[2] A Sunshine Day indeed. The day Anne had, during the joint monarchs' reign ten years ago, told Sarah Churchill she could await with Patience.

The new queen's subjects saw the fine, warm weather as a good omen. Yes, Anne had deserted her father the king even if to preserve her religion, defied her sister the queen in order to maintain her autonomy, and failed in her prime duty—to provide her country with a Protestant heir. She might be plump, middle-aged, and gout-ridden, but Anne was a fully English monarch. That gave people confidence in her; the queen would understand them.

Queen Anne faced the challenge of being a woman who wielded authority over men accustomed to view any female as weak, and of inferior ability. But although physically and emotionally diminished at age thirty-seven, Anne determined to fulfill all her responsibilities. The woman who had been the locus, no matter how carefully low-key, of Protestant opposition to Catholic King James her father; who had actively participated in revolution against him; who had resisted King William and Queen Mary's pressure, had already proved herself resolute. Indeed, the new queen's reserve, and retired lifestyle cloaked a firm, independent-minded female.

—⁜—

King James's recent death relieved Anne of any scruples she may have had over her father's exclusion from the throne; and parliamentary legislation banning a Catholic from becoming king eliminated her half-brother even had his birth been legitimate, which Anne still doubted. Hence, the queen could begin her reign as she meant to continue with a clear conscience.

Right away, Anne showed appreciation for the symbolic significance of royal ritual. She ordered new black mourning clothes in memory of her father's recent death, but these garments had only purple (mourning color worn by royalty for royalty) trimming for William, a pointed reminder of his refusing full mourning for James. And to emphasize the queen's Englishness, every court gentleman followed the lead of Anne's husband

Prince George. He wore a mourning hatband made of English silk rather than the customary Italian crepe imported from The Pope's Country.

With an untested woman heading the government, and the country on the cusp of a crucial war, many feared for the nation's welfare. Hence, the queen and her counselors agreed that their primary task must be reassurance.

The privy council immediately waited on Anne. Wearing her mourning dress of black figured silk with purple trim, and matching manto, her figure stately but still graceful, her face pleasant, Anne looked the personification of a queen.

With gravitas and authority, not to mention "softness of voice and sweetness of pronunciation that added much life to all she spoke,"[3] the queen expressed great respect for the late king's memory; promised to follow him in preserving church and state; opposing French power via fidelity to the Grand Alliance; and keeping the succession in the Protestant line. "Her declaration ... which she spoke all of it without book ... is highly applauded."[4]

Unlike her brusque predecessor, the new sovereign "received all that came to her in so gracious a manner that they went from her highly satisfied with her goodness and her obliging deportment, for she hearkened with attention to everything ... said to her."[5] Anne earned further accolades by answering "my lord mayor's speech so well. [And] the people like their new queen, thinking there will not so much of their money go out of England as the king carried out."[6]

—⁂—

The queen "is very unwieldy and lame; must she come in person to the house of lords, [Anne's advisor Sidney Godolphin asked parliamentary procedure expert Robert Harley] or may she send for the two houses to come to her"?[7]

She should come to parliament, said Harley, particularly as this would be Anne's first speech from the throne. "I suppose the queen will come ... but I doubt whether she has any robes,"[8] Godolphin replied.

Cognizant that this, her first formal appearance before the nation's representatives, would have major symbolic value, Anne showed her mettle. Magnificent in her crown glittering with diamonds, red velvet robe lined with ermine and edged with gold braid, her heavy gold chain bearing the badge of England's patron saint, St. George, and her broad, pale blue ribbon of England's highest order, the Garter, Anne modeled her garb on a portrait of her eminent and popular ancestor, Queen Elizabeth I.

The first monarch since Elizabeth born in England of an English mother, Anne, like Elizabeth, ruled alone in her own right, and would be the last of her line to reign.[9] Like Elizabeth, Anne had a royal father and commoner mother; events had estranged her from an older sister who, married to a foreigner, had been queen; and she had spent virtually all her life in England. A Protestant queen like Elizabeth, Anne also faced the challenge of guiding her country in a war against the mightiest Catholic king on earth.

As a fully English monarch, moreover, Anne felt she must restore Englishness to the crown. Dutch William who preceded her, had promoted his Dutch cronies and Dutch interests. The Hanoverians who succeeded her, might easily favor German concerns.

The queen gave her speech (which her ministers wrote, starting a tradition that continues to this day) without notes; and, as she would continue to do, Anne reviewed the speech beforehand and made some changes. Despite painful shyness and an embarrassing tendency to blush, the queen proved an excellent public speaker thanks to childhood elocution lessons from a professional actress. She spoke clearly but softly in a smooth musical contralto, her cadence pleasing. Anne's superb delivery helped create confidence in the new regime.

With her heart fully English, (a claim no sovereign could make since Elizabeth died a century ago) Anne promised readiness to do anything her subjects required of her, for England's happiness and prosperity. The new queen's adoption of Elizabeth's motto, *Semper Eadem*, (always the same) underlined this commitment.

Fully English resonated with the queen's patriotic audience, long resentful of King William favoring Dutch interests, to say nothing of foreign influence under Anne's uncle Charles and father, James, who had a French Catholic mother and foreign Catholic wives. But fully English Anne, whose fervent Anglicanism underlined her Englishness in contrast to William's continental Calvinism, seemed like one of the people. They called their blushing new queen, English Rose.

—⁂—

Fierce party rivalry figured as *the* basic fact of political life during Queen Anne's reign. The two major parties were not monolithic, but almost all politicians linked with either Whigs or Tories to some extent.

Party warfare permeated every aspect of life. Whigs and Tories rarely met in social or financial circles. Party affiliation affected popular meeting places like coffee houses, also shops, academia, the arts, marriage, military promotion, and professional choice like physician, architect, and lawyer; in towns and counties local officials were pawns in national party rivalry. Party spirit ruled in almost every diocese, thus affecting each citizen. And the press exacerbated the power and reach of England's political divide, for removal of press censorship in the previous reign made every print publication a medium of party propaganda.

King William had favored Whigs. Eager to curb the royal prerogative, Whigs had been mainly responsible for bringing him to England. Devoutly Anglican Anne preferred Tories, the pro–Church, anti-dissenter party that upheld the ruler's hereditary rights and prerogatives. Tories "made much noise with their zeal" for Anne, mainly after her son Gloucester's death, for Jacobites among them hoped she would make the "pretended" Prince of Wales her heir. But since Anne, as princess, had discouraged political activity at her court, Tories "came seldom to her. [Whigs kept] a great distance from [Anne throughout] the former reign."[10]

She wanted to avoid becoming a prisoner of either Tories or Whigs, to stay out of "the power of the merciless men of both parties."[11] Resolved to maintain the crown's political independence, Anne thought a moderate government, meaning a mixed ministry made up of moderates from both the Whig and Tory parties, would be in the nation's best interest. For the new queen equated party strife with national discord, which she judged would weaken her country.

The parties diverged over war policy. Tories, (most of whom were squires) thought the war unnecessarily entangled their country in Europe. Squires resented having to pay the land tax; it made up most of the government's annual revenue and fell especially heavily on landowners who relied on rental income. The mostly Whig men of commerce, on the other hand, had large incomes but little landed property, so they escaped the land tax with relative ease.

Tory squires thus hated the wealthy Whig merchants and bankers; besides, they threatened the squirearchy's political power by buying constituencies and bribing voters. As well, Tories suspected the influx of foreign Protestants fleeing war in their home countries; for, these immigrants tended to engage in business, and Tories sought to restrain the growth of the newer commercial classes.

Whigs—landed magnates, commercial interests, and all dissenters from Anglican orthodoxy saw the Grand Alliance as essential to Europe's balance of power and, thus, English domestic security. Hence, the alliance must be nurtured despite the faults of several allies. Whigs welcomed Protestant refugees because they infused the economy with energy, expertise, and foreign capital.

Fervently English and Protestant Anne saw defeat of France, whose king challenged not only her religion but also her right to reign, as her prime duty. She immediately dashed any expectation the French may have cherished that she lacked the guts to fight them.

—⁂—

Queen Anne dismissed most of King William's ministers. But she kept the Earl of Marlborough in the crucial military and diplomatic offices William had assigned him.

Despite having for years trusted Marlborough, beloved husband of her dearest friend, Anne's fondness for Sarah, per se, by no means guaranteed John's continuation in office. Rather, the new queen approved of his moderate Toryism, applauded his sincere religious sentiments, agreed with Marlborough's wish to stay above fiercely fighting political factions and work for national unity. As well, John's negotiation of the complex treaties of the Grand Alliance gave him a unique grasp of the intricacies prevalent in continental politics. And despite having never been given the chance to win a major battle, Marlborough had proved his military ability. Anne, therefore, judged him the best man to lead her armies against France.

The queen confirmed Marlborough, at the then advanced age of fifty-one, as captain general of British forces in Holland and ambassador extraordinary to the Dutch Republic. Anne also made him captain general of her armies at home and abroad, and master general of the ordnance, a lucrative post John had long sought. (Responsible for all army supplies, he got a commission from vendors.) And, ten years after William refused Princess Anne and Prince George's requests to grant Marlborough the Garter, the queen, on the fifth day of her reign, personally conferred England's most exalted order on him. With the new queen's favor thus prominently displayed, Marlborough at once left for The Hague to assure the Dutch and other allied envoys assembled there that England would honor its commitments to the Grand Alliance.

Queen Anne's endorsement of the Alliance fully engaged her country in the War of the Spanish Succession. Earlier, the nation had fought for its survival as a Protestant country and constitutional monarchy under a Dutch king and his Dutch generals. Now, an English queen and her English general led the nation in war.

—⁂—

Marlborough's responsibilities, not to mention his wife's intimate friendship with the queen, gave him a prominent place in Anne's government. She must next decide on who would be the best man to fill the crucial position of lord treasurer. Anne's hard-drinking uncle, fiery Earl Rochester, coveted the office he had held under James II; besides, Rochester thought the treasury his rightful due as Tory leader as well as the queen's close relation. Despite Rochester's refusal to help Anne over her allowance at the beginning of James's reign, as well as in her quarrel with Mary, the queen's sense of family loyalty inclined her to him. High Tory Rochester strongly advocated England focusing its war effort on the seas, where the nation could take advantage of its superior navy.

Moderate Tory[12] Marlborough held that France would never be curbed unless England committed her army to a major land war. He wanted his best friend and similarly moderate Tory, the able financial executive Lord Sidney Godolphin, to head the treasury; for, Marlborough knew that gold greases the wheels of war.

"A man of few words, but of remarkable thoughtfulness and sedateness of temper; of great application to business, and of such dispatch in it, as to give pleasure to those who attended him upon any affair,"[13] Godolphin understood England's relation to the Continent. The threat of French dominion, with its devastating effect on English commerce, must be defeated.

Marlborough could not achieve that, could not command the army overseas without the security of having sufficient funds, not to mention the assurance that the money would reach him on the Continent in a timely fashion. An efficient administrator and extremely competent financier, Godolphin, as treasury chief, could be guaranteed to provide that security. Nearing the venerable (for that time) age of sixty, Godolphin preferred his quiet private life of playing tennis, cards, and chess, breeding and racing thoroughbred horses. But yielded to Marlborough's appeal to his patriotism and sense of duty.

John now impressed on Anne how Godolphin had proved himself a reliable, able, and loyal servant to three kings—Charles, James, and William. As well, Godolphin held moderate Tory views and wished to stay above party strife. Besides, Marlborough had lately, and not without difficulty, succeeded in getting the Allies to agree to a new war aim that Anne fully endorsed—France must deny the Prince of Wales's claim to the British throne and recognize the Protestant succession. Anne trusted Marlborough; she had experience of Godolphin's dependability. The queen appointed him lord treasurer.[14]

—m—

She chose wisely. Sitting at his large mahogany desk in the ground floor lord treasurer's room at Whitehall with its four, silk curtained windows letting in large amounts of light, Godolphin at once put his talent and tenacity into reviving a financial system which had wilted under the weight of expenses incurred because of King William's continental wars. With the queen's backing, her new lord treasurer brought structure to guaranteeing parliamentary grants. Based on the trust he inspired in the Bank of England and financial community, Godolphin continued the policy begun under William of long-term government borrowing (funded mainly through the sale of annuities) to develop the country's wealth. His measures assured enough money to fund the War of the Spanish Succession.

Rochester became lord lieutenant of Ireland, thereby keeping his seat in the cabinet. But, rather than moving to Dublin, the queen's uncle stayed in London where he could better promote Tory interests. And to Tory satisfaction, the queen appointed as one of her two secretaries of state, Rochester's High Tory ally. Nicknamed Don Dismal, the tall, thin, swarthy and doleful Earl Nottingham's birth, experience, and pious lifestyle appealed to squires and country clergy.

Nottingham and Rochester openly challenged Marlborough's war strategy. England should deploy her powerful fleet to attack French weaknesses—colonies and navy. Unless

France were defeated at her strongest point—her continental army, Marlborough countered, French ambitions to rule Europe would never be checked.

Anne, Godolphin, and Marlborough invited their friend the moderate Whig Duke of Shrewsbury (one of the Immortal Seven who invited William to England, and a member of the Denmarks' Cockpit Circle) to join the cabinet. But Shrewsbury, whose hatred of partisan politics had driven him to resign his office under King William and flee to Rome, ostensibly for his health, preferred to remain there.

The queen saw cabinet unanimity on war, or, indeed, any other matter, as unnecessary, but did want moderation rather than extremes to prevail in governance. So, she backed Marlborough's prompting the cabinet to make resolute war plans. And yielded to Rochester in appointing a minimum of Whigs to places in court and ministry while resisting his efforts to purge Whigs from lower government positions.

Although not formally in the ministry, house of commons speaker Robert Harley worked closely with Marlborough and Godolphin. Outwardly amiable, Harley proved hard to fathom, especially as he spoke in an abstruse, opaque, and often insincere manner. This earned Harley the nickname, Robin the Trickster. Marlborough and Godolphin, who sat in the house of lords, relied on master parliamentarian Harley to manage the Commons.

Sidney, first Earl Godolphin, 1645–1712. Anne chose this "man of the clearest head ... calmest temper," and highest integrity as her first lord treasurer and prime minister. He attended Anne with "particular affection and zeal." The queen relied on Godolphin to keep her out of the hands of Merciless Men of both parties. Artist: John Smith after Sir Godfrey Kneller, 1707. © National Portrait Gallery, London.

———— ⁓⁓ ————

"The Prince of Denmark ... possessed sound good sense."[15] Queen Anne wanted to give her husband his due, especially after the insults he had endured under the joint monarchs. George should be her official consort. That, said Marlborough and Godolphin, would contravene the constitution, besides damage the English aspect of Anne's reign.

The queen then sought to have her husband become supreme allied commander. That would have foiled Marlborough's ambition, but neither he nor Sarah tried to dissuade Anne—because John's experience in negotiating the Grand Alliance made him familiar with politics at The Hague and Vienna. Knowing England's major allies, Holland and the Hapsburg Empire, would never accept George, Marlborough saw no need to oppose the queen himself. Indeed, the Dutch, with more troops in the allied army than England, refused to serve under the prince. (Britain had the smallest number of troops but English gold financed a large mercenary cadre and the armies of several allies.) Anne gave in. In return, Holland agreed that Marlborough become allied commander in chief. That made him the queen's de facto foreign minister for not only must Marlborough, via personal negotiation with foreign heads of state, fuse a group of fractious, envious, often inept allies and lead them to victory, but also, the war constituted *the* foreign policy issue of the day.

The queen contented herself by appointing George generalissimo of all her armed forces. This not only served to promote the prince's importance, but also spared his gout-plagued spouse the need to carry out royal military formalities like reviewing the troops. So, early in Anne's reign and before the War of the Spanish Succession officially began, George went to Portsmouth to review England's land and sea forces. "The magistrates, and the governor of that place [received the prince] with all the honor and respect due to his royal birth, his high station, and the dear consort of her majesty."[16]

The queen also made her husband lord high admiral and warden of the cinque ports (five port towns on England's southeast coast that were crucial to the nation's defense). The position of lord high admiral had always gone to a trusted member of the royal family—the most recent occupant had been Anne's father when Duke of York—and had a seat in the cabinet. Although that body set naval strategy, the prince and his council controlled naval administration, including naval expenses, which made up half of the military budget, as well as some military, civil, and judicial responsibilities. Because the navy formed England's first line of defense, and since the island nation's wealth depended on commerce, necessitating naval protection for merchant ships, the lord high admiral had substantial responsibilities, particularly in a time of war.

Prince George sensibly eschewed partisan strife, confining himself, rather, to his naval duties. But the prince's ability to appoint admiralty positions, as well as members of his household, gave George the power of patronage, which he used to build a core of support in the Lords as well as the Commons. The prince also wielded electoral influence, for the Cinque Ports each returned two members to parliament. Committed to the war and the Hanoverian succession—scarcely surprising for a zealous Protestant and former soldier, a prince related to the Elector of Hanover, and one whose position relied on the Revolutionary settlement—George's inclinations and naval responsibilities combined to make him reinforce Anne's policies.

This happily married couple lived, at least as far as the world could see, in a fashion contrary to contemporary custom. She, a member of the Weaker Sex, with supposedly inferior intellect, stood in a superior position to her husband, for Anne occupied the throne by herself. Nonetheless, she often consulted the prince. He "kept whisperers off and helped her judgment."[17]

—⚉—

Although several years her senior, and troubled by "asthma that every year had ill effects on his health,"[18] George, his wife decided, must have a secure and independent income, especially as she, hardly in robust health, could easily predecease him. Since "it became her to provide for all events,"[19] Anne asked parliament to settle an annual lifetime revenue of £100,000 on her husband.

Despite heavy war taxes, the Commons agreed, but included a clause limiting "the succession to the Hanover family,"[20] (George need have no illusion of kingship should he outlive Anne) and barring naturalized foreign-born persons from holding office. Since the latter clause would impact the prince's new responsibilities, let alone his sitting in the house of lords, the Commons proposed a clause to exempt him. But the Lords objected, claiming this constituted a Tack (irrelevant addition to a money bill). The queen "preferred it with the greatest earnestness she had yet showed in anything whatsoever. She thought it became her as a good wife."[21]

> I am sure the prince's bill passing after so much struggle is wholly owing to the pains you & Mr. Freeman have taken [Anne wrote Sarah.] I ought to say a great deal to both of you in return, but neither words nor actions can ever express the true sense Mr. Morley and I have of your sincere kindness in this & on all other occasions, and therefore I will not say any more on this subject but that to my last moment, your poor unfortunate, faithful Morley will be most passionately and tenderly yours.[22]

Because now, "whenever it please God to take me out of this world I shall die in quiet, which I should not have done if I had left him [George] unsettled."[23]

"Highly displeased with those that had opposed"[24] the Bill, Queen Anne never forgave the Whig opposition leader, Earl Sunderland. She had feared and hated his father, a Catholic advisor to King James, for prodding James into pro–Catholic excesses and suspected Lady Sunderland, whom James foisted on Anne as a lady-in-waiting, of spying on her.

—⁂—

Queen Anne "came to the crown with a universal joy. [This] good and gracious princess [showed] high virtue, merit, and sweetness of temper. [She proved to be] an excellent and pious queen."[25]

Anne chose to be crowned on the Festival of St. George, England's patron saint. But while members of the military marching band burnished their brass instruments and brushed minuscule specks of dust from their bright yellow uniforms, gout in the knee and foot lamed their queen. So a little after eleven in the morning on a bright and sunny April twenty-third, four specially selected yeomen of the guard had the honor of carrying Queen Anne from Westminster Hall to the Abbey, in a specially designed, carved, and gilded open chair of state with crimson velvet upholstery, fringed canopy, and low back to allow her six-yard train to flow to the Duchess of Somerset, (Anne's erstwhile landlady at Syon House) first noble lady in the land, and other aristocratic train-bearers walking at stately pace behind.

In front, privy councilors, gentlemen of the privy chamber, judges, peers, peeresses, bishops, and London aldermen marched slowly "on foot upon blue cloth … and the houses on each side being crowded with vast numbers of spectators, expressing their great joy and satisfaction by loud and repeated acclamations."[26]

Her "well-made … middle-sized"[27] figure still attractive, even if somewhat plump from pregnancies, her grey eyes and rounded face, grave, Anne, in contrast to her usual plain garb and lack of jewelry, (due to personal preference and gout, which made wearing the complex layers of fashionable dress difficult) wore a dress of gold tissue richly embroidered with gems, over it a crimson velvet cloak lined with ermine and trimmed with gold braid; her petticoat of gold tissue showed gold and silver lace between rows of fine diamonds. The blue ribbon of the Garter, and a thick gold chain carrying the badge of St. George, completed this toilette. Diamonds shone in Anne's luxuriant hair; "she wore a crimson velvet cap with ermine under the circlet, which was set with diamonds, and in the middle a sprig of diamond drops transparent hung in the form of a plume of feathers, for this is the Prince of Wales's Cap, which, till after the coronation that makes them legal king or queen they wear."[28]

With her customary detailed attention to the symbolic significance of royal regalia, Anne made sure everyone could see that she, and not her half-brother the Pretended Prince of Wales, was legitimate possessor of the throne.

On arrival at the Abbey, the queen, at this first chance to present herself formally to the nation, abandoned her chair and, despite gout, walked down the aisle to the altar. Seated, she listened to the service, then rose to give thanks for the sermon—whose text she had chosen—"And kings shall be thy nursing-fathers and queens thy nursing-mothers." (Isaiah 49: 23) Anne meant to be mother to her people.

She remained standing while the archbishop asked the packed congregation if it accepted Anne as sovereign. A roar of affirmation replied.

Before taking her coronation oath, Anne willingly complied with a novel requirement. Well aware that her religion constituted a crucial element in establishing her legitimacy as queen, Anne read a long statement against the doctrine of transubstantiation.

Having taken her oath, the queen accepted the gold spurs and sword of state, male monarchic symbols that only William, not Mary, received at their joint coronation. Anne slipped onto her finger the ring symbolizing marriage to her realm.

Still standing so that all could see her, Anne accepted the orb and scepter before the archbishop anointed her. As the Abbey rang with hurrahs, trumpets, and drumrolls, and guns boomed outside, the archbishop put a diamond encrusted crown on the new queen's head. After taking the sacrament, she sat enthroned to receive the homage of peers (first Prince George, first nobleman in the land due to his membership in the royal family) and bishops. Anne then retired to a small chapel for private prayer, emerging in her royal purple robe and specially commissioned crown of state clustered with magnificent diamonds, and topped with a diamond crowded cross that blazed with the least motion.

The whole procession then returned to Westminster Hall. There the queen "again quitted her chair [and walked to her table placed] on a great rise of steps" at one end of the great vaulted room with its pointed arches rising to a simple oak roof. Seated alone on her throne, as became a queen regnant, "under a fine canopy" of blue velvet supported by silver poles, with little bells at each end, Anne soon invited Prince George "to dine with her; so he came and at her request took his seat at her left hand without the canopy."[29] After dinner, "all things performed with great splendor and magnificence, about a half hour past eight in the evening her majesty returned to St. James's. The day concluded with bonfires, illuminations, ringing of bells, and other demonstrations of a general satisfaction and joy."[30]

—⁂—

Although fate prevented Queen Anne from mothering children of her body, she had consistently practiced the feminine art of nurture, and followed the tradition that an Englishwoman should provide for her family's well-being. Determined now to be mother to her people, while at the same time underlining her Englishness and turning royal ceremonial to political advantage, Anne revived an ancient monarchical custom—Touching for the King's Evil (scrofula, a tubercular infection of the lymph nodes that causes swellings in the neck, fever, and sickness).

The devout queen may have believed that, as anointed ruler and head of the Anglican church, putting her hands on an afflicted subject might really do good. Anne's subjects could have had faith in her power to heal, for scrofula's periods of remission lent credence to the efficacy of the queen's Touching. But certainly, the gold coins Anne hung around the necks of those she had touched, generated enthusiasm for the practice.

Thousands, from every social class, clamored to be touched. Not one of the queen's attendants "cares she should do it, for she fasts the day before, and abstains several days, which they think does her hurt."[31] Still, during the court season, Anne touched three hundred people twice weekly, although not before one of her physicians had screened applicants, and the queen placed protection between her Curing fingers and the sick person's affected skin.

Touching let Anne come into personal contact with many of her people. It also increased the queen's popularity and stimulated patriotism in time of war.

—m—

Ascent to the throne meant re-organization and expansion of Anne's household. She immediately set the tone for honesty and decency.

Horrified, as princess, to find her household comptroller selling places, Anne, as queen, forbad the practice. No official with power of employment could accept money or favors in exchange for position.

Daughter of frugal James II and his capable first wife, Anne Hyde, Queen Anne sought thrifty, sensible, household management. While princess she had examined accounts, ordered provisions, and noted poor service. Now, Anne would "look as much into all my affairs as I can."[32]

"Since there is nobody perfect but dear Mrs. Freeman," besides "there being nobody that will take that care to see all my things in order as you will,"[33] Anne appointed Sarah as groom of the stole; (the queen's closest household officer with control over the royal bedchamber and its staff, plus the right to spacious lodgings in all royal palaces) mistress of the robes; (responsible for the queen's clothes and those looking after them) and keeper of the privy purse. The latter duty put Sarah in charge of the queen's personal expenses, including management of the many petitions for places, pensions, and donations. As well, the queen confirmed Sarah as first lady of the bed chamber (senior lady-in-waiting).

Her new responsibilities enhanced Sarah's position and, as well, brought her a significant increase in salary. Chafing, nonetheless, at what she called the tedium of court, Sarah spent as much time as possible at her St. Albans country house. She delegated her cousin, Abigail Hill, whose duties in the queen's household brought Abigail into constant contact with Anne, to act as her eyes and ears. (Sarah had, in fact, got Abigail her menial position as a bedchamber-women[34]; for, on hearing about financial woes having impoverished Abigail's family, Sarah felt some responsibility.) Her absences disappointed the queen, but Anne prudently avoided confrontation.

The queen appointed all other high-ranking household members, (including ten ladies-in-waiting, among them the Marlboroughs' two married daughters) plus the most prominent and profitable intermediate positions. Anne favored old friends and faithful servants. For their loyalty during her standoff with Mary, the queen gave the moderate Whig Duke of Somerset (nicknamed Proud Duke for excessive pride in his rank, Somerset had four servants clear the road in front of his carriage to prevent the lower orders from sullying him with their stares) and his duchess important household places.

To make sure matters were arranged to her liking, Anne participated actively in household management. She altered the practice of contracting with suppliers for the entire reign; instead ordering an annual contract awarded the bidder with the best service at the most reasonable cost. Generous to those in real need irrespective of personal or political connection, the queen also took care not to overpay servants or expand her household without good cause.

In recognition of her subjects' heavy wartime tax burden Anne promised to apply £100,000 out of her household revenue to public service. This generous gesture had the added virtue of heading off any move to make her former £50,000 annual grant, which parliament had voted for Anne as heiress presumptive, from going out of the country to her successor Sophia of Hanover.

—⁜—

Determined not to be the figurehead that might all too easily fall to her lot as a female, Anne took her duties seriously. Hence, she became increasingly immersed in state business. Yes, the Glorious Revolution turned England's rulers into constitutional monarchs, but they retained some power. Anne's two secretaries of state, cabinet members with divided responsibility for both domestic and foreign affairs, waited on her every day; they presented a daily news précis; summarized important diplomatic and military dispatches so she could reply to her envoys in the field. (The queen corresponded frequently with Marlborough, who spent half the year abroad on campaign; she had definite ideas on the war, and in consultation with Marlborough and Godolphin, spent much time in its guidance.) Besides, Anne insisted on reviewing all state letters before signing them. She often made changes such as the "draft of the letter" her secretary gave her, intended for the Electress of Saxony. Anne liked it "very well and … only altered a few words."[35]

The queen presided over weekly cabinet meetings; met daily with lord treasurer Godolphin, her de facto prime minister, and several times each week with her treasury board. Anne wanted "to know what would be the cost of making the same provision for the families of sailors lost in the late storm as if they had been killed in the service."[36]

As titular head of the judiciary, the queen had power of executive clemency. And since so many crimes carried the death penalty, she received numerous pleas for mercy. Before making any decision, Anne first reviewed the documents, then asked judges personally to tell her about each case. She pardoned a convict because his youth gave hope that if gainfully employed, he would reform. She insisted that as soon as he possibly could, her secretary of state find out about a felon she considered a "case of compassion [because he had] a wife and six children … if you find it so, take care his life may be spared."[37] The queen ruled that hanging a pregnant woman would be barbaric, and when she heard that one of the literary lights of her reign had been sentenced to notorious Newgate prison for writing a scurrilous political pamphlet, Anne, although annoyed by Daniel Defoe's sarcasm, inquired "particularly … into my circumstances. [She then sent] a considerable supply to my wife and family and to … me to the prison, money to pay my fine and the expenses of the discharge."[38] But Anne showed no mercy towards two highwaymen who for years terrorized her subjects.

Despite the capture of several prominent Jacobites, Anne did not authorize any political executions. She remembered the horrors perpetrated in her father's name after the Monmouth rebellion as much for their needless cruelty, as for the hatred James reaped from them. His younger daughter ruled more wisely.

—⁜—

Whenever she could snatch a moment to herself, the queen sought Sarah's company.

Anne wanted to relax with her favorite, yearned to recreate their peaceful, cozy times at Syon House, when she and Sarah had chatted and gossiped together while they embroidered a bed-quilt.

"Confident I should have been the greatest hero that ever was known in the parliament house, if I had been so happy as to have been born a man,"[39] Sarah saw her private time with the queen differently. Anne's accession meant the chance to play an active role in politics. Sarah supported Whig principles. She favored rationalism vis-à-vis religious doctrine; preservation of a subject's liberties vis-à-vis the crown; and fair restraint on the ruler. Anne tended towards Tories, upholders of her revered Anglican church and the royal prerogative. The two friends' contrasting views of religion and politics were quiescent as long as they lived privately, but Anne's ascent to the throne changed everything.

Differences surfaced at once. Sarah advocated having a Whig archbishop preach Anne's coronation sermon. The queen chose a Tory.

Sarah reproached Anne for the loss of each Whig position, so the queen offered her favorite the lifetime post of ranger at Windsor Great Park[40]; the job included the handsome, high-roofed Great Lodge, an enchanting house which Sarah had often admired. From the Lodge's multi-windowed façade, she liked to contemplate the park's lovely green vistas and herds of grazing deer. Did Sarah want the Lodge for life, "because the warrant must be made accordingly, and anything that is of so much satisfaction as this poor place seems to be to you, I would give my dear Mrs. Freeman for all her days, which I pray God may be many and as truly happy as this world can make you."[41]

Happiness, for Sarah, included her husband's success. Whigs supported Marlborough's strategy of fighting the French on land. Tories pushed for a focus on naval warfare; besides, Sarah believed they meant to restore the Pretender.

Hence, Sarah took advantage of her private time with Anne to enlighten the queen about politics. But Sarah's anti–Tory tirades failed to move Anne, who thought both parties contained "knaves [as well as] good reasonable people, [and wished] there were more of that number in both parties."[42]

Political differences affected personal relations. Self-assured Sarah judged herself more intelligent and better read, especially as she had lately developed an interest in the classics. Frustration with her subordinate political role, and anger at Anne's rejection of her political advice, impelled Sarah, who took pride in being a true Whig, to advocate ever more fiercely for her Whig friends.

As a result, for the first time in her relationship with Sarah, Anne bluntly refuted her best friend—for being "mightily mistaken in your notion of a true Whig. [The] character you give of them does not in the least belong to them." The queen shrank from belaboring the point; she merely asked Sarah "for my poor sake [not to] show more countenance to those you seem to have so much inclination for than to the Church party."[43]

Far from wanting to have even the smallest difference of opinion with Sarah, Anne, nevertheless, concluded by declaring herself very familiar with the "principles of the Church of England, & I know those of the Whigs, and it is that and no other reason which makes me think as I do of the last."[44]

Cooling relations between the two women came less from Sarah's political beliefs per se, than from her candid and constant re-iteration of them while denying any validity to Anne's opinions. Always proud of her frankness, Sarah, now at the pinnacle of influence, gave unbridled rein to it. She failed to see how her outspoken lack of respect for clergy, and contempt for displays of devotion offended Anne's genuine religious faith. The queen resented Sarah's withering remarks about clerics and ridicule of church practices as much as her harangues on politics, her open contempt for Anne's mental ability and scorn for the queen's reasoning, to say nothing of Sarah's conviction that without her advice, Anne, could do nothing right.

Unrelenting in her attempts to convince Anne that Tories were secret Jacobites who would restore the Prince of Wales to her detriment, furious at High Tory Rochester's efforts to thwart Marlborough's war plans, Sarah did not, or would not, see that regardless of how pro–Tory Anne might appear, she had resolved not to let either party control her.

Actually, a moderate Tory, Anne disagreed with her uncle Rochester and his High Tory strategy of putting naval warfare before continental war. Like Marlborough, Godolphin, and, yes, Whigs, Queen Anne committed herself to land war as the best way to keep Catholic France from dominating not only the Continent, but also seizing her throne.

Seven

"A lady of intelligence and ambition"

"The wisdom of her counsels, and the success of her arms, were in some measure, owing to her just discernment in her first choice of prime minister and general."[1]—contemporary historian Abel Boyer

On a lovely late spring Sunday evening in 1702, as the setting sun spread a gentle glow over London and the scent of lilac and honeysuckle perfumed the park, Queen Anne presided over the weekly meeting of her cabinet.

She had come to the throne because England's Protestant parliament bypassed the direct heir, first offering the crown jointly to her older sister and Mary's husband; then providing for a Protestant succession should Anne die childless. Cognizant of parliament's power, the new queen, nonetheless, guarded her royal prerogative; believing, furthermore, that she ruled by hereditary right, Anne "immediately took exception to the expression that her right was divine."[2]

Monarchy, even if limited, functioned as a crucial part of government and politics. True, no administration could last without parliamentary cooperation. But the queen had power to select and retain ministers, a power that politicians must respect. Anne and the men she chose to fill her cabinet made all major decisions, which could only be revoked by her in cabinet. (Besides prime minister and lord treasurer Lord Sidney Godolphin, Anne's cabinet included, among others, the army and navy chiefs, Earl Marlborough and Prince George respectively, the Archbishop of Canterbury, and two secretaries of state.) No cabinet meeting could take place without the queen.

As this balmy spring evening drew to its close, the queen's imperious uncle Lord Rochester, Lord Lieutenant of Ireland, rose to address his cabinet colleagues. Foremost in urging that England use its superior navy to curb France, to focus the War of the Spanish Succession on the high seas, and to attack French colonies, rather than commit to a continental campaign, Rochester again condemned Marlborough for his war strategy of concentrating the anti–French effort on land, where France had greater strength. For Rochester still smarted over the queen's choice of Marlborough's close friend Godolphin, rather than himself, as treasury chief; hence, Anne's uncle resolved to challenge Marlborough's power.

Marlborough spent half the year campaigning on the Continent as commander in chief of the Grand Alliance; that gave him unique personal access to European decision makers. And since every member of the Alliance, to say nothing of those who opposed it, deemed the War of the Spanish Succession *the* major foreign policy issue, it dominated the diplomatic discussion. Expertise in military matters plus knowledge of continental politics made charismatic Marlborough, the consummate courtier, in effect England's foreign secretary.

Rochester resolved to diminish Marlborough and damage Godolphin—not only by tackling them in the cabinet, but also by undermining the ministry in parliament. There Rochester revealed cabinet secrets in open debate and tried to increase his authority in both Houses at the ministry's expense.

Exasperated at Rochester's moves against Marlborough and Godolphin, Anne ordered her uncle to carry out his duties as Ireland's lord lieutenant by living in Dublin. Rochester refused. Realizing he would prove less dangerous outside the ministry than in, the queen dismissed her ambitious, quick-tempered relative.

Rochester's ally, High Tory secretary of state Lord Nottingham, led his Tory cabinet cohorts in continuing to advocate use of the navy as Britain's key weapon against France. But although Anne and most of her ministers disagreed with a naval focus on fighting the war, Marlborough and Godolphin threatened to resign rather than carry on with High Tory colleagues who worked against them. Torn between reliance on her proven friends, and conviction that government should not be trusted wholly to men of one party, Anne convinced her friends to stay—and kept Nottingham.

"Having anything to do with these great men [proved] very troublesome, [the queen confided to her intimate, Sarah, Countess Marlborough] but one must have patience ... the only remedy for everything. The unreasonableness, impertinence, and brutality [Anne saw] in all sorts of people every day [made her appreciate the] great blessing God Almighty has given me in such friends as your dear self, Mr. Freeman, [Marlborough] and Mr. Montgomery [Godolphin]."[3]

—⟋ⱦⱦ⟍—

Queen Anne's gout had, meanwhile, improved but Prince George caused her great concern. He suffered an acute attack of asthma. The prince's doctors recommended recuperation at one of England's finest spas. So, in this, the first summer of her reign, Anne decided to accompany her ailing husband to Bath.

The queen used her journey to revive an important ceremony—the royal progress. Despite the road between London and Bath being "so rocky, unlevel, and narrow in places, that I am persuaded the *Alps* are to be passed with less danger,"[4] Anne and her entourage proceeded steadily, even if slowly. Eight sturdy, high-stepping horses drew the queen's comfortable, custom-built state coach, its body hung between huge wheels painted crimson and gold to match the carriage's elaborately carved body, and luxurious, upholstered interior. The liveried coachman and a footman sat at the front of the carriage, two footmen stood behind, and postilions kept the horses in stride.

All along the route huge crowds gathered to glimpse and cheer their queen; bells pealed from church towers; bonfires blazed; and everyone drank to her majesty's health in wine provided gratis as local luminaries spared no expense to mark the royal presence, let alone prove their loyalty. Anne's progress thus united queen, court, nobility, gentry, clergy, military, and ordinary people—important for a ministry fighting a costly and sometimes unpopular war. Indeed, Anne's progress through Bath's environs, a bastion of Tory squires who resented having to pay the extra land tax needed to fund the war, served a timely political purpose as well, for the queen had prorogued parliament shortly after her coronation and called for election of a new house of commons. The election would take place a few weeks after Anne's journey to Bath.

Bath's mayor and corporation outdid themselves in welcoming the royal couple. That stood in stark contrast to Anne's last visit when, on her sister Queen Mary's official orders, Bath dignitaries ignored her.

—m—

To avoid the crush of Bath in high season, not to mention the summer heat, Anne and her immediate entourage (which included Godolphin and one secretary of state) resided at a house outside the town where the queen carried on government business including the regular Sunday evening cabinet meeting.

Initially, Bath benefited the prince but within weeks asthma returned, bringing with it an alarming sleepiness. Anne nursed her husband devotedly, "would not be persuaded to lie from him during all his illness, though in many nights she had very little rest."[5] Regardless of lassitude, George retained his distrust of doctors, only letting them apply blisters to his back, nape of neck, and temples. Whether or not due to the dubious effect of this remedy the prince suddenly broke out in a sweat which moderated his symptoms. A week later George went "a hunting ... as the town said he was dead. [Courtiers hoped] he may live many years; and what is better news, the queen is healthfuller than ever."[6]

Eager to see the famous merchant exchange in the nearby port city of Bristol, the prince rode there with only a single officer as escort. George observed everything until all merchants, save one, went home to their well-deserved dinners.

> MERCHANT: Are you the husband of our good Queen Anne?
> PRINCE: Yes.
> MERCHANT: My colleagues were too bashful to offer you hospitality, but if you do not object to roast beef, plum pudding, and home brewed ale, I would be honored to have you and your escort come home to dinner with me.

Although he had already booked a succulent meal at Bristol's best inn, the prince good-naturedly accepted.

On bidding the merchant farewell, George asked if business ever brought him to London. It did. The prince invited his host and hostess to visit him at court. In due course, the couple arrived. George presented them to Anne. Thanking them for their hospitality to her husband, she bade the couple to dinner, the main meal of the day usually eaten at four o'clock in the afternoon. A stickler for court etiquette, which included correct dress for every event, the queen promised to provide appropriate raiment for the occasion.

Queen and prince usually dined privately, but that day sat down with their guests in public to eat the plain, plentiful food English and French chefs prepared in the royal kitchens. The two courses consisted of roasted lamb and pig, hot larded capons; soups enhanced with fresh herbs; a large variety of fresh vegetables including delicacies like asparagus; several fruits, some, like grapes, oranges, and lemons imported from abroad; and, of course, a large selection of wines.

The queen marked this repast by introducing the merchant and his wife as Bristol's most loyal citizens. Anne then knighted the merchant, and, when he refused the handsome sum of money she offered, the queen unpinned the gold watch she wore on her lace corsage and presented it to the merchant's wife.

MERCHANT'S WIFE: Oh, your majesty, I could never accept such a valuable gift.
ANNE: Your queen commands you to keep this watch.

—⟋ⱴⱴ⟍—

War, in the meantime, had begun in earnest. An Anglo-Dutch fleet failed to capture Spain's major Mediterranean port of Cadiz, but on its way home the fleet fought its way past French and Spanish warships guarding northern Spain's Vigo Bay. There, a flotilla of tall Spanish galleons stuffed with silks, spices, gold, and silver rode at anchor waiting to unload their cargo. The Allies destroyed or captured all the galleons.[7] And although Marlborough's main ally, the Dutch Republic, prevented him from luring the enemy into open engagement in the Netherlands, (fearing French invasion, Dutch generals insisted on keeping their army hunkered down in defense) he captured several key fortified towns—more than King William had achieved in nine years of war.

Tories were unimpressed. They touted Vigo Bay to justify their naval policy.

Resolved to show support for Marlborough's victories, Queen Anne ordered a special thanksgiving service. As venue, she chose the splendid, newly built (if not yet quite finished) St. Paul's Cathedral. And besides selecting all prayers and hymns, the queen graced the entire service with her presence, riding to and from the Cathedral in state.

Anne felt "very uneasy to think [she had] so very little in her power to show [her appreciation for all Marlborough's] kindness, especially at a time when he deserves all that a rich crown could give, [the queen wrote Sarah.] "But since there is nothing else at this time, [Anne hoped Sarah would let her] make him a duke. I know my dear Mrs. Freeman does not care for anything of that kind nor am I satisfied with it, because it does not enough express the value I have for Mr. Freeman."[8]

Sarah felt loath to accept the queen's offer, since the conspicuous consumption expected of a duke might overburden family finances, especially if her husband were killed in battle. Quailing at the concept of being an impoverished duchess, Sarah suggested waiting until she and John had accumulated more wealth. He agreed.

But decided, nonetheless, to consult his friend, judicious and honest Grand Pensionary Anthony Heinsius, head of Holland's government and Europe's premier non–French statesman. The personal relationship and mutual trust between charismatic courtier Marlborough and austere bachelor Heinsius proved vital to the efficacy of the Grand Alliance.

Having encouraged his friend to be frank, Marlborough wrote his wife, Heinsius advised that as regards the time of "taking the queen's favor, [were Marlborough to accept the dukedom now, in the] heat of everybody's being pleased with what I had done, [acceptance would be] a justice to the queen, and do her good with all the princes abroad, and especially in" Holland. If Marlborough postponed the award, it would be viewed as the result of "favor, which would not be so great an honor to my family nor to the queen's service."[9] Marlborough left the final decision to his wife and his best friend. Godolphin and Sarah agreed with Heinsius.

To support her captain general's dukedom, the queen sought to make permanent the £5,000 annual pension from post office revenue, already given to Marlborough for her lifetime. He asked that the pension be granted, as well, to his heirs in perpetuity.

House of commons speaker Robert Harley introduced the bill to make Marlborough's pension permanent. But Anne's uncle Rochester led Tories in such relentless opposition that the queen had to withdraw her request—the first reversal of her reign.

Furious, Anne offered the Marlboroughs £2,000 annually from her private purse. No envy would result, she told Sarah, "for nobody need know it"; [not that the queen would] disown what I give to people that deserve. [Sarah could decide whether or not to] keep it a secret [but in any case, Anne begged her] dear Mrs. Freeman [to] "comply with the desires of her poor, unfortunate, faithful Morley, that loves you most tenderly, and is with the sincerest passion imaginable yours."[10]

Sarah declined the queen's generosity.[11] Anne thus gave the third Marlborough daughter a liberal dowry and arranged for her intended to have a senior position in Prince George's household; because although the queen had no great opinion of the bridegroom's acumen, she thought his youth and demeanor gave hope of improvement.

—⁂—

On her first birthday as queen, (February 6, 1703) Anne reinvigorated the monarch's birthday ceremonial with a court whose magnificence had not been seen since the days of her uncle King Charles. As on all public occasions, the queen made an effort to appear in suitable splendor. London merchants dealing in Anne's preferred gold thread brocades and richly embroidered materials, applauded her decision no less than the queen's custom of ordering new clothes annually and letting her servants have her used raiment.

Aware of her dignity as well as the crown's heavy duties, especially in time of war, let alone acrid party dissent, Anne unified and popularized her court by reviving court ceremony and insisting on the correct dress and conduct that went with it. Easy to approach and listening to everyone considerately, the inarticulate queen confined herself to commonplace conversation. Some found it dull; others applauded Anne's discretion.

On this, her birthday morning the queen attended church service in full royal state; she and the entire court spent the afternoon listening to her poet laureate's paean of praise, for which the royal master of music had composed suitable accompaniment. In the evening, the queen, wearing an elegant pale grey Indian satin manto (one of two dozen she had ordered that year) embroidered with tiny flowers, over a blue, figured silk dress, presided over a formal drawing room crowded with nobility and gentry arrayed in splendid new clothes made specially for the occasion. A professionally performed ballet and a play, gambling at cards, and dancing entertained the assembled company.

Soon after, tragedy struck the new Duke and Duchess of Marlborough. Their favorite child and only surviving son (John, Lord Blandford) had been eager to enlist in the army and join his father on the Continent. But Sarah insisted on the teenager continuing his studies at Cambridge. Blandford eventually prevailed, and prepared to join his father. Sarah showed her displeasure by not writing.

Before Blandford could embark, smallpox struck Cambridge. Godolphin at once reassured the worried parents—he had moved Blandford and his tutor out of the beleaguered university town, and into a house he owned nearby. Regardless, the boy fell ill with smallpox. Duke, duchess, and their doctors hurried to him.

With memories of her two little daughters' deaths from smallpox still vivid, the anxious queen did her utmost to help her friends. Anne immediately sent two of her personal physicians in her own coach, with its distinctive, easily recognizable coat of arms emblazoned on the doors; she dispatched medicines via special currier.

In vain.

Anne's heart went out to Sarah. She, too, had lost her only son.

The queen remembered so well how the two boys loved to play soldiers together. How Gloucester admired the older Blandford.

Pale and with troubled mien, looking as if her own son had died, Anne immediately asked Sarah when "I may come to you, & who you would have come with me, [the queen could not travel alone] for I long to see my dear Mrs. Freeman, & would do everything that is most easy to you … therefore I beg you would not constrain yourself but let me know sincerely what you like best."[12]

Sarah refused to see Anne. Baffled and upset by her friend's rejection, Anne felt affronted as a queen and hurt as a friend. Feeling strongly about friendship—a very affectionate, non-sexual, emotionally close relationship—Anne thought the "unfortunate ought to come to the unfortunate."[13]

—◆◆—

The queen hoped Sarah's tragedy would heal the rift their political differences had opened and restore their former intimacy. But wallowing in grief, Sarah shunned everyone, even her daughters, and wandered around her house at St. Albans weeping with utter abandon. The death of her only surviving son proved particularly devastating for the ambitious duchess. It meant failure in her prime duty—to produce an heir to carry on the legacy she and the duke were building; besides, guilt entered into the equation. Had Blandford been on the Continent with his father, not, as his mother insisted, at Cambridge, the boy would have escaped smallpox.

Sarah's health started to suffer. Anne urged her ailing friend "to preserve your precious life, which is of more value to all your friends than can ever be expressed, but to none so much as to her that sincerely dotes on you, & will make it my daily prayer to God Almighty to support & comfort you under this heavy affliction."[14]

Piety and her husband's constant companionship had helped Anne when her son Gloucester died. Truly religious Marlborough took some comfort in his faith; besides, his military and diplomatic responsibilities distracted from sorrow and now took him to the Continent. Sarah scorned organized religion, never mind displays of devotion; and with only the youngest of her four daughters unmarried, her son dead, and her husband away at war, Sarah had little left but her political ambitions. She decided, therefore, to pour her considerable energy into politics.

—◆◆—

Heartbreak deepened the divide between duchess and queen rather than drawing them together. Sarah not only judged Anne to have suffered less deeply—she had wept only a little over Gloucester's death while Sarah expressed her grief by sobbing so uncontrolledly that those around her feared for her sanity—but also, the duchess's focus on politics meant continued conflict.

Still, concern for Sarah preoccupied Anne, even to the extent of putting her friend's health before her own.

> I give my dear Mrs. Freeman a thousand thanks for the satisfaction she has given me today of hearing from her, and I am very sorry to find by lord treasurer as well as by your letter that you have been more out of order than I knew, but I hope in God the worst is over since you find yourself better.
>
> For God's sake have a care of your dear self and do not only ask advice but follow it when it is reasonable. I shall be in pain until I have heard again how you do, which I hope you will be so kind as to

tell me by the first opportunity. I am I thank God very well in my health, & can walk a little with the help of two sticks, but I fear it will be a great while before I can walk alone.[15]

The queen, Marlborough, and Godolphin made allowances for Sarah's grief, but rejected her belief that Tories, many of them against Marlborough's maneuvers on the Continent, were working for France and the Pretender. Nor did Anne, John, and Sidney think Whigs would be any better at government. "You are so fixed in the good opinion you have of some, [the queen wrote Sarah in a vain attempt to end their argument,] & the ill opinion you have of other people that it is to no manner of purpose to argue anything with you, therefore I shall leave it to providence & time to convince you of mistakes you are in in several things."[16]

Aside from irritation at Sarah's aggressive tone, Anne felt offended "that difference of opinion should make you cold to your poor unfortunate faithful Morley & hinder you from coming to me, for whatever you say I can never take it ill, knowing as I have said already, that you mean it kindly."[17]

The queen's attitude inflamed Sarah into making acid remarks about Anne's apathetic or antagonistic answers to her advice. Discord and reserve entered their meetings, giving the queen a

heavy heart to see my dear Mrs. Freeman … so formal & cold…. How is it possible when one sees such a change to forbear asking the cause, for Christ Jesus sake tell me what's the matter, lay all the faults you think me guilty of before me, that I may vindicate myself & not be under your displeasure, which … I cannot support.

You told me once I had changed, I am sure I am not so in the least to my dear Mrs. Freeman … if I am altered in any one thing, however, I should be very glad to know … for few people know themselves & I am very sensible I have my failings as well as other people … open your dear heart freely, [Anne begged,] for I can have no ease till everything is set right between us.[18]

Sarah denied changing. She accused Anne of having changed, turned cold.

—⁓—

Anne had, indeed, changed since becoming queen. She had developed awareness of her authority and confidence in

Queen Anne. Politicians who thought the "kindest of queens" could be "hectored or frightened into compliance tho I am a woman" were "mighty mistaken in me." This engraving, executed early in her reign, shows Anne wearing the collar of the Order of the Garter; her crown is in the background. Artist: Robert White, 1702–1703 after Sir Godfrey Kneller. Royal Collection Trust/©Her Majesty Queen Elizabeth II 2018.

her judgment. The duchess found this hard to accept, especially as she begrudged, even envied, Anne's position—why should a woman less clever than herself one, besides, with less education (Sarah prided herself on pursuing her recently developed interest in the classics) have more power. As well, the duchess either failed, or refused, to recognize the subtle difference between a princess and a queen.

Princess Anne felt responsible for herself and her family. Queen Anne felt responsible for her realm. Before Anne's accession she and Sarah were two women focused on domesticity. After, they were two women focused on politics. The princess appreciated Sarah expressing frank opinions. The queen resented Sarah's attempts to influence her in favor of Whigs.

Consumed by her ambition to be a political force, Sarah deemed her time with Anne too precious to waste on trivialities like exerting herself to amuse, to be charming. The duchess could not accept that a woman younger and, as she thought, less astute than herself, had the power she craved. Aggravated and jealous, Sarah persisted in harassing Anne over politics.

> I own I cannot have the good opinion of some sort of people as you have, nor the ill one of others, [Anne replied to one particularly long screed] & let the Whigs brag never so much of their great services to their country and of their numbers, I believe the Revolution had never been, nor the succession settled as it is now, if the Church party had not joined with them, & why those people that agreed with them in those two things should all now be branded with the name of Jacobite I can't imagine, have they not great stakes [in the Revolution settlement] as well?[19]

Her patience waning, Anne promised to answer Sarah's counterargument when she had more time. But "one thing I cannot help saying now, is, I am very sorry to find that everybody who are not Whigs must be reckoned Jacobites."[20]

—⚹—

The forty-two-year-old duchess yearned for another child. Absence of menstruation gave her hope. "I cannot express how glad I am of the good news you send me of your dear self, [Anne replied to Sarah's news of her pregnancy.] Since my great misfortune of losing my dear child, I have not known so much real satisfaction in anything that has happened as this pleasing news has given me."[21]

The passage of time brought unhappy truth. No pregnancy. The duchess's missed menstrual periods meant menopause, with its bewildering physical changes and mental challenges. From his headquarters in The Hague, Marlborough urged the queen and Godolphin to make sure Sarah followed medical advice—to recover her strength at Bath. Anne and Sydney should take Sarah there with them. She must not, the duke insisted, be alone.

The duchess spent a month with the queen at Bath, but the stay improved neither her health nor her rift with Anne. Still, after Sarah left, the queen longed for "the satisfaction of hearing from you ... more than can be expressed, for oh my dear dear Mrs. Freeman you can never imagine how sincerely & tenderly I love you & be assured nothing can ever change me. I intend ... tomorrow morning ... to begin the waters, but they shall not hinder me from writing, it being impossible for me to hinder myself from telling you on all occasions, that I am unalterably yours."[22]

Anne yearned for a friend. Sarah yearned for political power.

—⚹—

Over a course of several weeks, the queen took her water cure at the Cross bath, most fashionable venue in the spa town, and most private. Even so, balconies ran along three sides, above the water, to allow bewigged men and powdered women to ogle bathers while musicians played and attendants served hot chocolate.

Daily, Anne donned a head-to-toe, finely woven yellow canvas gown to hide her body, and bonnet to protect her hair, before submerging in the bath's sulfurous warmth. Its water "bears you up … you generally sit [on a stone seat] up to the neck in water."[23] But some thought "it cannot be clean to go so many bodies together in the same water."[24]

After bathing, Anne moved into a private space where she shed her canvas clothing as her maid helped her into a flannel garment "made like a nightgown with great sleeves." The queen then removed to another private room with a fire, seated herself in a "padded, warm, curtained chair that servants carried [to her] lodging where she got into bed [and] sweated while her servants ministered to her."[25]

Soon after completing her water treatment, Anne suffered such an acute gout attack that she could hardly walk the "length of the room and that with two sticks, which makes me mightily afraid I shall hardly be able to go out alone"[26] by the day designated for her to open parliament with a speech from the throne. And a miasma of rumors that Tories meant to attack the ministry on the inutility of trying to wage offensive warfare in the Netherlands, made Anne confide to Sarah that she anticipated "nothing but uneasiness [in the coming parliamentary session; the duchess's] coldness [would, moreover,] make it insupportable."[27]

—◊◊◊—

Parliament confirmed Anne's fears. According to custom she had, soon after her accession, dissolved the legislature and called for new elections to the house of commons. Seeking to solidify, if not perpetuate, their victory by weakening the popular basis of Whig strength, Tories aimed to remove mostly Whig dissenters (also known as noncon-formists, these Protestants did not follow Anglican church ritual and doctrine) from office by enacting a bill banning Occasional Conformity. (The annual taking of Anglican communion to qualify for government service.)

Religion constituted *the* political passion of Anne's reign. Occasional Conformity bore the distinction of being the most vicious political battle of her first three years as queen.

Anne had favored the first Occasional Conformity bill; her chief ministers, Marl-borough and Godolphin, were neutral; Lutheran Prince George, an occasional conformist, opposed, but his wife convinced him to support the Bill from his seat in the house of lords. (George declined an attempt to exempt him from the Bill's strictures.) Whig members of the upper house were against the Bill but loath to defy the queen, so they added enough amendments intolerable to Tories, to assure the Bill's failure.

Now, a year later, as winter started to extend its icy clutch, the Tory Commons passed a second Occasional Conformity Bill. Tories despised dissenters as traitors. Mostly rich merchants and bankers, these nonconformist Whigs threatened the Tory squire's political power, because their wealth allowed them to influence elections; besides, dissenting Whig financiers insisted that the government, whose war policy they financed through the Bank of England and national debt, desist from enacting harassing religious laws.

The queen's High Tory ministers advised her to support the Bill. But Anne decided to put her country's welfare above her personal preference by opposing this second Occa-sional Conformity bill. True, the Bill would boost Church of England attendance and, thus, fortify the Church's position via increased income from tithing, but the queen judged the Bill inopportune. Because it provided a pretext for political conflict at a time when the nation should unite in focusing its energy on financing and fighting the war.

—◊◊—

Both parties threw themselves unstintingly into the fray. Both proved adept at propaganda, freely availing themselves of the diatribe and distortion afforded by a free press, not to mention the numerous and popular political pamphlets. "Tis the dirt each side throw at one another, and that in such plenty as some will stick; and the faults of a few on both sides, when the prejudices against each other are carried to such heights, make it very hard for either to wipe it off."[28]

Prince George told his wife that this time he would vote against the Bill. Anne made no objection. But she, Marlborough, and Godolphin did not want to alienate their Tory cabinet colleagues by open opposition. So, John and Sidney voted for the Bill, but quietly worked to have it rejected.

Sarah's vocal and energetic lobbying against the Bill dismayed Marlborough. "Having no private ends of my own [other than to serve the queen to his best ability, the duke refused to] meddle with [either party.] If she be satisfied with the sincerity of my intentions for her service I shall then be most happy, [for, the duke told his wife, he thought of] nothing but what may be most for the queen's service, and the good of the common cause. [If Sarah agreed with her husband's sentiments] which I promise you I can never be brought to alter from, I should then beg you would endeavor to bring yourself to the same temper."[29]

Unable or unwilling to control either her temper or her tongue, to bear restraint, opposition, or criticism, the duchess persisted in frankly airing her views to all and sundry. That included haranguing the queen on how the Bill would persecute nonconformists. Anne had refrained from mentioning that subject to Sarah, the queen confessed after parliament rejected the Bill, because she knew the duchess would disagree, but since Sarah gave the queen "this occasion, [Anne could not help but say she saw] nothing like persecution in this Bill; [the duchess might think Tory secretary of state Nottingham put this notion] into my head, but upon my word, it is my own thought." The queen promised to answer Sarah's missive in greater detail at another time; and concluded by imploring Sarah never to "let difference of opinion hinder us from living together as we used to do."[30]

—◊◊—

Angry that Their Queen had opposed the Bill, Tories raised propaganda pandemonium. Focused on dissenters' real or perceived threat to the Anglican church, Tories loudly asserted that the Church stood in danger.

As head of the Church of England, Anne felt personally affronted, but judged it wise to counter Tory criticism. She marked the second birthday of her reign (February 6, 1704) with a message to the house of commons. She would donate all her revenue from First Fruits (first year revenue of each Church of England benefice) and Tenths (one tenth of the annual revenue of each benefice) to the relief of the thousands of impoverished clergy. This generosity caused Anne significant financial sacrifice, but she thought she should share in the monetary burden that the war imposed on her subjects. And Queen Anne's Bounty[31] quelled Tory censure.

The Occasional Conformity fight ended when, some months later, the well-organized Whig majority in parliament's upper house rejected a third Bill.

—⟊—

On the other side of the Channel, Marlborough captured the important Rhineland city of Bonn, and pushed French armies further out of the Spanish Netherlands. But his Dutch allies continued to block the duke's efforts to bring France to a major battle. At the same time Louis XIV gained the alliance of south Germany's largest and strongest polity. Bavaria abutted England and Holland's key ally, the Hapsburg Empire. French armies now had a clear path to the imperial capital, Vienna.

Frustrated in the field, aggravated at home by constant Whig and Tory attempts to undermine Godolphin in parliament, and shake Anne's confidence in him, Marlborough returned to London when winter closed the campaign season. He had to face extensive discontent with the war. Whigs who had supported him and Godolphin despite political differences, now castigated the duke as inept for failing to win victories equal to parliament's generous war supplies; Tory ministerial colleagues critiqued his war strategy; other Tories accused Marlborough of helping himself to English, Dutch and assorted allies' funds. The charges were so spiteful that both the Marlboroughs and Godolphin contemplated resigning. Why struggle for the honor of being involved in a huge calamity, a Franco-Bavarian conquest of Vienna; why continue to carry the cares of office when paralyzed by fickle allies, abused by enemies in pamphlets and press, to say nothing of insults in parliament.

Joining in Sidney's miseries and John's exasperation, Sarah brought them to the queen. Godolphin and both the Marlboroughs idea of retiring gave Anne "no small uneasiness. [She could not but] wonder at all [that people in their positions] should be weary of the world, [people so] continually troubled with all the hurry and impertinencies of it. [But they must] consider your faithful friends & poor country, which must be ruined if ever you should put your melancholy thoughts into execution."[32]

Anne herself "could not bear it. [If duke, duchess, and treasurer resigned, the queen] would have nothing more to do with the world, but make another abdication, for what is a crown, when the support of it is gone. [Anne would] never forsake your dear self, Mr. Freeman nor Mr. Montgomery but always be your constant faithful servant & we four must never part."[33]

Eight

"So glorious a victory"

"Victorious Marlbro' conquers in your name;
His is the conquest, Madam, yours is the fame.
Your steady councils and discerning sight,
Let loose his glorious sword and show it where to fight.
The daring hearts that in your cause appear,
They fight the battle, but 'tis you make the war;
Their courage may exalt the English name,
But 'tis the scepter helps the sword to fame."[1]—Daniel Defoe.

Queen Anne's confidence in the Duke of Marlborough and Lord Godolphin restored their equilibrium. But England still faced the prospect of a debacle. French King Louis XIV planned to use his alliance with Bavaria as a springboard to attack Vienna, capital of England and Holland's key ally the Hapsburg Empire. Hence, as the sun began to lose its summer (1703) heat, the duke conceived a daring plan.

Convinced the Grand Alliance could not survive unless he defeated the joint armies of France and Bavaria before King Louis crossed Germany into Austria, Marlborough meant to march the British army to the Moselle river (bordering France and the Netherlands). That move, the duke planned to tell his Dutch allies, would give him command of the strategic Moselle. But once there, Marlborough would inform Holland that to save the Hapsburg Empire—and with it the Grand Alliance, he would march further into Germany to unite the men under his command with German troops paid by England and Holland. This would allow the duke to force battle on the Franco-Bavarian army. (He feared French spies might get wind of the plan if he divulged it to the Dutch before marching to the Moselle.) Marlborough impressed on his best friend and close colleague, prime minister Sidney Godolphin, that his plan "may be known to nobody but the queen and the prince."[2]

Queen Anne, her husband Prince George, and Godolphin endorsed the duke's strategy; but the Dutch balked at his marching to the Moselle because that would leave them as sole defenders of the Netherlands. "We shall be undone," Marlborough persisted from his headquarters in The Hague as the 1704 campaign got under way during an extremely chilly spring, if "we can't get the better of [France and Bavaria in Germany.] I shall want the queen's help in this matter."[3]

"The queen's help" consisted of an official communication, an order-in-council that the duke could show to his Dutch allies. Realizing the risk involved, for no assurance of victory existed and defeat would mean major trouble for her government, Anne, even so, had complete confidence in her captain general.

Seated at a rectangular rosewood writing-table in one of the large, "agreeably furnished,"[4] comfortable yet elegant rooms Anne had installed as part of her private apartment in St. James's Palace, overlooking the garden with its riot of spring flowers, and the park, which she had improved with new paths, tree plantings, and a herd of graceful deer, the queen took up her quill pen, pulled a piece of stiff parchment paper towards her, and began to write her order-in-council. It commanded the duke, acting jointly with England's Dutch ally, "to send speedy succor to His Imperial Majesty and the Empire."[5]

Presented with this document, Holland agreed that Marlborough march on the Moselle.

—⁂—

At the same time, the Duchess of Marlborough's testy relations with her queen moved Sidney Godolphin to write his close friend Sarah "one short word to your security and your quiet. The latter is much in your own power. [Sarah should not] abuse of that great indulgence of Mrs. Morley," Sidney warned, for she roused the queen's resentment with her incessant pro–Whig lobbying, to say nothing of removing herself from court—and her responsibilities in Anne's household—for weeks on end. The duchess's wish for security against a Jacobite invasion "you have if you will but think so. Why should you not believe me in this thing as well as in anything else? I know it better that I do most things, and without any vanity, ten to one better than anybody you talk with."[6]

Ignoring Godolphin's advice, Sarah continued to abuse Anne's "great indulgence" by focusing her energy on the removal of all Tories from office. So, when the queen's household comptroller died, Sarah lobbied to have her son-in-law Francis Godolphin (Sidney's only child) fill the position. Anne agreed.

> Tho one can scarce help being pleased at the first reading of a letter from your majesty which words is kind, [Sarah grudgingly acknowledged] that pleasure is very short when I consider the kindness of your heart is quite gone from me and for no cause that I can think of in the world but for being so faithful to you as always to tell you the truth, and a truth yourself must needs be sensible of from the testimony of your own eyes ... can you imagine it is possible for me to be persuaded of your kindness, only by a kind word or an expression now and then in a letter, when ... sincere kindness of the heart is wanting.[7]

"It is not in my nature to say I am tenderly fond of you (which is as true as Gospel) if I were not, [the queen replied.] I was once so happy to be believed by my dear Mrs. Freeman, oh, do not let me lose that credit which I cannot be conscious to myself, I have ever forfeited, but believe me that I really am unalterably yours."[8]

Encouraged, the duchess asked Anne to appoint a (Whig) low church cleric to high office. The queen agreed, but not, she warned Sarah, without first consulting her ecclesiastical advisors. Anne then decided to give the living to a high church man. Sarah accused her not only of succumbing to Tory influence, but also of dissembling—Anne had, from the start, meant to appoint a high church cleric. A sharp exchange ensued.

"Everything I say is imputed either to partiality or being imposed upon by knaves or fools, [Anne, finally, protested.] I am very sorry anybody should have either of those characters given them, for any fault in my understanding, since all I say proceeds purely from my own poor judgment, which though it may not be so good as other people, I'm sure is a very honest one."[9]

Sarah's heated reply moved her mistress to aver that

tho I am in the greatest haste imaginable, I must beg my dear Mrs. Freeman's pardon if I were too warm in my discourse last night, & that she would not give it the name of being angry, which I can never be with you, knowing that everything you say is meant kindly. [But Anne could not] help being very much concerned, to find after all the assurances I had formerly given you that I had no manner of value for [a particular Tory,] you still thought him one of my oracles, & that you seemed to think I would put anybody into a church preferment without being rightly informed...

I wish with all my soul God Almighty may inspire you with just and right thoughts of your poor unfortunate faithful Morley, who is not changed, nor never will, for I believe it will not be in the power of any mortal to convince you of that truth, as long as you have so very good opinion of some sort of people as you have now.[10]

Shifting her position Sarah trained her guns on getting Anne to dismiss the two High Tories still in her cabinet. The queen and Godolphin agreed to replace them with moderate Whigs. Still Sarah badgered the queen over her bias toward Tories, to say nothing of her altered personal attitude. Anne apologized, expressed a wish to return to their former intimate footing.

I am a little lame and therefore choose to stay here [Kensington Palace] rather than come to London, hoping by keeping myself still and quiet today, to be able to go thither tomorrow morning and I should be extremely glad if my dear Mrs. Freeman could come any time this evening to her poor unfortunate faithful Morley who is so far from being weary with your dear company as she is all impatience to enjoy more of it, and can never thank you enough for your kindness in staying so long yesterday, if you can make me happy again today, send me word, what hour you can come, if I may send my chariot to fetch my dear Mrs. Freeman, that she may come with as little uneasiness as it is possible this hot weather.[11]

The duchess used Anne's kindness to resume her denunciation of the queen's anti–Whig attitude. Exasperated, Anne said she did not mind having her faults pointed out, but from now on, Sarah should please do so in writing.

—◊◊◊—

As the days lengthened and a frivolous little breeze blew over London, Queen Anne bore multiple burdens. Besides estrangement from Sarah, pain from gout, and the unsure result of Marlborough's march across Europe, trouble simmered in her northern realm.

Sparsely populated Scotland, although under a joint crown in the Stuart line with England, functioned as an independent state. The country trailed England in agriculture, industry, and commerce. Under King William the Dutch muscled in on Scotland's most lucrative business—fish trade with the Baltic countries; and William's wars strangled Scottish commerce with France and Spain. Besides, the Scots resented England's refusal to grant mutual trade privileges. So, by the time Anne came to the throne, Scotland harbored a vociferous Jacobite party.

The queen's first speech to parliament endorsed the idea of union with Scotland. But differences over commerce and religion caused union discussions to die.[12] Scots particularly resented England's failure to support their participation in colonial trade, and England's parliament having omitted to consult its independent Scots counterpart before passing the Act of Succession, which stipulated that Protestant Sophia, Dowager Electress of Hanover, would succeed Anne.

Scotland's parliament refused to endorse the Act of Succession. The country did formally recognize Anne's sovereignty, but Scotland's failure to accept the succession settlement meant that the personal union of English and Scottish crowns presumably would end with childless Anne. Hence, Scotland's strident Jacobitism threatened England. For, if Scotland remained a separate kingdom, Scots could settle their crown on Anne's Catholic half-brother, the Pretended Prince of Wales.

Indeed, many Scots openly promoted the Pretender. Disturbed, English statesmen like Godolphin feared an attempt on the queen's life; further, England's leaders wanted Scotland to accept the Hanoverian succession. For if the poorly queen died before Marlborough won decisive victory, a disputed Scottish succession might well encourage France to invade Scotland, and from there, threaten England.

Of course, Louis XIV meddled. And convoluted Scottish politics muddied the waters as well. Whigs thus formed a parliamentary committee to examine whether a plot existed to raise a pro–Pretender rebellion in Scotland. No conclusive proof turned up, but the committee urged Anne's government to remove temptation by resolving the question of succession to the Scottish throne through union of the two kingdoms.

—※—

The queen agreed. She officially proposed union to parliament. Tories were lukewarm. Scotland's parliament passed the Act of Security: the country's next monarch must be a Protestant of the royal line, but not necessarily England's ruler. Interpreting this as an invitation to the Catholic Pretender if he converted, Scottish Jacobites supported the Act; as did Scottish politicians seeking to pressure England into ceding commercial concessions.

Anne's ministers advised her, as Queen of Scotland, to veto the Act. She did. But to soften her action and reward her supporters, Anne revived the highest honor a Scottish sovereign could confer on a Scot—the Order of the Thistle.

The queen also tried to mollify Scotland via official assurances of goodwill; she stood ready to believe seditious plots were confined to a few fanatics; she would approve any reasonable measure promoting good government, security of church and state. Anne further emphasized that settling the succession in the Protestant line would be vital for Scotland and England's peace and security, besides fortifying the Protestant cause overseas.

Scotland turned a deaf ear. Its parliament continued to demand trade concessions in return for rescinding the Act of Security. The Scottish parliament declined to vote money for the government or army—and refused to accept the offer of English money for those purposes since acceptance would compromise the country's independence

No money to carry on civil or military administration would certainly wreak enough havoc to raise Jacobite hopes. Scotland's army must be paid, Godolphin decided, in order at least to defend the country against invasion. So, with extreme reluctance, he advised Anne to accept the Act of Security.

Before she did so officially, England's house of lords must debate the Act. That opened Godolphin to criticism. The queen decided to act. For the first time she attended a Lords debate—incognita—Anne sat on the throne but did not wear her crown and royal robes or carry royal regalia. The queen intended her presence to help Godolphin by showing her support, as well as to soften the habitually raucous rhetoric. For three hours, Anne paid close attention, moving, as draughts chilled the chamber, from the throne to a bench near the fire. Her presence proved "serviceable in bringing the House into better order.... She diverted the storm by her endeavors, as well as she restrained it by her preference."[13]

The queen's subsequent presence at Lords debates gave her hands-on understanding of issues. This debate, in particular, gave Anne an appreciation of the dilemma she and Godolphin faced. With no word from Marlborough and the outcome of his march across Europe unclear, the queen and her prime minister feared that an increasingly nationalist, never mind Jacobite, Scotland might easily withdraw its several well-regarded regiments currently serving in Marlborough's army, welcome alliance with France, and open a path for the French to invade England.

With a heavy heart, Anne signed the Act of Security.

—⁂—

Concomitantly, reports reached her of a splendid al fresco banquet that a confident King Louis gave on the verdant, sun-dappled banks of the Seine in honor of the Pretender and his mother Mary Beatrice. Louis drank a toast to them as King and Queen of England. The entire French court dined off elegant new porcelain and crystal, specially commissioned for the occasion, and set on white marble tables. As the sun sank over the horizon, drums, cymbals, and trumpets heralded a magnificent display of fireworks.

On the other side of the Channel, grass in St. James's park turned brown as the long summer days dragged slowly by without any news from the army. Heat grew so intense that Anne and George left early for their annual stay at Windsor, but not before Sarah had supplied her sovereign with a large pile of pro–Whig pamphlets, designed, the defiant duchess told her queen, to improve Anne's political perception.

The duke, meanwhile, moved steadily southeast along two hundred and fifty miles of Germany's muddy, rutted roads, fully aware that the queen's reputation, not to mention his own destiny and that of Godolphin's ministry, depended on the battle he meant to force on the Franco-Bavarian army. But since Marlborough's plan depended on secrecy, only the duke and a handful of senior officers knew they were heading to the Danube.[14] There, the duke would join forces with his Austrian ally.

Inevitably, the French got wind of Marlborough's movements. As he had anticipated, the enemy began to advance parallel to him. But to reach adequate troop strength, Louis must divert men from his army in the Netherlands. This allowed the duke to convince his friend and ally, Dutch Grand Pensionary Heinsius, that Holland could now afford to transfer to him, some of its troops engaged in homeland defense. At the same time men from Hanover, Hesse, and Prussia joined the duke as he advanced eastward through the Germanies.

—⁂—

Queen Anne knew, but King Louis did not, that Marlborough had arranged to meet his imperial ally in south Germany. To confer suitable honor on the Hapsburg Emperor's commander in chief Marlborough, whose tastes on campaign were simple, hosted a magnificent formal dinner to mark his first meeting with Europe's most famous general.

Scion of the ducal house that later gave united Italy its kings, but born and brought up in Paris, Prince Eugene of Savoy rejected the church career chosen for him in favor of studying mathematics, fortifications, and warfare. Louis XIV refused the short, frail young man's request to join his army, so Prince Eugene decamped for Vienna where the emperor welcomed him and sent Eugene to join a force defending the city against a powerful Turkish army. Eugene so distinguished himself that he got command of a regiment, rose to became a major general at age twenty-two, and field marshal before his thirtieth birthday.

The ugly, plainly-dressed, blunt and opinionated warrior-prince and the handsome, urbane, circumspect and charismatic diplomat-general instantly took to each other. During that sumptuous dinner, their discussion ranged over the entire War of the Spanish Succession. The two men were of one mind: to energize the Alliance and destroy the French army's well-earned repute for invincibility, they must achieve a major victory.

The first step should, duke and prince decided, be defeat of France's Bavarian ally. The entry to Bavaria lay through Schellenberg fortress; it guarded Donauwerth, a strategic town sitting on flat ground where a minor river meets the mighty Danube. Marlborough shrank from causing the many casualties that would result from an assault on Donauwerth; but his spies revealed the need to move fast, before the Franco-Bavarians could complete Schellenberg's defenses. "It is very plain, [the duke subsequently wrote Sarah, that if] her majesty's troops had not been here, the Elector of Bavaria had been now in Vienna."[15]

Because Marlborough and Eugene's victory put all Bavaria in their power, the two generals sought to eliminate the Elector of Bavaria as France's ally by provoking him either into open battle or into making peace. "He may be sure that if he does not make peace, we will destroy [Bavaria] before we leave. [Certainly, the duke balked at having to] see so many fine places burnt, or that must be burnt, if the elector will not hinder it,"[16] but since the elector refused either to fight or to treat for peace, Marlborough had to make good his threat.

—⚬⚬—

No drumrolls roused the allied army shortly after midnight on Sunday, August 13, 1704. Leaving their tents intact, men from Austria, Britain, Denmark, Hanover, Hesse, Holland, and Prussia marched silently in a light early morning haze that hid them from French lookouts, to Blenheim village, at a strategic bend of the Danube. Unaware that Marlborough and Eugene's armies had united, let alone that they were nearby, French and Bavarian troops awoke as dawn cleared the mist, to find the allied regiments drawn up in front of them.

The enemy's generals scrambled to patch together a battle plan. Duke and prince already knew exactly what to do. The previous day, Marlborough and Eugene rode to a nearby church, climbed steep, narrow, winding stone steps to the top of its bell tower to survey the surrounding countryside and pinpoint the enemy position. Well placed enemy soldiers outnumbered the allied army, so, prince and duke agreed to attack before the Franco-Bavarian forces could fully fortify their site.

Striking in his red regimental coat sashed diagonally with the wide, pale blue ribbon of England's highest order—the Garter—which Anne had conferred on Marlborough during her first week as queen, the duke, astride a white horse, rode up and down the lines in front of his men as they waited for the order to attack heavily barricaded Blenheim village.

When dusk brought the Battle of Blenheim to a close, Marlborough, having spent seventeen straight hours in the saddle, lacked "time to say more, [he scrawled in pencil on the back of a tavern bill] but to beg [Sarah to] give my duty to the queen, and let her know her army has had a glorious victory.... The bearer, my aide de camp Colonel Parke, will give her an account of what has passed. I shall do it in another day or two."[17]

—⚬⚬—

Colonel Parke galloped across the Continent spreading his momentous news at every inn where he stopped to change horses or snatch a few hours of sleep. The colonel then waited impatiently for a favorable wind to speed his boat across the grey-green Channel. Arriving at Marlborough's London house seven days after he left its owner, the army's most distinguished-looking officer, now covered in dust, flung himself from the saddle of his sweating, mud-splashed horse, and gave Sarah her husband's hurriedly scribbled note. The duchess instantly sent Parke and his precious missive to Windsor.

Anne and George were savoring the cool evening breeze wafting across Windsor park and through the wide-open windows of a cozy, polygonal room; built in a turret above an old Norman gateway, this chamber served as the queen's boudoir. She and the prince were absorbed in a hotly contested game of dominoes.

The handsome colonel hastily brushed the dust from his scarlet regimental coat before clattering up the cobbled pathway to Windsor Castle's entrance gate. Parke demanded instant access to the queen. Bowing low, he handed her Marlborough's note; told Anne about seeing France's finest army put to flight; France's famous field marshals captured.

Anne instantly recognized the importance of Parke's news. Rather than giving him five hundred guineas,[18] the usual reward for bringing good tidings, the queen asked Parke to name his reward. The colonel requested her miniature. Anne gave him one set in diamonds, plus a thousand guineas.

> You will very easily believe that the good news Colonel Parke brought me yesterday was very welcome, [the queen wrote her captain general] but no more, I do assure you, than hearing you were well after so glorious a victory. It will not only humble our enemies abroad but contribute very much [to stopping the] ill designs of those at home. [Anne concluded with] sincere wishes that God Almighty will continue his protection over you, and send you safe home to the joy of your friends.[19]

After reading Marlborough's detailed description of the battle, Prince George could not

> content myself with having desired the queen to make my compliments to you upon your great and glorious victory but must give you this trouble to assure you nobody congratulates you more sincerely nor bears a greater share in everything that concerns you than I do. I hope this will find you perfectly recovered from your great fatigue, & that you will be so just as to believe, tho I cannot express myself so well as others, my heart is with all truth yours.[20]

—⁂—

Queen Anne acknowledged the Battle of Blenheim as a high point in her reign.

The man she had chosen to lead her army, contain France, defend the Protestant cause in Europe, and secure her throne, had justified her faith in him. Blenheim vindicated Marlborough's strategy of land war, which Anne backed against her High Tory ministers' advice. Blenheim damaged Louis XIV's power and prestige as nothing else had formerly done. Blenheim saved the Germanies and Vienna from French conquest; renewed the Allies' faith in their ultimate success; (the Grand Alliance had pledged to drive France out of Italy and the Spanish Netherlands) elevated Anne's captain general and her army onto the global stage; justified her right to rule; and damaged Jacobite pretensions.

The British public may not immediately have grasped Blenheim's larger meaning, but everyone understood their country to have won a great victory, a feat the nation had not experienced in decades. England erupted in joy. Church bells rang, cannon boomed, citizens eagerly snatched up the thousands of printed copies of Marlborough's scribbled note to his wife. Crowds thronged cobbled town squares, bonfires burned on village greens; men and women packed into taverns to drink health to the duke and the queen.

Anne decided to commemorate Blenheim by reviving with full royal ritual, a grand public thanksgiving for military victory. Like the royal progress, this ceremony required all political factions to attend the queen, giving them, as well as the general public, a chance to show their loyalty and support.

"One of the most serene and calm days that had been all year" followed a wet and stormy September night as the queen, in full royal regalia, entered her superb, comfortably cushioned, if cumbersome, gold and crimson state carriage drawn by eight, perfectly matched grey horses sporting red and white ribbons tied up to resemble roses. Prince George and the Duchess of Marlborough "in a very plain garment"[21] (to show that the brilliance of her husband's victory obviated the need for ornate raiment) sat in the carriage with Anne. Traversing St. James's quiet courtyard, the royal coach passed through the great arched gateway with its four octagonal towers at the corners, into a sea of sound. Spectators crammed the streets outside, cheered themselves hoarse, even, in their enthusiasm, threatening to breach the lines of city militia guarding the road to St. Paul's Cathedral.

London's lord mayor, sheriffs, and aldermen in "scarlet robes on their caparisoned[22] horses; the knights marshal and pensioners on horse ... great officers of the crown & nobility & bishops all in coach of 6 horses"[23] rode through streets decorated with flags, colorful carpets and costly tapestries hanging from house windows, to the Cathedral, its magnificent dome still swathed in scaffolding, to give thanks to God for Britain's glorious victory. Militia stood to attention, the city's professional bands, splendidly arrayed in new yellow and blue uniforms, played and crowds, standing on specially erected platforms, roared with delight as their queen rode slowly by.

On arrival, Prince George preceded his wife as stalwart guardsmen carefully carried Anne, suffering from a gouty knee, in an open chair from her carriage up the Cathedral steps into the choir where two arm chairs had been placed on a specially erected throne, placed so that everyone in the vast congregation could see their queen. She had supervised every detail of the thanksgiving ceremony, ordering it to include the Chapel Royal choir, which she had restored to the size it enjoyed before her father's reign, her private musicians, and "music composed by the best masters of that art, to accompany the church music and anthems."[24]

The service concluded with everyone singing the "*Te Deum*" (thanksgiving hymn to God for a special blessing). As its last notes faded, great guns on the banks of the Thames, in St. James's park, and at the Tower of London, boomed as they had done when the queen first entered her coach in the palace courtyard. And boomed again when Anne returned to the palace. Government-provided feasting for all classes, as well as bonfires and fireworks, continued far into the night.

—␣—

Such a significant victory merited a suitable memorial. Ministers and parliament argued themselves into an impasse. They appealed to the queen. She suggested that parliament make permanent (and thereby rectify its previous refusal) the annual grant of £5,000 she had already secured the duke for her lifetime.[25] Furthermore, having already rewarded Marlborough with a gift of the manor and its several thousand acres of royal park at Woodstock, Anne requested that parliament fund the duke's building a palace at Woodstock, as fitting tribute to Blenheim, for which it should be named.[26]

Not to be outdone, the Tory house of commons (whose members bore the brunt of the tax on agricultural incomes—the government's main revenue source) gratified Anne's ministry by voting, for the first time, extraordinary war supply in addition to supplies already passed. The queen then personally asked parliament for supply to exploit military advantages in Spain (a Tory admiral had, shortly before Blenheim, captured Gibraltar from Spain, and defeated the Franco-Spanish fleet off southern Spain's Malaga) so as to expedite the overthrow of Louis's grandson as king, and restore the country to the Hapsburgs in the person of the Austrian emperor's brother Charles (King Carlos of Spain).[27] The Commons not only agreed to the largest supply yet, but also gave the ministry discretionary use of it.

Austria's emperor wanted to create Marlborough a sovereign prince of his realm. Since no Englishman had ever received such an honor, Marlborough saw the emperor's gesture as a tribute to the queen as well as himself. Anne agreed. Sarah opposed—no foreign title could be more prestigious than an English dukedom. The duke silenced his duchess by saying that as a prince, he would better be able deal with the difficult princes of the Grand Alliance.

—m—

Basking in Blenheim's reflected glory, Sarah grew ever more impatient with Anne's rejection of her political advice. Granted, her close friend Sidney Godolphin consulted the duchess on political issues; but Sidney thought she could be most helpful to him by accepting the queen's wish that their friendship be personal. Not content to be Godolphin's cipher, still grieving over her son's death, and now worried about her husband's health, the duchess again raised the idea of retirement.

Marlborough refused. The oldest (age fifty-four) soldier on Blenheim's battlefield had so little time to himself that he had a debilitating and "continual fever on my spirits, which makes me very weak"[28]; and the duke had aged ten years since he last saw Sarah. Nevertheless, Marlborough decided that the queen's service demanded he stay with the army at least until the campaign season ended at the beginning of winter.

And Anne, seeking to save her friendship with Sarah, begged the duchess to return to court. "I cannot live without you, & tho I wish you and Mr. Freeman everything your own hearts can desire, you must not think to live out of the world as long as I am in it."[29]

The duchess failed to grace the court with her presence, confiding to the queen that concern for Anne and her interests caused her absence. Because, Sarah rationalized, she could no longer bear the queen's preferring Tories—who failed to support the war—nor could she stop herself from saying things Anne found disagreeable. But these worthy sentiments did not prevent Sarah from peppering the queen with such strident pro–Whig letters that Anne refused to counter-argue; for, what would be the use when the duchess consistently ascribed her sovereign's replies either to irrational bias, or to the result of listening to imbeciles. "I must again desire you would excuse my not answering some things in your letter, [Anne wrote,] "because I know it is better not to do it, for both our sakes."[30]

Her patience sorely tried, the queen confided to Godolphin that she very much feared her and Sarah's friendship could never regain its former intimacy. Feeling extremely "sorry to find Mrs. Morley & Mrs. Freeman cannot yet bring things quite right [although sure] they will do it at last, [Sidney told Sarah] when the case happens betwixt people that love one another so well, it is not impossible that both may be a little in the wrong."[31]

Godolphin's tact fell short. Driven by ambition to become a political force in her own right, the self-assured duchess refused to entertain any reason why she, a competent, intelligent, and well-read woman should not wield as much power as the queen, a female with less ability, brains, and learning.

While keeping up a steady bombardment on Anne, therefore, Sarah decided to shift her focus. She would train her heaviest guns on Sidney and her husband—because the duchess had greater influence over Godolphin and Marlborough than she had over the queen; besides, their support would be vital to advancing the Whig cause. So instead of using Blenheim to heal her breach with Anne, Sarah continued in her headlong course.

—⚅—

By the time bare trees in St. James's park stood in gaunt majesty against a pewter sky, and a knifing nor'easter swept over London almost daily, the gout that lamed the queen at Blenheim's thanksgiving service crippled her to such an extent that Anne could "not set her foot to the ground; has a chair made so well that it is lifted with her in it into the coach, and then she moves herself into the seat, and the chair taken away."[32] As well, the gout cramping Anne's right hand, plus sore eyes, impeded the queen's ability to write.

Yet, poor health failed to stop Anne from carrying out her duties, especially with her government under siege. Since only the Commons had power to levy and collect taxes, all tax bills must originate in that House. Tories held a majority in the Commons. They now proposed to Tack an occasional conformity amendment (immense fines and permanent ban from office for nonconformists taking Anglican communion once a year to qualify for government service) onto the bill imposing a tax on land, the main source of war funding. This would force the Whig dominated Lords either into accepting occasional conformity (which they opposed) in order to sanction financing for the war, (which they supported) or reject occasional conformity along with war funding.

The Tack would, moreover, set a dangerous precedent; for, if the Commons could add an unrelated amendment to a tax bill, which must start in that House, the Lords' ability to initiate legislation would be seriously, if not fatally, compromised. Godolphin thus agreed to oppose the Bill.

The queen concurred. Besides, by holding up a tax bill, the Tack hindered war planning. And the Tack threatened to fracture national unity by injecting acrid political partisanship over religion—*the* political obsession of the day—at a time when England needed to unite around a common cause: the war. So, Anne asked her husband, admiralty chief Prince George, to make sure MPs (members of parliament) dependent on admiralty patronage cast their votes against the Bill.

They did, joining a bloc of other court partisans, Whigs, and moderate Tories to defeat the Tack in the house of commons.

—⚅—

Still beautiful and sparkling, Sarah had seized on the Tack to favor the queen with a strongly worded letter praising all Whigs, not to mention their principles, and condemning all Tories as Jacobites. Anne's answer averred her opinion of Whig and Tory to be the same as ever. "I know their principles very well, and when I know myself to be in the right nothing can make me change. [Certainly, both parties contained good and bad people; the queen could see the] faults of the one as well as of the other. [Nor did those] calling themselves of Church [delude her; for,] God knows there are too many that talk of religion that have no true sense of it. [But because there were] some hot-headed men [among the Tories, Anne could see no reason] to brand them all with the name of Jacobite."[33]

Using a tone that could scarcely be considered appropriate for addressing one's queen, never mind one's friend, a tone that foreshadowed the tenor of Sarah's future letters and discourse, the duchess replied that she had

received yesterday a letter from my dear Mrs. Morley which has given me a great deal of satisfaction, tho I believe she thinks she has quite killed me with the firmness of her opinion which she says is, and ever will be, the same as to Whig and Tory, but then she goes on as if she … approved of such [Jacobites] as were for the liberty of their religion and country, by which I find plainly, that Mrs. Morley and her faithful Freeman differ only in the name.

I believe she has sucked in with her milk a great abhorrence of what they called in those days Whigs, [Sarah continued] and I don't at all wonder at it, I will allow they had cloven feet, [the duchess sarcastically conceded] but there is nothing more certain, than that you never heard the whole truth of that story, [the civil war, resulting in the beheading of Anne's grandfather Charles I] there being few that will venture to displease one they hope to have their fortunes made by.

This gratuitous insult suggested that the queen could not distinguish between toadies and truth-tellers. In fact, Anne, from birth surrounded by sycophants, had developed considerable skepticism towards them, which the duchess well knew not the least because Anne's letters revealed her lack of illusion about human nature.

Sarah Churchill, née Jennings, 1660–1744, Duchess of Marlborough. Anne's best friend, then most bitter enemy, beautiful, spirited, and confident Sarah never learned to curb her hot temper. She vilified Anne in voice and letter, but at the end of her long life had a change of heart. Artist: John Smith, 1705, after Sir Godfrey Kneller. © National Portrait Gallery, London.

I that have read every book little and great, that has been writ upon the civil war, [Sarah granted Anne the benefit of her superior knowledge] can assure the extreme weakness of that unfortunate king, contributed as much to his misfortunes, as all the malice of those ill men, nay I will venture to say more, that it had not been possible for them to have hurt him, if he had not been governed by almost as bad people without knowing it.

Not content with insulting the judgment of Anne's paternal grandfather, "that unfortunate king" Charles I, the duchess called the king's advisors, prominent among them Anne's paternal grandmother Queen Henrietta Maria and her maternal grandfather Edward Hyde, "bad people."

Sarah then referred to those "few" Tories Anne called "hot heads." With spurious innocence the duchess professed herself unable to understand

what dear Mrs. Morley means by saying a few of them…. I wish that were a little more clearly explained because I thought there had been still a majority to obstruct and trouble your business in the house of commons notwithstanding all the advantages your reign has, and all pains taken imaginable to prevent it, and I desire you would be pleased to ask anybody who has the character of sense and honesty, if these … people you are told by Jacobites, are Whigs … have ever failed in any one point to carry on effectually all things that could secure you from your enemies both abroad and at home.

Markedly omitting any respect for Anne as a sensible woman entitled to her opinion as much as Sarah, the duchess recommended that her sovereign compare

impartially the men they call Whigs, and Tories together, you will find more men of sense, estates, and that have ever been churchmen among those you have such a prejudice to, from the artifices of people that talk with you … therefore all that I beg, is only this justice, that since you have declared against Jacobites, and for those that are for the liberty of their religion and country you will give me leave for the time to come to call those that oppose whatever is good both for you and that, Whigs and those that are firm for a Protestant Succession, to all that concerns your welfare, and the good of England against France, Tories, and then we shall never more disagree, and if this be now a Tory, I beg you will give me his character in short, what that dear creature is, so extremely beloved, for I would fain to be in love too, [Sarah scoffed.] And if I can't compass it when you have made a right picture of him, I promise you I will never trouble you more upon this subject, but then you must be pleased to describe what the thing is that has so charmed you, for it will be very hard to impose such a blind passion upon me if you don't say something more, than that you will always think as you do of Whig and Tory.[34]

Sarah concluded with a threat to withdraw from court altogether.

Anne professed herself "very sorry dear Mrs. Freeman will be so unkind as not to come to her poor, unfortunate, faithful Morley who loves her sincerely, and will do so to the last moment. [Sarah must believe that] whenever you will be the same to me as you were five years ago you shall find me the same … as tenderly fond of you as ever. [Nothing, not even the duchess's] own unkindness, shall ever alter your own unfortunate, faithful Morley."[35]

The queen's letter proved notable not only for its brevity, but also for its omission. Anne had not begged the duchess to reconsider her threat.

—⁂—

Much water had flowed under London Bridge since Princess Anne, craving Sarah's company and determined to maintain her right to choose her servants as well as her friends, openly defied her sister Queen Mary, to say nothing of suffering the consequences, for steadfastly refusing to dismiss Sarah.

Nine

Moderation

"It is not the first time that women have governed in England, and indeed they have sometimes done this to better purpose than the men."[1]—Scotland Commissioner Sir John Clerk

The hot sun hovered over England during a summer (1705) singularly devoid of rain. This disconcerted many. Yet, the country continued on a steady course—Peace at Home War Abroad, thanks to the joint effort of political moderates—Queen Anne sitting on the throne, Lord Treasurer Sidney Godolphin leading the cabinet, Robert Harley crafting pro-ministry majorities in the Commons, and the Duke of Marlborough commanding on the battlefield.

Resolved to be the unifying influence in her divided realm as much as to maintain the crown's independence, the queen resisted becoming beholden to any one political party. Anne had cashiered High Tory secretary of state Nottingham over his insistence that she form an all-Tory ministry and replaced him with moderate Tory Harley; had withstood the Duchess of Marlborough's pressure to put Ultra Whigs into other cabinet places vacated by High Tories; had filled those positions with moderates. Anne thus achieved Moderation, her ideal of governance.

During that summer's election for the house of commons, party propaganda reached new extremes. High Tory pamphlets attacked the popular queen in person. The general Tory drumbeat of Church in Danger offended her; Anne thought it slandered her handling of Church business, let alone cast aspersion on her prerogative as head of the Church of England. "Willful and imperious [Lord Rochester, the queen's High Tory uncle, who passed for a] sincere man, and seems to have too much heat to be false (this natural heat is influenced by frequent excesses in drinking,)"[2] tried to grasp political initiative by moving in the Lords that under his niece's rule the Church faced serious peril. Anne attended the ensuing debate and, to her gratification, saw the "vote carried by a great majority: that the Church of England, under the queen's happy administration, was in a safe and flourishing condition. [And the Lords added a] severe censure [on the] spreaders of these reports of dangers; [they were] enemies of the queen and of her government. [Lords and Commons together] presented an address to the queen"[3] to that effect.

These rumblings confirmed Anne's conviction on the need for Moderation.

———∽∽∽———

To connect with her subjects, not to mention do a little electioneering, (Anne campaigned for moderates of both parties, and against Tackers, whom she despised for fomenting national disunity by Tacking occasional conformity onto a tax bill) the queen decided to make a royal progress to Cambridge. Local authorities built triumphal arches along Anne's entire flag-bedecked route across the flat fens countryside. Citizens turned out by the thousands to cheer their queen; aristocracy, nobility, and gentry clamored to kiss her hand. Church bells rang; flowers carpeted the queen's path; canons boomed; bonfires crackled; fireworks burst into thousands of colored lights; and free wine flowed.

At the university, kneeling scholars chanted Long Live the Queen. Trinity College gave a formal dinner; Anne sat on a specially provided throne. And since scientifically-minded Prince George had drawn his wife's attention to the work of Trinity's most famous Fellow, the queen knighted Isaac Newton.

Anne and her entourage then proceeded to Newmarket. She had inherited her uncle King Charles II's keen interest in horse racing. When Charles's regular attendance at the Newmarket races made the place popular, it consisted of two hundred houses set on the gentle slopes of a hill surrounded by flat green fields. The king's small, unremarkable residence stood at the center of town.

In preparation for her attendance at the Newmarket races, Anne "ordered her house … to be rebuilt, and gave £1000 towards paving the town." Once there, the queen, who owned a racing stable and ran her horses under her name, (sometimes that of her trainer) launched horse racing sweepstakes. She and George, also keen on the sport, had already given £100 gold cups as prizes at several racetracks too far north for them conveniently to attend. Anne now "bought a running horse [that] cost 1000 guineas, and gave it to the prince."[4] And refused to let a gouty knee interfere with her enjoyment of Newmarket.

—⁂—

The key political challenge for Queen Anne and her ministers consisted of creating a working relationship between crown and parliament. Mandatory elections at least once in every three years served to complicate the task.

The new parliament must, as its first duty, elect a speaker for the house of commons. The queen and her politically moderate prime minister, Sidney Godolphin, wanted moderate Whig John Smith. Anne had no doubt that a new MP, son of her childhood friend Frances Apsley, had "good inclinations to serve me. [She trusted the young man to vote for Smith, but also to] be careful never to engage himself so far into any party as not to be at liberty to leave them when he sees them running into things that are unreasonable, for I shall always depend upon his concurring in everything that is good for me and for the public."[5]

Smith's hairbreadth victory convinced Godolphin that Tories, who had lost a significant number of seats to Whigs in the recent election, would reject Moderation. Since he and the queen continued King William's policy of public borrowing to develop the nation's wealth and, thus, pay for the war, the government needed the support of Whig capitalists who controlled the nation's commerce as well as Whig MPs to assure a continued supply of funds for the war. Hence, Godolphin decided that the queen's government must work more closely with Whigs.

In exchange for their support, Whigs demanded more power. And because party hatred meant ministers could no longer rely on parliament to back measures purely out of national interest, the queen's ministers must yield to party leaders' demands for office in return for party votes.

Since only the queen could appoint ministers, Godolphin advised Anne to appoint popular, respected, Sir William Cowper, a talented orator and able lawyer, as lord keeper of the great seal. One of the five highest officers of state, the lord keeper had actual custody of the great seal of the realm, used to denote the ruler's approval of major state documents; the office came with a seat in the cabinet. Judged a moderate Whig, one aligned with but not a member of, the Junto, (Whig leadership) Cowper would be acceptable to all Whigs.

The queen considered her lord treasurer a personal friend as well as colleague; and candor, Anne believed, should prevail between friends. So, when Godolphin promoted Cowper's appointment, Anne thought she should be frank on such an important subject.

"I wish very much that there may be a moderate Tory found for this employment."[6] A moderate Tory would support Marlborough's land, rather than naval, war strategy; back the queen's agenda in parliament and cabinet without succumbing to party malice towards Whigs or pressure to pass partisan laws; favor the Protestant Hanoverian succession; respect monarchy and constitution. But above all, Anne sought a moderate Tory tolerant enough to accept dissenters' privileges while at the same time, reliably Anglican, a man she could trust to use the clerical patronage at his disposal with enough discernment to earn her approval.

Since Whigs had received so many favors from her, the queen concluded that a few more would put her "insensibly into their power"—a development Anne dreaded. Realizing, besides, the high opinion her "dear unkind friend" Sarah had of Whigs, Anne expected the duchess to do her utmost to get Godolphin to "prevail with me to put one of them into this great post."[7]

Of course, she would. Scarcely had Anne had time to settle herself on the throne when Sarah started to press her to appoint Whigs to the cabinet. And since Godolphin respected Sarah's political acumen, she could influence him.

Godolphin advocated Whig admission to positions of authority only when faced with Whig parliamentary power. Regardless, the queen put "entire confidence [in her prime minister.] There is nobody I can rely upon but yourself to bring me out of all my difficulties, [she wrote him. Anne trusted Godolphin] to do all you can to keep me out of the power of the merciless men of both parties."[8]

—⁂—

Godolphin agreed with Sarah that Cowper should get the lord keeper position. Anne declined to appoint him mainly because the lord keeper's office had a say in church appointments. That the queen saw as an integral part of her prerogative as head of the Anglican church. A Whig lord keeper might well disagree with his sovereign over choices for high church office.

This impasse provoked the duchess's decision to step in.

Sarah had been away from court for long stretches of time. Having her keeper of the privy purse, mistress of the robes, groom of the stole, and senior lady-in-waiting constantly absent caused the queen considerable inconvenience. Hence, Sarah's close friend Sidney Godolphin felt the need to advise not only a decrease in the frequency and intensity of her letters insisting Anne grant favors to Whigs, but also the duchess's immediate return to court.

Sarah did return. And managed to reconcile with Anne.

That pleased Marlborough. His wife should concentrate on being "easier with the queen, [the duke wrote] for the good of everything." Because Godolphin's letters indicated that harmonious relations between duchess and queen "would be of great use to him."[9]

The duchess agreed to accompany queen, prince, and court on another state visit, this time to the cathedral city of Winchester. Having marked the occasion by quarreling with one of Anne's ladies-in-waiting, Sarah again withdrew from court, although not before complaining to the queen about her attendant.

Some time went by before Anne claimed a disinclination to tolerate any member of her household insulting the duchess; and promised to do anything Sarah thought reasonable. But since the queen had "been so unfortunate as to be unjustly thought of by you for so long, [she worried that] what I say now will be no more credited than all the former assurances I have given you of my truth. [Still, Anne tempered her reproach by concluding that] since I have ever had a most sincere and tender kindness for my dear Mrs. Freeman, so I will preserve it to my grave."[10]

—⁂—

Rather than building on her harmony with Anne to restore their personal friendship, Sarah resumed her bombardment; she favored the queen with what she considered her superior understanding of politics, particularly the need to appoint Cowper to the cabinet. But where Princess Anne had valued Sarah's candor as a refreshing antidote to a kowtowing court, Queen Anne saw Sarah's lobbying as political opportunism. That not only roused the queen's resentment; it also increased her suspicion that the duchess had undue influence over Godolphin.

Focused on Cowper's cause even to the extent of casting aside concern for her husband who suffered from debilitating headaches, stomach trouble, and gout, which his heavy responsibilities hardly helped, Sarah shattered her vow not exacerbate Marlborough's military and diplomatic problems with domestic political tussles. She appealed to him for help.

The duke and his imperial Austrian ally, Prince Eugene of Savoy, had planned to start the 1705 campaign by opening the road to Paris via a march on the Moselle River. But because Blenheim had removed France's threat to Germany, its several independent princes were slow to send the duke promised troops; as well, vital supplies went awry when the Dutch engaged a cheap contractor who failed to deliver; and the emperor's Italian campaign kept Eugene busy. The French were thus able to penetrate the Spanish Netherlands.

Marlborough stopped the French advance, but his Dutch allies declined to join him in pressing the advantage against a poorly positioned enemy. So, the duke led British troops into fooling the French via a series of bold feints and bluffs, marches and countermarches, to demolish the enemy's Lines of Brabant, sixty miles of broad, deep, strongly fortified trenches extending across France's northern frontier bordering the Spanish Netherlands. His victory animated Marlborough to seek an end to the war via all out battle against France. Holland again refused to cooperate.

—⁂—

Temporarily shelving these problems, the duke hastened to tell his wife that he agreed with her and Godolphin—moderate Whig Cowper should be appointed to the cabinet. The queen appealed to Marlborough. "What I say is from my heart and soul for your service, [he answered. Were he with her, the duke would] beg on my knees [that Anne instantly ask Godolphin what needed to] be done, that you might be in the condition of carrying on the war, and of opposing the extravagances of these mad people"[11] (High Tories Rochester and Nottingham). Otherwise, the queen must ask them to form a ministry, which meant trouble, for High Tories would fail to wage the land war forcefully; besides they lacked popular support, and were so partisan that Whigs would certainly oppose them.

"Those two persons you mention, [Anne replied] have made it wholly impossible to employ them, if I had ever the much inclination to do it & as I am entirely satisfied of the sincerity and the capacity of him I trust, [Godolphin] then I shall never repent of the choice whatever my fortune may be."[12]

That being so, the duke implored Anne, for "your own sake and the happiness of your kingdoms … never [to let anyone harm Godolphin.] Besides his integrity for your service, his temper and his abilities [made him the] only man in England capable [of counseling Anne so as to keep her] out of the hands of both parties, [which should] at least make you happy, if quietness can be had in a country where there is so much faction."[13]

—〰—

Furious about Holland's refusal to join his plan to lure the enemy into a definitive engagement, worried that his various ailments indicated serious illness, Marlborough longed, as well, to return his wife and children. Hence, he spoke often and loudly of retiring at the end of the current campaign season. The queen concurred that all the "disagreeable things you have met with this summer" gave her friend ample cause for considering resignation. Exceedingly concerned about the duke's "uneasiness, [Anne, nonetheless, fervently hoped that for the] good of your country and the sake of your friends, who cannot support themselves without you, you will be persuaded to banish your melancholy thoughts. [She wished the] business abroad may give you leave to be soon at home, which all your friends [want, but] none … more than your humble servant."[14]

Consequently, instead of spending the few private moments he could snatch, in contemplating how his "greatest happiness [would be to live a quiet life with his] dearest soul,"[15] Marlborough confided to his wife—"I can't but love, and endeavor to serve, [the queen] as long as I have life."[16]

Since next year's campaign held out the possibility of ending the war satisfactorily, although not without help from the German states, Marlborough prepared to travel around the Continent to rally them, plus other allies. As well, the duke must confer with bankers at Frankfurt, a major financial center; and convince bankers in his Austrian ally's capital to advance the emperor (on English and Dutch security) enough funds to support Prince Eugene, fighting the French in Italy.

Not about to let her uneasy relations with the duchess impinge on matters of state, Queen Anne thought herself fortunate to have Marlborough functioning as quasi foreign minister, a sentiment reinforced by Prince George, whose continental background gave him a more cosmopolitan outlook than his wife. Since monarchs and ministers rarely traveled outside their realms in the early eighteenth century, the duke's journeys to continental capitals gave Britain a unique advantage. No one knew more about the war, *the* foreign policy issue of the day, than Marlborough; no Briton knew personally all the great players on the European stage who were most relevant to British interests; and no Briton stood higher in the queen's favor.

—⚉—

Realizing her need for Whig parliamentary support of the war, the queen recognized that Cowper's admission to the ministry seemed a fair price to pay. So, after delaying his appointment until she had wrested some ecclesiastical patronage from the lord keeper's office,[17] Anne graciously welcomed Cowper into her cabinet.

Lord Keeper Cowper soon endeared himself to the queen by refusing to accept the traditional New Year's Gifts—from counsel practicing at the chancery (commercial and property matters) bar—Cowper thought such Gifts smelt of corruption. And the new lord keeper made friends with all his colleagues, even the Tory ministers.

Cowper's appointment owed little, if anything, to the duchess's efforts. These served merely to increase the queen's distaste for what she saw as Sarah's unwarranted interference in politics. Rather than the duchess staying away from court for weeks on end, Anne thought Sarah should devote her energy to her responsibilities in the royal household.

Whigs, on the other hand, believed the duchess's influence caused Cowper's appointment. They deluged her with flattering praise. So, while Sarah further damaged her relations with the queen via futile attempts to impose what she deemed her superior political views, Whigs believed in Sarah's unlimited sway.

—⚉—

Anne continued to suffer from gout. No cure existed. Regardless, the queen's doctors prescribed the usual remedies—sweet and nourishing ass's milk, hiera picra, (a warm purgative made of aloes and canella bark ground into powder and mixed with honey) and oil of millipedes to relieve pain. In addition, Anne submitted to bleeding although she preferred cupping—which involved the doctor applying a glass cup from which the air had been drawn out, to the affected area, to bring blood to the surface. But only laudanum relieved the queen's agony. When she could no longer bear it, Anne consumed a little laudanum on toast floating in brandy.

Infirmity failed to stop the queen from carrying out her duties. But Anne's ailing health did focus the question of the succession.

Queen Anne supported the Protestant Hanoverian succession as the best guarantee not only against a challenge to her throne from her Catholic half-brother the Pretender, but also to keep her country Protestant. Yet, the queen refused to have her successor, Sophia, Dowager Electress of Hanover, live in England.

Experience as heir presumptive had taught Princess Anne the dangers of a rival court. Sophia would surely attract political discontent, to say nothing of intrigue, for had not Anne, during William and Mary's reign, been obliged to guard her court from developing into the center of opposition? Besides, from the moment William had introduced Sophia to the idea of succeeding Anne, the dowager electress initiated and maintained, correspondence with several people in England. Hence, the queen shuddered to think how, given current poisonous party rivalries, a competing court, particularly one headed by the redoubtable dowager, would exacerbate the challenge of maintaining a moderate ministry.

Adored for her goodness among the inhabitants of [Hanover, popular with] strangers by her unparalleled affability, [septuagenarian Sophia, with her firm, full-lipped mouth and determined chin, had] ever enjoyed extra-ordinary health, which keeps her still vigorous, of a cheerful countenance, and merry disposition. She steps as firm and erect as any young lady, has not one wrinkle in her face which is still very agreeable, nor one tooth out of her head, and reads without spectacles ... letters of a small character in the dusk of evening.... She's the most constant and greatest walker ... never missing a day ... for one or two hours, and often more...

She has long been admired by all the learned world, as a woman of incomparable knowledge in divinity, philosophy, history, and the subjects of all sorts of books, of which she has read a prodigious quantity. She speaks five languages so well, that by her accent it might be a dispute which of them was her first.... English ... she speaks as truly and easily as any native ... has a due veneration for the Church of England ... professes to admire our form of government and understands it very well.[18]

Determined to secure the throne for herself or, failing her survival, for her eldest son and his son, feeling miffed because she had not been accorded the privileges of an heir apparent—household, pension, and title—the dowager electress thought her dignity as successor demanded at least her residence in England. In this, Sophia chose to ignore the advice of her private agent in London. He assured the dowager that no one could force the queen to invite a Hanoverian to England; indeed, on that subject "the queen ... is extremely determined and very fierce."[19]

Regardless, the dowager electress thought it would be agreeable, let alone diverting, to live in London as courted successor to the throne. Not above meddling in English politics, which she understood "very well," acutely aware that Whigs were as one in their loyalty to the House of Hanover, Sophia planned to woo the less committed, less united Tories (one faction avowed Jacobitism; another wanted the Prince of Wales restored if he converted to Protestantism; other Tories gave the Hanoverian succession varying degrees of support). And this formidable female found a powerful ally.

—m—

Determined to wreak revenge on the niece who had dismissed him from her cabinet, Anne's High Tory uncle, Earl Rochester, sent an envoy to establish contact with Sophia. He planned to propose that parliament invite her to live in England. This would accrue to Tory advantage. The dowager electress could officially head the opposition; their opponents would no longer be able to tar Tories as Jacobites; and if Whigs were against Sophia's presence, they could handily be labeled as republicans. Furthermore, since the court had started "to look more favorably [on Whigs, their opposition to having the dowager in London] would cast a load on them as men, who after all the zeal they had expressed for the succession, did now, upon the hopes of favor at court, throw it up."[20] Finally, the queen would be humiliated.

For High Tories focused their fury on the queen personally. Not only had she cashiered their leader, Rochester, but Anne also dismissed from her cabinet his ally, Nottingham, as well as other High Tories. Hence, they enhanced Rochester's plan: the young Electoral Prince of Hanover should be made Britain's generalissimo—to embarrass the queen, Prince George (titular head of the armed forces) and Marlborough (Anne's captain general).

The pro–Hanoverian succession Whigs at first treated the "intention of sending for the old electress as a ridicule. [Whigs then said] they should not have moved anything so disagreeable to the queen, [but such a motion did contain] much security for England"[21]; for, if the ailing queen died suddenly, the Pretender, who lived in France, could come to England more quickly than anyone from Hanover. Hence, Whigs admitted the impossibility of their opposing the motion.

"Tis not imaginable how uneasy this will be to the queen, and I don't know how to prevent it." Godolphin begged his ally, parliamentary insider Robert Harley, recently appointed to the cabinet, to "find some expedient to keep the queen from so great a mortification as I know this will be to her."[22]

—⁂—

In the gloom of winter dusk, while a disagreeably dank chill suffused the air and rain drummed against the windows, Anne opened the weekly Sunday evening cabinet meeting. Its agenda included a letter, read aloud, about an "agent from the discontented party [who had arrived] in Hanover to invite over the Princess Sophia & electoral prince into England, i.e. to assure them a party in parliament here was ready to propose it. [Sophia had answered that] she judged the message come from such as were enemies to her family—that she would never hearken to such a proposal but when it came from the Queen of England: & had discouraged the attempt so much, that it was believed nothing more would come of it."[23]

Having a "temper always to fear the worst,"[24] besides mistrusting Sophia's glib assertion, Anne decided to take matters into her own hands. She appealed to Marlborough, about to embark on his mission to fortify the Grand Alliance via personal visits to continental capitals. The duke's itinerary included Hanover.

The "disagreeable proposal of bringing some of the House of Hanover into England, [a prospect the queen had long dreaded, now loomed as a motion] very near being brought into both houses of parliament, which gives me a great deal of uneasiness, [Anne wrote Marlborough. True, the Elector of Hanover had instructed his official envoy in London to] discourage the propositions; but as yet he has said nothing of them, which [made the queen worry] there may be some alterations in this resolution at the court of Hanover. [She thus relied on Marlborough's] kindness and friendship [to put the Hanoverian court] right, in notions of things here, and if they will be quiet, I may be so, too"; [otherwise, Anne] "must expect to meet with a great many mortifications."[25]

Having jolted for fifteen hours a day in a lumbering, even if well-upholstered, coach over eight hundred miles of Germany's pot-holed roads in mid-winter making his "side very sore,"[26] the duke, after satisfactory discussions at Berlin, found himself having to walk on eggshells in Hanover. Whigs and Tories would scrutinize his every step. The dowager wanted to visit London. The queen opposed.

Marlborough must convince Sophia that Tories meant the invitation purely for their political benefit. He thought it ill-advised to use Anne's aversion to the visit as an argument. The queen had no objection—everyone in England knew Tories were pushing the invitation to annoy her.

The day after his arrival, the duke had "a very long conversation with [the elector. He needed very few] arguments to convince him that his and the queen's interest were the same.[27] He has commanded me to assure her majesty that he will never have any thoughts"[28] that conflict with hers.

—⁂—

Marlborough's nimble diplomacy earned him a migraine. And failed to stop Tories from introducing a motion into the house of lords that Anne invite the electress to England. The queen had to summon all her dignity, every ounce of her resolve to come to the ensuing debates, (incognita) to say nothing of the fortitude to sit through them.

Weeping silently into her lace trimmed, white cambric handkerchief, Anne attended throughout—except—at mention of her son Gloucester's name, the queen had to withdraw until she could regain her composure.

Sparing Anne nothing, the debates centered on her inmost personal traumas—her dead daughters; her son's promise and tragic death; her stance vis-à-vis her father; her position regarding her half-brother; and her poor health. The queen showed amazement at the "behavior of some"[29] who sought even to arrange for the contingency of her becoming senile in old age.

Although Anne's presence at the Lords debates embarrassed several Tories advocating an invitation to the dowager electress, Anne's uncle Rochester unabashedly led his party in arguing "with great earnestness"[30] that national security mandated the Successor living England.[31] For the Pretender, in Paris, lived much closer to England than the Successor, in Hanover; besides, Scotland had recently passed the Act of Security averring the country's right to choose its own successor; and a bellicose, armed Scotland stood ready to receive the Pretender.

Whigs thought "this matter" should be left entirely up to the queen. The dignity and safety of both crown and nation demanded that the heir be fully dependent on the queen; for, "rivalry between two courts might throw us into great distractions and be attended with very ill consequences."[32]

Tories had trapped Marlborough, Godolphin, and Whigs. If they voted against the Hanoverian invitation, Tories would denounce them for disloyalty to the Protestant succession. If they voted for the invitation, Whigs would alienate Anne—an action to be avoided at all cost, for every politician, actual or aspiring, sought the queen's favor.

—m—

A small, close-knit group that, to the frustration and envy of fragmented Tories, led Whigs with order and efficiency, conceived a solution. The Whig Junto proposed a Regency Act—on the queen's death, a caretaker government would automatically be formed and parliament convened, to carry on the country's business until Anne's successor arrived.

Queen Anne disliked and distrusted the Whig Junto for its Whig values, to say nothing of its proficiency in effecting Whig causes. The party included great landed aristocrats, commercial classes, and all dissenters and free-thinkers. Common fear of Tory reaction to their religious freedoms, (Tories upheld strict adherence to the rules and ritual of the Anglican church and strove to suppress non-conformists) plus common principles (the monarch must rule according to the law[33]; the royal prerogative must be further limited; distinctions among Protestants should be removed) united Whigs. They supported Marlborough's land war strategy and the Hanoverian succession because Whigs held Louis XIV's Catholicizing policy, and control of the Spanish empire through his grandson currently sitting on the Spanish throne as King Philip V, to be existential threats to British freedom.

Strength of shared values, forceful pursuit of power, and fidelity to each other, bound the five, otherwise heterogeneous, Junto lords. Anne thought the morals—or lack of them—characterizing blunt, colorful and bold Junto member Lord Wharton, profane in the extreme and a proud atheist alleged to have defecated in a church pulpit to prove his point, unsuitable for public office. But this genius at electioneering who focused his immense wealth on getting Whigs into parliament, proved instrumental in steering the Regency Act through the legislature.

Anne's attendance at the Lords debates supported her and her ministry's acceptance of the Regency Act. Because by forestalling any need for Sophia or her heirs to reside in England during Anne's lifetime, the Act's passage resolved the transition issue and relieved the embattled queen of embarrassment. Hence, Anne agreed to an additional act naturalizing Dowager Electress Sophia and her heirs.

To show yet more support for the Protestant Hanoverian succession, the queen decided to confer England's highest honor, the Order of the Garter, on Sophia's grandson, the Electoral Prince of Hanover. And to thank Whigs for resolving the vexing issue of the Hanoverian invitation, the queen chose proud, prickly, pushy Junto member Lord Halifax[34] as her special envoy to Hanover, to present the Regency Act and Garter. Not content with this honor, however, the electoral prince, backed by his spirited grandmother Sophia, clamored to be created a duke. Anne hesitated—giving the young man a seat in the house of lords would reopen the residence matter. But Godolphin and Marlborough (the electoral prince served in the war under his command; besides, the elector did not want his son in England) reassured her. The queen thus created the electoral prince, Duke of Cambridge. And his patent of nobility specified that although war prevented the prince from visiting England or sitting in parliament, Anne wished to honor him and his family.

—⁓—

The queen recognized Whigs' role in the Regency Act, she told Sarah; and because Anne also recognized Tory "malice and insolence" she promised, in future, a more positive attitude towards Whigs. But despite the satisfaction Queen Anne professed to gain by not disagreeing with her "dear Mrs. Freeman ... as we have formerly done,"[35] Anne remained committed to a moderate, all-party ministry.

Ten

Queen Anne's War

"When she [the queen] thinks herself in the right, she needs no advice to help her to be very firm and positive."[1]—Duke of Marlborough

The new year (1706) brought Queen Anne crippling gout. She led the weekly cabinet meeting from her canopied, four poster bed, its crimson velvet curtains tied back with tasseled silken ropes. Wearing a nightgown of white mohair lined with black and white striped flowered silk, the queen took part in a lively discussion.

Gout failed to stop Anne from celebrating her birthday. "About eleven of the clock a fine ode was sung, in concert, before her majesty; at one of the clock in the afternoon the great guns of the Tower, and those of St. James's park, were fired. [In the evening the queen presided over a] numerous and extremely magnificent court."[2] Nobility, gentry, political notables, and every foreign envoy attended, all arrayed in new garments ordered specially for the event. Anne's guests observed her to wear a stylish manto of brocaded cream velvet, open below the bodice to reveal her underlying dress, richly embroidered in silver gilt; Anne's matching embroidered satin shoes, too, were in the latest style, tapered to a square toe of less than an inch wide, with high Louis heel, and fastened by satin straps tied over a high-instep tongue. And, of course, the queen carried the most important female accessory, a fan, Indian painted, with ivory sticks.

The evening featured a splendid ball. Hanging from the ceiling, a huge crystal chandelier containing hundreds of candles that made its cut-glass pendants sparkle like diamonds, illuminated the ballroom. Guests danced to the music Anne's court composer had written (as he did every year) to honor the queen's birthday. As well, the queen treated her guests to an Italian opera, and a play. Festivities "concluded with ringing of bells, bonfires, and other demonstrations of public joy."[3]

Next day, asthma attacked Prince George. He became gravely ill, spitting blood for several weeks. Although still ailing, Anne sat with her husband throughout the nights to help him fight for breath.

—⁂—

The queen had nursed her husband back to health by the time daffodils and tulips brightened London parks. But the War of the Spanish Succession reached its fourth year without bringing Anne and her allies enough gain to realize the goal their Grand Alliance held vital to European security—pushing France out of the Spanish Netherlands and Italy. True, the seas were rid of enemy fleets, and the French army sustained a blow at the Battle of Blenheim. But the war's heavy financial burden, let alone the impatience of each ally to satisfy its own interests, undermined the Alliance. It would crumble without another major victory.

The coming campaign gave little cause for optimism. Allied commander in chief the Duke of Marlborough waited at his headquarters in The Hague for early spring sunshine to melt enough snow on mountain passes to let him cross the Alps, and join his friend and colleague, the Hapsburg Empire's Prince Eugene of Savoy, fighting the French in Italy. France forestalled the duke's plan by defeating his and Eugene's ally, the Prince of Baden, thereby opening Germany to invasion. Instead, French King Louis XIV decided to force peace on his terms via a victory to his north. Elated that the enemy intended to leave its well-fortified bastions in the Spanish Netherlands to fight, Marlborough prepared to attack.

Before dawn (May 23, 1706) on a foggy, albeit mercifully dry day after hours of torrential rain, Marlborough's army (sixty thousand Britons, Danes, Dutch, and Swedes) marched over a four-mile front to meet the enemy on broad Ramillies plain.

The duke twice led cavalry charges, his scarlet uniform coat easily discernible amid the blue and grey uniformed Dutch he rallied to stop the French from breaking through his lines. Targeting the conspicuous allied commander in chief, French sharpshooters hit his horse. Marlborough jumped to safety, then immediately prepared to mount a fresh steed. While holding the stirrup for him, the duke's equerry had his head shot off. Unharmed, Marlborough instantly rejoined the battle.

By the time late afternoon light turned to dusk the decimated, dispirited French troops had been completely overpowered. Their commander described the Battle of Ramillies as the most shameful and calamitous of defeats.

—⚶—

It is impossible for me ever to say so much as I ought in return of your great & faithful services, [and] all the great successes you have had in this campaign, [Anne congratulated her captain general.] But I will endeavor by all the actions of my life to show you how truly sensible I am of them … the blessing of God is certainly with you, may He continue to protect you & make you the happy instrument of giving a lasting peace to Europe. And I beg though I cannot express myself so well as I would you would be so just … as to believe nobody is with more truth and affection your humble servant.[4]

A bad cold causing Prince George shortness of breath prevented him from immediately congratulating Marlborough. But as soon as the prince could put pen to paper, "nobody I am sure rejoices more sincerely than I do at your being well after the great dangers you have been in."[5]

Overjoyed at her army's success, the gout-plagued queen gritted her teeth, rose from her couch, and casting aside the poultices infused with a malodorous, dark brown unguent designed to ease the excruciating pain in her red and swollen foot, led her nation in thanksgiving. Anne donned a splendid gown and petticoat made from cloth of gold brocade. George wore a purple suit embroidered with silver. Eight horses, their coats brushed to a high gloss, their harnesses gleaming, their manes and tails decorated with knots of red, white, and blue ribbons, drew the royal couple's splendid, carved, crimson and gold state coach through streets lined with wildly cheering crowds, to a special three-hour service at St. Paul's Cathedral, packed with nobles, political luminaries, and foreign dignitaries.

Anne not only rewarded Marlborough monetarily, but also, since he had no sons to succeed him, asked parliament to provide for his dukedom to descend through the female line.

—⁓—

Ramillies resulted in the surrender of every major town in the Spanish Netherlands. Without one shot fired, provincial assemblies, fortresses, and cities declared for the Austrian House of Hapsburg's King Charles III, (brother of the Austrian emperor) as King of Spain, rather than Louis's grandson, the French House of Bourbon's King Philip V.

Ramillies compelled France to turn its attention to defense of its northern frontier; that necessitated troop redeployment, including removal of some French regiments from Italy. Consequently, English diplomacy and English gold cajoled the German states into joining Prince Eugene, fighting the French in Italy's north where the Dukedom of Savoy, a small but strategic independent polity, had recently abandoned its alliance with France in favor of the Allies. King Louis responded by besieging Savoy's capital, Turin. That challenged the Allies. Eugene's victory at Turin forced French withdrawal from northern Italy.

Marlborough found it "impossible … to express the joy [Turin gave him.] I do not only esteem but I really love that prince. [His victory delivered such a blow to France, that if Whigs could] be persuaded to carry the war on one year longer with vigor, [the Allies must, with] the blessing of God [achieve] such a peace, as would give us quiet in our days."[6] Sarah's husband knew she longed for a role in politics. He gave her one: make sure Whigs kept up their strong support of the war.

The queen saw Turin and Ramillies as a chance to negotiate for peace. She had always backed the war. But Anne also understood its burdens—the toll that casualties took on families, how wartime taxes affected almost every household. Ramillies and Turin meant that allied goals were met—France had been pushed out of the Spanish Netherlands and Italy.

But the queen's lord treasurer and prime minister, Sidney Godolphin, and Whig financiers whose backing sustained the war effort, saw Ramillies, Turin, and Blenheim as a chance to insist on France's unconditional surrender. For although the Treaty of the Grand Alliance accepted dividing Spain's empire between Bourbon Philip and Hapsburg Charles, outright French defeat would enable the Allies to demand all for Charles, nothing for Philip. And give England an opportunity to gain major trade concessions from France and a grateful Hapsburg king of Spain.

Anne acquiesced to No Peace Without Spain. But told Marlborough that as soon as Hapsburg Charles had ascended to the Spanish throne, she wanted peace.

—⁓—

Continued Whig support for the war came at a cost. Whig leaders, the five tightly-knit lords known as the Junto, wanted one of theirs in the cabinet, a notion that could scarcely be considered excessive since Whigs dominated parliament. Still, Whigs knew Anne, who wanted a moderate ministry, would resist.

Convinced, even if mistakenly, that Sarah, Duchess of Marlborough, had been mainly responsible for moderate Whig Sir William Cowper's recent appointment to the cabinet as lord keeper of the great seal, the Junto selected Marlborough son-in-law Charles Spencer, Earl Sunderland, as the most likely candidate to succeed in breaching Anne's defenses. For, the queen could surely not reject a close relative of her victorious general, one, moreover, backed by such a potent favorite as Sarah, her dearest friend. Sunderland must, his Junto cohorts insisted, receive a senior cabinet post; he should replace one of the two moderate Tory secretaries of state.

Republican in his youth, now an Ultra Whig outspokenly mistrustful of royal prerogatives in general, full of scorn for the queen in particular, arrogant, impetuous Sunderland, whose parents had roused loathing and dread in Anne as princess, could not be said to qualify as a strong candidate for her favor. For besides his frank views on the need to curb royal power and promote parliamentary control of government, this tall, well-built Marlborough son-in-law with the pockmarked face had led opposition to the bill granting Prince George a lifetime income. As well, Sunderland lauded foreign countries but disparaged his own, a sentiment not designed to endear him to his patriotic sovereign. Were Sunderland to become one of her secretaries of state, the queen must not only tolerate him in her cabinet, but the nature of his office would also necessitate her conferring with Sunderland almost daily.

Knowing Anne would object to having the Junto's most strident member in her ministry, Godolphin broached a compromise. Sunderland should be appointed envoy extraordinary to Vienna, to head a distinguished delegation bringing the new emperor England's official congratulations on his accession, condolences on his predecessor's death, and help to the British ambassador in mediating an end to Hungary's rebellion against Hapsburg rule.

The Junto declined this sop. So, Godolphin advised the queen to appoint Sunderland a secretary of state. No. To have any Junto member, let alone this Junto member, foisted on her offended Anne's dignity and impinged on her royal prerogative, her right to appoint ministers of her choosing.

—m—

Four years on the throne had increased the queen's trust in her judgment. True, her health had deteriorated; multiple pregnancies had slackened her muscles, the sedentary lifestyle that gout inflicted and dropsy (an abnormal accumulation of fluid) exacerbated, had ruined her once comely figure. Anne could no longer hunt on horseback in her close-fitting coat with its large cuffs, and matching three-cornered hat with feathers, as she had loved to do while princess. But Anne did still hunt hare and stag—in a light, strong, custom-made, high-wheeled, comfortably padded chaise, specially built for speed, and designed to hold only herself. Handling her carriage reins skillfully, driving swiftly over the rides her gardeners had cut through Windsor Forest, the queen often covered forty to fifty miles on a fine day.

And Anne knew her own mind. She would not have anyone she judged unfit for office forced upon her—and Junto membership disqualified Sunderland. Having escaped Rochester and Nottingham's ultra Toryism, the queen loathed the idea of having an Ultra Whig in her ministry, recoiled at the notion of being in the hands of one party; for once she appointed Sunderland to her cabinet, more Junto members would surely clamor for entry.

Marlborough, too, opposed Sunderland becoming a secretary of state. His abrasive manners were ill-suited to the queen; and Anne hated him. But more to the point, Marlborough thought such an extreme Whig would fail to fit into the moderate government he, Godolphin, and the queen wanted. So, despite the need to propitiate Whigs, the duke opposed his son-in-law's appointment to any high state office.

Whigs accused Marlborough and Godolphin, of not acting "sincerely." The duke thought he deserved better from his compatriots than to be suspected of not acting in the national interest, which he always had done, did, and "ever [would do] without being of a faction, [Marlborough wrote his pro–Whig wife. Since the Junto had decided to] vex or ruin the lord treasurer and me because the queen has not complied [about Sunderland, the duke would] henceforward despise all mankind; [for, he knew how zealously Godolphin had] pressed the queen in that matter."[7]

—⁂—

The duchess disagreed. Daily more convinced of her political acumen, Sarah considered herself, besides, as able as any minister. She thus charged the victor of Blenheim and Ramillies with timidity, railed against John's "tenderness" for Anne and tepidity towards Whigs—he must insist on the queen appointing Sunderland.

Since the "very sincere [queen had, as well,] a great many other good qualities, in which we ought to think ourselves happy," Marlborough counseled patience. Sunderland and his friends ought not to be miffed. Anne's growing awareness of the "undutiful and unkind usage she meets from the greatest part of the Tories, [would] bring her to what I am afraid she is yet uneasy at."[8]

Patience could not be considered among the virtues calculated to appeal to hot-tempered Sarah. Having for months refrained from political argument with her sovereign, the duchess, as a Whig and mother-in-law, jumped at Junto requests that she lobby Anne about Sunderland.

Seeing the duchess's political urgings as unjustified meddling, her partiality for Sunderland driven by family interest, (which Sarah fiercely denied) the queen put off answering Sarah's long pro–Sunderland screeds. The duchess stopped writing. "Not having heard from my dear Mrs. Freeman since my last two, [Anne reacted] I am almost afraid of venturing to trouble her with a few lines from her poor unfortunate ever faithful Morley. [Unconscious] of ever having done anything to deserve such coldness as you have shown of late, [the queen could not] help putting you in mind of her who you thought worthy of your esteem & will to her last moment be with all truth & tenderness my dear Mrs. Freeman's."[9]

Thus encouraged, Sarah pointed out that two Tory MPs who voted against the government, had kept their positions in Prince George's household. The queen induced her husband to replace them with Whigs.

—⁂—

No matter, the duchess continued to insist on Sunderland's appointment; for Anne must know she could not govern without the support of parliamentary Whigs and their capitalist allies who assured the steady flow of funds essential for war expenses. Sarah wanted the queen to "succeed by any sort of men in what is just and will prevent what has been done from being thrown away." The duchess thought Prince George and his deputy at the Admiralty, Tory George Churchill—the duke's brother—were behind Anne's resistance. "Your security and the nation's is my chief wish; [so, Sarah begged] God Almighty ... that Mr. and Mrs. Morley may see their errors as to this notion before it is too late."[10]

Misreading *notion* for *nation*, Anne felt insulted to the core of her queenship. How could the duchess question her commitment to her country. The queen did not reply; but, did convey her outrage to Sarah's close friend Sidney Godolphin.

He admitted that "the word *notion* was not so distinctly written, but that one might as naturally read it *nation*,"[11] Sidney told Sarah. Still, making the duchess aware of Anne's innocent mistake served little to abate either Sarah's fury at her former gentle, tender friend taking offense at one word, or Sarah's pro–Sunderland promptings.

The queen came to dread Sarah's tirades, especially during their occasional private times at Windsor Castle that summer. As the two women sat cozily in Anne's favorite, many-sided boudoir in a turret over the castle's Norman gateway, the queen presided over the tea-table. Set with freshly-baked ratafia (an almond flavored liqueur) biscuits, and the aniseed, cinnamon, citron, and orange brandy seasonings for Bohea, a black tea from China, the queen fended off political discussion by chatting about her clothes, her ever present lapdogs, and worries over George's asthma, all of which Anne liked to talk about in her rare moments of relaxation.

But the duchess viewed these private moments differently; they were political openings. Frustrated, not to say irritated, by what she called the queen's insipid conversation, Sarah went back to London.

"Very impatient to know of the reasons why [the duchess] would not see her last Saturday, [since Sarah] could have no good one, & as long as I know myself innocent I can yet better bear your unkindness, which is a greater mortification to me than can be expressed, [Anne wrote with noticeably less effusion than in former days. She wished the duchess] would ask some advice about your health for I fear it is not in good state, & nobody … wishes my dear Mrs. Freeman it & all other blessings more sincerely than her faithful Morley."[12]

—⚹—

Sarah's certitude about Anne's inability to think for herself grew parallel to the duchess's confidence in her political perception. There must be a reason, Sarah thought, for her sovereign's refusal to appoint Sunderland. The duchess found her reason. It also served as a convenient explanation for Sarah's waning favor.

Some time ago the duchess's cousin, Abigail Hill, had been forced by circumstance (her father had fallen on hard times) to become a maid in a nobleman's house. For, in the days when women were thought to be the weaker sex, inferior to men and incapable of undertaking a profession, females compelled to earn a living usually did so as domestics. On hearing of Abigail's plight, Sarah introduced her into the queen's household as a bedchamber-women. Since this position as one of Anne's personal maids put Abigail into daily contact with the queen, Sarah, during her long and frequent absences from court, relied on Abigail to be her eyes and ears.

A starker contrast to the imperious duchess would be hard to find. Beautiful, golden haired and azure eyed Sarah, vivacious and self-assured, wife of England's war hero, stood at the pinnacle of wealth and power, stood on such a unique footing with the queen that she could afford to criticize and argue, let alone pay scant attention to her court duties. Plain, red-nosed, meek, unmarried Abigail stood ready to perform any menial task for her ailing mistress.

Although a Tory, Abigail refrained from political argument; nor did she show the slightest disapproval of Anne's political judgment. And unlike Sarah who scoffed at organized religion per se, let alone its manifestations, deeply religious Abigail revered the principles of the Anglican Church.

Soothing and supportive, amiable and obliging, Abigail's calm and gentle ministrations made her an excellent nurse. Besides, Abigail discreetly tidied sickroom trash, brought refreshing tea to allay a sleepless night, and did her utmost to make the poorly queen comfortable. Furthermore, Abigail distracted Anne from gout's agonies via an amusing ability to mimic, as well as perform delightfully on the harpsichord.

Abigail often played compositions by the queen's favorite Henry Purcell when, in the late afternoon, George usually took a post-prandial nap, and his wife, free from public duties, retired to her prettily furnished green room. Anne would admit a select few to sit around her tea table, listening to the harpsichord, or chatting in low voices. The queen especially liked talking to moderate Tory Robert Harley, who had tutored her about the ways of parliament during the waning days of William's reign, and now served as one of her two secretaries of state.

—⧗—

Known as Robin the Trickster for his cagey, crafty ways and convoluted writing style, Harley, having invited several cabinet colleagues to dinner, "drank to love & friendship & everlasting union & wished he had more Tokay to drink it in, [as the company had already consumed two] good, but thick [bottles. One of the guests suggested Harley's] white Lisbon [for the toast,] it being very clear. [Everyone, including the host, took this remark] to relate to that humor of his, which was never to deal clearly and openly but always with reserve, if not dissimulation or rather simulation; & to love tricks even where not necessary, but from an inward satisfaction he took in applauding his own cunning."[13]

Nonetheless, incorruptible Harley held to high standards of public duty, harbored deep and sincere religious convictions. And, coincidentally Abigail's cousin on the other side of her family from Sarah, Harley had, like the duchess, assisted Abigail's relatives.

He echoed the queen's wish for a moderate ministry, one free of party extremes. Having so far seen eye-to-eye with Marlborough and Godolphin's policies, Harley now feared the latter's conciliation of Whigs would alienate moderate Tories; especially as Harley judged that the Junto could never be satisfied with only one cabinet appointment. He pressed this point on Anne whenever he could. And since this sentiment confirmed her own, the queen's appreciation of Harley grew. Whigs, on the other hand, held him responsible for the queen's steadfast opposition to Sunderland's appointment.

Sarah agreed but went one step further—she blamed Anne's attitude on the insidious influence of Tory Abigail—Sarah's treacherous cousin had not only usurped her position as favorite, but also manipulated the queen into taking her political advice. Here, the duchess made a major misjudgment.

She and the shy, motherless, insecure little princess who looked up to her stunning, magnetic, self-confident senior, had formed a friendship as close and equal as possible between sovereign and subject. The mature queen's feelings for Abigail never changed from those of mistress to servant, nurse, and social inferior.

Yes, Sarah did correctly assume Abigail would try to influence the queen politically. Indeed, in an age when partisan politics permeated every aspect of life, anyone having even the remotest contact with Anne would feel honor bound to try and exert some sway. Like Sarah, Abigail failed to get very far, even with the cogent arguments her cousin Harley fed her. Like Sarah, Abigail persisted. Unlike Sarah, Abigail knew when to stop.

"I had a great deal of discourse with the queen, [Abigail wrote her cousin Harley.] People think I am able to persuade her to anything I have a mind to have her do, but they will be convinced to the contrary one time or another."[14] Consumed with jealousy and rage, Sarah persisted in ascribing to Abigail far more power over Anne than actually existed; and Marlborough and Godolphin treated Sarah's exaggerated assertions seriously.

—⁓—

On the Continent, meanwhile, Ramillies brought several advantages, not the least of which freed the Spanish Netherlands from French control. That pleased neighboring Holland. Hence, Louis XIV's peace feelers encouraged the Dutch peace party, particularly as war had depleted the country's treasury.

Concomitantly, as early autumn sun shone brightly over England, the air felt crisp, and Queen Anne saw late roses blooming beside early chrysanthemums in St. James's park, her country faced a political crisis. War subsidies. They would be the key question facing parliament in the upcoming session. Whigs threatened to withhold support unless Sunderland came into the cabinet. The queen refused.

This impasse proved too much for lord treasurer and de facto prime minister Sidney Godolphin. He had given his health and most of his sixty plus years to working for the crown, had served the queen "faithfully to the best of my understanding, without any advantage to myself, except the honor of doing so, or without expecting any other favor than to end the small remainder of my days in liberty and quiet."[15] Fed up with the endless parliamentary criticism that came with his position, plus incessant Junto demands, besides Marlborough's misgivings about war and diplomacy, Sarah's tirades, and Anne's determination, Sidney, despite his affection for the queen, told her he would resign if she continued to hold out against Sunderland's appointment as secretary of state.

Friends, Anne replied, "should always speak ... freely" to one another. She had always valued true friendship, recognized its responsibilities, and sought to obey its laws. But sometimes, the queen wrote, one friend hoped matters might not reach "that extremity as to make it necessary to trouble [the other. In such a case, of course, one defers] doing so as long as one can."[16]

Now, her difficulties were "so great and so uneasy to me" that Anne could no longer keep her thoughts to herself. She would rather explain them in writing to Sidney, than try to

begin to speak and not be able to go on.
[Appointing] a party man secretary of state when [so many Whigs held government positions already, would be] throwing myself into the hands of a party, [something the queen wanted to] avoid, and which [she had heard both Marlborough and Godolphin] say I must never do.
[The queen wanted only her freedom] in encouraging and employing all those that concur faithfully in my service, whether they are called Whigs or Tories, not to be tied to one or the other. [Should she be so] unfortunate as to fall into the hands of either, [Anne would view herself] though I have the name of queen, to be in reality but their slave. [That would mean not only her] personal ruin; [it would mean, as well, the] destroying of all government, for instead of putting an end to faction, it will lay a lasting foundation for it.[17]

Since Godolphin had told her Whigs would withdraw parliamentary support unless she cashiered a current, and competent, secretary of state to make room for Sunderland, Anne asked why men of "sense and honor will not promote the good of their country, because everything in the world is not done that they desire"? Especially, the queen added, as she had promised Sunderland a position as soon as one became available.

And, why, Anne asked, must she, who had "no interest, no end, no thought, but for the good of my country, [be made] so miserable [by having to surrender to] the power of one set of men. [Why could she not be] trusted, since I mean nothing but what is equally for the good of all my subjects?…

"Consider, [Anne begged Sidney, how to resolve] my difficulties, and never leave my service for … that is a blow I could not bear."[18]

—m—

"It gives me all the grief and despair imaginable to find that your majesty shows inclination to have me continue in your service [Godolphin promptly replied,] and yet will make it impossible for me to do so. [He could not] struggle against the difficulties of your majesty's business, and yourself at the same time."[19]

All too aware Godolphin did "not serve for advantage or ambition, but with entire duty and affection, [Anne could not] bear the thoughts of parting with [him. She begged Godolphin to let Marlborough's] words plead"[20] for her. The treasurer's resignation would not only "disturb the affairs of England, [but also the] liberties of Europe, [Marlborough had written Godolphin. He must stay in office until] we have obtained a good peace. [Both of them were] in conscience bound to undergo all … dangers and troubles … to bring this war to a happy end…. Without flattery, as England is divided, [only you] can execute your place."[21] Anne would be "lost and undone, [she added, should Godolphin] pursue this cruel intention."[22]

Anne refused any more discussion of the subject. As her lord treasurer Godolphin kept a firm and honest hand on the nation's finances. As prime minister, he acted as a crucial liaison between queen, cabinet, and the politicians who controlled parliament.

The queen now begged Sarah not to push Sidney into leaving her ministry. But the duchess provided little comfort. She insisted that Whigs would fail to support the queen's government unless she gave Sunderland a cabinet office; Whigs were even ready, Sarah warned, to oppose the ministry. Hence, continued refusal would cause irreparable harm to queen and nation. Anne then consulted moderate Tory secretary of state Robert Harley. He advised resisting Sunderland's appointment for once the queen gave in, Whigs would demand more.

"The uneasiness betwixt the queen and myself continues, [Godolphin glumly wrote Marlborough.] Nor do I see how it can ever be mended, unless you are here to do it, either by your credit with the queen, or by your authority and influence with [Sunderland and his Junto friends.] And there is no reason to hope for the least assistance from Mrs. Freeman in this matter."[23]

Since losing Godolphin would be worse that swallowing Sunderland, the queen suggested he enter the cabinet council with a pension until a place in the ministry became vacant. The Junto refused. Sunderland must become secretary of state now, or Whigs would stop supporting the government.

—m—

Exasperated, Godolphin accused the queen of failing to realize the critical nature of the upcoming parliamentary session. Its most important task would be voting war supplies. With Holland's empty treasury making the Dutch receptive to Louis XIV's peace overtures, parliament must approve of significant war funding; otherwise, Ramillies and Blenheim would have been in vain. Pained by what she saw as Sidney's unjust accusation, Anne abruptly averred that she knew her country's circumstances very well.

The lord treasurer next proposed that Queen Anne at least grant Sunderland an audience to allow him personally to promise his goodwill. This suggestion upset Anne. Sidney then insisted on her appointing Sunderland to the cabinet. Bursting into tears, the queen reproached Godolphin for making her miserable.

Distressed by Anne's emotion, agitated by her resistance, not to mention having to deal with Sarah's fury over the whole issue, Godolphin agreed to revive the queen's suggestion: admit Sunderland to the cabinet council with a pension but without office, for now. But before making any further move in the matter, they agreed to await Marlborough's reply to Anne's proposal.

"Your reign has been so manifestly blessed by God, that one might reasonably think you [could govern without using the heads of either party, the duke wrote. This might work] if both parties sought your favor. [But since Tory leaders had] declared against" queen and government, Anne could not afford to offend Whigs.

Because it would be impossible to get almost five million pounds to wage "war with vigor, without which all is undone." Holland would make peace with France. But if parliament voted those millions, the Allies could fight forcefully next year. A favorable peace would ensue and Europe would acknowledge the queen as protector of its liberties. The alternative: French ascendancy and Anne's throne at risk. With "so much knowledge and experience [of Godolphin's] capacity and integrity, [Anne must know she could] safely rely upon his advice. [Those with] opinions different from [Godolphin neither knew as much about matters of state,] nor can they judge so well of them."[24]

Godolphin followed up by enlisting the duchess, agog to make sure her husband held firm. Yet, not content with this crucial assignment, Sarah continued to pressure the queen. Using words and tone that contrasted starkly with the duke's tact, not to mention were far less likely to sway Anne, Sarah began by reminding her sovereign of the risks Marlborough took in her service, of his sacrifices. The duchess then urged Anne to "reflect whether you have never heard that the greatest misfortunes that ever happened to any of your family [Anne's father James II, and grandfather Charles I, who lost throne and head respectively] has not been occasioned by having ill advices & an obstinacy in their tempers that is very unaccountable."

Sarah then recalled the days when Anne proved

> willing to take advice, and loved those that spoke freely to you; and that is not five years ago; and is it possible, that when you seriously reflect, that you believe you can do business ... without it? Can flatteries in so short a time have such power? or can you think it is safer to take it from those you have little or no experience of, [Abigail and Harley] than from those that have raised your glory higher than was ever expected? And let people talk what they please of luck, I am persuaded whoever governs with the best sense will be the most fortunate princess.[25]

Ten days later, Sarah received Anne's reply. The queen blamed this lapse on "apprehension ... of saying what might add to the ill impressions" Sarah already had of her. For although Anne believed she and Sarah were "of the same opinion in the main, [the queen could not, to her] misfortune ... agree exactly in everything, and therefore what I say is not thought to have the least color of reason in it. [That made the queen] really not care to enter into particulars. [Still, even if] unwilling to do it, [Anne thought she must give the duchess] some answer to your last letter, in which ... you think me insensible of everything."

Extremely sorry that Sarah, who had known her for so long, could "give way to such a thought as that I do not think the parting with my Lord Marlborough and my lord treasurer of much consequence, [Anne, furthermore, could not believe her] dear Mrs. Freeman [thought her] so stupid as not to be sensible of the great services [treasurer and duke] have done me, nor of the great misfortune it would be if they should quit my service"?[26]

The substance and tenor of Sarah's arguments angered the queen; Marlborough's reasoning convinced her. Having, in the interests of maintaining a moderate ministry, resisted the pressure surrounding her for eighteen months, Anne decided that if she meant to keep her promise to her subjects, made in her first speech to parliament as queen—to do anything they asked of her, to assure England's happiness and prosperity— she must give in to Whig demands. Because although Anne judged Sunderland's admission into her moderate ministry as not qualified to be in England's best interest, continued forceful prosecution of the war did so qualify. Hence, with extreme reluctance, let alone profound humiliation at having to surrender her royal prerogative, her ability to select her ministers, the queen put the welfare of her nation before personal preference.

—m—

The war over Sunderland constituted a watershed in Queen Anne's reign. Although less closely involved in the Sunderland struggle than Godolphin and the duchess, Marlborough made a misjudgment—he underrated the strength of Anne's opposition to having the Junto invade her cabinet. The duke also disillusioned his sovereign by acquiescing to pressure from Sidney and Sarah. Hence, despite Anne's awareness that Marlborough remained essential to her as long as the war lasted, he lost the queen's full trust.

So, too, did Godolphin. He had failed to recognize the queen's growth in political maturity. Sidney's attempts to overcome Anne's hostility to pleasing the Junto, whose members she despised and distrusted, to say nothing of having their most vocally Whig member in her ministry, offended Anne as monarch and shook her faith in their friendship. Godolphin had failed to stand by her as a friend should; as well, he had pressured Marlborough into supporting Sunderland's appointment.

True, as the sole female operating in a male dominated milieu, an extremely unusual situation for that time, and as an ailing female to boot, the queen needed a chief minister to manage both the administration and the relationship between herself, her cabinet, and parliament. But greater confidence in her judgment and authority decreased Anne's reliance on Godolphin. While unwilling to let him go, she ceased to see Sydney as essential. He had not protected her from Merciless Men.

Harley's situation improved. The queen concurred in his opposition to further Whig gains and approved of his parliamentary followers because they were moderate Tories. As well, master parliamentarian Harley, not for nothing called Robin the Trickster, took advantage of the circumstances of his office—it (unlike Godolphin's position as prime minister) did not require him to recommend hated actions to the queen. Hence, Harley took every opportunity to point out to Anne the injustice of Whig demands and futility of Godolphin's placating the Junto.

The tussle over her son-in-law exposed the extent of Sarah's alienation from Anne. The duchess's unbridled temper, imperious manner, and fierce pro–Whiggism, her adamant, arrogant, even wounding, oral and written lobbying for Sunderland roused the even-tempered queen's anger. By readily entering the fray on behalf of Whigs, never mind helping Godolphin convince the doubtful duke to back him over Sunderland, Sarah not only shattered the remains of her personal relationship with Anne but roused the queen's anxiety about her pro–Whig influence over Marlborough and Godolphin.

Nonetheless, Anne had reason to be satisfied with what her moderate ministry had achieved. Overseas, Ramillies and Blenheim liberated the Spanish Netherlands and Germany from French domination; carried the war to France's borders; and at Turin, allowed Austrian troops to break French power in Italy. At home, the ministry had, via passage of the Regency Act, secured the Protestant Succession. But, one crucial issue remained unsettled.

Eleven

Great Britain

"May our queen twice a conqueror prove;
Of her foes by her arms, and her subjects by love.
The last is the noblest we know of the two;
But I fear she will find 'tis the hardest to do.
Yet let not her majesty wholly despair,
The bravest attempts the most difficult are;
Who knows but our Anne may by heav'n be decreed
To close the wide wounds of a nation that bleed?
A victory equal to Blenheim success;
And justly deserving a triumph no less.
And what from her reign we must hope for alone:
For she by her sweetness must do it, or none."[1]—
Anonymous contemporary verse

Queen Anne's government stood on the cusp of singular success as the new year (1707) got underway. Her appointment of Whig Junto member Lord Sunderland to the cabinet, coming after that of moderate Whig Sir William Cowper, plus placement of several Whigs in lesser offices, earned the queen's ministry Junto support. Hence, parliament's passage of substantial war supplies empowered the queen's captain general, the Duke of Marlborough, on the Continent, and the queen's prime minister, Earl Godolphin,[2] at home. But like the imposing grey bulk of crenellated Edinburgh castle looming over Scotland's capital, the Scottish question loomed over Anne's government.

Because the Battles of Blenheim and Ramillies diminished, but did not eliminate, the threat of France invading Scotland. And from Scottish bases, French troops could easily attack England.

As queen of both England and Scotland, Anne had advocated union of the two countries in her first speech to parliament, and had supported the ensuing, disappointingly abortive, negotiations. Then, before Blenheim settled the uncertain result of Marlborough's march across Europe, the queen had, to neutralize Scottish nationalists, unwillingly signed Scotland's Act of Security, which specified that the country's next monarch must be Protestant and of the royal line, but not necessarily a Hanoverian. After Blenheim, England's parliament lost no time in retaliating against this display of Scots defiance.

The Alien Act choked off Scotland's lifeblood: its cross-border trade. If Scotland did not agree to Union, (or the Hanoverian succession to its crown) within three months, no native Scottish livestock, coal, or linen could be brought into England. Further, every native Scot residing illegally in England would be arrested and detained as an alien unless serving in the queen's armed forces.

After some political posturing, both countries proved ready for compromise. England wanted to secure its vulnerable northern border. Scotland wanted trading privileges with England as well as with her colonies.

The queen, Marlborough, Godolphin, and parliament's leaders, the Whig Junto, agreed that Union would be a better solution to the potential danger of Scotland acting independently, than the Scots simply endorsing the Hanoverian succession. All parties subsequently agreed that commissioners be appointed to negotiate a union treaty. In a victory for Moderation, Anne's preferred method of government, parliament gave her power to appoint England's commissioners. To the queen's satisfaction, Scotland's parliament followed suit.

—⚹—

Godolphin, Marlborough, and Robert Harley (his duties as secretary of state for the north included Scotland) conferred with Junto Lords Halifax, (financial expert) Somers, (Junto leader, respected jurist, and constitutional authority) and Wharton (who had guided the Regency Act, which settled the Succession, through parliament) to fashion a foundation for Union.

The English and Scottish commissioners then assembled at a venue with symbolic meaning—Anne's former residence—the Cockpit. Talks took place in the "great room, [which had] a long table, sufficient to hold all [fifty representatives,] being about 50 feet in length. At the head of the table, under a canopy, [stood] a large chair, ornamented with gold lace and crimson velvet, for the queen."[3]

She came "at our first or second meeting, to acquaint us of her intentions and ardent good wishes for our success and unanimity in this great transaction."[4] A month later, Anne "came again to enquire of our success, and had most of our minutes read to her."[5] She then "made a short speech, pressing [the commissioners] to finish the good work in their hands."[6]

Concurrently, Anne suffered "extreme pain and agony"[7] from a gouty foot. After her torture had eased, the queen moved, as she usually did in late spring, to Kensington Palace. Sitting in pleasant Kensington village, far from the sooty London fogs that aggravated Prince George's asthma, yet not too far to make ministers grumble at having to attend the queen there, Kensington had always pleased her. "I went to Kensington to walk in the garden, which would be a very pretty place if it were well kept but nothing can be worse, [the queen wrote her friend Sarah, Duchess of Marlborough, shortly after her accession.] It is a great deal of pity and indeed a great shame that there should be no better use made of so great an allowance, for I have been told the king [William] allowed four hundred pound a year for that one garden."[8]

Planning new gardens distracted Anne from the stress of politics. The queen and her husband Prince George made the improvement of Kensington's garden their joint project. King William had re-arranged the garden to reflect Dutch fashion; Anne hated his box hedges because of their smell. Queen and prince ordered thirty acres of new flowers and evergreens; half the area became a plotted wilderness; half, a small forest. Six shallow terraces planted with flower beds formed a sunken garden with dwarf yews, and a novelty—niches where one could sit in privacy. Newly graveled paths provided a pleasant stroll throughout the gardens; deer and antelope grazed in an adjacent paddock.

Anne commissioned England's leading architect, Christopher Wren, to build, to her specifications, a simple yet elegant summerhouse at Kensington. Standing in a sunken garden full of orange and myrtle trees, the Orangery boasted a modern convenience—underfloor heating—to combat the chilling damp of England's spring and summer.

—∿—

The union commissioners, meanwhile, wisely agreed to hold their negotiations in secret. As a result, they crafted a treaty with surprising speed.

The two nations would have the same (Hanoverian) succession. Scotland's parliament would merge into England's, which would become the legislature of Great Britain. Scotland would have freedom of trade with England and its colonies. A separate article guaranteed the security and integrity of Scotland's established (Presbyterian) church.

After duly signing the treaty, the fifty commissioners walked in procession from the Cockpit to St. James's Palace to present their work to the queen. Surrounded by ladies of her court, foreign ambassadors, and other notables, the queen received her commissioners in state. They entered the royal presence two by two, one Englishman, one Scotsman; a spokesman for each nation presented the proposed union treaty to their sovereign.

Parliamentary passage came next. The queen attended the daily Lords debates incognita. Tories opposed Union. They accused the treaty's guarantee of Presbyterianism as Scotland's official church, to be a danger to the Church of England. Anne blunted Tory objections by sponsoring an act for Church of England security. She also lobbied assiduously for passage of the union treaty.

The Act of Union, joining Scotland and England (Wales and Ireland) into one realm with one Protestant ruler, one legislature, and one free trade system, created Great Britain.

—∿—

On a crisp, clear, if blustery morning in the early spring of 1707, as a wan sun gilded Westminster and the wind ruffled surface of the Thames, Queen Anne, arrayed in full royal regalia, arrived at the house of lords. Once seated on the throne, she sent an official to the house of commons "requiring their attendance in the house of peers. The Commons being come hither accordingly, her majesty was pleased to give the royal assent to:

An act for an union of the two kingdoms of England *and* Scotland."

Speaking in her clear and pleasing contralto, the queen then made a "most gracious speech [to both Houses]."

> It is with the greatest satisfaction, [Anne concluded,] that I have given my assent to a Bill for uniting England and Scotland into one kingdom.... I desire and expect from all my subjects of both nations, that from henceforth they act with all possible respect and kindness to one another, that it so may appear to all the world, they have hearts disposed to be one people.... And I cannot but look upon it as a peculiar happiness, that in my reign so full a provision is made for the peace and quiet of my people, and for the security of our religion, by so firm an establishment of the Protestant succession throughout GREAT BRITAIN.[9]

The queen's long and steady support of Union made it a personal achievement. So, while fresh May sunshine frolicked over London, Anne formally launched Union with particular gratification. Wearing England's Order of the Garter and Scotland's Order of the Thistle to denote Union, the queen together with Prince George, all senior state officials, and both houses of the new union parliament marked the occasion "with the greatest splendor. A very numerous procession accompanied the queen to the cathedral church of St. Paul, at least 3 or 400 coaches." Congregants heard a musical composition that Anne had commissioned to mark the occasion, and her private musicians performed. An "exceptional sermon [followed,] and prayers of thanksgiving were very heartily put up for the success of the union, at least no body on this occasion appeared more sincerely devout and thankful than the queen herself."[10]

Never had the streets been more crowded with joyful citizens. Church bells rang, banquets abounded, and illuminations animated the night sky as England expressed relief at no longer having to fear menace from the north.

—ɯ—

Although Anne arranged state ceremonies with meticulous care, her court could hardly qualify as brilliant since a gout-plagued queen and chronically asthmatic prince headed it. But Anne did attend court drawing rooms two or three times a week and made a special effort on public occasions. For the third consecutive year, her birthday featured an opera. Lamed by gout and buried under business, Anne had not yet seen the production that daily packed her subjects into the Drury Lane theatre; so, she invited the performers of Bononcini's *Camilla* to bring the opera to court. That conferred the seal of approval on opera,

Queen Anne, wearing as her only jewelry the Order of the Garter on its broad blue ribbon, the medallion partly concealed by her hand. The artist persuaded Anne to this pose in order to paint her lovely white forearms and hands. The queen's crown is in the background. Artist: Sir Godfrey Kneller, painted circa 1705; this is a mid-nineteenth century copy. Royal Collection Trust/©Her Majesty Queen Elizabeth II 2018.

accepted as a musical form on the Continent for decades, but not in England until opera enjoyed the queen's patronage.

Still, queen and prince preferred to entertain a select group of friends privately at Kensington palace. On those spring evenings, countless candles illuminated the Orangery and showed to advantage the exquisite creations of England's finest wood carver; Grinling Gibbons had decorated the rooms with baroque garlands that gave wood the loose, airy lightness of leaves and flowers. Round walnut tables were set with oriental china, and silver candlesticks. Dinner included a large selection of fresh fruits and vegetables, for Anne and George's garden renovation included a sizeable plot for produce. Over a dozen sorts of peas and eight varieties of beans, among other legumes, grew; plus, cabbages and cauliflower, asparagus, artichokes and lettuce. Flowering fruit trees provided the palace with peaches, plums, apples, pears, cherries, nectarines, apricots and figs; strawberries transplanted from nearby woods, raspberries and gooseberries, tempted the royal palate.

After dinner the stout host and hostess led their guests through the white drawing room to a circular music space at one end of the Orangery. There high- backed chairs faced the harpsichords that accompanied performers of a pastorale, or medley of popular songs.

—⁓—

The Sunderland appointment had marked a watershed in Anne's relations with Marlborough, his duchess, and Godolphin. It also marked a watershed in the ruler's place within government. The queen had fought for her right to appoint ministers. Defeat dented the royal prerogative.

That made Anne doubly determined to defend her right of appointment. She headed the Church of England. The queen resolved to protect her power to choose clerics. As a profoundly religious woman, she believed only good, spiritual men merited Christian office.

Anne's would-be political mentor and former intimate, Sarah, Duchess of Marlborough, to say nothing of Sarah's Whig friends, saw clerical appointments as an integral part of political patronage. That viewpoint offended the queen.

Her political knowledge and ability had grown during five years on the throne. And since Anne's forecast about the effect of Sunderland's appointment (it would inspire the Junto to make more demands) proved correct, the queen's trust in her judgment intensified.

Inspired by their success at pushing Sunderland into the cabinet despite Anne's opposition, the Whig Junto coveted England's richest diocese for a Whig. The queen's prime minister, Lord Treasurer Sidney Godolphin, had long since promised Winchester to a Tory. So, to placate the Junto, a different but still lucrative bishopric went to a Whig.

Death then opened two other bishoprics. Godolphin nominated Whig clerics. Anne had already promised the bishoprics to Tories. She refused to retract her word.

Once more caught between Junto fury and royal resolve, Godolphin decided to keep the bishoprics open until Marlborough returned from campaigning overseas. His presence at court could help Godolphin change the queen's mind.

Marlborough, meanwhile, agreed with Anne that both parties vied to govern. But since Whig interest "obliges them to be more governed by you," the queen must consider the best way of making Whigs depend on, and be governed by, her and those she trusted. Queen and country's interests demanded a solution; otherwise, Anne would "put it out of the power of the honestest and best minister any prince ever had, I mean lord treasurer.… Your majesty has by God's blessing obtained a greater reputation, and power in foreign courts than any of your predecessors … continuance is so absolutely necessary both for the good of our religion and your prosperity."[11]

Marlborough implored the queen soon to appoint Whigs to the vacant bishoprics, so that parliament would continue to vote enough money to wage forceful war. This, the duke had good cause to know, had become pressing in view of events on the Continent.

—⁓—

Blenheim certainly blighted French ambitions in Bavaria; Ramillies lost France the Spanish Netherlands; Turin cleared the French from Italy; and English gold glued the fractious Alliance. But the 1707 campaign opened with a disastrous Allied defeat.

Led by Anne's (bastard) half-brother, the English Jacobite Duke of Berwick, son of James II and his longtime lover Arabella Churchill (Marlborough's sister) a Franco-Spanish army defeated an allied force (British, Dutch, Huguenot, and Portuguese) outside northwestern Spain's walled town of Almanza. (April 25, 1707) France then won a victory on the Rhine and prepared to penetrate into Germany.

Having managed to stop the enemy's excursion into Germany, Marlborough sought to end the war with a decisive blow during next year's campaign. In preparation, he wanted to weaken the French position in Spain this year. The duke's colleague and friend, Prince Eugene of Savoy, should lead a land attack on France's great Mediterranean naval base at Toulon while an Anglo-Dutch fleet attacked Toulon by sea. Victory would enable the Allies to invade France from the south and facilitate the entry of allied troops into northern Spain.

The queen privately instructed her envoy extraordinary to Savoy. "Press the Duke of Savoy to embark on board our fleet sent to the Mediterranean five or six thousand men who may attempt Toulon ... by land, at the same time that our fleet shall attempt [Toulon] by sea; promising him in all events the expense of his troops, and in case of success fifty thousand pounds."[12]

French King Louis XIV moved thousands of troops into Toulon. That discouraged Eugene from attacking; in any case, he felt averse to a plan involving naval warfare about which he knew little. Yet, despite the allied failure to take Toulon, the Anglo-Dutch flotilla poised offshore decimated the French fleet. The Allies now controlled the Mediterranean.

—⁂—

The nautical triumph at Toulon, not to mention the debacle at Almanza, encouraged Tories to step up opposition to Marlborough's focus on land war and push, instead, for a naval attack against France's colonies. This roused the Duchess of Marlborough's anti–Tory hackles, which aggravated her already damaged relations with the queen. For Sarah's robust pro–Sunderland activities still rankled; and now the duchess opposed Anne's Tory nominations for the vacant bishoprics.

Sarah ascribed her sovereign's firmness on that fraught issue to the sinister influence of Abigail Hill, the queen's favored chambermaid and Sarah's cousin, whom the duchess had introduced into Anne's household out of, said Sarah, pure altruism. Yet, by putting Abigail, whom she had rescued from poverty and whose family she helped, close to the queen as a maidservant, Sarah sought to ease her own position. For the duchess had long chafed against having constantly to attend Anne and thought she could count on her cousin's loyalty and gratitude to report on everything occurring at court and about the queen's person. This Abigail did so faithfully that Sarah felt less and less need to come to court. Judging her favor with the queen too strong to be in danger, the duchess never dreamed that a lowly, unattractive, and dull dependent, one lacking in any abilities besides, who owed her position to Sarah and kept it because of her protection, would pose any threat.

But Abigail started to develop ambitions. She saw the bickering between queen and duchess, "observed the queen's temper with so much application that she got far into her heart,"[13] and rose steadily in the queen's favor. A capable nurse and amusing companion, Abigail mutated from Sarah's humble dependent to Anne's favored attendant—but never her friend, never her equal. The queen saw Abigail as nothing more than "a useful servant about her person."[14]

As the duchess reveled in the reflected glory of her husband's victories, she grew haughtier, more imperious, and less able to admit any fault in herself. Sarah accused Abigail of undermining her as favorite; and denounced Abigail for augmenting moderate Tory secretary of state Harley's support for what the duchess denounced as Anne's anti–Whig bias. Increasingly blinded by jealousy, Sarah went further; she imputed all the queen's political views to Abigail's evil influence, for how, the duchess reasoned, could such a stupid woman as Anne have an independent thought. During her rare appearances at court, and in her frequent letters to the queen, Sarah showed hatred and scorn for Abigail, which roused Anne's resentment.

The queen felt obliged to tell Sarah why she had denied being angry during their last meeting, why she could not bring herself to tell Sarah the cause. Had Anne started to speak, upset and tears would have made her not "fit to be seen by anybody. [Far] better to let it alone."[15]

Finding it easier to express her feelings on paper, wishing, as well, to avoid an emotional encounter, the queen wrote Sarah that by look and word she made Anne think "you have hard and wrong thoughts of me. [Hence, the queen's anger. She wanted to know what these thoughts were,] that I might clear myself, but let it be in writing, for I dare not venture to speak with you for the reason I have told you."[16]

—◊—

Anne did not turn from Sarah to Abigail; the queen found Abigail waiting while Sarah made a habit not only of absenting herself from court, but antagonizing Anne over politics. Certainly, both women struggled to sway the queen politically. In fact, they sustained her private life. Sarah satisfied Anne's hunger for a friend. Abigail satisfied the ailing queen's need for a nurse.

Marlborough advised his wife to talk to Abigail—she had good cause to be grateful to Sarah for finding her a place in Anne's household, as well as for helping her family. But the duchess preferred to tackle the queen. How, Sarah accused Anne, could she let a servant who spoke only to Jacobites and disgruntled Tories, influence her politics. How, when the duke defended her throne on the field

> shall anybody that is secretly undermining him, remain near your person? It is not enough for your majesty to say, you know of no such servant about you: Your subjects, madam, know *who it is*; and so do your allies & your house of commons…. If the door through which the enemies of the government have so long entered, & at which they have still the impudence to appear barefaced, be not immediately shut, it is easy to foresee such consequences as I will rather pray to God to avert, than go about to describe.[17]

"I give my dear Mrs. Freeman many thanks for her letter … as I must always do for everything that comes from her, not doubting but what you say, is sincerely meant in kindness to me, [the queen replied.] But I have so often been unfortunate in what I have said to you, that I think the less I say to your last letter the better."

Anne confined her comments to Sarah's

> explanation of the suspicions you seemed to have concerning your cousin [Abigail] Hill, who is very far from being the occasion of feeding Mrs. Morley in her passion,[18] (as you are pleased to call it) [appointing Tories to the vacant bishoprics] she never meddling with anything.
>
> Others … in her station in former reigns have been tattling & very impertinent, but she is not at all that temper, & as for the company she keeps … for one that is so much in the way of company, she has less acquaintance than anyone upon earth. I hope, since in some part of your letter you seem to give credit to a thing, because I said it was so, you will be as just in what I have said now, about Hill;

for I would not have any one hardly thought of by my dear Mrs. Freeman, for your poor un-fortunate, but ever faithful Morley's notions or actions.[19]

Despite the duchess's increasingly bitter letters, she and the queen kept a façade of cordiality. Anne had, from childhood, been both inarticulate and adept at hiding her feelings; Sarah had too much pride to show her chagrin. But little episodes indicated the two women's estrangement. Keeper of the privy purse Sarah met her queen's request for a small amount of cash by retorting that Anne should not squander money during a costly war (this while the government paid huge sums to build Marlborough's Blenheim Palace). So, when one of King James's servants died in poverty, Anne, rather than pro-voking her keeper of the privy purse, paid for the funeral with funds borrowed from one of her ladies-in-waiting.

—⁂—

Abigail, meanwhile, wanted to marry but lacked the requisites—fortune, youth, or beauty. She did, however, manage to attract the attentions of Captain Masham, several years her junior and a member of Prince George's household. But since Abigail had only her position as the queen's chambermaid—even if favored yet still a chambermaid—to commend her, the captain balked at marriage. Abigail asked secretary of state Robert Harley, her cousin on the non–Sarah side of her family, to help. He wangled Masham's rise to rank of colonel, as well as promotion in the prince's household.

Always generous to servants she judged deserving, Anne gave Abigail a handsome dowry. And since the wedding would take place in secret, the queen advised Abigail to tell Sarah beforehand. Abigail did not. When Sarah finally heard about her cousin's mar-riage, she saw it as proof of Abigail's deceit. And the clandestine nature of the Masham nuptials, not to mention Anne's prior knowledge, furnished the duchess with added proof of Abigail's ambition to supplant her as favorite; further, Sarah reasoned, the chamber-maid's devious influence, which flattery of Anne's Tory bias and distortion of Sarah's wise counsel compounded, had turned the queen away from the duchess. Refusing to see how her manner of giving political advice did more to alienate Anne than did its content, Sarah's rashness added personal acrimony to her political tussle with the queen.

Anne now received such a torrent of anti–Abigail venom that she begged the duchess not to mention "that person any more who you are pleased to call the object of my favor, for whatever character the malicious world may give her, [would never] have any weight with me. [Anne knew Abigail] did not deserve it."[20]

—⁂—

Sarah maintained her drumbeat against Abigail by accusing the queen of letting secret, unnamed influences turn Anne against her.

> By what my dear Mrs. Freeman said a little before she went from me this evening, I cannot help fear-ing she may have heard some new lie of her poor unfortunate faithful Morley, and therefore I beg you to open your dear heart, hide nothing, but tell me every least thing that gives you any hard thoughts of me, that I may justify myself, which I am sure I can do, never having done anything willingly to deserve your displeasure.
>
> I would have made this request when I parted from you, but I found my heart and eyes growing so full, I durst not attempt it, being sure if I had, I should not have been fit to have been seen by any-body, for the same reason I desire an answer to this in writing, and yet for Jesus sake as soon it is as possible for I am on the rack and cannot bear living as we do now.[21]

Sarah replied with a repetition of her charge that the queen had changed towards her. Anne found these

> unkind & unjust thoughts … extremely [troubling.] I have the same sincere tender passion for you as ever … as for my having any reserve I have none upon my word but will open my heart as freely to you at any time as I used to do.
>
> I have of late been a little afraid to speak of any subject we differed upon, because you have been pleased to think I have shut my eyes, that I am infatuated, that I am fond of some people (who I care no more for than I do for the pen in my hand) & when I happen not to agree in the very good opinion you have of some, & the very ill of others that you think it proceeds from the wrong information & notions that some sort of people give me, & all I can say to justify myself is not to be believed; these are the reasons that have made me seem reserved though I am not so in my heart.[22]

Citing instances of Anne's favor to Abigail, and of Abigail's contacts with Harley, which the queen denied, Sarah asked for a private meeting.

—⁂—

The duchess opened hostilities by attacking Anne's Tory candidates for the two vacant bishoprics; moved on to accuse Harley of secretly plotting against Marlborough and Godolphin; (they suspected Harley but had not yet divulged their distrust) and concluded with condemnation of Abigail for inducing Anne to favor Harley. In any case, said the duchess, all Tories (Harley and Abigail included) were Jacobites bent on harming the queen. Sarah concluded with her preferred self-portrayal—the hurt yet always faithful servant.

Greatly offended, the queen replied that Abigail did not meddle in politics; indeed, she never stoked what Sarah chose to call Anne's "passion"[23] for Tories. The queen then asserted her right as ruler to choose ministerial servants; her right as a private individual to choose, and protect, her personal servants. Little wonder that in her rare private moments, Anne preferred Abigail's pliant personality, amusing mimicry, melodious harpsichord playing, and soothing ministrations to the haughty duchess's harsh, peremptory, and insistent harangues.

Certainly, Abigail helped smooth Harley's path to the queen, such as letting him know when would be a good, or bad, time to approach her. Actually, Abigail had little influence. For Anne never discussed affairs of state with her maidservant. And in keeping with her policy to be free of party or ministerial control, to maintain the crown's independence, the queen sometimes invited politicians who did not serve in her ministry to visit her privately. Because female servants, like Abigail, conducted visitors into the queen's presence, these women were thought to control access to Anne, to wield influence. But the queen's maids did not decide who came to see her. Anne did.

—⁂—

Focused on her goal of furthering the Whig cause, Sarah fused Abigail and Harley into a single foe whose nefarious influence cultivated the queen's dislike of Whigs. This, the duchess impressed on Marlborough, damaged Great Britain. If, the duke replied, Sarah had sound reasons for professing the queen's "kindness and esteem [for Harley and Abigail, Marlborough and Godolphin must tell the queen] what is good for herself. [If that] will not prevail, [the two ministers must] be quiet, [and let Abigail and Harley] do what they please."

Marlborough hoped Godolphin would agree; for, then "we shall be much happier than by being in perpetual struggle." If the two ministers had lost Anne's confidence, they would be foolish to act as they did now, when everyone thought "it is in our power to do everything; [such conduct would make Godolphin and Marlborough] uneasy, [and lose them their] reputation both at home and abroad."[24]

Godolphin thought Marlborough should return home secretly, before the campaign season ended. The two ministers could thus together confront the queen and counter the arguments Godolphin believed Harley fed Abigail to hold Anne firm on her Tory clerical appointments.

—⁓—

Instead, the duke marshaled his forces at his headquarters in The Hague. Having dosed himself with licorice and rhubarb to ease his aching stomach after a debilitating bout of diarrhea, (stopped with nips of brandy) Marlborough took up his pen. "As a friend, [her husband warned Sarah, he would predict the] unavoidable consequences if the Whigs mortify the court; that Godolphin will be disheartened, and Harley have the power and credit of doing what he pleases. [This, the duke emphasized to the Junto's helpmate] will hurt both the queen and England."[25]

Deaf to her husband's counsel, Sarah continued to badger the queen. As a result, the fissure between the two women widened.

Marlborough admitted to Godolphin that, yes, if Sidney stayed at his post, he would be blamed for all that went wrong. But quitting would be worse, for that would damage both domestic and foreign affairs; the Allies would think they could no longer rely on England if Godolphin and Marlborough, having served with success, lost their credit with the queen.

And to Anne—

> If you do not alter the resolution you seem to have taken, by which you will make it impossible for Godolphin to serve you with any success, you will not only disturb the quiet of your own life, but also ruin the Protestant religion and all the liberties of Europe.
>
> The credit and power I have in this country [Holland] proceeds ... solely from the opinion they have of your having an entire confidence in me, so that when they shall see that a man with whom I have had a friendship these 30 years, and who has so great merit of his own, is not able to continue in your service, they can put no other construction but that of you being guided by other hands, which must make me of no use to you...
>
> [After] the faithful services for so many years performed with success by Godolphin and Marlborough [what would Britain and the world think if] they have not credit enough left to persuade you to do what is good for yourself.... I should not write with this earnestness, were it not for the duty I have for you.[26]

Anne failed to see how her selection of two Tory bishops, "being worthy men and all the clamor [raised against them only due] to the malice of the Whigs," which Marlborough would see very plainly were he in London, breached the procedures she, Godolphin, and the duke previously agreed on. The queen knew that the bishops' nomination had been "otherwise represented [to Marlborough, that he had] been told, [as had she, that Harley recommended] these two persons ... which is so far from being true, that he knew nothing of it, till it was the talk of the town. I do assure you these men were my own choice."

Sarah said Anne had "an entire confidence [in Harley. The queen certainly had] a very good opinion of him. [But questioned how the duchess] could say such a thing, when she has so often been assured from me, that I relied on none but Mr. Freeman and Mr. Montgomery."

The queen concluded by "begging [her friend and captain general always to] tell me your mind freely in everything. [Anne would] desire the same favor [from Godolphin]; when I know both your thoughts, I will give you my poor opinion."[27]

—⁘—

A long and frank talk between queen and prime minister followed. Their discussion focused on the main point at issue—the war—which, they agreed, would be damaged if Marlborough came home early. Still, Sidney impressed on Anne, she must weigh the importance of a few clerical appointments against winning the war—in which continued Whig support in voting military supplies would be crucial; for the queen surely remembered parliamentary problems over "the extraordinary expenses of the war in the last year, tho' that was a year [Ramillies and Turin] of greater success than had ever been known before; the present is a year of great misfortunes [Almanza and failure to take Toulon] … yet the extraordinary expense … is greater than [last. How, then, could the ministry hope for backing] unless there be a considerable majority in either House that will show the warmth and spirit to support your majesty and your administration in all your zealous endeavors towards the good and speedy conclusion of the war."[28]

Godolphin urged the queen to compromise—revoke her promise on one of the bishoprics and give it to a Whig. No. Godolphin offered to resign. No. He "must not think any more of that cruel request. [Anne could] never consent to it. [If Godolphin left her service] it will be my death."[29]

—⁘—

Whoever among Whigs thought their queen could be "hectored or frightened into compliance tho I am a woman, [Anne told Godolphin, were] mighty mistaken in me. [She thanked] God I have a soul above that & am too much concerned for my reputation to do anything to forfeit it."[30]

The bishoprics battle signaled Anne's opposition to Whig rule and stiffened her resolve to maintain a moderate ministry. Humiliation at having to accept Sunderland, resentment at Whigs riding roughshod over her royal prerogative to appoint ministers, reinforced Anne's determination to keep her promise to the two Tory clerics she had chosen to fill the vacant bishoprics, men who were sincerely religious rather than mere political partisans. Nonetheless, after their confirmation, the queen did agree not to promote and more Tories to senior Church positions without due consultation.

Encouraged, Whig pressure for office grew, particularly as the party proved useful to Anne's government on issues other than the Church, such as war supplies, the Regency Act, and a key achievement of Queen Anne's reign, one she had consistently supported from the start—Union with Scotland.

Thus, on a soft grey day when London spires were golden in the evening light, the queen derived profound personal satisfaction from officially opening Great Britain's first union parliament. It ratified the united nation's war aim: No Peace Without Spain (a Whig initiative). And in her speech from the throne, Queen Anne affirmed her commitment to Moderation.

Twelve

"A disagreeable noise"

"All I desire is my liberty in encouraging and employing all those that concur faithfully in my service whether they are called Whigs or Tories."[1]— Queen Anne

Dense, cold rain falling from a leaden sky, soaked London as the new year (1708) opened. At the same time, Queen Anne sanctioned a new plan for Moderation. It had been hammered out by Anne's captain general the Duke of Marlborough, her prime minister and lord treasurer Earl Sidney Godolphin, and her secretary of state Robert Harley. His temperate Tory followers in the Commons would unite with moderate Whig magnates and Tory peers in the Lords, as well as senior treasury officials, to form a new ministry designed to end party faction and guarantee the queen's freedom from future coercion over ministerial appointments.

Actually, however, Harley sought to take advantage of Marlborough and Godolphin's fear of Whig domination to form his own ministry—mostly made up of moderate Tories, plus some moderate Whigs. This ministry would include Marlborough, (still vital to win the War of the Spanish Succession) but exclude Godolphin. For Harley believed Godolphin would fail to garner Whig support for war funding while still retaining control of a moderate ministry.

Harley's success depended on Anne's support. She faced a dilemma. The queen had a horror of Whigs as ruthless men willing to oust one sovereign (as in the case of her father) in favor of another when their policies demanded it; Tories supported the monarchy and guarded the Church. But Whigs backed the war, crucial for the Protestant cause at home and abroad. The queen thus wanted a moderate ministry that would combine the best of both parties while eschewing their extremes.

January's bleak, short days brought Godolphin and Marlborough proof of Harley's planned coup. For ample reason known as Robin the Trickster, Harley had, besides, been sympathizing with Anne over Whig attempts to wrest power from her ever since the Sunderland affair; in addition, he now disparaged Marlborough and Godolphin's handling of the war. And worse. Harley publicly gave credence to a comment already circulating about war management—the vast discrepancy between the troop numbers parliament had voted for Spain, and the actual number present at the Allies' recent defeat at Almanza.

Tories moved for a parliamentary request to examine reasons for the troop shortage. Still smarting over Anne's appointment of the two Tory bishops, (despite her later elevation of two Whig clerics) Whig leadership let the Tory motion pass. Harley's ally, war secretary and cabinet member Henry St. John, whose oratorical ability had gained him political attention, told the Commons that few of the soldiers it had authorized were present at Almanza; further, money to pay and equip the troops had mysteriously vanished—a dig at Marlborough, master of the ordnance, and at Godolphin, head of the treasury.

Tories pounded the ministry. Harley and St. John failed to defend the government of which they were members. A Whig motion to adjourn rescued Queen Anne's ministry.

—∽∽—

Sarah, Duchess of Marlborough had for some time been scolding the queen for favoring Tories over Whigs. Lately, the duchess ascribed the rise in Anne's regard for Harley to the influence of Tory Abigail Masham, the queen's preferred bedchamber woman. Sarah now intensified her criticism of Tories and Harley, but trained her heaviest guns on Abigail for causing Anne to favor them. This strategy served merely to widen the breach between queen and duchess, not to mention driving Anne to defend Abigail.

Affronted, the duchess offered to withdraw from court altogether, but not before favoring her sovereign with a lengthy diatribe. Its gist informed Anne that since Marlborough and Godolphin would soon be forced out of her service, Sarah, too, would resign—but—the duchess asked that her three daughters, already serving as ladies of the bedchamber, be assigned her well paid, senior offices in the queen's household. Anne at first demurred—as a matter of policy she discouraged her servants from viewing their positions as a disposable asset, but to silence the duchess, let alone lay to rest a dread of what her hot temper might drive her to do if thwarted, Anne eventually agreed.

Concomitantly, evidence came to light that one of Harley's clerks, William Greg, had been selling confidential state papers to France. Although Greg insisted (even on the scaffold) that Harley knew nothing of his clerk's treason, the affair damaged Harley—he had shown poor judgment in hiring Greg. Hence, Harley hinted at resignation; meanwhile, he continued to plot against the lord treasurer.

Godolphin accused Harley of deceit. Harley denied the charge and appealed to Marlborough. But while Harley assured both treasurer and duke of his esteem and support, he strove to turn the queen against them.

—∽∽—

Marlborough refused to abandon his best friend and political ally Godolphin. And although the duke dreaded Whig Junto domination, he balked at cooperating with Harley after that master of parliamentary management neglected to stop the Commons from voting to censure the ministry over Almanza.

Duke and treasurer decided to put their case before the queen. "She would believe nothing [they] suggested [against Harley,] nor would she enter into any examination of his ill conduct." (Harley cultivated High Tories—anathema to queen, duke, and treasurer—to join his fledgling ministry.) So, Marlborough and Godolphin wrote to Anne that if Harley continued in office "they could serve her no longer."[2]

Anne showed more concern over losing Marlborough than Godolphin; for, the duke's military skills were vital to ending the war on terms satisfactory to Great Britain. She agreed with Harley that Godolphin proved too willing to oblige Whigs; besides, the queen thought Harley could fill the treasurer's position. Still, Anne begged her two old friends to reconcile with Harley, to bring about the moderate plan they had all agreed. "No consideration can make me serve any longer with that man, [Marlborough declared. The queen must] look upon me, from this moment, as forced out of your service, as long as you think fit to continue him in it."[3]

Marlborough's proviso challenged the queen's royal prerogative—her right to select ministers. Loth to give up Harley—he had promised her a moderate ministry made up mostly of temperate Tories—Anne, nonetheless, quailed at parting with two such proven friends as Marlborough and Godolphin. Her quandary brought the queen to tears; indeed, Anne became so ill that she failed to attend her forty-third birthday celebrations. But the queen did promise that two days after, when the cabinet met, she give would give the duke, his duchess, and the treasurer (the three offered to resign together) her answer.

—∞—

In the early afternoon of a frigid February day, the Marlboroughs and Godolphin drove the short distance to Kensington Palace on a road rendered iron hard by frost. The sun shone from pale, cloudless skies, but with little warmth, and only a few brave snow-drops showed under the hedges lining the road. Anne received the three privately, in a small parlor next door to the large salon where cabinet ministers were already assembling. A wood fire crackled in the parlor grate; candles burned brightly in several gilded wall sconces and a pair of branched silver candelabra set on the handsome white marble man-telpiece; the heavy, yellow silk brocade window curtains were already drawn.

> GODOLPHIN: Serving your majesty any "longer with one so perfidious as Mr. Harley [is] impossible."
> ANNE: Because of your "long service, [I will give you] till tomorrow to consider. [Then you may do as you please, for I can] find enough glad" to take your place.
> SARAH: "With great duty and submission." I have always served you "with affection and tender-ness. [My utmost has been my duty and I have] been faithful in it."
> ANNE: "You shall consider of this till tomorrow, then if you desire it, I shall then advise you to go to your little house in St. Albans and there stay till Blenheim house is ready."
> MARLBOROUGH: "With his utmost address." I have ever served you "with obedience and fidelity. [I have] used that sword [I must now resign to you, to your] honor and advantage. [I lament to have] come in competition with so vile a creature as Harley. [My] fidelity and duty should con-tinue so long as [I breathe. It is my duty] to be speedy in resigning [my] commands that [you] might put the sword into some other hand immediately. [It is also my duty to tell you I fear the Dutch will] immediately on that news make a peace very ruinous for England."
> ANNE: "And then, my lord … will you resign me your sword. Let me tell you … your service I have regarded to the utmost of my power, and if you do, my lord, resign your sword, let me tell you, you run it through my head."

The queen turned to go "to the council, begging him [the duke] to follow; he refusing, so the scene ended."[4]

—∞—

Queen Anne entered the adjacent salon to find her husband, Lord High Admiral Prince George, and other cabinet ministers already seated around the mahogany table. Two chairs were empty.

Anne opened the meeting. The first order of business consisted of an update on the war. In his capacity as secretary of state, Harley rose give a report. His colleagues seemed sunk in thought. As Harley spoke, some ministers started to mutter. Others fidgeted.

The moderate Whig Duke of Somerset stood up. "I do not see, [he interrupted Harley] how we can discuss the war when the commander in chief and lord treasurer are absent."[5] If the queen tolerated Harley discussing the war without Marlborough and Godolphin, Somerset could not continue to serve her.

Somerset's words sent a signal to Harley: the moderate Whigs he had been counting on to become part of his ministry, would not support him without Marlborough. Indeed, no ministry could survive without the duke.

The queen remained silent. She "saw that the rest of her ministers, and the chief officers, were resolved to withdraw from her service, if she did not recall the two that had left it. [Anne would have risked that] if Harley himself had not apprehended his danger."[6] He offered to resign. Preserving her royal privilege to select ministers, Anne refused.

Angry and upset, she left the room. The meeting ended. Refusing to give up Harley, the queen began to canvass every possible Tory supporter.

Rumors instantly cropped up and as quickly ballooned: the queen had dismissed Marlborough and Godolphin in favor of Harley; the Commons refused to consider voting for any war supplies pending definite information; the Lords were preparing to impeach Harley over the treasonous conduct of his clerk, Greg. Alarm gripped the City, London's financial center.

Monetary panic, public agitation, moderate Whig desertion, Junto (Whig leadership) hatred, and a miasma of suspicion hovering over him, (political duplicity plus the Greg affair) made Harley realize the futility of trying to form a ministry.

Horrified, meanwhile, at all the commotion and concerned about the smooth advance of war management, Prince George, who "although a foreigner born was become so hardy an Englishman that it was visible to all … looking on … this kingdom as his own country,"[7] opposed discharging Marlborough and Godolphin. The prince counseled his wife that in the nation's best interest, she must dismiss Harley and recall them.

"The queen sent the next day for the Duke of Marlborough … but … seemed to carry a deep resentment of his and Lord Godolphin's behavior on this occasion; and though they went on with her business, they found they had not her confidence."[8]

—m—

As February wept and blustered its way into March, Harley, his ally the energetic and able war secretary St. John, and two other moderate Tories, left the cabinet. Whigs replaced them. Whigs now had a majority in the ministry. This erosion of her moderate government mortified the queen, and increased her loathing of the Junto, especially as its five members not only gloated at having prevailed over her, but also pressed to have more of them in the cabinet.

At the same time a handful of anti–Union Scottish peers encouraged French King Louis XIV to send the all too willing Pretender (Anne's Catholic half-brother) to Scotland at the head of an invasion force. Success would at least divert British troops from the Continent, at most install a grateful king on the British throne, in any case enable France to force a favorable peace on the Allies. But when the tall, dark young Pretender arrived in Dunkirk to board the French flotilla's flagship, he suddenly succumbed to a virulent bout of measles. The resulting delay gave British and Dutch spies time to report on invasion plans although not before the Pretender issued a proclamation announcing his intent to dethrone his half-sister.

"The queen came to the House. [Her speech informed of] an express [she received] this morning … from Ostend that the Dunkirk squadron sailed with the Pretender on board, and that [Admiral] Sir George Byng had gone after him, and that ten battalions of her troops were embarking at Ostend. The Commons voted to make good any sum of money she should make use of on this occasion."[9]

The putative invasion caused panic in London. Godolphin, Marlborough, and the queen had to deposit large sums in the Bank of England to avoid a bank run. And in an age when news took several days to travel from one end of Anne's realm to the other, ten alarm filled days elapsed before intelligence arrived that Admiral Byng's fleet, having followed the French squadron to Scotland's east coast, harried the enemy back to France before any soldiers could disembark.

Fear of invasion had been serious. Reprisals were slight. A few French prisoners were brought to London, lodged in the Tower, then released unharmed. Anne pardoned the Scottish peer most prominently involved.

Ascendant Whigs used the abortive invasion to tar Tories with unproven and exaggerated accusations of being Jacobite sympathizers, and to portray themselves as the party loyal to the queen and to the war. Hence, when the English countryside smelled sweetly of honeysuckle, and gentle breezes caressed London, Whigs won the general election.

—⟶⟵—

The Junto declared that continued Whig support would come at a cost. Had not Whig majorities in the Lords rejected the Occasional Conformity Bills; were not Whig financial interests vital to Marlborough's victories; did not Whig input and backing prove crucial to passage of the Regency Act and Act of Union? The Junto lords felt justified in demanding that the queen appoint their leader, Lord Somers, to one of the cabinet's most prestigious positions—lord president of the council.

Again besieged over her right to select ministers, Anne refused to admit any more of the Junto into her ministry, especially in view of a recent scandal involving the last Junto member foisted on her. Secretary of state Sunderland, responsible for Scotland since Harley's recent departure from government, used his office to strike a bargain on behalf of Whigs: Jacobite prisoners taken during the latest invasion scare, were freed in return for Scottish peers promising to vote, in the Lords, against Godolphin's nominees to receive a peerage (the new peers were expected to support the government). Enraged at this maneuver, the queen accused Sunderland of disloyalty to the ministry and abuse of office. Only her esteem for Marlborough stopped Anne from dismissing his son-in-law, but the incident crystallized her fury at having had to accept Sunderland in the first place; never mind having to endure his rudeness to, and neglect of, her, and his ridicule of her political ideas.

Scarcely in the same category as abrasive, stridently Whig Sunderland, mild-mannered, charming and courteous Somers, a notable orator and sound lawyer with a good grasp of constitutional and diplomatic matters, interested himself in fine arts and science. As president of the Royal Society, (national academy of science) Somers came into contact with another man drawn to science—Prince George—whose interest in the work of Isaac Newton motivated the prince, to Somers's appreciation, to fund some of Newton's research.

Nonetheless, Anne viewed Somers askance, not least because he had, as one of King William's closest advisors, counseled the king against appointing her as regent during his absences on the continent. But the queen did recognize Somers as having been mainly responsible for the Regency Act; (by settling the Succession, it spared Anne the dreaded specter of a visit from one of the Hanoverian electoral family) besides, Somers respected Marlborough and his military plans; esteemed Godolphin's financial ability and integrity; and despite her Whiggism, winced at Sarah's personality. Still, the duchess had the last word. "Lord Somers could not have supported so long to have been the head of the party, if he had not had good talents. But there was one thing that appeared to be a great blemish … he lived as publicly with another man's wife as if she had been his own."[10]

—⁂—

Once more a woman defied Merciless Men. Throughout spring and early summer, the Junto pressed Anne to appoint Somers, as well as Whigs to lesser positions. Godolphin, and Marlborough from his headquarters in The Hague, advised the queen to comply. To complicate matters, Hanover's dowager electress still craved to be received in England as Anne's successor. Failing that, Sophia thought recognition should come via an allowance. She secretly plotted with Tories. To embarrass the ministry, they again floated the idea of a parliamentary invitation.

Loth to be left behind in using the Hanoverian issue for their own ends, Whigs planned to introduce a motion in parliament asking Sophia and her son the elector to allow the electoral prince, recently created Duke of Cambridge, to visit England to take his seat in the house of lords.

"I have heard of the court they [Whigs] make to the electress from several people," Tory Abigail Masham informed her cousin Harley, who had retired to the country immediately after the failure of his attempted coup, "and told her [Anne] all, while she is hearing it she is very melancholy but says little to the matter."[11] Always hesitant to express herself, the queen, in any case, would hardly be likely to share concerns of state with one she considered a servant.

Instead, Anne appealed to a friend. "If this matter should be brought into parliament, [she wrote Marlborough,] whoever proposed it whether Whig or Tory, *I should look upon neither of them as my friends nor would never make any invitation neither to the young man, nor his father, nor his grandmother.*"

The queen begged the duke to

find out whether there is any design where you are, [the electoral prince and his father the elector, served in the allied army under Marlborough's command] that the young man should make a visit in the winter & contrive some way to put any such thoughts out of their heads, that the difficulty may not be brought upon me of refusing him leave to come if he should ask it, or of forbidding him to come if he should attempt it without asking, for one of these two things I must do if either he or his father should have any desires to have him in this country, it being a thing I cannot bear to have any successor here though but for a week.

Anne feared the effect of a rival court on the already poisonous political climate. She relied on Marlborough "to do everything on the other side of the water to prevent this mortification."[12]

No matter how dissatisfied with his sovereign's conduct over Somers, Marlborough responded to Anne's appeal to his loyalty and friendship. The duke's refusal to defy her over the Hanoverian invitation ended the matter—at least for now.

—⁂—

"Your majesty will be neither surprised nor displeased to hear I am gone into the country, [Sarah informed the queen,] since by your very hard and uncommon usage of me, [Anne's preference for Abigail's soothing company over the duchess's angry tirades] you have convinced all sorts of people, as well as myself, that nothing would be so uneasy to you as my near attendance."[13] If, the duchess continued, "your majesty thinks fit to dispose of my employments according to the solemn assurances you have been pleased to give me, you shall meet with all the submission & acknowledgments imaginable."[14]

By solemn assurances Sarah meant Anne's unwilling, not to say tepid, agreement to Sarah's insistence that she appoint the Marlborough daughters to their mother's offices if the duchess resigned. "If I should outlive you, your faithful Morley will remember her promise,"[15] the queen replied. If I should outlive you. Anne would give Sarah's offices to her daughters if Sarah died, not if she resigned.

Regardless, the queen declined Sarah's resignation offer. An open breach with her erstwhile favorite would adversely affect Marlborough, since much of his credibility in foreign capitals rested on realization that he had the queen's full trust.

Sarah duly decamped for the country. There, she solidified a friendship. Playwright, pamphleteer, and Ultra Whig Sir Arthur Maynwaring, a government auditor and MP close to the Junto, now styled himself as the duchess's secretary; she called him her political advisor. Maynwaring cajoled the duchess into confiding tales of life with Princess Anne; Sarah even showed him Anne's early letters. They inspired malicious, clever Maynwaring to float the idea that in her youth the queen showed lesbian tendencies, that these were now focused on her favorite bedchamber woman, Abigail Masham.

—⁓—

Queen Anne's early letters to Sarah were certainly fulsome, although inside the parameters of a style close female friends used to address each other; in fact, well within contemporary norms used to express passionate platonic love between women. Ordinarily, therefore, the duchess would have dismissed as absurd any idea that genuinely devout Anne indulged in anything then deemed wicked, a vice.

No female, moreover, except possibly Anne's mother, had been closer to Anne than Sarah. And the duchess knew Anne harbored no lesbian leanings for she had never shown any such tendency towards her closest friend. As well, the accusation of lesbianism ignored the loving relationship Anne and her husband enjoyed from the first days of their marriage.

If Sarah had suspected a lesbian liaison between Anne and Abigail, she would have launched the charge before Maynwaring's fertile brain hit upon lesbianism as the motive for the queen favoring her maid. But now, anger at the queen's rejection of her political advice and envy at Abigail's rise in Anne's esteem, caused Sarah to deny any fault in her own conduct towards the queen as the reason for her fall from favor; far simpler for the duchess to use lesbianism as the explanation of Anne's preference for Abigail, and the latter's (according to Sarah) political influence.

—⁓—

Mainwaring urged the duchess to return to court, but not to reclaim her position as favorite. He envisioned another role for Sarah. She should use her sway over Marlborough and Godolphin to broker an alliance between cabinet and Junto.

The duke also wanted his wife at court; she must not leave the field to Abigail. And the queen assured Sarah that if she were ready to resume their old relationship, Anne would be, too. But peace between the two former intimates did not last long.

Marlborough knew, the queen wrote him, that she often "had the misfortune of falling under [Sarah's] displeasure. [Now, after] several reconciliations, [the duchess had again] relapsed into her cold, unkind way." Sarah refused to attend the queen when she sat alone, and thought no one would notice this change. Sarah might "impose upon some poor simple people, but how can she imagine she can on any that have a grain of sense? [Would not the] tattling voice … in a little time make us the jest of the town? Some people will blame her, others me, and a great many both. What a disagreeable noise she will be the occasion of making in the world besides. God knows of what ill consequences it may be."

For all their sakes, the queen begged Marlborough to "endeavor all you can to persuade Mrs. Freeman out of this strange unreasonable resolution."[16]

—⟋ⱴⱴ⟍—

No one could reason with the duchess. Her husband, plus everyone else, got a taste of Sarah's temper. In the meantime, Maynwaring provoked her to still greater heights of insolence towards Anne than the duchess achieved on her own. He and Sarah delighted in composing long, anonymous letters to Abigail, which may or may not have been sent, accusing her of a lesbian relationship with Anne. Sarah went so far as to favor the queen with one of Maynwaring's ballads, set to a popular tune, and, the duchess assured Anne, currently enjoying wide circulation "in town and country."[17] The duchess enjoyed entertaining her friends with a rendition of the ballad. Its thirty-one verses began:

> Whenas Queen Anne of great renown
> Great Britain's scepter sway'd,
> Besides the Church, she dearly lov'd
> A dirty chambermaid.
>
> Oh! Abigail that was her name,
> She starched and stitched full well,
> But how she pierc'd this royal heart,
> No mortal man can tell.
>
> However, for sweet service done
> And causes of great weight,
> Her royal mistress made her, Oh!
> A minister of state.
>
> Her secretary she was not,
> Because she could not write;
> But had the conduct and the care
> Of some dark deeds at night.[18]

To charge one's queen, never mind former dear friend, with dark deeds at night at a time when society judged lesbianism as a sin, constituted a huge offense. Besides, the duchess knew, from personal experience, that Anne's concept of intimate friendship between females did not include sexual relations; just as she knew the queen's early letters merely reflected the hyperbole common in current writing style between close female friends. But because Sarah had convinced herself that the queen's affection for her came from esteem for Sarah's intellect and frankness, Abigail, who lacked those qualities, must have attracted Anne for other reasons. Sexual gratification presented itself as a convenient rationale.

The duchess reasoned correctly up to a point. Abigail did lack Sarah's attributes; but Abigail had others, which the duchess overlooked—she nursed the ailing queen with skill and patience, diverting Anne, as well, with soothing music and amusing mimicry;

and Abigail respected the queen's desire not to bring up politics. Nonetheless, Anne failed to harbor the same strong feeling of friendship for Abigail as she had for Sarah. The queen never urged Abigail to treat her as an equal; (Mrs. Freeman, Mrs. Morley) instead, the queen kept their gap in rank and, to the end of her life addressed Abigail as Masham, her surname—the typical way a lady spoke to and of, a female servant.

The duchess's charge of lesbianism also insulted Anne because the queen had purposefully set an example for her people by promoting a happy domestic milieu. This Anne achieved by creating an efficient household and relaxed, relatively private atmosphere, appointing people she liked to posts near her person, and assigning household positions to people of proven loyalty.

Further, Sarah knew how deeply the religious queen respected Christian morality; yet, the duchess persisted in accusing Anne of indulging in conduct contemporaries considered sinful. And Sarah knew how much the queen prized loyalty; but, accused Anne of betraying her husband.

And not only that. The duchess's allegation that the queen preferred to have sexual relations with women, ignored the love that existed between Anne and George. This, in particular, hurt the queen's feelings. Her subjects routinely wished bridal couples to Love Like the Queen and Prince; for, they were "a perfect pattern of conjugal love."[19]

—✵—

"I found plainly when I had the honor to show your majesty the new ballads," Sarah wrote at the end of a twelve-page screed on politics, that although the ballads circulated openly throughout the realm, "you never see any of them but from me. [So, to edify her sovereign, the duchess took] the liberty to send [Anne yet another oeuvre,] for there are more to be expected."[20]

Hoping her revelation of Maynwaring's insulting verses, not to mention her continued emphasis on their theme, would mortify the queen into dismissing Abigail, Sarah achieved a different result. She destroyed the last shreds of Anne's affection for her.

But since the queen judged France not yet ready for peace on terms favorable to Britain, she wanted to keep Marlborough. Weary of his demanding responsibilities, the duke had several times expressed his wish to retire. If Anne dismissed the duchess, thus exposing the extent of their breach, Marlborough might well resign immediately. The queen had no choice but to keep Sarah.

Fully aware of this, the duchess kept up her bombardment. Pointedly recollecting Anne having said

> that of all things in this world, you value most your reputation, which I confess surprised me very much that your majesty should ... mention this word after having conceived so great a passion for such a woman for there can be no great reputation in a thing so strange and unaccountable ... nor can I think the having no inclination for any but one's own sex is enough to maintain such a character as I wish may still be yours, but to the preserving a great reputation general greatnesses are certainly necessary such as justice and wisdom and constancy.[21]

The queen did not deign to reply. That, Marlborough warned his wife, showed the extent of Anne's anger. But Sarah's unbridled temper consumed her. The duchess could not, would not, see that her satisfaction in berating Anne carried consequences.

—✵—

Queen Anne's keeper of the privy purse now helped herself to a large sum from that account to help finance the building of her new London residence, Marlborough house, situated close to Anne's official London dwelling, St. James Palace. The queen had granted Sarah's request for a long lease of the crown land even though this meant ceding part of her palace garden; and Anne added two acres when the duke judged the original parcel of land not large enough for a suitable townhouse. Building it meant felling the oak tree King Charles II had planted to honor the oak that saved his life in the civil war. Sarah ordered the tree destroyed. The queen, a careful housekeeper, regularly reviewed Sarah's account books. In the interest of peace, Anne refrained from mentioning the duchess's withdrawal.

At the same time, stirring events took place on the Continent. France opened the 1708 campaign with a successful offensive. But although the quick French conquest of strategic fortified towns (Ghent and Bruges) gave the enemy most of Flanders, to secure it they must tackle the allied garrison at Oudenarde (south of Ghent on the Scheldt river). Marlborough fortified Oudenarde and urged his friend and fellow general, Prince Eugene of Savoy, to join him in a bold plan. It would force battle on the enemy even though the French were numerically superior and held a more favorable position.

Eugene arrived to find Marlborough ill with headaches and high fever. Depressed, as well, by discord with Anne over the Somers appointment, let alone Sarah's relations with the queen, the duke spoke as if all were lost. "Unless [he] lost his life we should with God's help obtain satisfaction, [the prince told Marlborough]; his affairs were not in anything like so bad a state as he saw them."[22]

Marching their armies to the Scheldt at top speed, duke and prince astonished the enemy even more by effecting the difficult river crossing with apparent ease. Working in perfect harmony Marlborough and Eugene were thus able to form their armies in battle lines before the squabbling French generals could agree on a common course of action.

The battle of Oudenarde (July 11, 1708) consisted of fierce, frantic, hand-to-hand combat fought through village streets and vegetable gardens, across ditches and hedges, as duke and prince slowly yet steadily surrounded the French army. Darkness and a downpour could not disguise complete allied victory with relatively little loss of life.

Oudenarde obliterated French power in the southern Netherlands. Oudenarde opened Lille, France's second largest city, to allied armies.

Anne lacked "words to express the joy I have, [she told the duke. Although her thanks were inadequate for this and] all the great and faithful services you have ever done me, [Marlborough must believe the queen] as truly sensible of them as a grateful heart can be…. I hope you cannot doubt of my esteem and friendship for you, nor think that because I differ … in some things, it is for want of either."[23]

—〰—

"I do and you must give thanks to God for his goodness in protecting and making me the instrument of so much happiness to the queen and nation, [Marlborough hastily scrawled to Sarah from the battlefield,] if she will please to make use of it."[24]

Time and again the duke had warned his wife that their letters were private. Sarah shared this note with Anne.

The queen instantly asked Marlborough to explain what he meant when he wrote of thankfulness, for being the instrument of so much good to the nation and queen, if she would please to make use of it. Certainly, Anne would never "make an ill use of so great a blessing, but according to the best of my understanding, make the best use of it

I can." What use, Anne wanted to know, would the duke have her make of his victory at Oudenarde? Her reply would tell him her "thoughts very freely and sincerely."[25]

> DUKE: Take Godolphin's advice—do not trust Tories; [i.e., Abigail and Harley] reconcile with Whigs who will continue to wage war forcefully.
> QUEEN: Were you in London, you would not judge me wrong to resist appointing Somers to the cabinet.
> DUKE: I wish to continue serving you in the army, but not as a minister.

Although her "sore eye [made] it uneasy to me to write,"[26] Anne picked up her newly sharpened quill pen and dipped it into the inkwell standing on her white marble writing table.

Extremely sorry to find Marlborough adamant in not wanting to advise her on domestic affairs, Anne begged his "pardon for disobeying your commands in that particular. [Since she had always] spoke and writ my mind very freely, as I think every friend ought to do to one another, [the queen could not stop doing the same now. She wanted to ask the duke's] opinion in everything; there being nobody but you and lord treasurer that I do advise with, nor can rely on. [The queen hoped Marlborough would believe her,] since I tell you so."

Daily, the queen must bear with Sarah's scolding about having succumbed to Harley's influence via his cousin Abigail Masham. And since the duke wrote that unless "there were not something very extraordinary," Anne would follow his and Godolphin's advice, she worried that Marlborough no longer had "a thorough good opinion of me."

Why, the queen asked, should "my not complying with some things that are desired, and which you know I have ever been against … be imputed to something extraordinary? Is not one a body of opinion and one of another? And why, then, should it be wonderful [that queen and duke] differ in some things, as well as other people, especially [as Anne's views on Whigs had not changed ever since the time she became] capable of having notions of things and people, and I must own I can see no reason to alter mine."[27]

The duke insisted that Anne hold firm against Harley and heed Godolphin, "so long faithful to you. [Any other advisors led her into a] labyrinth, to play their own game at your expense. Nothing but your commands should have obliged me to say so much."[28]

—◊◊—

If, during this exchange, the duchess expected her interference to help the duke, she expected in vain. Oblivious of the effect her lengthy political diatribes had on the queen, Sarah's letters now lamented that despite his decisive victories at Blenheim, Ramillies, and lately Oudenarde, Marlborough had no choice but to conclude that he had little credit with Anne. How could he reason otherwise when she let a lowly bedchamber woman sway her against the duke, not to mention her other prominent and experienced servants. Angrily denying Marlborough had lost her trust, the queen commanded Sarah never again to mention Abigail. The duchess instantly replied: Anne had made a mistake in assuming she alluded to Abigail.

"I am very sorry whenever I happen to make any mistakes in what dear Mrs. Freeman says to me, [Anne replied.] I hope you will not think it unreasonable if I defer answering it [Sarah's letter] till tomorrow to have time to read it over & over again before I begin to write for fear of making any more mistakes."[29]

—◊◊—

The queen had, according to habit, spent the summer at Windsor, but this year she forsook the great Norman castle. As princess, Anne had bought a small residence located on the edge of Windsor park. Living at the Little House facilitated hunting in Anne's favorite venue despite Queen Mary's having forbidden her the castle. Now the modest Little House, with its dormer windows and rooms of "plain unvarnished oak wainscot,"[30] gave Anne an escape from the formality of court.

Consequently, the queen brought her ailing husband to the Little House that summer, (1708) the better to concentrate on nursing him through a series of severe asthma attacks. Prince George's rooms, decorated in yellow damask and, like all the rooms, with marble chimney piece and large mirrors, were directly below Anne's apartment; bedecked in

Queen Anne. "The best defender" the Church "will ever see." This statue stands in front of St. Paul's Cathedral. Artists: R.C. Belt and L.A. Malempré 1886, copy of the weather-damaged original by Francis Bird, erected in 1712 to commemorate the completion of the cathedral during Anne's reign. Author photograph.

crimson velvet, the queen's rooms faced the garden with its shaved green lawns, comfortable benches, graveled walks, and abundance of trees and flowers. Both queen and prince's dressing-rooms boasted the latest modern convenience—a small adjacent room with "marble seats of easement with sluices of water to wash all down."[31]

Anne rose at four each morning to hunt during the cool hours. Wearing a riding-coat of light brown worsted lined with yellow silk, the queen, seated in her custom-built, high-speed carriage, would review her officials and hunting dogs assembled under the branches of a giant oak tree. After hunting, the queen returned to state business and household duties. Besides, Anne nursed her husband through ever more acute asthma attacks.

—∞—

On a still, sultry August morning the queen left her gravely ill prince, and the comfort of Windsor's cool, clear country air, for sweltering, dusty London. Anne wanted to emphasize the importance of Marlborough's latest victory by personally attending the special thanksgiving service she had ordered to mark the Battle of Oudenarde.

On arrival at St. James's Palace after a tiring journey, the queen found that Sarah, her groom of the stole, had laid out a scarlet velvet robe, heavily trimmed with gold braid, for her to wear. As well, the duchess thought the occasion merited Anne donning elaborate state jewelry.

Gout and obesity made wearing heavy state clothing burdensome for the queen at best of times. But London heat and exhaustion due to worrying about, and constant nursing of, George, failed to deter the queen from putting on the dress Sarah selected. Anne did, however, decline the state jewelry Sarah laid out, in favor of lighter gems.

Anne and Sarah rode to St. Paul's alone together in the queen's open state carriage. But the duchess's smiles and waves to the cheering crowds lining the route hid rage and humiliation. For when she had settled herself in the carriage, Sarah saw the queen sitting beside her with those heavy state gems conspicuously lacking. A deliberate omission, the duchess concluded, meant to show the world that Marlborough, as well as his wife, had lost favor; to shame both Marlboroughs in front of all the domestic and foreign dignitaries packed into the great cathedral, to say nothing of the throngs outside.

Rather than waiting for a private moment to discuss the matter, the duchess began to berate the queen as soon as the carriage clattered out of St. James's Palace courtyard. Reprimanding Anne for her dislike of Whigs and lack of trust in her old friends, Sarah proceeded to accuse the queen of having favored Abigail's choice of jewelry—Abigail had selected gems that would show Anne's apathy for Oudenarde and Marlborough—in fact, Abigail had left London some weeks before to prepare for her imminent confinement at the Masham country house.

The duchess's tirade continued until the coach drew up in front of St. Paul's. Two stalwart, bewigged, and white-gloved footmen carefully lowered the carriage steps for the two ladies to alight. As queen and duchess ascended the Cathedral's shallow marble steps, lined with serried rows of attentive courtiers and dignitaries, Anne opened her mouth to answer Sarah's accusations. But before the queen could say a word, the duchess hissed, Be Quiet.

Thirteen

"That good man"

"And thus we've lost the pillar of our state
Both good and virtuous, wise as well as great;
The best of men who led the best of lives,
The best of husbands to the best of wives:
The best of queens ne'er loved a better man,
Then show me such another if you can."[1]—
Anonymous contemporary verse

The drama enacted in front of St. Paul's Cathedral on that dusty, humid August day (1708) caused a sensation. News spread quickly. It confirmed rumors swirling for months—an abyss yawned between Queen Anne and the Duchess of Marlborough.

The two women returned to St. James's Palace in the queen's gilded, carved state coach. While they waved and smiled graciously to the cheering citizens crowding their route, the duchess resumed her rant in favor of Whig policies; as well, she continued to chastise Anne for openly insulting both Marlboroughs by not wearing the gems she, Sarah, groom of the stole, had selected. Further, Sarah could not refrain from scolding the queen about her (supposed) lesbian relationship with favorite chambermaid Abigail Masham. "I should find myself wanting in the duty I owe you, [Sarah justified herself,] if I saw you so much in the wrong (as with one passion or prejudice you certainly have) and did not tell you of it … because nobody else could so speak upon … such a subject."[2]

The duchess continued her harangue in a letter. It included a missive from Marlborough (one he warned her not to show to anyone) delineating the domestic political situation and accentuating the need for Anne to acquiesce to Whig Junto demands—that their leader, Lord Somers, be appointed to the cabinet as lord president of the (privy) council, one of the four highest offices of state. As well, the duke reiterated weariness with his demanding military and diplomatic duties, as well as his wish for peace.

"After the commands you gave me on the thanksgiving day of not answering you, [the queen replied, she would not have] troubled [Sarah] with these lines but to return [Marlborough's] letter safe into your hands. [For the same reason, Anne did] not say anything to that nor to yours which enclosed it."[3]

This reply provoked Sarah into a lengthy self-validation whose opening paragraph set the tone for what followed.

I have had the honor to receive a letter from your majesty written is so different a manner from what you have formerly used, that if I had not been so well acquainted with the hand I would not have believed it possible to have come from you, and having had the occasion to compare some of the expressions in it with those that are in your other letters, I have found it difficult to conceive how they could ever happen to be used by the same person.[4]

—⚏—

The duchess demanded an interview. She used the occasion to accuse Anne of heeding only the advice of moderate Tory Robert Harley, even if in self-imposed retirement at his country house following his failed coup attempt earlier in the year, (1708) and of Tory Abigail Masham. Anne hotly denied the duchess's charge. Fierce words flew between the two former friends. Attendants in the queen's ante-chamber could hear the duchess shouting. Both women were reduced to tears. Sarah had to have the last word—how could Anne so angrily and scornfully tell her to leave the room. News of this scene spread like wildfire, dispelling any lingering doubt about the duchess's loss of favor.

Furious at her failure to impose her political opinions on the queen, Sarah decided to stop lobbying. Marlborough greeted this resolve with relief—he had often warned his wife that her political pressure antagonized Anne. Observing the duchess's loss of favor, fearing her efforts on their behalf might now do more harm than good, Whigs echoed the duke.

Had she yielded to personal preference, the queen would instantly have dismissed her groom of the stole, first lady of the bedchamber, and keeper of the privy purse, a woman whose conduct had gradually destroyed Anne's affection for her, a woman who now provided only upset and anguish. But as queen, Anne could not afford to indulge in personal sentiment. Hence, she again sacrificed private emotion to state concerns. The queen neither wanted nor could afford, to have Marlborough leave her service. He alone had the military talent to secure victory against France and the diplomatic ability to keep the fractious Grand Alliance together. The duchess must, therefore, stay in office as the price of keeping the duke; and the queen must maintain some semblance of cordiality towards Sarah as her duties directly affected the queen's private business and well-being.

—⚏—

The recent allied victory at Oudenarde fortified Whig resolve to make the queen acknowledge their contribution to the war effort, not to mention their support in other matters important to Anne, like union with Scotland, and the Regency Act, which secured the Hanoverian succession and spared the queen the distress of having to receive her successor, the Dowager Electress of Hanover. Hence, the Whig leadership (Junto) stepped up pressure to have their chief, Lord Somers, appointed to the cabinet as lord president, albeit with growing anger at the Duke of Marlborough and Lord Treasurer Sidney Godolphin for their inability to overcome the queen's opposition to admitting additional Junto members to her cabinet.

Godolphin and Marlborough were, in fact, doing their utmost to advance Whig interests as the price for continued Whig parliamentary support of the war. But although the cabinet had been depleted of moderate Tories since the resignation of secretary of state Robert Harley and his cohorts after Harley's unsuccessful attempt to unseat the ministry, the queen clung to her conviction that Moderation—a ministry made up of moderates from each party—or at least a cabinet that excluded extremists, remained in the best interests of her country.

Anne strove to maintain the crown's political independence. As queen, she must represent the whole of her divided nation. Anne loathed the united, powerful five-man

Junto who tirelessly tried to erode her royal rights. She could never be certain the Junto meant her well. "They have been disputing my authority and are certainly designing tear that little prerogative the crown has to pieces. [Nobody more than Anne wanted] to encourage those Whig friends that behave themselves well. [But the queen did] not care to have anything to do with those that have shown themselves to be of so tyrannizing a temper. [In short, Anne believed matters now stood as to whether] I shall submit to the five tyrannizing lords, or they to me."[5]

Faulted by Whigs for failing to convince the queen to give them office, castigated by Tories for trying too hard to please Whigs, Marlborough and Godolphin again contemplated resignation. Anne hoped they both would "think better of it, [not choose an action that would throw queen and] country into confusion. Is there no consideration to be had for either? [Anne thought her commander in chief and prime minister might] flatter yourselves that people would approve of your quitting; [but, should they] persist in these cruel and unjust resolutions, [the queen predicted that] where one will say you are in the right, hundreds will blame you."[6]

The queen later wrote privately to Marlborough. "When, after all the glorious successes God Almighty has blessed you with, he is happy to make you the happy instrument of giving a lasting peace to Europe, you are bound in conscience, both to God and man, to lend your helping hand; and how can you do that if you retire from business"?[7]

The duchess and her longtime friend Sidney Godolphin, meanwhile, drew closer; for with his close friend Marlborough fighting on the Continent, Sidney, under constant pressure from Junto demands, felt isolated in the cabinet. At the end of his letter summarizing various business communications received that day, the treasurer and prime minister confided to Sarah (now staying the country) that he saw "so many difficulties coming upon me from all sides, that unless I would have recourse to you oftener, upon many occasions, than it is possible for me to have at this distance when the ways grow bad and the moon fails, then I am afraid they must needs be too hard for me; besides that, I would not willingly take *any step but what is first approved by you.*"[8]

Since the duchess supported Godolphin in pressing Marlborough to urge Whig appointments on the queen, the prime minister depended on Sarah's sway over her husband. Indeed, Sidney and Sarah drafted many of the duke's political letters to Anne. So besides disagreeing with the duchess's strong pro–Whiggism, the queen distrusted Sarah's influence over the two ministers and, as a result, lost some faith in them both.

—⚹—

Aside from constant concern over politics, Anne faced a greater anxiety as the last days of summer (1708) brought a nip to the air and began to burnish the leaves. She had, for weeks, been devotedly nursing her cherished husband. Still, Prince George of Denmark failed to regain his health.

As if that were not enough, politics directly relating to the prince beset his wife. Not only did the Whig Junto continue to insist that their leader, Lord Somers, be given a senior cabinet position as the price for continued Whig support of the war, but, to increase pressure on Anne, Whigs also accelerated their long-simmering censure of George's management of naval matters.

When she ascended the throne, Anne appointed her husband as lord high admiral, a crucial position for her island nation because, unlike other countries who invested heavily in standing armies, England relied, rather, on its navy as the first line of defense. And since the country's wealth came from commerce, sophisticated naval convoy arrangements must be made to protect British merchant ships. The nation thus devoted ample resources to the navy, as well as naval support services and infrastructure[9]; naval supply absorbed one quarter of the naval budget. Administration of this vital outlay demanded efficient organization.

From the day of his appointment, Prince George showed interest in, and knowledge of, naval matters, particularly ship design and naval management. The prince conferred daily with his admiralty secretary and personally supervised admiralty replies to numerous requests for the protection of merchant shipping, as well as war-related matters like the composition of naval squadrons.

As his deputy the prince chose a bluff, corpulent, and pock-marked admiral. High Tory George Churchill, Marlborough's younger brother, had been friends with Prince George since boyhood. (When George's brother visited London on his Grand Tour, young Churchill entered his service as a page. The crown prince brought him back to Denmark where Churchill and Prince George shared an interest in the navy of that seafaring nation. Churchill returned to England in Prince George's retinue.)

The prince gave Admiral Churchill considerable leeway so as to let Marlborough have the naval control he needed via his loyal brother. But blunt, hearty Churchill proved not firm enough to be effective de facto ruler of the queen's navy. Merchants complained to their MPs that lax admiralty orders caused commercial losses; that their ships lacked convoys; that pirates plundered with impunity even in England's home waters.

Seething about Somers, let alone their defeat over the bishopric appointments in the previous year, Whigs now aimed to cause the queen maximum embarrassment via her husband. Initiating a parliamentary assault, Whigs accused the admiralty of gross ineptitude. This charge proved popular since admiralty neglect had undeniably caused large shipping losses to French pirates. But as Prince George pointed out in the house of lords, creating a complex convoy system proved difficult because war-related naval needs in the Mediterranean and Caribbean stretched naval resources; besides, England's maritime victories had resulted in the French navy targeting commercial vessels instead of warships. Concomitantly, the war caused explosive growth in England's international trade—English cloth enjoyed a world-wide market, English ships brought back lacquer and porcelain from China and the Indies, carpets from the Levant, silks and velvets from Genoa and Venice. Wealthy merchants and landowners bought these imported luxuries to furnish the elegant, comfortable Queen Anne Style houses they were building all over England.

Since politics drove parliamentary complaints against the admiralty, the legislature agreed that a committee should examine them. Detractors failed to find significant instances of egregious neglect so, after hearing the committee's conclusions, the Commons decided "to lay the whole matter before the queen. [She assured] that the trade should be carefully looked into; but nothing else followed upon it; and the queen seemed highly offended at the whole proceeding."[10]

Nevertheless, "everyone [knew] that not only the prince, but the queen likewise concerned herself much [about criticism of the admiralty.] And both looked on it as a design, leveled at their authority."[11]

Reluctant to incur Anne's wrath by attacking George directly, the Junto blamed admiralty failings on Churchill. Whigs hated him. They believed this High Tory had brainwashed his chief on behalf of Toryism. Prince George would, naturally, influence his wife.

Certainly, Churchill "had a great sway in the Prince of Denmark's affection, and governed the admiralty under him,"[12] but the admiral did not necessarily influence George's political opinions. The prince had, when his wife became queen, counseled her to appoint some moderate Whigs to the cabinet and to senior government posts. George himself appointed moderate Whig Lord Westmoreland to a senior naval position. Churchill accused Westmoreland of committing "some heinous thing. [Prince George] informed Mr. Churchill it was a lie. [And told Westmoreland] he was very well satisfied in the integrity of my actions, and ... should not direct me."[13]

At the same time Anne's de facto prime minister, lord treasurer Sidney Godolphin, in despair at her continued refusal to have Somers in the cabinet, appealed to Marlborough, mired in diplomatic maneuvers to maintain the Alliance. The duke must, Godolphin insisted, find time to tell his brother the admiral to stop lobbying Prince George and through George, the queen, against appointing Somers. But the admiral assured Marlborough "he would behave himself in everything as [Godolphin would like.] I verily believe, [the duke told the treasurer, that since Churchill] would take pains not to offend ... there must be somebody else that does mischief."[14]

Somebody else pointed to Robert Harley, fittingly nicknamed Robin the Trickster. Godolphin confronted the queen. Without mincing words, he asked if she kept up contact with Harley. No. She discussed politics with nobody but the prince. The treasurer believed her. He, like many, assumed that since Prince George did not speak fluent or non-accented English, he must either be stupid or unduly susceptible to the influence of others; besides, Sarah, whose opinion Godolphin valued, believed George, like his wife, incapable of independent thought. Hence, the treasurer reasoned, Whigs must be right to blame the queen's stand against Somers on Admiral Churchill's influence instilled into Anne via her husband.

The queen's secretary of state, strident Ultra Whig and Junto member Lord Sunderland, a vocal critic of naval management, now convinced his mother-in-law the Duchess of Marlborough, to get the duke to gag his brother George. Marlborough told the admiral that if he failed to resign, he must face dismissal.

The queen and her husband saw these Junto maneuvers as a direct attack on them personally, as well as on Anne's royal prerogative to appoint ministers of her choice. Hence, the queen backed her husband's refusal to remove Churchill.

At this juncture, the queen became preoccupied with her husband's worsening health. Rather than move him from Windsor to St. James's Palace as chilly autumn winds began to whistle through London and a sooty dampness clogged the air, Anne took George to Kensington Palace. She hoped Kensington's pure country air would ease the alarming congestion in Prince George's asthma-weakened lungs.

—⚊—

Queen and prince occupied Kensington's ground floor rooms; from them, George could more easily reach the gardens he and Anne had taken such pleasure in improving together. Painful gout now assailed the prince, as well as dropsy, (now known as edema) which grossly swelled his body; on mellow, golden autumn days he had to be helped along Kensington garden's graveled path to a seat in one of the secluded niches the royal couple had introduced. There, the prince could rest his eyes on a vista of pink and orange dahlias, purple verbena, sprays of lavender-blue and yellow daisies, and close-cut green lawns.

As George's asthma deteriorated, the

> violence of the cough produced a spitting of blood, and an increase of the coma or sleepiness, with an addition of convulsive motions of the tendons; which symptoms not yielding to the remedies administered by his own and several other learned physicians ... his royal highness fell into a suffocation, from which neither bleeding, nor a vomit ... could relieve him, her majesty assisting ... during his whole illness, in the most mournful and most affecting manner.[15]

Day and night the queen held her husband as he battled for breath. When her strength failed, Anne's preferred chambermaid Abigail Masham, who slept in the anteroom of the queen's bedchamber and proved to be a competent nurse, helped.

Enraged, meanwhile, at Prince George for supposedly inducing the queen to oppose the Somers cabinet appointment, and resolved to push themselves into power, the Junto threatened to stop backing the government unless moderate Lord Pembroke, currently president of the council and lord lieutenant of Ireland, replace the prince at the admiralty. Pembroke would thereby retain his cabinet seat but leave his current cabinet posts open for Junto members Somers and Wharton.

Godolphin tried to compromise. The Junto refused. If Somers were not admitted to the cabinet now, Whigs would mount an all-out personal and political attack on Prince George in the upcoming session of parliament. To spare Anne this embarrassment, Marlborough again told his brother the admiral to resign.

But the careworn queen, dog-tired to boot, concluded that George must be shielded at any cost. She acquiesced to Marlborough's reasoning: royal refusal to appoint Somers would declare to the world that Marlborough and Godolphin had lost credit with the queen; which might well cause Holland to initiate peace talks with France. Anne thus promised to appoint Somers to her cabinet—but—suspended making her decision official because of the prince's acute illness.

—⁂—

The Duchess of Marlborough had not graced the court for weeks. But encouraged by her Whig friends, Sarah sent a torrent of letters; they urged the queen to admit Junto members to her cabinet. As well, the duchess twice made a lightning descent on Kensington to scold Anne for allowing her chambermaid Abigail Masham to occupy rooms originally assigned to the duchess. All this ado took its toll on the queen, drained by worry over her husband, exhausted from sleepless nights spent nursing him, and hardly in robust health herself.

George had declined so badly, Godolphin told the duchess, that even Anne, used to nursing him through serious illness, now despaired. That alarmed Sarah. Her absence from court at such a crucial time for the queen, would risk censure; besides, in her capacity as first lady of the bedchamber, Sarah preferred to wait on the queen rather than leave Abigail Masham in sole attendance. So, the duchess informed Anne that despite her unjustifiable severity, Sarah would come to Kensington to do her utmost for her mistress during this, the prince's critical illness.

Anne did not leave her husband's bedside, not for a proper meal, not for a few hours of unbroken sleep. Early on a dreary day at the end of October, as gusty winds hurled rain against the windows, Prince George lapsed into a coma. Overcome with sorrow, the queen knelt at his bedside. Sarah entered the room. Ignoring the dying prince, she instantly began to scold. Anne asked her to leave. Sarah withdrew to the back of the room. Anne stayed with her husband until the end came in early afternoon, kissing him even as the breath left his body.

—⁓—

"An extraordinary tender and affectionate wife: and in all his illness, which lasted some years, she would never leave his bed; but sat up sometimes half the night in the bed by him, and with such care and concern, that she was looked on very deservedly as a pattern in this respect."[16]

As soon as the prince had breathed his last, Sarah emerged from the shadows at the back of his bedroom. Dismissing George's servants, she instantly took control.

Insensitive to the devout queen's wish for a few private moments with her dear husband's body, the duchess urged Anne to leave Kensington Palace immediately for St. James's. Craving a little time to adjust to her final parting from George, the queen "answered that she wanted to stay there. [Impossible, Sarah declared,] what could she do in such a dismal place. [The duchess then launched into what, according to her, were] all reasonable arguments"[17] against Anne remaining. The queen "seemed not to mind me, but clapped her hands together, with other marks of passion."[18]

This conduct led the duchess to conclude that Anne's "chief difficulty in removing was her fear that she could not have so much [of Abigail's company. Nobody] ever continued in a place where a dead husband lay, [Sarah tells us,] and where she could be within a room or two of his dismal body."[19]

If the queen removed to St. James's Palace, Sarah persisted, she "need not see anybody that was uneasy to her; [but could as easily as at Kensington see] anyone that might be of any comfort. [The queen's face showed] satisfaction in that, and so I went on, saying she might go away privately in my coach, with the curtains down, and see nobody.... Upon which she consented to go."[20]

But not before asking Sarah to send for Abigail, a request the duchess instantly took as proof of Anne and Abigail's lesbian relationship, besides showing a "very shocking" instance of favoritism when bishops and ladies of the bedchamber were asking to see the queen. Although "resolved not to say the least wry word to displease"[21] Anne, Sarah did not summon Abigail.

The duchess pulled Anne to her feet and led her out of the room. "Her arm was upon mine, which she had leaned upon, I found she had strength to bend down towards Mrs. Masham like a sail, and in passing by, went some steps more than was necessary, to be nearer her."[22] The duchess took this gesture as a personal insult.

As she and Anne "came into the coach, [the queen had what struck Sarah as] a very extraordinary thought. [Anne asked her to] send to my lord treasurer, and to beg of him to take care and examine whether there was room in some vault, to bury the prince at Westminster, and to leave room for her too. [In case not enough room existed] for the prince and her too, she directed another place for him to be buried in."[23]

—⁓—

On arrival at St. James's, the duchess installed Anne in her favorite, prettily furnished green room overlooking the park, and gave her a cup of broth. "Afterwards she ate a very good dinner, and at night I found her at table again, where she had been eating."[24] And as would be natural for a preferred maidservant, Abigail attended the queen on the latter occasion. But Sarah took her rival's presence as an offense. Because the duchess failed to see that Abigail's amenable personality and solicitous care had more to do with her displacing Sarah as the queen's favored attendant, than any intrigues on the chambermaid's part.

The queen then "passed a good deal of time looking into [recent royal burial] precedents, that she might order how it should be performed. [This, Sarah considered a] peculiar pleasure. [Indeed, the duchess judged Anne's sorrow as superficial because she only saw] tears in her eyes two or three times after his death. [That proved, Sarah concluded, that Anne only] fancied she loved him … her nature was very hard."[25]

The queen had missed regular meals for days on end, so of course she felt hungry; besides, many people take comfort from eating when in distress. Many of the bereaved find comfort in planning a final gesture of love, a last farewell—the dear one's funeral; many mourners find comfort in tears. (Sarah wept so unrestrainedly and for so long after her son Blandford's death, that her friends feared for her sanity.) Others, like Anne, do not.

Before withdrawing, the duchess ordered all necessary arrangements for the queen, and adjured Anne to call her at any time. The queen then admitted Godolphin to discuss the prince's funeral arrangements.

Barely had her chief minister bowed himself out of her presence when Anne had an afterthought. Hoping "to have spoke one more word [with Godolphin, the queen] scratched twice at dear Mrs. Freeman's door" but no one answered. Unwilling to send what she had to say by word of mouth, Anne wrote. When Godolphin sent orders to Kensington, the queen wanted him to make sure there were a "great many yeomen of the guards to carry the prince's dear body, that it may not be let fall, the great stairs being very steep and slippery."[26]

—◈—

Having managed to get "some rest [at night, the widowed queen applied] herself already to business"[27] two days after her husband's death. Anne understood her responsibilities. She sat on the throne as queen regnant. She had always resisted the idea of becoming a figurehead. She would not be one now.

But the queen's distress showed when Godolphin first asked her to review and sign admiralty documents that formerly went to the prince. Still, Anne undertook the onus of supervising the admiralty. (George's death had resulted in Admiral Churchill's resignation.)

While sympathetic to the queen's "affliction," Godolphin admitted that it complicated his work. George's death caused a "difficulty of speaking with that freedom and plainness to her, which her service requires, while she has so tender a concern."[28] The Merciless Men of the Whig party had no such qualms. They were hell-bent on taking advantage of the queen's vulnerability.

Her husband's death, let alone the upsetting weeks leading up to it, had their effect on Anne. A cabinet reshuffle took place. At Junto insistence, moderate Lord Pembroke moved from his cabinet position as president of the council, to head the admiralty. That allowed Junto chief Lord Somers to enter the cabinet as council president. Like Prince George, Somers interested himself in science, and esteemed Marlborough and Godolphin. Courteous and affable, his charm, to say nothing of Somers's ability as a politician and legal scholar, soon mollified the queen.

Not so the other addition to her cabinet. Since his days as King William's advisor, Anne had judged foul-mouthed Lord Wharton unfit for public office. This deft, gutsy Junto member, a rake par excellence as well as an atheist, delighted in baiting High Church Tories. But at least the queen could be thankful that the duties of her new lord lieutenant for Ireland meant he must spend part of the year in Dublin.

Anne presided over a meeting of her reconstituted cabinet a couple of weeks after the prince's death; but she felt unable to participate in the elaborate ceremony of formally opening parliament. No matter, parliament lost little time in formally addressing the queen. After expressing condolences, both houses of the all-male legislature petitioned their forty-three-year-old female, newly widowed sovereign to consider re-marriage in order to present her country with a Protestant heir of the direct Stuart line.

Parliament surely did not expect her to re-marry, Anne replied. Her wounds were still too fresh and ached too much (and this reminder of her failure in her most important duty—to bear royal children—would scarcely be expected to soothe her hurt; nor would a ballad, *The Hasty Widow or the Sooner the Better*). However, the queen assured parliament that the provision she had made for the Protestant succession (Regency Act) proved her profound concern for the nation's welfare.

—⁓—

"Free from all vice ... a prince of a familiar, easy disposition, with a good sound understanding, but modest in showing it,"[29] Prince George had "meddled little in business."[30] Nevertheless, many rued his passing.

After twenty-five years of friendship, George's death "made such an impression on [Marlborough] that I have not been well for several days, insomuch that I was obliged to march last night in a litter."[31] Prince and duke had been on excellent terms since the days when King Charles sent young Colonel John Churchill to Denmark to escort Princess Anne's bridegroom to England. The two men shared a keen interest in military matters; indeed, a few weeks before the prince's death, Marlborough, after outlining to George his reasons for attacking a strategic fortification that evening, enclosed the sketch plan "made for it, that your R.H. [royal highness] may please to see at your leisure how difficult a task it is."[32]

"Our misfortune at home, [motivated Marlborough to honor George with a] vigorous resolution in forcing a passage which the enemy has boasted was impossible."[33] And the officers and men of the British army, on hearing "the sad news ... with the greatest concern imaginable,"[34] wanted to win one for the prince.

He buttressed the war effort. "I am very glad the Danish troops have been assisting you, [George wrote the duke,] and hope that they will always do their duty however others behave themselves; nothing shall be wanting on my part to persuade their master to follow the interest of England in everything."[35]

The prince played a key part in greasing the wheels of the Anne-Marlborough-Godolphin government. George's friendship with the duke and respect for the treasurer made him see Marlborough and Godolphin's shift towards Whigs with less alarm that did his wife. But the Junto's charge of egregious ineptitude against admiralty de facto chief George Churchill decided the prince to back Anne in her resistance to further intrusion of Whig leaders into the cabinet. This shift notwithstanding, George continued to support both treasurer and duke.

The prince had been an active Fellow of the Royal Society. Interested, particularly, in navigation and seafaring, George underwrote publication of scientific works such as the royal astronomer's report, and, in general, encouraged interest in mathematics and physical sciences.

"I am not capable to set forth the just praise due to that good man," mourned moderate Whig Lord Westmoreland, a senior member of Prince George's household and his deputy warden of the cinque ports. "He was mighty easy towards all his servants, affected not popularity. [Careful not to act without] first acquainting him with it as I was of a different sentiment to all the rest of his family ... especially Mr. Churchill,"[36] Westmoreland earned the fair-minded prince's trust.

—m—

> This terrible misfortune has overwhelmed us with such deep sorrow, [the widowed queen wrote to her Dutch ally,] that we would willingly remain in profound silence, if the close ties which we have with your state did not oblige us to communicate everything that occurs to us, by God's will, either good or bad. You can imagine the magnitude of our affliction because he was an inestimable treasure of a husband, who loved us with such great and faithful tenderness over the course of so many years. You, too, have lost in him a true friend, who cherished your interests on every occasion.[37]

How many had loved Anne with such great and faithful tenderness for over twenty years? No one. Not even her oldest friend who, despite their political differences, could reasonably be expected to give the queen some support as she stood alone at a time of such great need. But Sarah's attitude, let alone her behavior, proved her friendship hollow. The duchess would be no crutch for the queen.

To be pitied, Abigail told her cousin Robert Harley, "for this last misfortune of losing all that is dear to her, the only comfort of her life. I hope in God this affliction will have no ill effect upon her health."[38]

Emotionally and physically drained, the queen succumbed to an extremely painful onslaught of gout. She spent the cheerless, increasingly frigid weeks following George's death in seclusion at St. James's Palace. Often, Anne locked the door to her rooms. No one, not even the duchess or Abigail, had keys.

Wearing a plain, purple (mourning color for royals) nightgown of warm heavy silk and matching robe, her gouty limbs wrapped in ointment-smeared bandages and covered with a cozy purple velvet quilt, Anne ensconced herself in her huge four-poster bed hung in unadorned purple and black. Weekly, the queen held an audience so that courtiers and foreign dignitaries could pay their respects.

The only person able to coax a smile, sometimes even a laugh, from the grieving widow during those doleful weeks after George's death, proved to be a newcomer at court, a beautiful, lively Italian lady, famous for her wit and cultured conversation. She had been the (moderate Whig) Duke of Shrewsbury's lover during his voluntary exile at Rome, but her Catholicism precluded their marrying. After Marlborough convinced his friend that he could as easily eschew partisan politics by retiring to his English country estate as by living in Rome, Shrewsbury took tender leave of his lover, and embarked on the long homeward journey. The lady followed. She finally ran her quarry to earth at Augsburg, where she declared her readiness to convert to Protestantism. Shrewsbury had been a member of Anne and George's Cockpit Circle, had often visited them during Anne's banishment from court during William and Mary's reign. Of course, Shrewsbury brought his bride to court to pay their respects to the bereaved queen.

—m—

"There is care taken she shall not be alone, [Abigail told Harley.] Since the misfortune Lady Marlborough has hardly left her so long as to let her say her private prayers but stays constantly with her … to keep [me] from her."[39]

The queen ordered fires lit in the little room George often used for his hobby of building miniature model ships. His work table and tools still stood there. Anne often sat alone for several hours in this bleak small space, sometimes praying, sometimes reading from the Bible—as she and George had done together after their son Gloucester's death. But the duchess, whose overblown suspicions of Abigail Masham clouded her perception, whose completely unfounded belief in the queen and her favorite chambermaid's lesbian liaison overcame her judgment, thought the "true reason [for Anne] choosing this closet to sit in, was, that the backstairs belonging to it [connected with] Mrs. Masham's lodgings."[40]

Sarah failed to comprehend why the queen constantly sought reminders of her husband. Without consulting Anne, the duchess removed George's portrait from the queen's bedroom immediately after his death. Not knowing where Sarah had put the precious painting, Anne several times implored her to restore it. But the duchess had already left court in a huff because the queen refused to assign Marlborough some extra stables at St. James's Palace.

> When dear Mrs. Freeman spoke to me about the stables I had so little of anything of that sort in my thoughts that I did not know very well what answer to give you, but upon considering of it since, I believe there are several of the dear prince's servants have lodgings in the stables. I intend to order an account of the stables and what servants are in them, to be laid before me. [When Marlborough returned,] he may see whether there are conveniences enough for him besides, & if there be, I shall be very glad to gratify him in his desires.
>
> Now that I have a pen in my hand I must desire you to bespeak a purple quilt and three cushions against I see company but they must not be of any glossy thing, & if you please send one of your servants to the upholsterer to know the size of the bed that they may be made fit.
>
> I cannot end this without begging you once more for God sake to let the dear picture [of George] you have of mine be put into my bedchamber for I cannot be without it any longer.[41]

—⚜—

Desperate for a modicum of comfort now that her husband's death had left her to face the world alone, the queen could derive little solace from her political situation. Since the departure of moderate Tory Robert Harley and his cohorts from her cabinet, Anne had been battling to keep some semblance of Moderation. But George's death, to say nothing of the punishing period prior to it, sapped her energy. Three members (Somers, Sunderland, and Wharton) of the hated five-man Whig Junto now occupied senior positions in the queen's almost all Whig cabinet, while others clamored and jostled for entry.

Fourteen

Murdering Malplaquet

"Nobody was ever so used by a friend as I have been by her ever since my coming to the crown. I desire nothing but that she should leave off teasing and tormenting me and behave herself with the decency she ought both to her friend and queen."[1]—Queen Anne

Skaters swooped and swirled across the frozen Thames, and apple-cheeked children skipped rope and played ball on frost-bitten ground as the new year (1709) gripped all Europe with glacial fingers. Ice floated in the Channel and North Sea surrounding Great Britain, major rivers like the Seine froze, as did all the canals in Venice, and the ruby-red claret at Versailles.

Hardy British souls skimming across ice-bound ponds and rivers were clad completely in black. Coaches crunching through the frozen slush were banned from displaying polished nails. Queen Anne had ordered the entire nation to observe deep mourning for her husband, Prince George.

The court went into mourning for the maximum twenty-five months. Courtiers must wear black, even use black handkerchiefs.

Laid up with severe gout from January to June, the queen kept to her private rooms in St. James's Palace. Her hair free of powder to mark her mourning, her face blotched with pain, her afflicted limbs wrapped in bandages, her black and purple garments plain, Anne admitted only strictly necessary visitors.

—⁂—

The queen's anguish at losing her husband had given the Whig leadership an opening. Junto members bullied their worn-out sovereign into accepting a Whig ministry. But in honor of Prince George's memory, Anne resisted Whig demands that a Junto member replace him as lord high admiral. The queen assumed control of the admiralty.

"If the queen be governed by the cabinet" in important matters, Anne's captain general the Duke of Marlborough wrote his jubilant spouse Sarah, "everything might mend, especially as you think that [lord treasurer and prime minister] Godolphin is as well with the queen as ever. If that continues, Mrs. Masham may vex, but never do much mischief."[2] Actually, Abigail Masham had little, if any, political influence; for regardless of partiality for Abigail's soothing attentions, Anne never discussed business with her favorite chambermaid.

During that frigid winter, ascendant Whigs initiated an address to the queen. She should "conclude no peace with France, till" that country recognize Anne's lawful title

159

as Queen of Great Britain, "disown the Pretender, and send him out of that kingdom, and till the Protestant succession should be universally owned, and that a guarantee should be settled among the Allies for securing it."[3]

No Tory dared to oppose. Hence, the address sailed through both houses of parliament. The house of commons added "that the demolishing of Dunkirk [from which fortified naval base French pirates freely plundered English ships] should be likewise insisted on, before any peace were concluded."[4]

Both houses then formally presented their address to the queen. Anne "received and answered it very favorably [to the satisfaction of] the whole nation, and to all our allies."[5]

—⁂—

As Queen Anne suffered agonies of body and soul, and her subjects shivered under arctic conditions, Britain's foe in the War of the Spanish Succession fared worse. French harvests had failed the previous year. (1708) Now, weeks of icy wind and hard frost killed people weakened by hunger, also livestock, trees, and vines, even seed corn planted underground. This year would see no harvest either.

King Louis XIV faced the prospect of an empty treasury. The Allies organized a naval blockade that exacerbated French misery. At Versailles, king and courtiers were reduced to dining on oat bread. Starving soldiers deserted; hungry garrisons guarding France's northern border with the Spanish Netherlands, mutinied.

By this time the battles of Blenheim, Ramillies, and Oudenarde, followed by the successful siege of France's northern bastion, Lille, had won the war against France. But Spain remained a stumbling block. The only way to wrest the country from Louis's grandson, (Bourbon) King Philip V, and secure it for the Hapsburg claimant Archduke Charles, (King Carlos III) would be, according to allied commander in chief Marlborough, if the allied armies ended the war with a march on Paris.

To forestall this dread prospect, and with his freezing, famished army in rags, the French king, on a clear day in early spring when towering clouds moved regally in the light breeze, sent his secretary of state to The Hague in secret, to initiate peace negotiations. Peace overtures to Holland, Louis thought, would drive a wedge in the Grand Alliance thus giving him a better chance for favorable terms. But the Alliance's three major signatories, Great Britain represented by Marlborough; Holland by Grand Pensionary Heinsius; and the Hapsburg Empire by Prince Eugene of Savoy, had been working so harmoniously together that they confounded the French king by negotiating as one.

Louis indicated willingness to trade his grandson King Philip V's claim to Spain for peace, in return for Philip receiving Spanish possessions in southern Italy. Marlborough received the French king's overture with skepticism because Philip refused to cede his right to Spain; besides, by now he controlled the whole country so it would be difficult to dislodge him. Furthermore, five years of fighting under Philip's leadership had caused Spaniards to see him not as the French candidate for their country's throne, but as their king. Hence, Louis commanding Philip what to do meant one thing; Louis making Philip do it, meant quite another.

The Allies demanded that France immediately cede three fortified northern border towns; within two months of an armistice King Louis must make his grandson Philip V cede Spain's crown; if Philip did not, the Allies, now in possession of the three French border fortresses, would resume war. Louis agreed to surrender the towns, agreed that all Spain's European holdings would go to Austrian Hapsburg Archduke Charles, (who claimed Spain as King Carlos III) and agreed to finance—but not fight in—an allied army to take Spain.

—⚒—

Marlborough had a better grasp of continental politics than any of his countrymen. He judged the Whig goal of No Peace Without Spain unrealistic. So, the duke asked Queen Anne's Whig ministers to send one of their own (Lord Townshend) to attend peace talks with him. The Junto gladly complied; they did not entirely trust the duke to negotiate in good faith for them. Townshend thus went to The Hague ostensibly to help Marlborough, actually to assure robust exposition of Whig peace terms.

Smug about their power in parliament and cabinet, let alone having Queen Anne their pockets, Whigs instructed Townshend to insist that the Allies add further demands. Louis must not only recognize the Protestant succession, but also expel Anne's half-brother, the Catholic Pretender, from France. He must agree to No Peace without Spain—the country and its entire empire must go to Hapsburg Charles (who had secretly promised Whigs to give Britain valuable trading concessions in Spain's colonies).

Although France faced famine and likely invasion, King Louis refused allied demands that he go to war against his grandson. Besides, Louis had recently replenished his coffers with a fresh supply of Spanish silver from South America, which allowed him to buy foreign grain despite the allied blockade. The king could now feed his starving troops.

Queen Anne's Whig ministry did not feel sorry to see peace talks collapse. Even had the French king conceded over his grandson Philip, Britain faced danger. For, Holland would take the three fortified towns ceded by Louis, withdraw from the war, and leave Britain to confront French ambitions with a weakened alliance.

Whigs and prime minister (lord treasurer Sidney Godolphin) failed to grasp that war had been won against France, but war against Spain had been lost. Spaniards were loyal to their king—Philip V. Spain should, therefore, be left to him, and the Spanish empire partitioned.

Tories saw the situation accurately. That gave them a weapon against the ministry. Tories now promoted peace and disarmament—against the Whigs and Marlborough—all warmongers working for a military dictatorship. So, the parties battled over how and when to end the war. And fought constantly over three elements of peace-making: how urgently did Britain need peace; what were the basics of a Good Peace; and how best to negotiate a settlement.

Failure of the peace talks disappointed Anne. Acutely aware of the war's human costs, (she wept when reviewing the lists of killed and wounded) the queen also appreciated her subjects' economic sacrifices. These had recently escalated; for winter's arctic conditions, although not so dire as in France, caused rising corn prices and domestic privation. As well, the government policy of letting Protestants fleeing religious persecution in German states settle in England, where they flooded the weak job market and burdened already overstretched English charities, made Britons begin to think their country put upon.

—⚒—

Pink and purple phlox carpeted flower beds, calla lilies, sweet peas, and carnations filled the air with a heady scent, the sun shone, a fresh breeze blew, and small puffs of cloud rode high in the blue sky. But Anne ordered her Little House at Windsor hung in black during that sad summer following Prince George's death.

Like the queen, all members of the royal household and court must continue to observe deep mourning. Anne ordered new, plain, black or purple silk dresses, matching mantoes and satin mules. And since none of the fans in Anne's superb collection proved appropriate for mourning, the queen arranged for a new fan in plain black silk, with delicate ebony sticks.

The first to sport gaily colored ribbons on her drab black dress, Sarah, Duchess of Marlborough, the queen's groom of the stole and senior lady of the bedchamber defied mourning even further. The duchess powdered her heavy, honey-colored hair and placed silk patches on her face.

Sarah felt entitled to extra leeway because the failure of peace talks underlined Anne's need for Marlborough to command her army and bring the war to a satisfactory close. Defying queen and duke's wishes that she stop her political lobbying vis-à-vis Anne, the duchess focused her ardent, not to say arrogant, pro–Whig arguments on persuading Anne to appoint Whig Junto Lord Orford to Prince George's position of lord high admiral. Further, Sarah seized every chance to criticize her cousin and the queen's favorite chambermaid, Abigail Masham, and what Sarah wrongly supposed but nonetheless stoutly claimed, to be Abigail's pro–Tory influence over Anne. The duchess's efforts amplified the queen's aversion to a political party she already abhorred and fanned the flames of Anne's anger at her former friend.

As a result, the queen, usually respectful of etiquette, deliberately defied it. Without consulting her a groom of the stole, as Anne normally would have done, she ordered a daily bottle of wine for a sick laundress, then raised the woman's salary. Ignoring the privileges of Sarah's office yet again, this time her role as first lady of the bedchamber, the queen hired an additional bedchamber woman—not the duchess's candidate, but, as it happened, the daughter of a woman who disliked her.

Sarah complained in public about the queen's lack of consideration.

No one thought the duchess ill-used but herself, Anne told her.

—⁂—

"You are pleased to say that nobody thinks me ill-used but myself, [the duchess riposted.] Your majesty is very wrong informed in that matter, & I can assure you my Lord Marlborough thinks so," his wife declared, for the first time bringing the duke directly into her conflict with the queen. "If he has not yet complained of it to you, it is because he has so many other things to do that are of more consequence to the public, tho none I have reason to think that are of more concern to himself."[6]

His wife's bluster notwithstanding, Marlborough tried to restrain her; he saw no advantage in further riling Anne. But the duke's advice had no effect. Sarah persisted in justifying her every action to the queen, professing her inability to understand Anne's transfer of favor from her superior self to a menial like Abigail.

The queen's reply described Sarah's seven years of harassment in detail, her attempts to convert Anne to Ultra Whiggism, her instances of bad temper and rudeness. All this had lost the duchess her sovereign's favor.

Anne's letter does not survive, but Sarah's paraphrase of salient passages does.

> She complains of my inveteracy as she calls it to poor [Abigail] Masham & says 'tis very plain I have
> nothing so much in my heart as the ruin of my cousin, & advises me for my soul's sake to lay aside

my malice. Next, she mentions the misunderstanding that has been between us, for nothing that she knows of but that she could not see with my eyes & hear with my ears.... She says I have been often several months without coming near her & when I have come again looked with all the disdain & ill humor imaginable & said a great many shocking things.

[It would be impossible for Sarah to recover Anne's] former kindnesses, but that she would always behave herself to me as the D. of Marlborough's wife & as her groom of the stole & she desires me once more not to torment her about Masham.... In the very same letter her majesty uses these remarkable words. "You have asked me once or twice if you have committed any fault that I was so changed, and I told you no, because I do not think it a crime in any one not to be of my mind."[7]

In finding this sentence remarkable the duchess showed her inability to see the difference between *what* she said to convince the queen in favor of Whigs, and *how* she said it.

—✦—

The two women now agreed to confine their contact to matters concerning the duchess's duties in the queen's household—but not before Anne asked Sarah to return all her private letters. That, the duchess mendaciously tells us, gave her the idea of printing them; for, Sarah reasoned, why be so foolish as to part with such a potent weapon. She might never publish what the queen called her "strange scrawls,"[8] but the mere threat could prove a valuable weapon.

Anne's early letters to Sarah were certainly effusive, although as certainly, well within the bounds of a style bosom friends used to address one another. But those letters, if made public twenty years later when Anne sat on the throne, would provide ample fodder for satirists, would expose the queen to innuendo and derision.

The duchess showed a few of the letters to Anne's calm and sensible physician, moderate Whig David Hamilton. The doctor quoted them to the queen. "When people are fond of one another, they say many things, however indifferent, they would not desire the world to know,"[9] she commented. Anne realized that if the letters were published in her lifetime, she would become the laughingstock of Europe. That, Hamilton thought, would gratify Sarah who "took more pleasure in justifying herself than the queen did in wearing her crown."[10]

—✦—

On the other side of the grey-green Channel, warmer weather had finally brought a welcome thaw. So, when France's tall, slender poplar trees slowly unfurled their leaves in the late spring sunshine, King Louis sent emissaries to read a special proclamation in every French city, town, and village. The king's manifesto exhorted his exhausted subjects to rally to the defense of their homeland. Louis's promise to feed soldiers stopped desertions and increased enlistment. A large and enthusiastic, if poorly trained and still somewhat hungry army gathered under the command of Marshal Villars, the only French general with enough military talent to mount a serious challenge to Marlborough.

Villars entrenched his army so well that the duke and his Austrian ally Prince Eugene decided against immediate attack; rather, they would first besiege strategic Tournai in the Spanish Netherlands. The allied armies arrived via an all-night march that took the enemy by surprise. After seizing Tournai, duke and prince turned southeast to besiege Mons, a Belgian town under French control.

The loss of Tournai and threat to Mons made the French king rethink his strategy. Loath to risk his army in all-out battle, Louis had also feared defeat would expose France to invasion, and victory would be of little value to his famine-enfeebled nation. Then Villars, who had shared the army's winter hardships, reported that further scarcity of food would result in mass desertions. The king decided to fight.

Villars deployed his army in a strong defensive position at Malplaquet Gap (a small ridge running along the border between France and the Spanish Netherlands) and the woods on either side. Marlborough planned, as at Blenheim, and Ramillies when his victory left Queen Anne without enough words to express her pleasure, to attack the two flanks, forcing the enemy to weaken its center; there the duke would deliver his knockout punch.

—m—

Both armies were told that this battle, and only this battle, would decide the war. The allied army had more men; for Queen Anne's Whig ministry convinced the house of commons to vote extra troops. Holland contributed the largest contingent ever. Eugene led an unusually strong imperial and German contingent. The French were extremely well entrenched. Both sides used heavy artillery. Fierce, often hand-to-hand fighting contested every inch of ground. When matters looked grim for the Allies, Marlborough personally led British and Prussian cavalry squadrons. A ferocious engagement ended the battle. The French were forced to retreat. The Allies were too exhausted to chase them.

Immense losses marred the allied victory; but, duke and prince had again proved the Grand Alliance's military superiority. They had driven the enemy from such a strong position that Marlborough, on inspecting the ground next day, marveled at his success. Nonetheless, the duke mourned the loss of so many brave men on both sides. In their memory he spent every available penny on care for the wounded, regardless of nationality. "I believe it the chief cause of my illness, [return of severe headaches] to see so many brave men killed with whom I have lived these eight years when we thought ourselves sure of a peace."[11] Marlborough called Malplaquet (September 11, 1709) a murdering battle.

France acknowledged defeat; but, unlike previous battles against Marlborough, could be satisfied that the army retreated in good order, battalions intact. Malplaquet proved French will, not to mention ability, (the duke had never seen them fight so well) for future battles. Malplaquet restored France's military honor, stopped invasion of its territory, and prevented the Allies from imposing harsh peace terms. King Louis could afford to reject the Whig ministry's draconian terms. He judged time now to be on his side.

Malplaquet discouraged Holland who suffered heavy losses; besides, the Dutch had little interest in backing Britain's demand of No Peace Without Spain.

Malplaquet fortified Whig resolve to push for No Peace Without Spain. That insistence and the battle's heavy losses fueled anti-war sentiment in Britain. After seven years of fighting, Queen Anne's subjects grumbled about the army policy of pressing unemployed men into service, about war taxes, (Britain paid the lion's share of allied war expenses including the funding of foreign armies) and about rising food prices. Many began to think Marlborough and Godolphin continued to wage war against the nation's interest.

Anne did not congratulate either duke or duchess on Malplaquet. "I do agree with you, [Marlborough wrote his wife,] that the queen might have taken notice to you of the victory and have shown some concern for my being safe."[12] Nor did the queen mention Marlborough's victory in front of her bedchamber ladies—among them his daughters.

"When will all this bloodshed ever end"? Anne reputedly responded to news of her army's victory at Malplaquet. Her words may have owed more to fable than fact, but they reflected her country's attitude and expressed her own.

—◠◠—

Queen Anne could do little to change her Whig ministry's view that continued war would achieve No Peace Without Spain. To attain it, to secure Spain and its empire for a grateful Hapsburg Charles, Britain needed Dutch support. Having suffered massive losses at Malplaquet, however, and with depleted treasury besides, Holland seemed ready to make a separate peace with France; for the Dutch fought mainly to win a military barrier[13] against France, and to get guarantees of commercial supremacy in the Spanish Netherlands. Peace now, would gain both.

The Whig cabinet decided that Holland must be kept happy. Hence, Britain abandoned its goal of monopoly on trade with Spanish America. And defied her ally Austria, who sought to expand into the Spanish Netherlands, to say nothing of Hapsburg Charles whom Britain backed for the Spanish throne, by offering Holland full military and economic control over the Spanish Netherlands.

Tories objected to the Barrier Treaty (October 1709) as a blow to British commercial interests and damned the ministry if it continued the war. Whigs damned the ministry were it to make peace without securing Spain for Hapsburg Charles. Since Whigs controlled both houses of parliament and supported continued war, the queen's prime minister, lord treasurer Sidney Godolphin, had no choice but to advise Anne to agree to the treaty.

—◠◠—

On a shimmering September morning Anne's preferred bedchamber woman, Abigail Masham, left London for the country, to prepare for the birth of her second child. Sarah, Duchess of Marlborough, seized on Abigail's absence to favor the queen with angry speech. Maintaining a stoic silence, Anne rose to leave the room. Sarah clapped her back against the door. The queen must and should, hear her out.

For two hours and at the top of her lungs besides, Sarah scolded her sovereign for what she, Sarah, condemned as Abigail's political influence, to say nothing of her brazen intrusion into the duchess's Kensington Palace lodgings. Sarah rued Anne's reluctance to appoint Junto Lord Orford as lord high admiral. The duchess railed against her sovereign's refusal to give Sarah an extension of her St. James's Palace apartment—the duchess felt sure public opinion would condemn Anne for denying military hero Marlborough, victor at Malplaquet, a few more small rooms in the palace. Sarah's tirade culminated with a threat to publicize, via the effusive expressions in Anne's early letters to her, what she implied were the queen's intrinsic lesbian leanings, now manifest in her lesbian liaison with Abigail. This latter accusation especially upset Anne, her grief over the death of her beloved prince still raw. Turning from the light to hide her reddened face, (the queen had always suffered from an embarrassing tendency to blush) Anne promised her torturer a written reply to all arguments.

As soon as she had curtsied herself out of the queen's presence, Sarah covered nine extra-large size sheets of stationery with an accusatory screed. It concluded by asking Anne "to admit [in] your own words ... which you should do, [that Sarah had always been] a faithful subject and friend. [For that reason, the duchess appealed to] your majesty if I have not often asked you what my fault was, for I was sure I could mend. [The queen had not replied until] one day upon such pressing you said it was that I believed you had such an intimacy with Masham."[14]

The queen remained silent. So, Sarah got her friend, Ultra Whig MP and satirist Arthur Maynwaring, to help her write a reminder. Although fulminating against Abigail, this missive focused on Anne's failure to give the duchess a valid reason for her loss of favor.

—⁂—

By this time a year had passed since Prince George's death. As Anne's first pangs of grief mellowed into a permanent and leaden ache, she resolved to free herself of Whig control. Hatred of the Junto, continual Whig pressure for further concessions, to say nothing of acrid relations with pro–Whig Sarah, made the queen receptive to her former secretary of state, the man who had initiated her into the workings of parliament during the last weeks of King William's life.

Moderate Tory Robert Harley, aptly named Robin the Trickster, returned to London from self-imposed retirement in the country after the failure of his coup attempt at the beginning of the previous year. Still an MP, Harley now connived with Tories dismayed at Marlborough and Godolphin's alliance with Whigs. At the same time, Harley intrigued with Whigs including members of the cabinet and royal household. He wanted to form a moderate ministry, a goal that appealed to Anne.

Nonetheless, she had been burned once before. A year ago, the queen had been forced to withdraw her backing of Harley in a similar undertaking—creation of a moderate ministry—because he failed to secure a strong enough position from which to withstand Marlborough and Godolphin. Hence, Anne now hesitated to support Harley. But that did not stop her from listening to his advice—or discourage him from giving it.

Harley used every method to impress his opinions on the queen. "I received yours, [his Tory cousin Abigail Masham wrote,] and desire I may not burn [it]…till I have read it to the queen, who [could use] such good instructions, and though she has had the same advice last year yet I think it cannot be too often repeated."[15]

Despite Anne's failure to follow the advice Harley gave last year, Sarah continued to paint Abigail as the all-powerful favorite who could manipulate her sovereign at will. But Abigail achieved little, if anything, in the way of political influence because the queen refused to discuss business with her maidservant. Besides, Abigail often left court for weeks on end to give birth to her children or supervise their upbringing; Anne showed no signs of longing for her return. And no evidence exists of any correspondence between the two women.

"I can't tell you what the queen has made of the advice given her in your letter, [Abigail wrote Harley,] but she heard it over and over. She keeps me in ignorance and is very reserved, does not care to tell me anything."[16]

—⁂—

Abigail's lack of power notwithstanding, Whigs resolved to wring what they could out of the perception that Anne's chambermaid controlled her. Sarah's cohort, literary light and aggressive Whig MP Arthur Maynwaring, led the charge. Whigs threatened a parliamentary address petitioning Anne to dismiss Abigail, a move not made for four hundred years when parliament forced Edward II to discharge his favorite—and male lover.

Never one to sit on the sidelines, the duchess, in a veiled threat to expose Anne and Abigail's supposed lesbian relations, told the queen about a new book currently in fashion. Featuring lesbianism, the book also included dialog between Louis XIV's mistress, Madame de Maintenon, and Abigail Masham, in which the former thanked the latter for her efforts on the French king's behalf.

The semi-invalid queen, meanwhile, decided that since Abigail had too much work, she would hire her sister (Alice Hill) as an additional bedchamber woman. Some time ago Sarah had been the first to ask that Alice be appointed to Anne's household; the duchess now took her entry as a personal affront.

The likely demise of a royal seamstress then gave the duchess a chance to defend her position. Fearing Abigail would recommend her crony for a post under Sarah's control, the duchess demanded to be consulted.

The seamstress recovered. Anne hoped she would live a long healthy life, but if not, the queen told Sarah,

> I shall hearken to nobody's recommendation but my own … that being a post that next to my bedchamber women is the nearest to my person of any of my servants, & I believe nobody, nay not even you yourself if you would judge impartially, could think it unreasonable that I should take one in a place so near my person that were agreeable to me.
>
> I know this place is reckoned under your office, but there is no office whatsoever that has that entire disposal of anything under them, but I may put in any one I please when I have a mind to it.[17]

—✠—

The duchess's reply consisted of a long, written Narrative that enumerated her services since Anne's earliest days of marriage. Full of appeals to the queen's piety and conscience, the Narrative blamed Tories, and their plots to return the Pretender, for Sarah's warnings that the queen must beware a Tory ministry—it could well threaten her life; referred to the malign influence Tory Admiral Churchill (the duchess defamed him as a Jacobite) exerted over Prince George; included copies of Anne's early letters to Sarah, to remind the queen of her former feelings for the duchess, let alone Sarah's threat to publish; plus a summary of Abigail's rise to full power—how Anne had done "extraordinary things [for a woman who combed her hair] and did the necessary offices. [Such conduct by a queen] and the very hard things she has done to Mrs. Freeman so contrary to all her professions, [gave the duchess no choice but to believe] (as all the world does) that such things can proceed from nothing but extravagant passion."[18]

The queen's only reply to Sarah's Narrative, and letters of similar ilk written at about the same time, came at the end of a brief note asking the duchess, as Anne's keeper of the privy purse, to pay for two of her purchases. "I have not yet had leisure to read all your papers but as soon as I have I will write you some answer."[19]

None came. That caused the duchess to send her husband several of Anne recent missives. He declined to say much "concerning the queen's letter, which was by no means obliging." Extremely concerned about his wife's loss of favor, not only for herself but also for its effect on his position, the duke convinced Sarah to forbear sending the queen any more letters. "If you can't regain her affections,"[20] further correspondence would prove futile.

The duke then promised Anne that Sarah's missives on politics and Abigail would stop. But that did not entirely halt the headstrong duchess. She entertained "her confidants with telling them what a praying godly idiot the queen was," to say nothing of regaling them with a spirited rendition of Maynwaring's scurrilous ballad featuring Anne and Abigail's Dark Deeds at Night. Sarah thought her friends "would keep such a secret for her."[21]

They did not.

Regardless, the queen must maintain a façade. If she dismissed the duchess, the duke would surely resign, thus precipitating a parliamentary crisis, let alone catastrophe within the Alliance. The queen did not yet feel strong enough emotionally (barely one year after her husband's death) and politically to face the duke's departure. Anne first wanted to remove hated Whigs like strident Sunderland from her cabinet but needed time to garner adequate support. So, she reiterated her willingness to keep up a friendly front if Sarah did her duties respectfully, avoided fraught subjects, and stayed away from court as much as possible.

—⁂—

Seven consecutive years of war and diplomacy had taken their toll on Queen Anne's oldest and most trusted advisor. Weary, unwell, and depressed about domestic politics, Marlborough knew that in letting Whigs dominate the government he had alienated the queen. She still sought to uphold the crown's independence, act in her country's best interests via a balanced ministry, via Moderation.

Marlborough knew his support of Whigs exposed him to the party politics he detested; knew his influence with Anne had suffered over the Sunderland appointment, never mind forcing her to dismiss Harley after his coup attempt; knew that should the queen cashier her current ministry, Tories would make sure he lost his position. And Marlborough knew Harley connived to turn the queen against him. "I am in no ways surprised that the queen did not inquire after me, [Marlborough told his wife,] for I know very well there is no more kindness."[22] The death of Prince George, who had steadfastly supported the duke, plus the acrimony between queen and duchess, made matters worse.

Marlborough, therefore, resolved to make himself independent of the throne and the perfidious political scene, to create an autonomous position as head of the Alliance before his influence evaporated at home. Further, the duke wanted to safeguard the splendid reputation he enjoyed on the Continent; show the world he still enjoyed Anne's favor; and, in view of the probable return of Tories to office, secure his military status and the lucrative offices that went with it.

Without confiding in Sarah, without consulting his oldest and closest friend, his colleague Sidney Godolphin, the duke asked Queen Anne for an unprecedented mark of favor—to appoint him captain general of her armed forces for life.

She must have time to consider, the queen replied; and she wanted to take legal advice. Actually, Marlborough's request alarmed Anne. Granting him such unparalleled, not to mention powerful, status beyond her lifetime would need an act of parliament, which, in the interest of No Peace Without Spain, Whig majorities in both houses would surely support. The result: Great Britain permanently militarized under Whig aegis, and Marlborough set outside the crown's control.

The duke, meanwhile, consulted his lawyer and talked to his friend, legal expert Cowper, moderate Whig cabinet member and keeper of the great seal. The duke's lawyer advised against requesting the captain-generalcy for life. Cowper could find no legal precedent; besides, he would never countenance such a commission, never stamp the great seal on it.

The queen consulted her senior legal authority, Whig Junto chief and eminent jurist Lord Somers, recent entrant into the cabinet as lord president of the council. Somers told the queen that making command of the army irreversible would contravene the spirit of the constitution; harm her prerogative; and, by making the military independent of civilian power, damage the nation's liberties.

Somers's counsel confirmed Anne's innate aversion to granting the duke's wish—no subject should have permanent control over the army. Somers's counsel fortified the queen's concern that the war promoted a perilous protraction of military power in British society; and his counsel earned Somers the queen's respect for putting the national interest before partisan preference. Queen Anne denied the duke's request.

—⁓—

The allied victory at Malplaquet failed to improve Marlborough's domestic political position. And rising anti-war feeling at home, not to mention Harley's use of every opening to pour censure of the duke into Anne's ear, hardly helped. Hence, despite his lawyer's advice, Cowper's opposition, and the queen's refusal, Marlborough renewed his request that she appoint him captain general for life.

The duke's request roused a storm of criticism. And gave Tories a gift. Already scheming to overthrow the ministry, Harley now had an excellent pretext for hammering home to the queen, the evils of Whig ascendancy. Tory MPs, most of them squires chafing under the onerous land tax, (main source of war funding) were already trying to topple the government via a campaign of peace and disarmament. Marlborough's request handed them the ability to claim that the duke and his Whig allies were militarists aspiring to a military dictatorship.

This time Anne refused the duke's request point-blank.

"God Almighty knows with what zeal and duty I have served you for all this many years, and all Europe as well as yourself are witnesses how far God has blessed my endeavors ever since your accession to the crown,"[23] Marlborough reproached.

Ignoring his own advice to Sarah to avoid antagonizing the queen with unnecessary criticism, the duke proceeded to insert himself squarely into his wife's personal quarrel. "For some time with the greatest mortification imaginable, [Marlborough averred, he had] observed your majesty's change from Lady Marlborough to Mrs. Masham, and the several indignities Mrs. Masham has made her suffer, of which I am much more sensible than of any misfortune that could have befallen myself."[24]

As if jumping into that battle were not enough, the duke displayed unusual indiscretion by affirming his belief in what he had been told on good authority: Abigail had assured Harley "that let my services or success be whatever they would, from thenceforward I should receive no encouragement from your majesty. [This, Abigail felt] very confident, [would] oblige me to retire."[25]

To determine how much Anne agreed with Abigail's guarantee to Harley of the duke having to retire because the queen had lost faith in him, Marlborough requested, as a "mark of your favor that my commissions might be for my life. You were pleased to judge it not proper. This made me very uneasy but no ways lessened my zeal; witness my actions in this campaign which I hope will put a happy end to this war."[26]

Marlborough concluded his letter with atypical clumsiness. He promised to leave Anne's ministry at war's end unless she recognized "the long and faithful services of Lady Marlborough. [The duke further hoped] God will bless you with the opening of your eyes, so that you may avoid the danger these people are running you into, before it be too late."[27]

—⚘—

"The illness in my eyes has hindered me so long from writing to you, that I have now four of your letters to answer," Anne replied.

"I am very sorry for the resolution you have taken of quitting my service when the war is ended," the queen wrote with marked coolness. "But I hope when you have talked with your best friends here you will be prevailed to alter it."[28]

As for the duke's dissatisfaction with Anne's conduct towards Sarah, the queen did "not love complaining," but the occasion demanded her saying that "nobody was ever so used by a friend as I have been by her ever since my coming to the crown. I desire nothing but that she should leave off teasing and tormenting me and behave herself with the decency she ought both to her friend and queen." Anne hoped the duke would prevail on his wife to comply with this wholly reasonable request. But "whatever her behavior is to me, mine to her shall always be as becomes me."[29]

Marlborough's anger "against poor Masham" did not surprise the queen because the duchess, aside from her fury against Abigail, "used her so very hardly," which Anne knew her chambermaid did not deserve. Any attempt to vindicate Abigail would be futile in the face of Sarah's extreme bias; but, the duke wronged Abigail "most extremely [in blaming her for Anne's refusal to appoint him captain general for life.] Upon my word she knows nothing of it. [The queen's decision had been based on her] own thoughts."[30]

In a separate letter written at about the same time, that dealt with business matters, the queen briefly referred to Marlborough's "uneasiness at my refusing the mark of favor you desired. [She still thought it not] for your service or mine to do a thing of that nature; however," if, when the duke returned to England, Anne wrote with manifest lack of enthusiasm, "you still continue in the same mind I will comply with your desires."[31]

Lukewarm agreement plus deferral of a final decision spared Anne further painful confrontation with her oldest and most trusted counselor. In addition, the nation's and her own war weariness, plus the fluid political situation, led the queen to hope she might yet be spared the distressing eventuality of having to give Marlborough a definitive No.

—⚘—

Although too grief-stricken immediately after Prince George's death to resist Junto pressure for cabinet positions the queen had, nonetheless, summoned enough stamina to withstand one particularly painful Whig demand. Anne refused to appoint the man she loathed for having led parliamentary censure of George's admiralty management, to replace her cherished husband as lord high admiral.

Blunt, able Junto Lord Orford had been one of the Immortal Seven who invited William of Orange to England; formerly Admiral Russell, victor at the naval battle of La Hogue, (1692) which routed a French invasion fleet carrying the Pretender to Scotland, Orford had for months been jockeying for position. His naval experience, the support of naval officers and admiralty officials as well as numerous and devoted family connections sitting in the Commons had always constituted, and still did constitute, an effective resource for the Whig leadership.

Commanding a solid majority in parliament, and having backed the ministry all year, Whig leaders insisted on Orford becoming head of the admiralty (with a seat in the cabinet). Anne's aversion to admitting a Whig to the only government department that party had not yet penetrated, gave Godolphin enough leeway to evade Whig pressure—until Whigs insisted that their continued support depended on Orford's appointment.

The queen appealed to Marlborough.

He wanted to avoid any more disputes with her.

But the duke swallowed his dislike of Orford and backed him, if apathetically, in return for Whig support. This tepid stance earned Marlborough reproaches from his wife and his best friend, Sidney Godolphin. The duke defended himself by citing his respect for the queen and gratitude for past favors. Unconvinced, Sarah and Sidney's censure intensified. The duke gave in. He sent draft letters to duchess and treasurer until they agreed on the exact wording of Marlborough's letter to Anne. As she had often done before, the queen took his advice.

Whigs then pushed for their members to fill the admiralty's six-man governing board. Anne balked. The duke mediated. Compromise prevailed.

Orford's appointment proved especially galling for the queen. Her husband's most vocal and effective critic had succeeded in displacing him; and just as bad, a Junto lord filled the position traditionally assigned to a trusted member of the royal family. Orford's promotion denoted defeat for Anne's defense of the royal right to select ministers; the hated Junto had again succeeded in violating her prerogative.

On a blustery November day when ragged low clouds raced across the sky and a determined rain slanted over the steel grey Thames, Queen Anne opened parliament. Her speech, which Godolphin had written and Anne's Whig cabinet approved, referred to Malplaquet as a most remarkable victory, and suggested that since it made France more vulnerable to invasion than ever before, the enemy would prove more amenable to making peace. But many in parliament noted that the queen's pure and pleasing contralto lacked its customary conviction—connoting that Anne might not necessarily concur with her cabinet's rosy predictions.

The queen indeed felt she had been reduced to a cypher, something she had vowed from the start of her reign never to become. Four members of the five-man Junto were in Anne's cabinet. Two other Whigs held important ministerial posts. Whigs also filled junior positions and had taken control of key house of commons committees. But Whigs gave up demands to have Abigail Masham and three other royal servants dismissed because the queen threatened to make her opposition public—that would expose frosty relations between Anne and her ministers, a revelation Whigs wanted to avoid. They had dented Queen Anne's prerogative, but her favor still counted.

"There is no one party, nay not both of them, can stand against the queen's frowns."[32]

Fifteen

"We four must never part"

"Whoever of the Whigs thinks I am to be hectored or frightened into compliance tho I am a woman are mighty mistaken in me."[1]—Queen Anne

When the cold, clear light of a weak winter sun launched 1710, Queen Anne's support for the War of the Spanish Succession wavered. Disappointed at the failure of peace talks in the previous spring, distressed over so many losses at the ensuing Battle of Malplaquet, the queen shared her subjects' war weariness. Anne wanted peace, but a peace beneficial for Great Britain. She believed only her captain general, the Duke of Marlborough, commander in chief of the anti–French Grand Alliance army, capable of achieving the victory essential to that peace.

Whigs and their City friends backed the war and the duke. Yet, the queen chafed under the control of her Whig cabinet. Anne detested the five-man Whig leadership; the Junto had ripped into her royal prerogative to select ministers, forced themselves into her ministry. Their most raucous member, Earl Sunderland, had been the first to rupture Anne's defenses; later, Junto chief Lord Somers; then Earl Wharton, whose atheism she deplored no less than his libertine lifestyle. Most humiliating of all, her cherished husband's nemesis, Lord Orford, replaced him as lord high admiral. As well, the queen resented Whig pressure to admit their associates to every echelon of Church and government. But, if Whigs were to leave her ministry and Marlborough, too, the Alliance might crumble, the City collapse.

Anne wanted a moderate, all-party ministry. It would enable her to preserve the crown's independence and keep out of the clutches of ruthless party extremists.

—⁂—

This scenario provided fertile ground for the machinations of moderate Tory Robert Harley, not for nothing known as Robin the Trickster. Gunning to become head of the ministry, Harley knew Anne's support would be crucial. He shared her aversion to a Junto ministry, to say nothing of the limitless Whig lust for power. Like Anne sincerely religious; like Anne, Harley wanted a moderate government. Still an MP after his failed coup attempt two years ago, Harley held no other office. The queen sometimes sought counsel from this expert in parliamentary machinery who had tutored her about the legislature, served her well as secretary of state.

Harley aimed to attract some Whigs and join them with temperate Tories to form a moderate government. Anne wanted to jettison Whig ability to force her hand by presenting a united front but wanted to retain Whig ministers she respected.

A canny politician, intuitively able to discern what motivated an individual, Robin the Trickster cobbled together political support. He wooed tentative Whigs, those who sought more power, or disliked the Junto. He courted Tories by openly advocating peace and disarmament—Tory policy since failure of the recent peace talks for which Tories, like most people, blamed Whigs. Tory squires resented the hefty wartime taxes that fell most heavily on them; and with memories of civil war and military rule still ripe, feared Marlborough, commander of a strong army, could be tempted to become Britain's military dictator.

His failed coup taught Harley that Marlborough must be included in any ministry; moreover, the duke would not join a cabinet Harley headed. Hence, Harley decided to maneuver Marlborough out—but in a timely fashion. For, the duke's removal would energize France, disturb the coming (1710) campaign, and tempt Holland into a separate peace. Harley knew the queen would countenance nothing but a good peace for Britain. So, Marlborough must stay for now; Harley would, meanwhile, chip away at him via propaganda, and undermine the duke with Anne by convincing her that he, Harley, could be as effective a first minister and lord treasurer as the current incumbent and Marlborough's ally, Sidney Godolphin.

Harley spread propaganda via the numerous, eagerly read[2] pamphlets and newspapers proliferating during the Age of Anne following the end of press censorship in the previous reign. His publicists painted Marlborough as waging war for personal gain— most egregiously—he prolonged Malplaquet so that more officers would be killed and he could sell their commissions; (in fact, the duke had banned selling commissions to forestall promotion of inept officers) Whigs wanted war because they and their City friends benefited from the resulting accrual of government debt; the Duke and Duchess of Marlborough had enslaved Queen Anne.

—〰—

A death in the army's upper ranks played into Harley's hands. He urged the queen to assert her right to make appointments and at the same time, affirm her ultimate control over the military. Recalling her alarm when Marlborough, not many months ago, asked her to designate him captain general for life, Anne took Harley's advice. Without consulting Marlborough, she designated a new lieutenant of the Tower (a position in the duke's power of appointment). And the queen promoted Jack Hill, brother of her favorite maidservant Abigail Masham, as colonel of the dead man's regiment.

Hill's appointment posed a singular challenge. True, he had fought bravely in recent battles, but Hill had less field experience than other, longer-serving and higher-ranking officers. However, the right connections still counted in army promotions, and this constituted only the second one Anne had made, so she stood well within her prerogative.

Marlborough had no great opinion of Hill's ability. His promotion would, the duke wrote his sovereign, not only be "a great mortification [to him, but also] a real prejudice to her service. [Besides, the] showing of so extraordinary and partial a favor to a brother of Mrs. Masham's was in effect setting up a banner for all unreasonable discontented people in the army to fly to."[3]

"Nothing, [the Duchess of Marlborough, not without reason, tells us] could be more disagreeable to the duke than" Anne's choice of Hill. Nothing would tend more to diminish his authority in the army, and, thus, at home as well. For Marlborough's yielding would "sow discontent among the officers" and open a door for his opponents to enter the army. The duke's non-compliance or grudging compliance would provide an "excellent pretense for grievous complaints."[4]

—⁓—

Angry at Anne's refusal to reconsider, the duke left London to join his wife at Windsor, where she liked staying at the charming Lodge. (Early in her reign, the queen appointed the duchess lifetime Ranger of Windsor park; the position came with residence rights to the Lodge.) Its intimate confines allowed Sarah's friend, satirist and Ultra Whig MP Arthur Maynwaring, to buttonhole Marlborough. In any case sure Hill's promotion proved Abigail Masham's ascendancy over Anne, the duke let Maynwaring convince him that Abigail's removal must be made a condition of Marlborough's remaining in office. Maynwaring and the duke's son-in-law, Ultra Whig cabinet minister Sunderland, then arranged that the house of commons petition Anne to dismiss Abigail.

Setting the Commons against her enraged the queen. Parliamentary meddling in her household outdid any of William and Mary's attempts to have her dismiss a favored lady-in-waiting (Sarah Marlborough). Further, the sole precedent for such legislative intrusion, especially galling in view of Sarah's groundless charge that Anne and Abigail were lovers, had occurred four hundred years before over a king's favorite—his male lover.

The queen waged coordinated political warfare over her right, as an Englishwoman, to decide about her bedchamber personnel. Whig demands to dismiss Abigail signified an inexcusable invasion of her private life. Anne told her supporters to impress on each MP who employed servants, (i.e., everyone) that limiting her ability to select personal servants affected her as it would any British subject. The queen's prime minister and treasurer, Sidney Godolphin, plus Whig Junto chief and cabinet member Somers, and moderate Whig cabinet member Cowper supported her. As did Tory luminaries, some of them not always friendly to Anne, like her uncle, Earl Rochester. The queen canvassed nobles and gentry from both parties, "persuading them with tears in her eyes to show their adherence to her service by opposing the motion."[5] Anne made sure these interviews got broad circulation. She also spoke to Maynwaring with unusual bluntness.

The queen's efforts, plus lack of unanimous cabinet support, caused Marlborough to drop the parliamentary address about Abigail. Anne withdrew Jack Hill's promotion.

To eliminate the risk of more distress from conflict with Marlborough, the queen ordered him to The Hague before the opening of the campaign season would naturally take the duke there. He should participate in the upcoming round of peace talks, which again, were to founder on the rocks of Whig insistence on No Peace Without Spain—French King Louis XIV must use force of arms to drive his grandson from the Spanish throne.

Nobody knew better than the duchess, given her experience during the joint monarchs' reign, how fiercely Anne could defend her right to choose her servants. Yet, Sarah insisted that this latest episode "exposed … the queen's misfortune … to be the talk of all courts and countries for so wrong a thing as having such a fondness for a bedchamber woman."[6]

Hence, before the duke left London, Anne extracted his promise that Sarah would avoid court as much as possible, and, as well, cease sending letters on politics or Abigail. The duchess, therefore, declared her intent to retire to the country the better to focus on writing her memoirs—a prospect hardly likely to afford the queen much comfort since the duchess's story would certainly be self-serving.

—⁓—

On a grey winter day, with no wind to stir the heavy clouds and whip the bare tree branches, Londoners packed into their city's largest church, to hear a celebrated clergyman deliver the Sunday morning sermon. Imposing Oxford theologian Dr. Henry Sacheverell preached in St. Paul's Cathedral at the invitation of London's Tory lord mayor.

Tories had, for some years, been fearmongering about The Church in Danger, a mantra conceived to counter Whig influence. For Whig leaders lobbied to have moderate rather than high Church prelates fill senior clerical positions. Rumors then spread that the Whig ministry and Whig parliamentary majority meant to repeal the Test Act, thereby breaking the hold Church of England members had on all public offices, even the universities, by opening them to nonconformists.

Sacheverell had been preaching hatred of dissenters and Whigs with dramatic effect in prominent churches throughout the land. He denounced low Church men; (moderate Tory and Whig clerics) moral degeneracy; intellectual arrogance; (rationalism, atheism) and deplored what he called Britain's alien (Whig) government, which paid mere lip service to Church and gentry interests while gagging high Church clerics and Tory squires.

Thundering from the pulpit in St. Paul's, Sacheverell accused toleration of putting The Church in Danger. Enemies Within—False Brethren—used moderation and occasional conformity to destroy the established order. Sacheverell belittled the 1688 Revolution settlement and thus, by inference, the Hanoverian succession. He insulted prime minister Godolphin; suggested that believers in rationalism and atheism like the Duchess of Marlborough weakened the Anglican church as well as the British constitution; charged Whigs with republican leanings and with offending the queen whose divine hereditary right to the throne they denied for the sole purpose of getting her in their grasp.

Sacheverell had his sizzling sermon printed (at his own expense) despite lacking the necessary license. And in an affront to the Whig majority in both national and London governments, ordered reprints. One hundred thousand copies soon sold out; more circulated to every corner of the realm.

—m—

Alarmed at Sacheverell's riveting effect on public opinion, Queen Anne's Whig cabinet resolved to stop the firebrand cleric from becoming a dangerous agitator. They would impeach him for railing against Revolution principles.

A swift trial for treason, before parliament, resulting in a deterrent sentence would, the cabinet reasoned, calm clerical fury, not to say fright, as well as satisfy unprecedented public interest. Sacheverell's conviction would, furthermore, affirm religious toleration; justify the Revolution settlement and Protestant succession; cast doubt on Tory loyalty to the queen and Hanoverian succession; and taint high Church clerics plus their Tory cohorts with the charge of being secret Jacobites. Above all, a guilty verdict would fortify the Whig ministry. Because everyone blamed it for something; for high grain prices due to the previous year's hard winter; for the flood of Protestant refugees who were (supposedly) draining the economy; for heavy war taxes; for French piracy that damaged commerce; for failure of the victory at Malplaquet to bring peace; and for Whigs' No Peace Without Spain, which prolonged the war. Consequently, condemnation of Sacheverell would constitute a Whig triumph and curtail Tory momentum.

Did the legitimacy of Britain's monarchy rest on heredity right or parliamentary sanction? Impeachment centered on that question. Whigs said James II's breach of his basic contract with the English people (setting himself above the law; deserting his country in the face of foreign invasion) justified their rejecting him; hence, William and Mary, and Anne, owed their crowns to parliament. To fortify their case, let alone prove Anne's legality as a parliamentary monarch vis-à-vis her Catholic half-brother's hereditary claim, Whigs declared the charge against the legitimacy of James's son a convenient lie created to justify the 1688 Revolution.

Anne disparaged Whigs for discarding the warming pan theory which, by now, she judged as at least a useful piece of anti–Jacobite propaganda. But the queen agreed with her Whig ministers that Sacheverell deserved a penalty for his sermon since such incendiary conduct must not be condoned.

When pressed to voice personal judgment about punishment, Anne refused. "I was with the queen last night on purpose to speak to her about Dr. Sacheverell," the queen's chambermaid, Abigail Masham, reported to her cousin Robert Harley. Abigail asked if Anne "let people know her mind in the matter. She said, no, she did not meddle one way or other."[7] But Queen Anne favored mild punishment.

—⚋—

To Junto surprise, the Commons rejected holding Sacheverell's trial in their house. Scenting potential disaster, prime minister Godolphin sought to drop the case; but Ultra Whig Sunderland convinced the cabinet to make an example of Sacheverell. He must stand trial for an insulting and disloyal sermon that questioned the legality of queen, ministry, Revolution, and Protestant succession. The Lords agreed to have the trial in their house.

Two thousand spectators from all classes crammed into gothic Westminster Hall. Members of parliament sat on nine tiered benches built along the hall's left-hand side, bishops in the front row. Lesser gentry occupied similar seats on the right, ladies in front. Rows of peers sat in the center; the rest of the audience sat on specially built scaffolding.

To the left and slightly behind the lord chancellor and twelve judges stood a custombuilt, canopied box for the queen and her ladies-in-waiting. Anne attended the entire three-week trial. In like fashion to Lords debates, her presence curbed the intensity of partisan rhetoric.

Absorbed in the opening arguments, the seated queen omitted to give her ladies, standing in attendance behind her, leave to sit. After a couple of hours on their feet in the enclosed box, some ladies signaled senior lady-in-waiting Sarah Marlborough to request Anne's consent to sit. Sarah whispered her wish. The queen nodded. To forestall claims that she insulted the queen by sitting, Sarah asked Anne to repeat her permission for all to hear. The queen promptly complied. But the Duchess of Somerset, Best Bred and Best Born Lady in England, who had defied King William to rent Syon House to Princess Anne during her exile from court, remained standing. This, Sarah took as an insult aimed at her; she accused Elizabeth Somerset of standing to make it seem as if Sarah sat without the queen's leave.

—⚋—

"Invidious Whigs, since you have made your boast,
That you a Church of England priest will roast,
Blame not the mob for having a desire
With Presbyterian tubs to light a fire."[8]

Anne's subjects gave vent to their anti-government feelings. A huge and rowdy mob daily turned out to cheer Sacheverell's coach enroute to and from Westminster Hall. Reveling in this unique notoriety, the tall, elegant, and youthful cleric strode confidently into the Hall while his smartly liveried footmen strewed coins amongst the adoring crowds.

They booed and insulted Whig ministers, roughed-up any hapless passerby who failed to doff his hat and salute Sacheverell with a hearty God Bless You. But whenever the queen appeared, cheering throngs surrounded her chair shouting "God bless your majesty; we hope you're for Sacheverell."[9]

Pro-Sacheverell mobs soon turned to violence and arson. They torched and looted buildings in central London. Several people died. Constables were ineffective. Fearing the horde would turn on their houses next, ministers decided to act. But they faced a quandary: no time existed to raise the militia; few regular troops were readily available except those on reserve at Whitehall (seat of government) or on guard duty at St. James's Palace (Anne's residence). If those guards were removed from the palace, mobs could easily sack it.

In his official capacity as secretary of state, Sunderland informed the queen. She blanched and began to tremble. But instantly replied.

QUEEN: My horse and foot guards are at the ministry's disposal.
SUNDERLAND: Madam, do you realize that will leave you unprotected?
QUEEN: God will guard me.

Military discipline and hard work soon suppressed the Sacheverell riots without a shot and only few casualties. Nonetheless, almost a hundred rioters were thrown in jail, soldiers patrolled the streets, and London did not return to normal until the trial ended.

The Lords took ten days to reach a verdict. An extremely narrow majority voted with the government to declare Sacheverell guilty. Another day of debate resulted in a light sentence: three years suspension from the pulpit; copies of all his sermons destroyed.

Sentence and verdict signified defeat for the Whig government. Tories exulted. London streets filled with ecstatic crowds. Queen Anne personally ordered civilian and military authorities to restore calm.

—⟋⟍⟍—

The Sacheverell affair dismayed Sarah, Duchess of Marlborough. Aghast at the outpouring of public support for Tories, angry at losing the queen's favor, annoyed over the Sacheverell trial seating episode, the duchess asked that once the war ended, Anne would let her resign and appoint her daughters to her offices at court—which, Sarah claimed, the queen had promised.

Anne frowned on the Marlboroughs' "silly and imprudent [eldest daughter, Henrietta Godolphin, for having lost her] "reputation" over an affair with the poet Congreve, let alone bearing his daughter; the queen disliked her namesake, "cunning and dangerous" Ultra Whig Anne Sunderland for herself as well as her husband; and thought Mary Montagu worst of all because she exactly resembled "her mother."[10]

Regardless, the queen said she had promised Sarah's court places to her daughters if the duchess predeceased her, not if Sarah resigned. Anne then declared the subject closed.

Sarah demanded "a private hour [with Anne. She had heard on] good authority [that the queen had been told] very false and malicious stories [about her,] and some instances were named of vile inventions that had never entered into my thoughts."[11] These "thousand lies" forced Sarah "to go about to clear myself."[12]

The duchess must not "trouble [herself to stay] a minute longer [in London than] you have a mind to on my account, [Anne replied. Whatever Sarah had to say could as easily be done] in a letter, and more to your ease as well as mine. [Sarah should] gratify" herself by going to the country when she wished, and let the queen know her thoughts "in writing. [Anne promised to answer] without delay."[13]

The duchess insisted on a personal interview; what she had to say would need no reply. Anne gave in. Then, weary and ailing, the queen changed her mind—her health "so absolutely [needed the] refreshment of air and a little quiet after the fatigues"[14] she had undergone during the past months.

Hence, Anne decided, if her gout would allow, to leave London for Kensington Palace where she meant to spend as much time as possible for the next three days. Bearing in mind that Sarah's communication could be "as well writ as said, [the queen again asked the duchess to put her] thoughts in writing."[15]

To forestall receiving "another harsh letter"[16] from the queen, Sarah followed her to Kensington, vowing to wait on her mistress every day until Anne granted her a private meeting. She assured the queen that "what she had to say would not create any dispute or uneasiness, relating only to the clearing herself from some things which she had heard had very wrongfully been laid to her charge, and could have no consequences either in obliging her majesty to answer, or to see her oftener than would be easy to her."[17]

Note: The queen would not be obliged to answer.

—⟋⟍⟍—

Illness and pregnancies had aged forty-five-year-old Anne prematurely, coarsened her once comely figure, turned her into a semi-invalid; gout had reddened and swollen Anne's once slender white hands so that she often found it hard to hold a pen. Spa waters, remedies like oil of millipedes, quinine, laudanum, bleeding, and cupping failed to cure the queen's gout. Hence, she must live a sedentary life—no more hunting on horseback or taking her dogs for a brisk walk along the pleasant paths she and George had installed through Kensington's planted acres.

Sarah found fodder for her derisive tongue in the queen's physical debility, although to do her justice, the duchess, unlike some, did not blame Anne's obesity on over indulgence in food and drink; in fact, Sarah said the queen ate and drank only in the modest amounts her doctors recommended. Still, the duchess could barely bring herself to mention Anne without insult. Letters to friends, like pro–Whig satirist Maynwaring and the queen's prime minister Sidney Godolphin, condemned Anne's stupidity, bogus piety, and lesbianism. Sarah entertained friends with stories about the queen's inanity, mocked her religious devotion, and gave a lively musical rendition of Maynwaring's slanderous ballad about the queen's supposed lesbian love for her maidservant Abigail Masham.

On Good Friday, (April 6, 1710) as a fresh wind propelled cotton-wool clouds across the rain-washed sky, Sarah succeeded in seeing Anne in her private parlor. This cozy room featured a handsome stucco ceiling; yellow damask tapestry with a foliage pattern adorned the walls and covered sofa and chairs; several small oak-paneled tables conveniently placed for tea, cards, or writing stood about the room. It opened onto a lawn with trees and flowers; an orchard stretched beyond.

The duchess started to speak. The queen interrupted: "whatever you have to say, you may put it in writing." Sarah went on talking. Anne turned her face away.

> SARAH: "There is a thousand lies made of me, which are so ridiculous that I should never have thought it necessary to go about to clear myself of what never entered my head.... I do assure your majesty ... there is several things.... I have heard has been told to [you] that I have said of you, that I am no more capable of, than I am of killing my children."
> ANNE: "Without doubt there were many lies told."
> SARAH: Of what, specifically, have I been accused? I want to clear myself.
> ANNE: I do not wish to name gossips, or repeat tittle-tattle. One of your recent letters says you seek only to vindicate yourself and need no reply.' "You desired no answer and should have none."[18]

The queen knew she could not match Sarah in verbal sparring, especially Sarah in full spate. Always a woman of few words, Anne took refuge in repeating "you desired no answer and should have none," as the simplest way out of a stressful meeting she had tried hard to avoid. Besides, eight years of experience had taught the queen that expressing her opinions had no effect on Sarah other than to rouse her temper. Far better, therefore, to avoid further painful acrimony. Anne moved towards the door.

Uncontrollable tears stopped Sarah from "speaking for some time. At length she recovered and appealed to the queen, in the vehemence of her concern, whether she might still have not been happy in her majesty's favor, if she could have contradicted or dissembled, her real opinion of men, or things." The duchess then reiterated her innocence of any malice towards Anne, begging her to reveal what she had been told about Sarah only so that she could clear herself. "You desired no answer and you shall have none,"[19] the queen repeated.

This went on for some time, one woman refusing to speak, the other talking through her tears. Sarah then "reproached [Anne] for above an hour with her own and her family's services, in so loud and shrill a voice, that the footman at the bottom of the backstairs could hear her.... The queen, seeing her so outrageous, got up, to have gone out of the room; the duchess clapped her back against the door, and told her she should hear her out, for that was the least favor she could do her, in return for having set and kept the crown upon her head."[20]

Faced with the queen's refusal to be drawn into an altercation, the overwrought duchess expressed confidence that "her majesty would suffer, either in this world or the next, for such an instance of inhumanity. [Anne quietly replied]: that will be to myself."[21]

Sarah "flounced out of the room and said she did not care if she never saw her more; to which the queen replied very calmly, that she thought the seldomer the better."[22]

So ended the last meeting between Anne and the woman she once swore she could not live without.

—⁂—

The duchess must go. The duke must stay. The beneficial peace Queen Anne wanted could be reached only by continuing the war. Despite her wish to exchange Whig diktat for the moderate ministry Robert Harley promised, Anne thus resolved to move cautiously.

Riding the crest of the pro–Tory groundswell released by thė Sacheverell affair, Harley coveted full power, and at once. Aiming to replace Godolphin as lord treasurer and first minister, Harley knew that first, he must shatter the queen's confidence in Marlborough. Hence, Harley came around to her viewpoint—government change should be gradual.

He saw Anne several times, albeit secretly, like all non-ministers the queen consulted from time to time. Sarah and her Whig friends insisted that Tory Abigail Masham, the queen's favorite chambermaid, worked hand-in-hand with her cousin Harley to manipulate the queen. Abigail's actual function consisted of passing Anne's letters summoning Harley, to under-gardeners who delivered them; then leading Harley up the backstairs to visit the queen. Indeed, Anne controlled her maid, not the reverse. For although Abigail "had a great deal of discourse with the queen [and] desired her to let me see you, [Abigail wrote Harley, Anne] would not consent to that … she is angry with me and said I was in a passion [because Anne appointed two moderate Whigs to senior clerical posts] perhaps I might speak a little too warm but who can help that when one sees plainly she is giving her best friends up to the rage of their enemies."[23]

Consulting with Harley when she sent for him—yes. Constantly having to hear her maid spouting Tory propaganda—no. Anne withheld "consent [for weeks, making Abigail] very uneasy to see"[24] Harley.

—m—

Harley managed to cobble together a coalition. Its core consisted of protégés who left office with him when his coup attempt failed; Ultra Tory leaders who disliked Harley's moderation but joined him to regain political power; and most crucially, three moderate Whig landed magnates—the Dukes of Argyll, Somerset, and Shrewsbury—who had what Harley lacked—open access to the queen.[25]

Charming Shrewsbury, King of Hearts, member of the Denmarks' Cockpit Circle and one of The Seven who had invited William of Orange to England, had always favored a moderate ministry (he declined to join Anne's first cabinet because it included too many Tories). Since returning from self-imposed exile at Rome, Shrewsbury had several times fulfilled the queen's request for advice; and she liked his droll Italian duchess. For years close to Marlborough and Godolphin, Shrewsbury opposed the Junto and faulted Whigs for failing to make peace a year ago. He, Harley, and Anne agreed that her ministers should be above party, should govern through her favor as representatives of the queen's mostly moderate subjects.

On her own initiative and without consulting her cabinet or prime minister Godolphin, the queen dismissed her lord chamberlain, one of three top household positions carrying cabinet rank, and appointed Shrewsbury. His selection signaled Anne's move from Junto to moderate Whigs willing to work with Harley.

The queen judged her first step in ministerial change to suffice for the present. She had no intention of trading Junto control for Tory tyranny.

Anne refused any action that might make Marlborough resign; for that, the queen knew, would not bring Britain closer to the peace she sought. Nonetheless, Shrewsbury's appointment "gave great alarm, [for everybody] concluded that a total change of the ministry would quickly follow."[26]

—m—

On a hot, still May morning, while lilac plumes, stately tulips, and forget-me-nots shimmered in the blue haze, news of Shrewsbury's imminent appointment surprised Anne's prime minister. Horse racing enthusiast Godolphin, seeking distraction from politics, had gone to Newmarket to attend the races. He returned to London at once. And confronted the queen with: Harley and his cadre wanted peace at any price; by appointing

Shrewsbury, who voted against the government at Sacheverell's trial, Anne invited France to foist the Pretender on Britain. The queen did not reply. Godolphin requested consent to resign. No. Godolphin acquiesced.

Anne's next move consisted of dismissing her despised secretary of state, Junto member and Ultra Whig Sunderland. Shrewsbury and Harley supported her.

Discharging Marlborough's son-in-law would damage the duke's position as commander in chief abroad and humiliate him at home, Godolphin warned. Marlborough had too much sense to resign over such a minor matter, answered Anne; besides, he and Godolphin both knew how much, how often, Sunderland had angered her. A long argument ensued. Consequently, the queen agreed that Godolphin could notify the duke before she officially cashiered Sunderland.

Shrewsbury's "consideration for you, and the fear of justly *choquing* [shocking] you, has been the only reason that ... hindered" the Sunderland business from concluding, Godolphin wrote. So, Marlborough should tell Shrewsbury that Sunderland's dismissal "might not only affect [the duke personally but would certainly render him] incapable of being of any use afterwards, either where you are, [with the army in the Netherlands] or with the Dutch,] who would [not fail to take care of themselves, by making their own terms. [Marlborough must write that he] thought it necessary to say this to.... Shrewsbury for the queen's sake; [for, anything Godolphin said to her] of this kind ... would be imputed to ... my partiality."[27]

The duke answered Godolphin with a letter to be given to Anne. Marlborough asked the queen to defer Sunderland's dismissal until the campaign closed at year end. "Then she may have the winter before her to take measures with the allies for the command of this army, on which, in a very great measure, depends not only the welfare of England, but of all Europe. This is what I beg, in reward for all my faithful services."[28]

The queen failed to "see why.... Marlborough's letter should make me alter my resolution, unless I could agree with him, that I had done him hardships, [appointing a new lieutenant of the Tower without consulting the duke, and Jack Hill, later rescinded] which I am not conscious.... I have. [Certainly, removing a son-in-law from] his office may be a mortification ... but must the fate of Europe depend on that; [must Sunderland] be gratified in all his desires, and I not in so reasonable a thing, as parting with a man whom I took into my service [with the greatest] uneasiness ... whose behavior to me has been so wrong, [a man] obnoxious to all people, except a few."[29]

Godolphin said he would resign if Marlborough did. Anne appealed to her treasurer's patriotism, plus Godolphin's concern for his close friend's reputation. "I have no thoughts of taking the Duke of Marlborough from the head of the army. If he and you should do so wrong a thing ... as to desert my service, what confusion might happen must lie at your doors, and you alone would be answerable, and nobody else. But I hope you will both consider better of it."[30]

They did.

—◊—

The queen thought Sunderland's exit need not jar the ministry. She wanted to keep Godolphin, as well as Whig ministers like moderate Cowper and Junto chief Somers whom she had grown to respect; indeed, Anne reassured both men that moderation remained her governing principle. That satisfied them.

It did not satisfy the duchess. Her son-in-law's imminent dismissal prompted Sarah to re-enter the lists. She favored the queen with an eight page, closely-scrawled diatribe. It stressed Anne's unkindness to her; deplored Sunderland's ouster as an insult to both Marlboroughs, let alone a blow to queen and country since his son-in-law's dismissal could easily drive the duke to resign. An account of his services plus Sarah's zeal and value followed; then a reminder of Anne's former kindness to them with copies of Princess Anne's letters written at the acme of her affection for the duchess, as well as a copy of the queen's joyful letter to Marlborough after Blenheim, as proof. The duchess blamed her disgrace on her forthright pro–Whig opinions; and reminded Anne that Whigs had, after all, put her on the throne. Sarah blamed Abigail for all past, present, and future trouble, and accused the queen of being so afraid to lose her favorite bedchamber woman, that she rewarded her loyal friends with ingratitude and rash conduct. Furthermore, many people "had several passions, & if, instead of disguising your last, [Abigail] you had said plainly you did love her but that you would never be unjust to me, it had been a short business & you would have saved yourself a great deal of trouble. But instead of that you have said there was no such thing, & then let her affront me."[31] Prince George, declared the duchess in a final thrust, would never have let his wife surround herself with the sort of people she now meant to do.

> Having had assurances from yourself & the Duke of Marlborough just before he went into Holland that you would never speak to me of politics or mention Masham's name again, [Anne replied,] I was very much surprised at receiving a long letter upon both, but I shall trouble you with a very short answer, looking upon it to be a continuation of the ill usage I have so often met with, which shows me very plainly what I am to expect for the future.... I do not return the letters, knowing they can be of no use to you but must desire all my strange scrawls be sent back to me, it being impossible they can now be agreeable to you.[32]

The duchess instantly replied with another insulting expostulation. It ended by imploring Anne to defer Sunderland's dismissal until peace had been signed, or the campaign closed. The queen's reply repeated her request that Sarah return her "strange scrawls." The duchess refused. This last exchange solidified not only Anne's decision to get rid of Sarah, but also decreased her inclination to listen to Marlborough on the subject of Sunderland.

When early English summer beamed its brief, entrancing smile that erased memories of fog, downpour, and gale the queen rejected Harley and Shrewsbury's candidates to replace Sunderland. Anne chose the diligent, reliable, moderate Tory Earl of Dartmouth, son of a Jacobite, as her new secretary of state.

—m—

Sunderland's dismissal stoked Sarah's fury. She renewed the idea of publishing Anne's early letters. Horrified at his duchess's conduct vis-à-vis the queen, Marlborough begged her to lie low, do nothing without first consulting him. But unstoppable Sarah had found a direct conduit to the queen.

Scion of minor Scottish nobility, educated at the Continent's finest medical schools, David Hamilton had already established a large and lucrative practice in London when his fame in obstetrics and gynecology brought him to the queen's notice. Calm and common-sensical, Hamilton rose rapidly in her confidence, professionally as well as personally. For although a Whig, Hamilton abhorred party fervor, although a dissenter he felt profoundly Christian. Ahead of his time as a psychologist, Hamilton advised his royal patient to avoid worry since it exacerbated her gout by eroding her spirits and weakening her nerves.

Perfectly placed to transmit information to the queen, Hamilton provided the duchess with an opening. She asked him to advise Anne of her intent to publish. Her letters, Hamilton told the queen, could be used to prove "breaches of promise [and other] asseverations [damaging to her good name. For, a quarrel] between a prince and a favorite" did not equate with a quarrel between two private persons. The former kind of quarrel would "spread through all countries, [which could very well tarnish Anne's universally and] so justly acquired ... reputation for piety, sense, and good nature."[33]

She had so often tried to mollify Sarah, said the queen, but in vain. That could be "remedied by not provoking [the duchess in the] method [of her dismissal, not] putting her out by herself, [but waiting until Marlborough left office, which, the doctor suggested, would be] much more acceptable"[34] to Sarah.

Anne's readiness to listen to Hamilton because she knew he put her health before everything else, Sarah's use of Hamilton's access to the queen, and the doctor's tact and patience, made him chief mediator in the delicate matter of getting the duchess to resign without causing a major kerfuffle. In fact, Hamilton convinced Anne to keep the duchess until Marlborough returned from campaigning at year end, for who could possibly have the ability to restrain Sarah, but her husband.

—⁂—

On a golden summer Sunday, London basked in warm sunshine under a clear blue sky as Queen Anne attended a service at the Chapel Royal. Looking "tolerably fresh, though she often suffers, especially from the gout, [Anne] walked with great ceremony up the center aisle into a seat near the altar.... Most of her retinue preceded her, a sword and four great scepters with crowns being carried in front of her. Then came the queen with her *dames d'honneur* behind her."[35]

Royal pomp and Sunday calm belied the City's reaction to Sunderland's dismissal. Most money men were Whigs. Would the treasurer be next to go? Businessmen valued Godolphin—he kept his word, brought integrity to the treasury, and understood financial complexities.

The stock market fell, confidence in public credit wavered, and a City delegation waited on the queen. She had, Anne told her visitors, "for some time resolved to remove the Earl of Sunderland, for particular reasons of state. [At this time, the queen assured, she had no] intention to make any farther changes; but should I alter any of my ministers, it shall be no prejudice to the Bank [of England] or to the common cause."[36]

London took these words to mean that Godolphin and the current Whig dominated parliament, would stay. Financial confidence returned.

—⁂—

Short, stout Godolphin had reached the venerable (for that time) age of sixty-five, and the pressures of office, not to mention frequent tussles with the queen, had had their inevitable effect. He now spoke less cautiously to Anne; bluntly told her dissolution of parliament would cause "ruin and distraction" since an election might easily lose Whigs their majority, thus leaving the way open for Tories to force the queen into accepting a premature peace. Godolphin asked to resign if Anne should decide to prorogue the legislature against his advice. Such a matter must be "very well considered,"[37] the queen replied.

Her guarded answer decided Godolphin to ask Marlborough to apply to Britain's allies for aid—the duke should ask his friend Heinsius, head of Holland's government, and Austria's Hapsburg emperor, (via Marlborough's friend and fellow general Prince Eugene of Savoy) to ask the queen not to make any more cabinet changes or dissolve parliament until the war had been won. Against his better judgment, the duke complied.

Foreign powers were meddling in British politics, roared the outraged Tories. Anne ordered her secretary of state to advise the Dutch of her extreme surprise "at so extraordinary a proceeding. [Her] affection [for Holland would not decrease, but as Heinsius's letter represented] the first of this kind, she hoped it would be the last. [The queen commanded her minister] to show her the letter before he sent it."[38]

—⁂—

Anne wanted to keep Godolphin. She valued his years of loyal, able, and honest service; his assiduous care of the public interest.[39] One of Harley's most prominent propagandists opined that Godolphin "managed the finances with great and unusual dexterity and has acquired thereby the fame of the best officer, that has for many years acted in that post."[40]

The queen respected Godolphin's financial capability, thought his leaving her cabinet might roil the City. And Anne appreciated Godolphin not supporting Marlborough over the recent parliamentary address asking that she remove Abigail Masham. Further, the queen knew that despite their differences, Godolphin had her best interests at heart. Having bumped into Dr. Hamilton, the treasurer asked after Anne's health. Godolphin could prolong her life, by informing the queen of as "few disquieting things as possible, [but if the] necessity [arose, Godolphin might] shun it at least at some certain seasons, [the doctor replied. Godolphin promised, adding that if Hamilton would alert him to each] such season, [he would do his utmost to] keep her easy. [And at year-end, Godolphin told the queen he would not bring up business until after Christmas,] which shows how readily he kept ... disquiet [from Anne and acted like a] kind friend as well as a minister of state."[41]

Anne did not object to Godolphin's frankness. The queen *did* object to Sarah's sway over the treasurer. It shook her faith in Godolphin's advice. Unyoking treasurer and duchess would "be one of the happiest things imaginable."[42] Anne asked Hamilton to make the attempt, but his best efforts fell short.

Family (Godolphin's only child married a Marlborough daughter) and politics tied the two long-time friends. Anne knew the Junto relied on Sarah "to animate" Godolphin "to do what is right"[43]; knew that even if treasurer and queen together came to a decision, when Godolphin saw the duchess, she often "impressed him to the contrary."[44]

—⁂—

On a mellow, late summer afternoon, bees buzzed busily among the flowers growing outside Queen Anne's windows. Inside, she presided over the weekly cabinet meeting. Godolphin and Shrewsbury expressed different opinions. Anne sided with Shrewsbury. Godolphin administered a sharp rebuke; no record exists of its exact nature, but the queen took her prime minister's words as a personal affront. Next day Anne and Godolphin had a long and constructive meeting. He asked if she wanted him to stay in office. Yes.

Satisfied, Godolphin took his leave. But he noted atypical signs of unease, even gloom, in the queen's manner.

That evening, the westering sun suffused Kensington Palace's gardens, gardens whose planning had diverted Anne at other times of stress. Now, as she sat at a small inlaid writing table in her pretty, private, oak-paneled parlor, the queen drew a sheet of paper towards her, dipped her pen in the standish, and wrote.

> The uneasiness which you have showed for some time has given me very much trouble, though I have borne it; had your behavior continued the same as it was for a few years after my coming to the crown, I could have no dispute with myself what to do. But the many unkind returns I have received since, especially what you said to me personally before the lords, [cabinet] makes it impossible for me to continue you any longer in my service.
>
> I will give you a pension of four thousand a year, and I desire, that instead of bringing the staff [of office] to me, you will break it, which, I believe, will be easier to us both.[45]

No expression of personal feeling, no compassion for Godolphin, no courtesy of a last interview, no thanks for a lifetime of impeccable service, of guidance, and of friendship. Anne's peremptory letter merely complained of unkind returns.

A "groom of the queen's stables [delivered her letter to Godolphin's porter. Godolphin] broke his staff, and flung the pieces in the chimney, desiring [a chance visitor] to be witness that he had obeyed the queen's commands."[46]

Having for some time shown "a great deal of uneasiness [in the queen's service, and] his behavior not being to me the same as ... formerly, [gave Anne no choice but to ask Godolphin to give up the] white staff ... and therefore I ordered him to break it, which I acquaint you with now, [she wrote Marlborough,] that you may receive this news first from me, and I do assure you I will take care the army shall want for nothing."[47]

Next day Anne put the treasury in charge of a board of commissioners. And she acceded to Robin the Trickster's months of subtle chipping away at Godolphin by making Harley chancellor of the exchequer, although not lord treasurer. Still, Harley, in effect, became the queen's chief minister.

—⟋⟍—

Queen Anne had decided that, his good points notwithstanding, her old friend and faithful counselor must go. Godolphin had become too closely connected to Whigs for her comfort. Anne's confidence in him started to wane over Godolphin's pivotal role in the Sunderland

Robert Harley, 1661–1724, later first Earl of Oxford. Queen Anne's second lord treasurer and prime minister. Known as Robin the Trickster because he loved "deceits ... even where not necessary, but from an inward satisfaction he took in applauding his own cunning." Artist: John Smith, 1714, after Sir Godfrey Kneller. © National Portrait Gallery, London.

appointment, continued to ebb as Godolphin facilitated the Junto push into her cabinet; and his tendency to succumb to Sarah's influence scarcely served to increase the queen's trust in Godolphin's judgment. To crown all, the prime minister's failure to take note of her growth in political maturity had most recently translated into open criticism. Nonetheless, Anne found it impossible to dismiss Godolphin in person. On cashiering Sunderland, certainly no friend, the queen asked his co-secretary of state to collect Sunderland's seals of office; when the co-secretary balked because he and Sunderland were friends, Anne replied that a friend could best handle such matters. The queen valued and understood friendship, had often shown friendship for Godolphin by encouraging him to be frank, for friends, she believed, should be forthright with each other. Now Anne could not face what would be nothing less than an extremely painful interview. "I can never express myself in words."[48]

Despite all, the queen and Godolphin's friendship continued. She often sought his advice, which Godolphin readily gave.

Sometime later, while visiting the Marlboroughs at their country estate, Godolphin came under attack from his old enemy—kidney stones. Since the sole cure consisted of being tied to a table to let the surgeon cut (without anesthetic) between anus and scrotum, insert a catheter, and suck out the stones, it is scarcely surprising that Godolphin refused treatment. Sarah nursed him devotedly, but after a few weeks Godolphin died—without uttering one uncivil word against Anne.

The queen "could not help [being affected by the death of her friend and counselor,] for she had a long acquaintance with him."[49] Anne shed many tears for Godolphin; his so-called insults, she believed, were due to the duchess.

Anne asked secretary of state Dartmouth to "hinder, as much as [possible,] any scurrilities coming out upon" Godolphin. The secretary did. And told the queen he had heard that her former treasurer "died very poor." (Sarah's exaggeration, circulated to embarrass the queen. Recent inheritance of the family estate had increased Godolphin's modest income although the pension Anne promised never materialized, probably because Harley, now de facto treasury chief, failed to pay it as well as money owing to several other of the queen's servants.) Anne felt "very sorry [Godolphin] had suffered so much in her service."[50]

She later admitted having been "dealt insincerely with and teased to do many things against her own inclination, particularly"[51] dismissing Godolphin.

—⁂—

Charismatic Dr. Sacheverell had, meanwhile, spent the summer months traveling to his new living with minimum speed and maximum exposure. Adoring crowds dogged Sacheverell's every step. All expressed joy at his narrow conviction and mild sentence; cavalcades escorted him from village to village, town to town; spectators lined rutted roads and dusty rural lanes, sat atop green hedgerows and climbed up trees to get a glimpse of their hero.

Local Tory officials augmented the excitement by providing fireworks, illuminations and feasts. London Tories jostled each other in their eagerness to pay respects to the queen. And Tories coordinated a grassroots campaign to have loyal addresses sent to Anne. From every corner of the realm effusions of patriotism, pro–Church zeal, and pleas for new elections poured into the palace. Ninety-seven petitions proved the ministry's unpopularity and convinced the queen that elections would help her shed Junto shackles.

Anne prorogued parliament with a speech from the throne on a clear, vivid afternoon when glossy brown chestnuts rolled on the ground. In her melodious contralto, the queen voiced her sanction of Sacheverell's trial, and rejected as false the claim that her administration imperiled the Church.

"Wonderfully inflamed by a multitude of licentious writings [representing Whigs] as *atheists* and *republicans*, [hyper-confident crowds] as it were, armed with authority, [appeared at the polling stations to express their support for] church and monarchy. [By] reproachful language, and odious epithets ... even by blows, [Tory mobs] deterred those who came to vote contrary to *the voice of the people*; insomuch that if the Whigs had not ... practiced ... *moderation*, these new elections might have ended in"[52] civil war.

They ended in a Tory landslide. Anne reacted with mixed feelings. Certainly, she wanted to drop her Whig cabinet, but not in exchange for Tory control. The queen meant to maintain Moderation as her governing principle.

Sixteen

"I cannot change my resolution"

"I have no thoughts but what is good for England. I am sure I have no other, nor never can, but will always to the best of my understanding promote its true interest & serve my country faithfully which I look upon to be as much of duty of a sovereign as of the meanest subject."[1]—Queen Anne

Queen Anne decided to mark the Christmas-New Year (1710–1711) season by ending the official mourning she had, for the past two years, observed in honor of her husband, Prince George. Hence, the queen needed new clothes.

Under normal circumstances Anne's groom of the stole, Sarah, Duchess of Marlborough, would order the queen's raiment at her sovereign's behest. But circumstances were not normal. The breach between queen and duchess had deteriorated beyond repair. Anne wanted to be rid of Sarah, and as soon as possible without raising the ruckus that surely would result from dismissing the duchess. She, judging the queen's emergence from mourning to require her presence at court regardless, anxious to preserve at least the façade of having Anne's favor, asked the queen's physician for help.

Dr. David Hamilton had taken on the role of mediator in effecting the duchess's dismissal without it causing a brouhaha. He now received the duchess's lengthy accounts of "what had passed, justifying myself, and exposing the ingratitude as well as malice of my enemies."[2] Enemies meant Abigail Masham, the queen's favorite bedchamber woman who, according to Sarah, had insinuated herself into Anne's favor with the evil intent of supplanting the duchess. On hearing about a new Italian creation called caricature drawing, therefore, Sarah asked an Englishman who had studied art in Italy to depict Abigail covered in festering sores. The duchess appended this oeuvre to one of her letters to Hamilton.

The doctor gave Anne as much of the duchess's self-serving explanation as he thought the queen's health could tolerate. Hamilton gave Sarah as many of Anne's comments as he judged would be least likely to rouse the duchess's temper.

Anxious to avoid further scenes with Sarah that, the queen knew with the certitude of experience, would result in a tantrum distressing to herself, Anne told Hamilton to advise the duchess not to return to court.

Sarah, however, still toyed with the tempting thought of publishing Princess Anne's early letters. True, their avowal of eternal and platonic love for Sarah used effusive language; equally true, Anne's words did not exceed the limits women adopted when writing to intimate female friends. But the duchess knew Queen Anne, twenty years later, could ill afford to expose herself to the ridicule and innuendo that public scrutiny would produce. How, Sarah asked Hamilton, when Anne stood so "much in her power, [could the queen] treat her so."[3]

He replied by advising Anne to dismiss the duchess from all her offices with the least possible provocation. An intelligent and temperamental woman like Sarah, when provoked, could often turned "malicious, [which might well] force her to print what has happened, for her own justification."[4]

If Sarah "offered to kill me, must I not put her away? [The duchess threatened to] take away my name and reputation, [which Anne saw as] all one"[5] with death. Now more than ever, the queen resolved to rid herself of the woman she detested, let alone dreaded.

—∞—

Since the Tory election triumph at the end of the previous (1710) year, Anne had focused on choosing her new cabinet. This, she carried out in close consultation with moderate Tory Robert Harley, in effect prime minister after Earl Godolphin's dismissal, and her longtime friend, the moderate Whig Duke of Shrewsbury, cabinet member since before the Tory victory. Like his sovereign deploring party strife, Shrewsbury agreed with her and Harley that the new ministry should not rely fully on one party.

Harley refrained from dismissing large numbers of Whig officials and civil servants. Anne did not want to part with all Whig cabinet ministers—some—like Junto chief Lord Somers, had earned her respect; others—like moderate Lord Cowper, keeper of the great seal, had become personal favorites. Somers refused the queen's offer to stay—he could not desert his Junto colleagues. Anne spent an hour trying to convince Cowper to keep the great seal. He tried to hand it over five times; as many times, Anne returned it. Cowper finally took the seal under condition that Anne would accept it next day. She did. But asked Cowper to visit her from time to time, to give advice. He did.

The queen appointed her choleric, hard-drinking, High Tory uncle Earl Rochester to a senior position—lord president of the council. He surprised her and his colleagues with political moderation.

Moderate Tory Lord Dartmouth, whom Anne had chosen to replace Ultra Whig Lord Sunderland as one of her two secretaries of state, remained; the other secretary position went to able, energetic Henry St. John. He had refused the minor post Harley (now de facto head of the splintered Tory party) originally offered him; but although alarmed at the younger man's ambition and outspoken political views, Harley could not afford to ignore St. John's standing with Tory squires in the house of commons, so, he became a secretary of state.

Strapping and handsome, St. John entered parliament after a wild youth spent living openly with one of England's most notorious prostitutes, and, when drunk, running naked through the park. His talents attracted attention in parliament. Harley helped St. John become admiralty secretary to Prince George and facilitated his entry into Anne's first moderate (1705–1708) cabinet as secretary of war.

An efficient minister, intelligent, well-read, and charming with graceful manners and ready wit, St. John soon mastered the details of his duties. He resigned with Harley after the latter's failed (1708) coup attempt, then moved closer to Tories more conservative than moderate Harley.

The queen had little enthusiasm for her new secretary of state. She disapproved of St. John's lifestyle for, despite marriage, he continued to prefer the company of prostitutes, propositioned any likely-looking female regardless of what occupied him at the time—

such as conversing with a friend when walking in the street—and enjoyed drunken binges in the company of riffraff. As well, Anne mistrusted St. John's flashiness and tendency to grab attention.

—⚹—

Robin the Trickster had achieved his goal of becoming the queen's prime minister; but, she had not yet appointed him first lord of the treasury, like his predecessor Sidney Godolphin. Harley sought complete power. That meant cutting the tie of mutual affection and political affinity between Anne and the Duke of Marlborough, commander in chief of her armed forces, leader of the Grand Alliance armies against France, and member of the queen's ministry. The abyss between Anne and the duke's wife, let alone dismissal of his close friend and colleague Godolphin, had diminished Marlborough's position. But since the queen meant to govern with a moderate ministry and wanted the duke to continue as commander in chief, she hoped he would cooperate with her new cabinet.

Out to wreck the queen's trust in Marlborough, Harley used public humiliation to provoke the duke into imprudent action. Harley wangled dismissal of Marlborough's private secretary, replacing him with a man the duke disliked. In the queen's name Harley cashiered three generals devoted to Marlborough on the pretext of their having drunk damnation to the new ministry. Anne backed Harley because disruptive conduct could not be condoned. Besides, she already disliked one of the three who, not content with mistreating his wife, had raped his housekeeper, a clergyman's widow. A trial ensued. The judge imposed a light sentence. Anne intervened after the Bishop of London brought the woman's plight to her attention. Marlborough and Godolphin (then still in office) talked the queen out of her intention to dismiss the general. But the queen said she would remember his ill treatment of women. Now, although Anne meant no slight to Marlborough by cashiering the three generals, she could not, she confided to Hamilton, accept their insult to her ministry, and, thus, to herself.

Harley asked the Elector of Hanover, (second in line to succeed Anne after his mother the dowager electress) serving under Marlborough in the allied army, to take supreme command. Tired, unwell, and depressed over domestic politics and his wife's loss of favor, Marlborough hoped the elector would accept, but doubted Holland or the Hapsburg Empire would agree to serve under him.

The elector not only declined but, in concert with the King of Prussia, threatened to remove all troops from the Alliance if Marlborough resigned. The duke's friend and fellow general, Austria's Prince Eugene of Savoy, refused to serve in the Netherlands without him.

Undeterred, Harley got his press allies to pour charges of avarice and financial irregularity onto the duke—who got government money to pay British troops, British-funded foreign soldiers, and to buy provision contracts. The pro-government *Examiner* featured satirist Jonathan Swift's "British Ingratitude." With caustic wit and cruel irony Swift voiced the rage of squires (who had to pay heavy wartime land taxes) at powerful Whig financiers and their associates (the Marlboroughs) who profited from the war and, thus, wished it to continue. Swift pilloried the duke as greedy, crooked, and excessively ambitious; accused the duchess of enriching herself by pocketing large sums out of Anne's privy purse; and portrayed the popular queen as to be congratulated for having emerged from Whig bondage to reign in freedom with her new Tory ministry.

The duchess sent Hamilton a copy of "British Ingratitude" despite his having asked her to stop writing him about the queen. Sarah thought Swift's article justified her making sure Anne saw it, because "to be printed and cried about the country for a common cheat & pickpocket is too much for human nature to bear. [The duchess begged Hamilton to show her letter to the queen.] It is so much in my power to publish other papers of a very different kind, I do not mean those that are full of professions of endless kindness & friendship, & of dreadful imprecations if ever it were otherwise, but those in which Mrs. Morley had acknowledged my care & frugality in her service."[6]

"Everyone knows that cheating is not the Duchess of Marlborough's fault,"[7] the queen said. Sarah certainly had faults, but not that one.

—☓☓—

Anne, meanwhile, faced a dilemma. Sarah's husband had left his troops at their Dutch winter quarters and set sail across the choppy, chilly Channel. Marlborough's imminent arrival in London meant the queen must resolve how to get rid of the duchess but keep the duke.

Anne still needed him. She wanted peace, but a peace advantageous to Britain. The duke now served in a ministry hostile to him. The queen's continental allies urged Whigs and Tories not to let political rivalry interfere with Marlborough commanding the allied army for what would, everyone hoped, be the War of the Spanish Succession's final campaign. The duchess had influence over her husband. If Sarah got him to resign and go into opposition, the Alliance would crumble before a beneficial peace could be reached. The queen "ordered [Hamilton] to insist [that the duchess] not inflame the duke."[8]

Wildly cheering crowds lined slushy London streets under a lowering sky that promised more snow, to welcome the duke home; but since Tory propaganda cast him as the new Cromwell, (army chief who, within living memory, made himself military head of government) Marlborough felt ill at ease. He might well.

In anticipation of her interview with the duke, Anne told Hamilton about her long relationship with Sarah. Hamilton then spoke to Marlborough's best friend, Godolphin. Both men subsequently told the duke of his wife's most recent conduct towards the queen. What shocked Marlborough particularly, were Sarah's persistent allusions to a sexual relationship between the queen and her chambermaid Abigail Masham, allusions that sealed Anne's resolve to dismiss the duchess.

The duke "complained of his wife, who, he said, acted strangely, but there was no help for that, and a man must bear with a good deal, to be quiet at home."[9] At home and in society Sarah, "railing in a most extravagant manner against the queen, [averred] she had always hated and despised her."[10] A woman incapable of "original thoughts on any subject, [Anne had] much love & passion, while pleased, for those who pleased her; and can write pretty affectionate letters; but do nothing else well."[11] One "must not mind what she said, [Marlborough excused, since his wife] spoke like that when in a passion, [something] she was very apt to fall into, and there was no way to help it."[12]

—☓☓—

The duke arrived at St. James's Palace in late afternoon. A curtain of sleet slammed against the windows but in Anne's private reception room, drapes of crimson damask lined with figured white silk were drawn to shut out the weather, and the applewood log crackling in the fire place emitted a pleasant scent.

Marlborough wanted to spare his wife the disgrace of dismissal. This would be obviated if they voluntarily left the queen's service together when the war concluded at the end of the next campaign. So, Marlborough aimed to convince the queen to let Sarah keep her offices for a few more months.

> DUKE: I want to carry the war to its conclusion, but, my "great uneasiness" is to have my wife "made easy," which I hope might be brought about "by her having more patience, and" your majesty "more goodness."[13]
>
> QUEEN: "I am desirous you should continue to serve me and will answer for the conduct of all my ministers towards you." But, Anne added firmly, even severely, "I must request you would not suffer any vote of thanks to you to be moved in parliament this year, because my ministers will certainly oppose it."
>
> DUKE: "I shall always be ready to serve your majesty, if what has recently passed [ministerial change] should not incapacitate me."[14]

Having bowed himself out of the queen's presence, Marlborough assured Hamilton that only "duty and submission [to the queen motivated him. Nor would he] intrigue with any ministry, [but serve to his best ability] in the state of war."[15]

Hamilton at once conveyed the duke's words to Anne, told her how "affectionately he spoke of her, which melted her. [Bearing in mind what Sarah disclosed—if the queen] smiled or said anything pleasant he [the duke] thinks nothing amiss," Hamilton then told Anne her smiles would ease Marlborough's mind. Sorry to see the duke "so broken, [the queen assured Hamilton she had] no thought of putting him out."[16]

—⚍—

Marlborough's trusted friends like Godolphin, Austria's Prince Eugene, Holland's Grand Pensionary Heinsius, plus foreign envoys in London, Whigs, and the City all pleaded with the duke to stay, rather than fracture the Alliance. Caught between these pleas and his wish to protect Sarah by resigning with her, Marlborough fell ill.

Concomitantly, the queen, clad in a colorfully embroidered blue satin nightgown lined with taffeta eased her gout-swollen limbs by sitting up against a bank of brocade pillows on her four-poster canopied bed. And spoke to Hamilton about the duke.

> DOCTOR: "However the duchess was passionate, yet I [am] satisfied of *his* tenderness and affection toward [your] majesty."
>
> QUEEN: "It would be no more disgrace to him to have the duchess out than in."
>
> DOCTOR: "His concern was lest the noise of it abroad should lessen him." If he were not so much in the queen's favor, he would be less able to serve her. For the "character of the queen's favor to him," made him "so successful, they from thence trusting his promise, as if it had been her majesty's own."[17]

Marlborough's illness, meanwhile, alarmed Sarah. Her interests must not interfere with her husband's honor and his country's welfare. Hence, Hamilton and Shrewsbury, one of the duke's old friends, convinced him to "talk and carry affectionately [as] suitable [preparation for gaining what might be possible—Anne's] forgiveness upon the duchess's owning her faults by letter."[18]

—⚍—

Marlborough must appeal to the queen on Sarah's behalf at an auspicious moment, Hamilton advised. So, on a day the doctor judged his royal patient to be in a benign mood, the duke personally delivered the letter he had persuaded his duchess to write.

She

never thought of troubling [Anne,] yet the circumstances [in which Marlborough stood, and Sarah's fears] that he cannot live [without] some end put to his sufferings, on my account, [made it] impossible [for her to] resist doing everything in my power to ease him. [Were the duchess] still so unlucky as not to make use of any expressions [that might move Anne,] want of understanding [would be the cause; for Sarah expressed herself as] very sorry ... ever I did anything ... uneasy to your majesty.

Ready to promise anything that you can think reasonable, [the duchess, knowing of only two things she] ever did, that were disagreeable ... solemnly [promised that so long as she remained in Anne's service,] I will never mention either of those subjects [Abigail and politics or, indeed, do] any one thing that can give you the least disturbance or uneasiness.[19]

Sarah wanted the queen to have these promises in her own handwriting to prove that she would omit nothing that saved her husband from "the greatest mortification ... and avoid the greatest mischief ... to your majesty and my country. [The duchess concluded by signing herself] with all submission and respect imaginable, your majesty's most dutiful and most obedient subject and servant."[20]

The queen refused to look at Sarah's letter.

Marlborough cajoled.

After carefully reading the duchess's close written pages Anne said, "I cannot change my resolution."[21]

The duke countered by pledging to convince his wife to resign; if, after two weeks he failed, the queen should do as she wished. But for all their sakes, Anne should not "adopt a harsher proceeding than any prince ever used towards persons of less faithful and long continued services, who had been guilty of greater faults, [especially as Sarah had asked for pardon, and promised to reform.] Still more, [the queen's refusal to change her resolution would] reflect on [Anne's] "generosity to deny so trifling an indulgence to one who has been honored by your friendship, and ... has given no substantial cause."[22]

Anxious to end so distressing a matter, the queen insisted on receiving Sarah's symbolic gold key of office within three days.

What were his wife's sins to merit such treatment, asked the duke. Anne did not reply. Marlborough begged her to postpone dismissing Sarah until the coming campaign ended, so that he and Sarah could retire together. He reminded Anne of her former affection for Sarah, of his service; and, as he had done a year ago, the duke promised his wife's silence on Abigail and politics—a promise the queen knew all too well Sarah had broken.

Unwilling to risk more upset, Anne refused to give the duchess another chance. She demanded Sarah's gold key within three days. Marlborough pleaded for ten days. Three.

Turning to other tactics, the duke raised some army issues. Having already talked with him for an hour, Anne sought to end a scene she found painful. The queen declined to speak about business until she had Sarah's gold key.

Defeated, Marlborough returned home to his wife. Sarah flung her gold key on the floor. Her husband could bring Anne the key at once.

The queen received it with a low inarticulate murmur. Marlborough thought she wished to say something. Actually, emotion overcame Anne. She had never found it easy to put her feelings into words, especially deep feelings. Having already borne so much tragedy, now the unhappy ending of her oldest, most intimate friendship, the queen must see another longtime friend, her trusted counselor, humiliated over his wife's conduct. Anne found it impossible to speak.

—m—

The queen celebrated her birthday in grand style that (1711) February. Clad in a stylish new gown of green flowered satin embellished with gold and matching deep shoulder cape whose broad ends fell to her knees in front, embroidered green satin shoes with tapered toe and fastened with straps tied over a high-instep tongue, Anne carried a green-papered Indian fan decorated with delicate gold tracery, and mounted on gilt sticks.

She had already resumed the private concerts that took place in her bedroom while Prince George lived, but had not yet heard the great Italian countertenor who had been mesmerizing London audiences for months. Hence, the queen commanded him to perform at her birthday entertainment. And she commissioned a new opera from a young German musician, formerly employed by her cousin the Elector of Hanover, but currently seeking his fortune in London. Anne delighted in George Frederic Handel's *Rinaldo* no less than Handel's setting to music her poet laureate's ode of praise.

Despite the "extraordinary pomp and magnificence" of the queen's birthday revels, to say nothing of the many richly robed, bejeweled Tories, (two peeresses were so laden with gems that they could scarcely move) "it was observed [that most Whigs as well as "the Duke of Marlborough, were absent.] With her majesty's leave, [the duke had] set out four days before for Blenheim,"[23] the palace a grateful nation had undertaken to build for him on land given by the queen, in honor of Marlborough's first great victory.

—m—

The few Whigs who did attend Queen Anne's birthday festivities included the Duke and Duchess of Somerset, both senior members of Anne's household since her accession to the throne. He held cabinet rank. She served as a lady-in-waiting.

The queen's Tory ministers pressured her to dismiss the Somersets. But Anne, as always, insisted on selecting her personal servants; besides, experience with Sarah taught Anne the advisability of balancing her favors. The queen gave the least important of Sarah's positions, keeper of the privy purse, to Tory Abigail Masham, who had been executing this duty unofficially during the duchess's long and frequent absences from court. Anne appointed Whig Elizabeth Somerset to Sarah's positions as first lady of the bedchamber and groom of the stole.

Two years younger than the queen, last of an ancient, noble, and powerful family, and extremely wealthy besides, Elizabeth Percy had been much sought after in the matrimonial stakes. Her grandmother and guardian arranged the girl's marriage at age twelve. Widowed a year later, then married to a man many years her senior, thirteen-year-old Elizabeth decamped—whether with or without her husband's consent remains unclear—to The Hague. Within a year widowed again because a disappointed former suitor killed her spouse, Elizabeth eventually married Somerset. His pride and pomposity did little to contribute to their conjugal bliss.

First noble lady of the realm, universally respected for her gracious nature and flawless manners, Elizabeth Somerset had always appealed to the queen. During the time that Sarah's conduct caused her to lose Anne's friendship, Elizabeth became her sovereign's favored companion.

The queen chose well. Friendships can, and do, exist between "persons without suitableness; [but this friendship had] suitableness of quality, of temper calm, and of breeding and of natural affection; [that made the two women's attachment much] more comfortable without interruption and lasting." Elizabeth never tried to foist her political opinions on Anne, never spoke of anything containing "unsuitableness, [never pressed the queen] hard, nothing [made Anne] more uneasy than that."[24]

Hamilton hoped this friendship would "draw [the queen] outward," for the ability to confide in a friend would bring Anne much needed peace of mind, essential, the doctor judged, for her health. And if the queen shed her "reservedness, [confided her] disquiets [to Elizabeth, Anne would gain the] greatest pleasure of conversation."[25] But experience with Sarah curbed any tendency the taciturn queen may have had to unburden herself to Elizabeth.

Nonetheless, the two women developed a genuine bond. Anne resisted overt and covert Tory efforts to remove her friend. When Elizabeth failed to respond to the queen's requests to attend her even when not on duty, Anne, chiding gently, ascertained that her messages failed to reach Elizabeth. The queen thus used a special courier and insisted on a receipt for delivery of each message.

Anne treated Elizabeth Somerset as a friend, a companion. Anne treated Abigail Masham as a servant. And when Abigail left court for the country to give birth, or spend time with her children, the queen showed no longing for her. As well, Abigail's absences limited any influence she may have had; in fact, the chambermaid's political utility consisted of alerting Harley to a propitious time for visiting the queen.

Beginning, meanwhile, to vacate her apartment in St. James's Palace, Sarah wanted to store some furniture in the palace until completion of the Marlboroughs' new London residence. Since a serving woman currently occupied the space chosen by the duchess for storage, she asked Anne's permission to use the rooms. Irked at having recently paid the duchess a handsome sum,[26] the queen replied that rather than trouble the serving woman, Sarah could rent storage space outside the palace for a pittance. Enraged, the duchess proceeded to take every moveable fixture from her apartment, including marble mantels, custom-crafted locks and brass door knobs. Anne countered by ordering a halt to construction at Blenheim—why should her government build the Marlboroughs a house while Sarah eviscerated hers.

—⁊⁊—

The queen resisted Tory attempts to have her dismiss moderate Whig Somerset from the cabinet; and often consulted Whig leaders like Somers and Cowper in private. As well, Anne continued to talk over everything with Shrewsbury, above party, skilled in domestic as well as foreign politics, and like herself, cautious.

He and Harley favored peace. As did queen and country. After nine years, the War of the Spanish Succession had drained Anne's realm of money and men; and her allies' demands for gold to fund their war efforts increased annually. Queen, ministry, and nation were satisfied with Marlborough's four major victories against France; for, they had enhanced the status of crown and country.

Harley "resolved to strike up a peace as soon as"[27] possible, because that would give him a chance to get the bulk of the booty for Britain. Another major military defeat in the Peninsula (Battle of Brihuega) sealed Tory determination to free Great Britain from No Peace Without Spain, the Whig conceived and Grand Alliance adopted, war aim.

(French King Louis XIV's Bourbon grandson could not continue to sit on the Spanish throne.) Anne thought Brihuega rendered No Peace Without Spain unrealistic.

Fate then took a hand. Austria's Holy Roman Emperor died suddenly. His brother Charles (Hapsburg claimant to the Spanish throne as King Carlos III) succeeded to the imperial throne. "I made war, [Queen Anne declared,] to prevent the crown of Spain being on the head of the [French] House of Bourbon, for to keep the balance in Europe, and for that same reason I am not for the crown aforesaid to be on the head of him that is become emperor on his brother's death."[28]

No Peace Without Spain had become untenable. The need for peace had become palpable.

—◊◊◊—

Initial peace negotiations must be secret. Whigs would oppose making peace now. The Allies would object to Britain breaking their pledge to negotiate jointly.

Shrewsbury and Harley chose the Earl of Jersey to initiate the secret talks. Suspected, not without reason, of Jacobite leanings, Jersey had contacts in France at both King Louis and the Pretender's courts. Anne objected to Jersey because of his Jacobitism, but Harley and Shrewsbury convinced her that peace would be harder to negotiate without him.[29]

Harley instructed Jersey to present certain conditions to his counterpart, the rotund, urbane Abbé François Gaultier, a Jesuit at the Austrian embassy's chapel; he had, for some time, also been an agent for the French foreign minister. Preliminary talks must, Harley stipulated, take place between England and France only; these talks must be secret because they broke Britain's pledge to the Grand Alliance not to make a separate peace; but, Jersey must assure Gaultier, the threat of Anglo-French peace would force Allied acceptance of any Anglo-French agreement. Louis XIV's grandson, Bourbon King Philip V of Spain, could keep his throne as well as the Spanish empire; in return, France and Spain must cede to Britain broad and exclusive commercial benefits in Europe and the Americas. Britain would choose a new barrier for Holland to replace the Anglo-Dutch Barrier Treaty, (1709) which, to assure continued Dutch participation in the war, gave Holland a barrier to protect the country from French invasion plus commercial privileges in the Spanish Netherlands. Lastly, because these secret discussions would betray the Allies, (including Hanover, home of Anne's successor) and thus, endanger Harley after Anne's death, he proposed to restore the Pretender if he converted to Protestantism.

Harley did not tell Anne about this last condition.

—◊◊◊—

With secret peace talks well underway and a brisk spring breeze tousling the dark surface of the Thames, Queen Anne received a personal petition from handsome Marquis de Guiscard. Having convinced power brokers in every major allied country of his ability to foment pro–Allied rebellion in certain areas of France, the marquis landed in London, finagled himself a government pension, and continued to weave his schemes. Indulgence in a well-deserved reputation for debauchery prompted Guiscard to petition the queen to increase his stipend; instead, de facto head of treasury Harley cut it in half to register his disgust at Guiscard's lifestyle. (Among other escapades, Guiscard and his most consistent drinking buddy, cabinet minister St. John, shared a mistress, and liked to banter over the paternity of her child.)

Anger at Harley turned Guiscard towards plotting with France. A crony betrayed him. Harley put him under observation. Incriminating letters surfaced. Arrest on a charge of treason followed. Guiscard faced formal questioning.

Shortly before the appointed hour, guards escorted Guiscard into the privy council[30] ante-chamber. Having removed his sword, they left. Guiscard "took up a penknife, which lay among pens in the standish. [Summoned before the council, he asked to] speak in private with secretary St. John, who refused it; and he being placed out of his reach, whereas Harley sat near him, he struck him in the breast with the penknife, again and again, till it broke; and indeed wounded him as much as could be done, with so small a tool."[31]

Harley wore the same silver-fringed, heavy waistcoat his devoted sister had lavishly embroidered with gold brocade flowers on a silver and blue background, for the queen's birthday gala a few weeks before. And because Harley had recently recovered from a feverish cold, he sported a thick flannel shirt under his waistcoat; over it, to further ward off the piercing dampness of an early English spring, a sturdy beige coat stylishly stiffened across the chest.

Guiscard's penknife penetrated Harley's clothing to the skin, and the force of the blow sent the queen's prime minister staggering back in his chair. But a gold brocade flower saved him. It broke the penknife. Still, Guiscard continued to stab with the shortened blade.

> "As soon as the noble Harley found
> The knife in his breast had made a wound,
> The council did to battle sound
> Like claps of summer thunder:
> Chairs and standish, inks and pen,
> To fly about the room were seen."[32]

Ministers drew their swords. Guards were hastily summoned. Together, they subdued the prime minister's would-be assassin.

Despite "the suddenness of the blow, the sharpness of the wound, the confusion which followed,"[33] Harley's sangfroid roused widespread admiration. His hurt seemed "to be a slight one, yet he was long in the surgeon's hands. Some imputed this to an ill habit of body; others thought it [Robin the Trickster's] artifice, to make it seem more dangerous."[34] Regardless, Guiscard's incision inspired Harley's doctor, for reasons best known to contemporary medical science, if science one can call it, to cut Harley six or seven times more, bleed him, and put on twelve dressings.

Ministers and guards inflicted so many stab wounds on Guiscard that he died within days. Prison officials embalmed the corpse in brine and, for a modest fee, admitted the curious public to view. When Queen Anne heard about that, she ordered Guiscard's immediate burial.

—⚉—

"The queen's health was at this time in some disorder ... probably heightened by"[35] Guiscard's attempt to assassinate Harley. Anne wept for two hours on receipt of the news, suffered a sleepless night, then "three fits of" [ague—regularly recurring chills, fever, and sweating—the last attack] severe"[36] enough to require emergency attention from four doctors. And the queen worried over her prime minister's recovery.

No wonder. The queen considered him her friend. Since she had been in so much pain all last night and today, "it is not easy to me now to write." Anne hoped Harley would excuse her for not having yet thanked him for his letter and assuring him she harbored no doubt about the "sincerity [of his friendship for her who stood] with all sincerity, your very affectionate friend."[37] After Prince George's death, personal friendships were, aside from religion, Anne's only comfort. Further, with her longtime trusted counselor and friend Godolphin gone, Marlborough estranged and in any case on the Continent with the army, the queen depended on Harley.

Anne recovered slowly from the shock, first of believing Harley dead, then agitating herself over his health. Nonetheless, ague could easily have resulted from the queen driving herself in her custom-built open carriage at breakneck speed through the special, twenty mile rides her landscapers had cut through Windsor Forest to allow Anne to drive year-round.

Having recovered her health, the queen commanded her coachman to take her through St. James's park to see the daffodils, their yellow trumpets swaying in the cool, pale sunlight. These excursions also served to let those subjects see the queen who could not gain entry to her Touching sessions or visit the palace to attend her twice-weekly drawing room evenings.

Gambling drew "a prodigious crowd and the table quite full before [Anne saw an old acquaintance.] She was not at rest till they brought me a stool over everybody's head and made them set quite close to her own chair."[38]

When the queen moved to Windsor that summer, (1711) she entertained her court with gambling and dancing. Anne hunted daily in Windsor forest. Sometimes she rose at dawn to drive herself through the avenue of limes and elms, expressly created to connect the castle to the queen's main hunting grounds; sometimes Anne hunted for forty miles, not returning until late afternoon. During fine weather she handled the reins of her one-horse, two-wheeled chaise, specially built for comfort and speed; on rainy days the queen followed the hunt in a coach. Still, fresh air and exercise failed to prevent gout.

It stopped the queen from going to Newmarket for one of her favorite amusements— horse racing. But while driving her chaise through Windsor forest, Anne happened on a tract of open heath near the Castle. She judged it perfect for horses galloping all out. So that summer the queen, accompanied by her entire court, initiated a tradition that persists until this day. Queen and court drove the short distance to Ascot, to attend races organized at Anne's command. She presented a prize—Her Majesty's Plate—to the winner of the first race. Today, Royal Ascot opens with Queen Anne's Stakes.

—⚏—

The attempt on Harley's life boosted his waning popularity. Even High Tories critical of his moderation were "ashamed to push a man [thus] assassinated by one [intending] to recommend himself to the court of France, (after having been expelled by it some years before for stirring up dissention in the south!) [and even] believed to have formed a design against the queen's person."[39]

But slow recovery did nothing to diminish Harley's anti–Marlborough activities. He paid the pro-government press to vilify the duke. Who protested. Robin the Trickster replied that he, too, deplored the printed insults and would try to curb the newspapers. Actually, Harley and his henchman, satirist Jonathan Swift, hatched anti–Marlborough press strategies; and Harley invited Swift to his Kitchen Cabinets (informal Saturday evening dinners preceding the official Sunday cabinet meeting) to further the satirist's political knowledge.

Although Harley and Marlborough maintained a façade of cooperation, the prime minister failed to share the fact of the secret peace talks. The duke's efficient intelligence service alerted him of their existence but could not provide details. Although "there is nothing upon earth I wish more than an end of the war,"[40] the duke still believed marching to Paris would yield the best terms for all Allies. He prepared to attack well-barricaded Bouchain fortress, key to France's northern border defenses and guardian of the best invasion route into France.

Harley opposed. Crushing France would prevent her from pressuring Spain to give Britain the special concessions currently in secret negotiation. Anne saw the siege of Bouchain as proving the duke's opposition to peace. She hoped successful negotiations would nullify "his power to prevent it."[41]

—⁂—

Secretary of state St. John took advantage of Harley's convalescence. The secretary contravened Harley's wishes by executing a costly military maneuver—the Quebec expedition.[42] (Failure to deprive France of its civil and military bastion in north America, nonetheless, netted St. John a fortune from army and navy contracts.) He also assumed a greater role in the peace negotiations. St. John's knowledge of French and European politics, let alone his vigor and ability, made the secretary a crucial participant.

Concomitantly, the unexpected death of Anne's uncle Rochester necessitated a cabinet reshuffle. The queen promoted Harley to lord treasurer and created him Earl of Oxford and Mortimer. She recognized St. John's role in the peace talks by creating him Viscount Bolingbroke[43]—not—to his intense regret, an earl. Because Anne believed St. John's ostentation and hunger for the limelight, let alone his libertine way of life (ignoring his loyal wife in favor of constant, not to mention, indiscriminate, womanizing) made him a less than ideal public servant.

Oxford asked Anne to give Britain's peace negotiator, Lord Jersey, a place in the cabinet. The queen had qualms; she disapproved of Jersey's Jacobitism. His appointment would, Oxford argued, facilitate discussions with France. Anne resisted. Jersey then produced what he called justification for his Jacobitism. That and Oxford's urgings caused the queen to yield. But on the day arranged for official notice of Jersey's appointment, he died of a stroke.

To expedite peace talks, the queen officially approved of poet and diplomat Matthew Prior going to Paris in secret, to negotiate directly with French foreign minister Marquis de Torcy. His reception of Prior signified France's de facto recognition of Anne as Britain's ruler. Prior returned with Torcy's senior commercial authority; Nicholas Mesnager spent several weeks in London incognito, hammering out trade concessions with Oxford and Bolingbroke.

The queen followed every detail of their discussions, sometimes reviewing them with Oxford for several hours. Anne summoned Prior to hear his version of the talks with Torcy, and asked him to convey to Mesnager, her delight at his arrival, a delight only dimmed by her inability to receive him officially. When Mesnager got new instructions from Paris, the queen instantly received copies. And gout failed to stop her from presiding over the cabinet until late into the night while ministers debated peace. Very glad "the great affair [made such good progress, Anne prayed that] God send a happy conclusion to it."[44]

Negotiations were almost complete, King Louis had authorized Mesnager formally to recognize Anne and her Protestant successors as legitimate rulers of Great Britain, when Shrewsbury and Bolingbroke raised a new issue. Parliament had, two years before, banned any agreement with France unless Louis expelled the Pretender from his realm.

"I have this business of the peace so much at heart, that I cannot help giving you this trouble, [the queen wrote Oxford,] to ask if it may not be proper to order [Boling-broke, if he found Mesnager] very averse to the new proposition not to insist upon it, & if you think it right I hope you will [give Bolingbroke] such an order in my name, for I think there is nothing so much to be feared as the letting the treaty go out of our hands."[45]

Mesnager suggested shelving the issue until formal peace treaty negotiations were underway. Anne and her cabinet agreed.

—⁂—

In the gentle golden light of September, (1711) Britain and France agreed on prelim-inary peace articles. They consisted of three documents.

Britain and France shared the first document with the Allies. It included King Louis XIV's promise to recognize as Great Britain's legitimate sovereigns both Anne, and her Hanoverian successors; prevent union of the French and Spanish crowns; satisfy all nations at the upcoming formal peace conference; restore international commerce; and give Holland barriers. (This displeased the Dutch; it implied abolition of their advanta-geous Barrier treaty. But since the war had cost Holland dearly in men and money, the government complied with the country's wish for peace.) Only French representative Mesnager signed this document.

France and Britain kept the second document secret. Only Mesnager signed it. France would cooperate in securing for the Duke of Savoy those sections of Italy that Britain judged essential to fortify northern Italy against any future French aggression. (This showed disloyalty to Britain's ally, Austria, who wanted to acquire territory in northern Italy.)

The third document focused on specific French concessions to Britain. They included France's formal recognition of Queen Anne as legitimate sovereign of Great Britain, plus the legitimacy of her Hanoverian successors; negotiations for an Anglo-French commercial treaty; conditional destruction of Dunkirk; (French fortress providing a home port for pirates plundering British ships) British retention of booty won in naval battles (the strategic Mediterranean outposts of Gibraltar, and Port Mahon, Minorca) Britain to have a thirty-year exclusive right to the *Asiento*; (the profitable trade in African slaves for Spain's American colonies) and Britain to have commercial advantages in Spain equal to those of France. Mesnager, as well as British secretaries of state Dartmouth and Bolingbroke signed this third article. It would be kept secret until Britain and France decided to divulge its contents.

Queen Anne declared herself extremely pleased.

—⁂—

A foreign diplomat promptly leaked the public preliminaries to the press. Predictable outrage erupted.

Oxford had sought to avoid it by negotiating both public and secret preliminaries. He planned to reveal the true nature of Britain's accord with France in stages, because he judged that by securing advantages for his country before any formal peace congress and keeping them secret, Britain could more easily coerce unwilling Allies to agree to peace. But the public preliminaries sufficed to distress the Allies. They feared Britain had extracted better conditions than she would admit. And since the public preliminaries concealed the strategic and commercial concessions Britain did win, they disappointed the bulk of Queen Anne's subjects.

Whigs were furious. The war must continue until Bourbon King Philip V of Spain had been driven from his throne. The Whig majority house of lords prepared to challenge passage of the preliminaries. Whigs felt confident of support from the queen's popular captain general, her longtime friend and counselor the Duke of Marlborough; he believed invasion of France would get Britain better peace terms.

Regardless, on a cool, damp October day, Britain and France formally signed the preliminaries.

All combatants in the War of the Spanish Succession had, meanwhile, agreed that their official peace conference would get underway early in the new year (1712) at Holland's handsome old canal city of Utrecht. That timeline presented Queen Anne's cabinet with a challenge. For, a far from willing parliament must first ratify the peace preliminaries.

Seventeen

Peace

"As long as I live" I shall try "to make my country and my friends easy and though those that come after me may be more capable of so great a trust as it has pleased God to put into my poor hands, I am sure they can never discharge it more faithfully."[1]—Queen Anne

Queen Anne attended "the chapel last Sunday and was so well as to see company in her bedchamber afterwards. [A courtier gave] this good news" as chilly rain drummed against the palace window panes on a dreary November (1711) day, "because some people have made it their business to spread abroad a report as if she was dangerously ill."[2]

Many expected the queen's frail health to cause her early death, but Anne opened the last parliament of 1711 with a speech from the throne delivered in her characteristically cadenced contralto. "I never saw an audience more affected, [one attendee noted. The queen's delivery] was a sort of charm."[3]

Anne's chief minister, the Earl of Oxford, wrote the queen's speech; she, as always, reviewed it. Most notably, her speech faulted those in favor of war. Anne may not have relished the idea of deserting her allies to negotiate a separate peace with France. But in her first speech to parliament as queen, Anne promised her subjects to do anything they demanded of her for the nation's happiness and prosperity; she had vowed never to deviate from her pledge; her motto would be *Semper Eadem*. So, with the country ready for peace, Anne supported the tactic of abandoning one principle of the Grand Alliance—that the Allies would treat with France as one. Besides, entering into separate peace talks with France presented Great Britain with the best chance for a beneficial peace.

Queen and nation wanted peace. But the parliamentary debate following Anne's speech, made clear that passage of the peace preliminaries would not be easy.

—⁓—

Worried about the opposition's strength, let alone Oxford's failure to win over some key peers, the queen lobbied several opposition lords including Whig former ministers she had come to respect. Anne received Cowper "very kindly; she heard me above ½ an hour on the intended peace; could not persuade me to promise to vote with her ministers."[4] But the queen did succeed in persuading several other peers to vote for the preliminaries. And she lobbied bishops because they sat in the house of lords. Anne hoped bishops would back the peace preliminaries, she told the Whig Bishop of Salisbury, scholar and historian Gilbert Burnet, formerly tutor to her son Gloucester.

202

BURNET: The bishops "prayed daily" for "a good peace," but the preliminaries "gave no hopes of such an one; and the trusting to the King of France's faith, after all that had passed, would seem a strange thing."

ANNE: You must disregard "the preliminaries; we should have a peace" that would in no way "rely on the King of France's word." The bishops must "suspend [their] opinions," until "acquainted ... with the whole matter."

BURNET: May I have leave "to speak my mind plainly"?

ANNE: Granted.

BURNET: "Any treaty by which Spain and the West Indies were left to King Philip, must in a little while deliver up all Europe into French hands." Any such peace would betray the queen and ruin her compatriots; for "in less than three years time she would be murdered," the Pretender return, and Catholicism reign as the country's official religion. "I pursued this long, till I saw she grew uneasy."[5]

—m—

"It will be best for me just to begin to open the matter of the peace to [the Duke of Marlborough, then refer him] to you and [secretary of state Bolingbroke] for a fuller account of all that is passed,"[6] Anne wrote Oxford as her captain general's ship approached the English coast at the close of a successful campaign season. Marlborough had left London in the spring with parliamentary support for war supplies. Suffering migraine headaches aggravated by labyrinthitis, (causing vertigo and vomiting) the duke focused on calming sticky allies and corresponding regularly with Oxford and Bolingbroke who pledged full backing, which included Marlborough making plans for his march on Paris. The duke thus asked that the army go into winter quarters at recently captured Bouchain fortress, (easiest path to Paris) rather than the usual Holland, so as to get an early start when the coming campaign season opened. (1712) Oxford agreed but had no intention of letting the duke invade France. Were Louis XIV to be flattened, Britain must share the spoils with her Allies, rather than reap exclusive benefits.

Still aching from the after effects of a gout attack, Anne, clad in a new nightgown of quilted scarlet satin lined with red and white striped silk, received the duke in her bedroom. Her gaily-colored, long-tailed pet macaw perched on a brocaded Indian screen placed behind the queen's bed.

The duke had already informed his fiercely pro–Whig wife of his resolve to cast his lot with Whigs. Much gratified, Sarah, who for years had seen her husband struggle to stay above party, let alone resist her Whiggism, could scarcely be expected to keep such news to herself. Although out of favor at court, she had plenty of friends who, the duchess made sure, would convey the duke's decision to Anne.

The queen told Marlborough she wished him to stay in her cabinet, but also support the peace proposals. He "spoke very plainly to the queen against the steps already made."[7] These steps, the peace preliminaries, indicated Oxford's intent to restore the Pretender, which would subject Anne to Catholic plots against her life. Dismissing the duke's warning about Catholic assassination conspiracies, the queen felt confident that "God Almighty's protection is above all things, and as He has hitherto been infinitely gracious to me, I hope he will continue."[8]

Marlborough thought Anne "so possessed [by the possibility of peace] that what he said made no impression. [The duke thus asked to be excused from coming to the cabinet meeting] since he must oppose every step [made] in that affair."[9]

Her meeting with Marlborough confirmed, to the queen, his alliance with Whigs.

For Anne knew, at least from her conversation with Bishop Burnet, if not with Cowper and other Whigs, that the duke's words echoed the Whig position. This, she resented. The queen had, for years, relied on the duke's judgment with the confidence that it would be independent.

Marlborough had not behaved well about politics although she found his personal manner pleasing, Anne confided to her physician Dr. David Hamilton. Hence, when the duke asked the doctor what people said about his conduct to queen and country, Hamilton replied that some gave him "as great or greater character for that victory over himself under provocation than for all his other victories."[10]

—⚏—

Anne's popular captain general spoke against the peace preliminaries in parliament—crushing France would yield a better peace for all members of the Grand Alliance. The duke's prestige made his opposition a boon to the anti-peace party. As well, Marlborough marshaled allied political power against a separate peace, using, particularly, his influence at Hanover through his excellent personal relations with Anne's successor, the dowager electress and her son the elector.

The duke's leadership of the anti-peace movement made him a dangerous enemy. Hence, Oxford and his chief peace negotiator, Viscount Bolingbroke, resolved that Marlborough must be diminished, his popularity dented to make the peace preliminaries palatable. But the two ministers had to tread warily for the house of commons regularly praised Marlborough's military achievements, and cheering crowds followed the duke whenever he appeared in public. Further, the queen had a long-standing personal and political bond with Marlborough.

The threat he posed to peace, plus shrill Whig anti-peace propaganda playing on public fears of a Jacobite restoration by asserting Oxford and Bolingbroke to have secretly promised France to bring back the Catholic Pretender after Anne's death, prompted Oxford to act. He engaged the pen of England's foremost political satirist.

Jonathan Swift's "On the Conduct of the Allies" appeared at year end. (1711) With insidiously simple prose that gave the appearance of accuracy, Swift made credible the government's charges that Anne's captain general and allied commander in chief, victor of four vital battles in the War of the Spanish Succession, had embezzled public funds. And more. This courtier who had succeeded due to his mistresses, not to mention his fawning conduct, this man married to a fanatical Whig, had created a costly conflict he now sought to prolong at all costs to assure continued public funding for his extremely expensive Blenheim Palace. Consequently, the war—caused either by the Marlboroughs' friendship with Queen Anne, or a (Whig) bankers' conspiracy—should be deemed pointless. Marlborough must be crushed to achieve peace.

"The Conduct of the Allies" soon sold out in every urban center. Swift had thousands more copies delivered to country estates to make sure his polemic's natural constituents, Tory squires, read it. Like the recent Sacheverell trial, "Conduct" capitalized on anger and energized the political power of rural Tories.

Further, by blurring the line between Marlborough's supposed abuse of the system and public doubt about government efficacy per se, "Conduct" shifted the latter disquiet onto qualms about Marlborough. And because his domestic foes deplored the duke's wish to perpetuate the war even as they acclaimed Marlborough's achievement—containment of France changed the European balance of power and made Britain a major player—they agreed that he must be destroyed in order to convince parliament to endorse the greater goal—peace.

Other attack pamphlets followed. They shocked all Europe. How, Britain's allies asked, could the queen's ministry condone such an assault on the country's greatest man. The Elector of Hanover, second in line to succeed Anne after his mother the dowager electress, and one of Marlborough's subordinate generals in the allied army, sent his advisor, Baron Bothmer, as a special representative to London personally to convey his objection to the peace preliminaries.

—⁂—

Warnings from old friends like Marlborough and Bishop Burnet troubled Queen Anne. Important allies like Holland and Austria urged her to reject the peace preliminaries. And the Elector of Hanover wrote a memorandum. It supported Marlborough; disparaged the peace as a betrayal of Britain's allies; refuted Tory pro-peace propaganda, with particular attention to "The Conduct of the Allies"; stressed the need to maintain good inter-allied relations, guarantee the interests of all, and stop a Bourbon prince from ruling Spain and the Americas. All allies, the elector assured his audience, could get good peace terms if they kept military pressure on exhausted France.

Baron Bothmer presented his master's memorandum to Oxford and Bolingbroke. He then circulated it among several people of influence. Besides stiffening Whig resistance to the peace preliminaries, the memorandum found its way into one of London's major newspapers. Thousands of copies quickly sold out.

Anne knew nothing of the memorandum. Oxford and Bolingbroke had purposely kept it from her. But the queen's friend and favorite lady-in-waiting, red-haired Elizabeth, Duchess of Somerset, showed her mistress a newspaper copy. The elector's opposition alarmed Anne; her ministers' silence about it, annoyed her. Nonetheless, Queen Anne stayed committed to peace.

—⁂—

As the year (1711) drew to a close, Marlborough joined majority Whigs in the house of lords to vote in favor of the motion: no peace could be ethical or secure if Spain and its empire went to a Bourbon. The motion carried.

Led by Oxford and Bolingbroke, some of Anne's ministers reasoned that since peace would improve relations with France, the need for Marlborough to command the army would disappear and the Alliance (as they desired) would dissolve. These ministers thus agreed that the duke must be destroyed—to kill the anti-peace coalition, achieve peace, and perpetuate the ministers' continuity in office.

Oxford and Bolingbroke initiated an official inquiry into disposal of the huge sums of money parliament had, for nine years, voted to conduct the war. Heavily weighted with Tories thirsting to demolish the duke, the commission of public accounts exposed enough possible misuse of public money to enable the ministry to bring two fraud charges before the Commons.

Marlborough had accepted an annual commission for the contract to supply bread to the army. Certainly, said the duke. This money had all been spent on the secret service; (a crucial investment since much of his success depended on hoodwinking the enemy) besides, everyone knew Marlborough's troops were well fed and his intelligence the best in Europe. But because the duke could not reveal the names of those he had paid for information, or show receipts, he had no way of proving exactly where the money had gone.

The commission further accused Marlborough of keeping for himself two and a half percent of the money Britain paid foreign troops. Yes, said the duke, this constituted the usual way for a commander in chief to finance his secret service; King William III and Queen Anne had both officially authorized the practice. And allied rulers, especially the Elector of Hanover, backed the legality of the deduction.

Oxford had the commission's report on the embezzlement charges published. Derisive mobs gathered outside the Marlboroughs' splendid new London residence. While waiting for the ducal carriage to emerge, enraged citizens amused themselves by hurling stones against the windows of stately Marlborough house. Anonymous and libelous anti-Marlborough screeds deluged the reading public; one Tory pamphlet alleged that the duke murdered his soldiers for profit. Marlborough challenged the author to a duel. Sarah intervened. She notified the authorities. They arrested the man for his own protection.

Furthermore, the duchess circulated copies of her memoirs privately. They lost no opportunity to vilify the queen as a mere cipher, a weakling incapable of independent thought, a religious hypocrite who freely broke every promise.

A compliant Commons found Marlborough to have lined his purse at public expense. That gave Oxford enough ammunition to urge Queen Anne to strip her captain general of all his offices.

—m—

Her ministry's charges against Marlborough shocked the queen; they may not have convinced her of his having committed crimes. But guilty or not, the duke endangered peace. Anne agreed with her ministers that he must be silenced.

The cabinet met on the last day of 1711. Anne's ministers prevailed on her to order an entry in the official record. "Being informed that an information against the Duke of Marlborough was laid before the house of commons, by the commissioner of the public accounts, her majesty thought fit to dismiss him from all his employments, that the matter might undergo an impartial investigation."[11]

The queen felt extremely uncomfortable about dismissing her old friend and trusted counselor, to say nothing of her unease at Oxford's method of effecting Marlborough's fall. True, the queen's confidence in him had started to wane several years before when the duke supported Godolphin and Whigs over the Sunderland appointment. And since her "memory was exceeding great, almost to a wonder,"[12] Anne easily recalled her alarm over Marlborough's more recent request that she appoint him captain general for life, an alarm confirmed when her senior legal advisor assured Anne that the duke's request would flout the spirit of the constitution, damage her prerogative, and injure the nation's liberties. Still, even Anne's decision to dismiss Sarah had scarcely dented her affection for the charismatic duke, whose "manner was irresistible, by either man or woman,"[13] who "knew the arts of living in a court beyond any man in it."[14]

Unable to face dismissing Marlborough in person, the saddened, tongue-tied queen, as in the case of another longtime friend and trusted counselor—Sidney Godolphin—took refuge in the written word. "To see himself treated in such a manner [gave the duke] such present commotion of mind, that he threw the letter into the fire, with a mixture of just disdain, and resentment at such usage. But he presently recovered his usual calmness, and immediately wrote the queen."[15]

After blaming his dismissal on Oxford's malice, the duke avowed himself "much more concerned at an expression in your majesty's letter, which seems to complain of the treatment you had met with. I know not how to understand that word, nor what construction to make of it. I know, I have always endeavored to serve your majesty faithfully, and zealously, through many undeserved mortifications."[16]

If, by treatment, Anne meant Marlborough's absence from the last cabinet meeting, he declared himself "very free to acknowledge [that duty to queen and country] would not give me leave to join in the councils of that man, [Oxford] who, in my opinion, puts your majesty upon all manner of extremities, [for France's government and religion must make its] friendship ... destructive to your majesty."[17]

Even such Marlborough detractors as Jonathan Swift conceded that the duke's dismissal might yet prove an unwise move; for "we have had constant success in arms when he commanded. [Since] opinion is a mighty matter in war, [Swift felt sure] the French think it impossible to conquer an army that he leads, and our soldiers think the same: and how far this step may encourage the French to play tricks with us, no man knows."[18]

Concomitantly, Tory ministers increased their pressure on the queen to dismiss the moderate Whig Duke and Duchess of Somerset. That offended Anne's strong sense of prerogative. Dislike of Whigs had provoked the queen into cashiering her Whig cabinet. If Tories meant to enslave her, she may as well have kept her former jailors, Anne told Oxford who, under stress, could stray across the subtle line separating an offer of respectful advice from an attempt at coercion. "I told you my thoughts freely, as I always have, and ever will continue to do on all occasions, [Anne wrote her prime minister after one of their rare disputes.] You cannot wonder that I who have been ill used so many years should desire to keep myself from being again enslaved; and if I must always comply and not be complied with, [it] is I think very hard and what I cannot submit to, and what I believe you would not have me."[19]

The Somersets had served Anne for years. First noble lady in the land Elizabeth Somerset had defied the joint monarchs to let Anne live in Syon House during her banishment from court, had served the queen as lady-in-waiting since her accession, had lately become Anne's first lady of the bedchamber and groom of the stole, but above all, her personal friend. And Elizabeth had recently shown the queen what her ministers withheld—the Elector of Hanover's memorandum refuting Tory propaganda in favor of the peace preliminaries.

The Duke of Somerset had served in Anne's household and cabinet since her accession. But Somerset now advocated against the peace preliminaries in the house of lords. That made it impossible for the queen to keep him in her cabinet. So, the first moderate Whig to desert Harley lost his prestigious post as Queen Anne's master of the horse.

This victory motivated Tory ministers to mount a concerted campaign to remove Elizabeth Somerset. And asked Jonathan Swift to help. "Windsor Prophecy" resulted.

> Dear England, if aught I understand
> Beware of carrots [Elizabeth's red hair] from Northumberland. [Her birthplace]
> Carrots sown there a deep root may get,
> If so be they are in summer set:
> Their conyngs mark [play on Konigsmark, the rival suitor who killed Elizabeth's
>   second husband] thou, for I have been told,
> They assassine when young and poison when old.

Root out these carrots, O thou, whose name
Is backwards and forwards always the same: [Anna]
And keep close to thee always that name,
Which backwards and forwards is almost the same. [Masham]
And England wouldst thou be happy still,
Bury those carrots under a hill.[20]

The queen refused to part with her friend and favorite companion. And when haughty Somerset pressed his duchess to resign her court appointments, to return her gold key of office, Anne "ordered" her trusted physician, David Hamilton, to ask moderate Whig former cabinet minister Cowper "to use all interest [with Somerset, so that he would let his wife] "continue her charge." The queen even instructed Hamilton on how to press his case—the doctor should to use her health. It would be "greatly impaired, if it happened that the duke would not let her stay."[21]

Hamilton then "presumed [to tell Anne that if she liked Elizabeth Somerset] it was pity she did not act her own will. For she needed an agreeable friend to open to, in order to lessen the ill effects of her disputes. [Furthermore, if the queen failed to use her power to keep Elizabeth] for her own quiet, [Sarah would gain a] handle to say ... it was not her fault that her majesty parted with her, but her majesty's own circumstances which occasioned it."[22]

Elizabeth Somerset stayed.

Whigs now sought to use Anne's friendship with Elizabeth as a political conduit to royal power. Having deluded themselves into believing Sarah Marlborough had political influence over the queen, Whigs were, however, similarly disappointed—scarcely surprising given Elizabeth's discretion and Anne's aversion to being badgered by her personal attendants.

The Duchess of Somerset kept Anne's affection. Swift paid for his "Windsor Prophecy." It had infuriated the queen. She proved loyal to her friend by rejecting Oxford's urgent plea that she appoint the satirist, ordained in the Established Church of Ireland, (his native land) to a senior position in the Church of England.

—⁂—

A stiff north wind propelled arctic air over London when Queen Anne, dressed in full royal regalia and swathed in furs, drove the short distance from St. James's Palace to Westminster, to open the first parliament of the new year. (1712) Her speech from the throne expressed joy in announcing the place (historic Dutch city of Utrecht) and time (January 29, 1712) for opening formal peace negotiations.

The Tory majority in the house of commons promptly voted that the gratuity which army bread contractors had given Marlborough, constituted an illegal and unjustifiable act; his subtraction from the pay of foreign troops represented unwarranted use of public money.[23] Consequently, the ministry threatened to impeach Marlborough, certain this menace would discourage the duke from further opposition to the peace preliminaries.

At the same time, the Whig dominated house of lords voted in favor of another motion against the preliminaries. So, Oxford turned his talents towards convincing the queen to create enough new peers to assure the government a majority in the Lords. Disinclined to dilute the peerage, (she thought the house of lords full enough) Anne had "made fewer lords than any of her predecessors."[24] But if the ministry fell, Whigs would return to power and continue the war.

The queen "must do what she could to help herself."[25] Behaving like a "pattern of patience, [Anne denied her] own inclination [so as not to provoke Oxford, Bolingbroke, and their allies, and by such] provocation be made uneasy in her own mind."[26]

In the interest of peace, the queen agreed to Oxford's request that she ennoble twelve Tory stalwarts, enough to assure government control of the Lords. Nevertheless, Anne, protected her prerogative; for, if given an opening, ministers proved "too apt to encroach upon my right."[27] The queen did not consult her cabinet over creation of the new peers.

But she did balk at one name on the list of candidates Oxford presented for ennoblement: Colonel Masham. The queen objected to having the husband of her favorite chambermaid become a peer—and Abigail Masham, in consequence, a peeress. Anne "never had any design to make a great lady of her and should lose a useful servant about her person: for it would give offense to have a peeress lie upon the floor and do several other inferior offices." But since Oxford could not find a reliable replacement for Masham, the queen "consented, upon condition [that Abigail] did as she used to do."[28]

The queen had never considered Abigail Masham a friend, merely a good nurse and amusing companion. Hence, Anne told her chambermaid to live privately, refrain from partaking in the formal visits usual for a peeress. Indeed, the queen suspected Abigail, "or her sister [Alice Hill] listened at the door all the time. [That and] some disrespects shown to the Duchess of Somerset, gave her majesty some thoughts of easing her [Abigail] and her sister out of the household."[29]

Abigail confided to Anne that she had heard about some carriages recently imported from Paris—that one might well become hers. "Do not take any notice of it to her, [the queen wrote Oxford, but find out if it were true and try to] prevent it; for I think it would not be right."[30]

The new Tory majority in the house of lords, meanwhile, passed a motion to censure Marlborough.

—⁂—

Soon thereafter, one of Europe's greatest generals arrived in London. Even before he teamed with Marlborough to win victories at Blenheim, Oudenarde, and Malplaquet, the Austrian Empire's Prince Eugene of Savoy held the status of hero in England due to his defeat of the Turks.[31] Now Marlborough, Whigs, and the Allies placed their hopes in Prince Eugene.

The queen's ministers viewed the advent of their distinguished visitor with dismay. Because Great Britain would be going to the peace congress at Utrecht certain that her Austrian ally opposed the peace preliminaries; and because the emperor proposed to send an army into Spain. Prince Eugene would surely urge the queen to do likewise. Thus, Anne's ministers not only tried their utmost to discourage Eugene's visit, but also sent an emissary to meet his ship. Along with his official welcome, the envoy conveyed a warning: the less Eugene saw of his friend and colleague Marlborough, the better.

Prince Eugene stayed with the Marlboroughs at their elegant new London residence throughout his two-month stay in England. And openly declared himself a Whig. On his first full day in London, the queen granted Eugene an audience, and most gracious reception. Eugene presented the personal letter he had brought from the emperor. It urged the queen to join her allies in continuing war against France.

Reluctant to tackle the issue of peace directly, the queen pleaded poor health as a pretext for delegating discussion of the emperor's letter to Oxford and Bolingbroke.

They listened politely to Eugene's protest, on behalf of his sovereign, against the peace preliminaries. But Anne's ministers breathed easy; for, Eugene had arrived too late either to save Marlborough, or stop the peace conference from opening, on schedule, at Utrecht.

London mobs loved Prince Eugene. They followed him everywhere, but cheered most loudly when prince and duke rode out together. Whig as well as Tory notables who thronged to visit him, soon discovered the prince unwilling to listen to any criticism of his friend and co-general. Sarah planned a magnificent ball in Eugene's honor. It would take place on the queen's birthday, and, besides, showcase Marlborough house. Newspapers began to hint that the ball cloaked a seditious plot. Fearing mob violence, the duchess canceled her invitations.

Despite gout in knee and foot, the queen marked her forty-seventh birthday (February 6, 1712) with a full court that sported "as much fine clothes as ever. [Most Whigs chose not to attend. The queen] appeared both morning and afternoon as usual,"[32] first attending chapel in state; later listening to an instrumental concert and the ode she had commissioned Handel to set to music.

Having been "carried in her chair from her dressing room to the great drawing room" in the evening, Anne played a hand of basset with Prince Eugene. She then bestowed on him a splendid dress sword, its gold hilt gleaming with twenty diamonds. Another concert followed—the finest Italian vocalists sang excerpts from popular Italian operas. And since "the next day had got no cold but was rather better than before, [Anne ventured] "out to take the air in Hyde Park."[33]

Discussions with Oxford and Bolingbroke, meanwhile, showed Eugene their lack of interest in continuing the war despite the emperor's promise to double his contribution to it. And although the queen received Eugene several times, the prince became convinced that Britain wanted peace, would make it with France regardless of the Allies to reap valuable commercial concessions.

—⁂—

The popular queen's support for peace and a Tory majority in the house of lords gave Oxford confidence to face parliament. He managed the house of commons so as to get approval of the peace preliminaries despite general reluctance to see Spain and its empire go to a Bourbon prince. Lords approval followed. Assured of the country's commitment to peace, therefore, the government could meet its irate allies at Utrecht, irate because Britain had ignored one vital aspect of the Treaty of the Grand Alliance. It stipulated that the Allies would negotiate with the enemy as one; but Britain had preferred to secure her interests in separate negotiation with France and, fumed the Allies, since France had almost certainly conceded much to England, she would concede less to them.

Marlborough, meanwhile, faced formal impeachment and possible subsequent loss of his fortune. (Government lawyers were preparing to sue the duke for repayment of the bread commission and deduction from foreign troop payments, not to mention demand his returning part of the public money spent to build Blenheim.) Since Marlborough still had a sterling reputation on the Continent, he decided to preserve his person and his wealth by going into voluntary exile; besides, the duke feared that if he stayed in England, he risked becoming embroiled in factional violence or a Jacobite invasion sparked by Anne's uncertain health and a Hanoverian succession.

Marlborough asked his wife's friend, the Ultra Whig MP and satirist Arthur Maynwaring, to apply on his behalf to Oxford, for a passport to travel through the Netherlands and Germanies. There the Marlboroughs would be among friends.

The duke presented his wish to leave England as a means to avoid further rousing Anne's ire, let alone his enemies' harassment. But in fact, Marlborough, the ministry's most active and menacing opponent, harbored ideas about persuading the Allies to invade Britain, oust the ministry, and foil the Jacobite restoration that he and Whigs feared would result from either peace or the queen's death.

Regardless, Oxford had always wanted to get rid of Marlborough. The prime minister now had his chance. Bolingbroke and France both opposed giving the duke a pass to leave England and travel on the Continent. But Oxford prevailed.

Please "assure our friend ... with my most humble service [that despite] endeavors from both sides to obstruct granting the pass desired, yet I shall have the honor to put it into his hands, [Oxford wrote Maynwaring.] I did not think it worthwhile to trouble you with the obstruction one meets with; for when I undertook it, I was resolved not to be deterred from finishing it."[34]

Having accepted the political need for Marlborough's dismissal but recognizing his role in limiting France, securing her throne, and achieving Britain's current status as great power, the queen personally signed Marlborough's pass. She decided against granting him a final interview. Such a meeting would only cause them both a great deal of pain and, besides, serve no practical purpose. Anne did, however, do her utmost to ease the duke's exile.

She made sure his passport gave Marlborough permission to travel at will. The queen made sure the pass recommended him, in her name, not only to all her subjects abroad, but also to the rulers of and commanders in, the places he visited. And Anne agreed that the duke's longtime quartermaster general and righthand, get leave from the army to continue to serve him.

The queen thought Marlborough "did wisely" in going into exile. Friend of both Marlborough and Anne, Cowper took her words to mean "twas a kind of composition between him & the ministry, as well as for other reasons"[35] relating to the bonds of friendship between duke and queen.

Eighteen

"The kindest of queens"

> "The queen ... had all the goodness of temper, of courtesy and breeding, of compassion and inclination to serve the world."
>
> "A mind ... pious towards God, willing to please all its fellow creatures, calm and courteous in conversation, unwilling to believe reproaches of others, or to cast upon them any; dutiful to a husband, and one of the best mistresses to servants."[1]—Dr. David Hamilton

Queen Anne's de facto prime minister, Robert Harley, Earl of Oxford, brought her a magnificent diamond. It had originally belonged to a senior British official who acquired it during his service in India.

> OXFORD: A foreign buyer has shown great interest in having this jewel. "Several gentlemen of the house of commons said it was a pity it should go out of the kingdom and had a mind to move in their House to have it presented to [your] majesty."
>
> QUEEN: I wish you to stop this motion. I "should be very sorry to see the people's money thrown away upon such a bauble for"[2] me. Far better to use the funds to finish construction of Greenwich hospital. (For those serving in the navy and merchant marine.)

Anne later told her secretary of state, the Earl of Dartmouth, that "she never had bought a jewel for her own use in her whole life, and of all the vanities in the world looked upon jewels as the greatest. [But the queen thought they were] proper for presents, because a great value in a small compass."[3]

—⁓—

Queen Anne committed to the War of the Spanish Succession on the day she ascended the throne; indeed, the war defined her reign. But Queen Anne's War did not end with parliament's passage of the peace preliminaries. The prematurely aged queen waged war against pain and debility, not to mention the efforts Merciless Men of both parties made to control her.

A gouty hand gave Anne such pain at Christmas (1712) that the court despaired of seeing her on New Year's Day. But the queen honored the occasion by donning a new nightgown of royal blue mohair lined with matching blue taffeta, to greet the well-wishers who crowded into her bedroom. Two weeks later Anne resumed holding court three times a week, rose from her armchair to welcome the ambassador sent by French King Louis XIV, played basset with the Spanish ambassador, and defied 1713's cold and snow to drive in the park.

Anne refused to let her subjects realize that Their Queen did not enjoy robust health. During a winter that surpassed itself in spreading frigid temperatures across the land, Anne went out daily. What her doctors diagnosed as gout of the stomach made the queen extremely ill for some days, but she soon had herself carried outside in her specially built chair to get fresh air and let herself be seen.

On her birthday, (February 6) the queen savored the French truffles her secretary of state Henry St. John, Viscount Bolingbroke, brought from Paris. But she heard with scarcely veiled disapproval that while there, the married viscount had a flagrant affair with a lapsed nun. And worse. As Bolingbroke waited for the curtain to rise at the Paris Opera, Anne's half-brother, the Pretender to her throne, Prince James Stuart, entered a nearby box. Far from letting this advent disturb his pleasure in the performance, Bolingbroke stayed throughout. The queen thought her minister should have left the theater when the Pretender arrived.

A splendid ball took place on the evening of Anne's birthday. Gout and obesity made her avoid the formal, old-fashioned court dress that French royal females were turning into the accepted

Queen Anne in later life. Neither brilliant in mind nor schooled in statecraft, the popular queen applied pragmatism, common sense, and a kind heart to governing. Artist: John Faber the Elder, 1711. © The Trustees of the British Museum.

European mode; in fact, gout made wearing the stylish layers of any evening dress difficult, but for formal events Anne rose to the occasion. Tightly corseted, clad in a new, old-gold silk dress embroidered in silver thread with a pattern of leaves and flowers, matching satin shoes with a high Louis heel, and carrying a fan of frosted crape mounted on ivory sticks, the queen had herself carried, in her armchair, into her formal reception room to greet her guests. Afterwards, Anne played cards with the French and Spanish ambassadors, and the Duchess of Somerset, her friend and favorite lady-in-waiting.

—∞—

Continuing disagreement in her ministry, meanwhile, distressed Queen Anne. She had never asked for cabinet unanimity but did expect a modicum of harmony.

The queen approved of her temperate Tory prime minister's desire for Moderation, to govern with a mixed ministry that would be above party. Oxford sought to conciliate Whigs so as to save the government from Tory domination. His rival, secretary of state Bolingbroke, wanted a purely Tory government.

Oxford thus sought to replace Bolingbroke, chief British negotiator at the official peace conference taking place in the Dutch city of Utrecht, with his fellow secretary of state, moderate Tory Lord Dartmouth. A vicious dispute convulsed the cabinet meeting. The queen cried for hours afterwards.

Dartmouth failed to match Bolingbroke either in knowledge or ability, so Oxford had to accept defeat. Dartmouth threatened to resign. The queen convinced Oxford to join her in dissuading him. Yet, the Oxford-Bolingbroke rivalry continued unabated, causing Anne to weep and worry throughout many nights.

—⁓—

This situation troubled the queen's physician, moderate Whig David Hamilton. Ahead of his time as a psychologist, Hamilton believed the Oxford-Bolingbroke battle had a negative effect on his royal patient's health. The doctor planned to ask Oxford, he told Anne when gout tortured her, not to bother his sovereign with business, to say nothing of troublesome business. Hamilton "need not do that," murmured the queen. He countered that she kept all worries to herself when nothing could be "so injurious as disquiet lodged within one's self."[4]

Anne's refusal to articulate her anxieties, refusal, even, to admit she had them "unless drawn by some conversation which forced her to," made Hamilton wish the queen's friend and favored companion, Elizabeth, Duchess of Somerset, had not left court to spend time in the country with her husband and children.

The doctor thought Elizabeth a "perfect companion" for the queen. Calm and poised, of the highest noble birth, Elizabeth never tried to meddle, to pry into another's business; besides, she had great "affection" for Anne. Had Elizabeth taken the liberty of asking the queen about business, Anne might have got some peace of mind; Elizabeth lacked ulterior motive; her questioning would have "given relief to her majesty's mind when she had so much uneasiness elsewhere from other hands."[5]

Surrounded since infancy by flatterers and self-servers, Anne had learned how to value discretion. Naturally taciturn, she had lost, with the death of her cherished husband, the only person she could fully trust; besides, the queen had seen how politics could corrode even the closest friendship—as it had hers with Sarah, Duchess of Marlborough. Yes, Anne appreciated Elizabeth's attributes, but because she valued their friendship, the queen judged that in the best interest of keeping it, the relationship should be free of politics.

Had Sarah been like Elizabeth, whose serenity "made her a most suitable companion, [said Hamilton,] she would never have lost favor."[6] Anne agreed.

She also agreed to Hamilton's suggestion that he urge Elizabeth to be with the queen as much as possible. Hence, the doctor told Elizabeth how much he "loved the queen, [would do] everything for her quiet; [and knew Anne derived] great delight [from Elizabeth's company. Hamilton tried to] convince [Elizabeth of Anne's] affectionateness to her, [that the queen had] uneasiness, and feels the advantage of having your grace to converse with."[7]

Elizabeth replied that she always took account of her duty. "Neither the frowns nor the smiles of a court should hinder her from doing that." Because she owed a duty to her husband and children, she must devote all the time spared from "her duty to the queen [to domestic responsibilities.] Impossible, [therefore, that Elizabeth] spend all her time with the queen."[8]

Anne understood duty. She respected Elizabeth's reasoning.

The queen's favorite bedchamber woman Abigail Masham, although agreeable and capable, could scarcely be expected to fill the void left by Elizabeth Somerset's absence. Actually, courtiers noticed a waning in whatever sway Abigail may have enjoyed. The queen refused to allow her chambermaid to assert her new position as wife of a peer, disapproved of anyone approaching Abigail in hope of gaining access to the royal ear. The queen told Dartmouth (who disliked Abigail) that the chambermaid did not favor him because he got on well with Elizabeth Somerset which, Anne trusted, he would continue to do despite Abigail's scowls. Hamilton feared that fiercely Tory Abigail's attempts to exert political influence over the queen upset Anne; but the queen held to her policy of refusing to listen to Abigail's pro–Tory arguments. Nonetheless, when heavily pregnant Abigail stood in danger of losing her baby, Anne kept a three-hour, late night vigil at her bedchamber woman's bedside.

—⁂—

By the time a stronger sun spread warmth, the southeast wind puffed large white clouds across broad spaces of blue sky, and shadows flitted over the budding flower beds beneath Anne's windows, "the queen seems to be very well. [She] goes to take the air, and to church three times a week."[9]

Spring meant the start of a new campaign season on the Continent. Concomitantly, diplomats had gathered around the negotiating table at Holland's canal city of Utrecht to hammer out a peace agreement. Nonetheless, the Allies were still contemplating a march on Paris; they had a larger, better-equipped army than France could muster. Regardless, the Duke of Marlborough's dismissal motivated King Louis XIV to raise his demands at the peace table to such an extent that the Allies decided to resume hostilities.

Oxford and Bolingbroke shuddered at the prospect of another allied victory. Because if the Allies imposed general peace on a completely beaten France, Britain would lose the lucrative trade concessions France and Spain had made in the secret peace preliminaries.

Besides, peace faced enough jeopardy. Recent deaths in the French royal family left King Louis with only a frail toddler grandson as heir, which, considering the high rate of early childhood mortality, scarcely inspired confidence that this little boy would survive; if he did not, Louis's grandson Philip, the current king of Spain, stood next in line. Philip's accession to Louis's throne meant union of the Spanish and French crowns. That would not only upset the European balance of power, but also nullify the effect of the nine-year war waged to prevent exactly that.

Anne expressed much sympathy for the French king on a personal level. But the good of her country came first. Peace must prevail. The queen and her prime minister agreed that, as part of a general peace, Philip's formal renunciation of his right to the French throne would be the most effective way to prevent a union of the two crowns. Intense diplomatic activity ensued.

—⁂—

While British and French diplomats awaited Philip's reply to their proposal that he relinquish his claim to the French throne, the general Queen Anne had appointed to succeed Marlborough as captain general of her army arrived in Holland. The Duke of Ormonde carried prime minister Oxford's orders to confer with the other allied generals on the coming campaign even though Oxford had no intention of allowing the war to continue.

The queen agreed with her prime minister that another allied victory would not be in Britain's best interests. Anne's reaction to the carnage at Malplaquet, last major battle of the war, made her sentiments clear: enough blood had been spilled. Why, therefore, risk the added slaughter more battles would bring. The queen also reasoned, like her ministers, that further allied military success did not necessarily mean a swift end to the war. Louis could be counted on to resist harsher peace terms, and wealthy Spain would back him, thereby entangling the Allies in problematic operations on the Peninsula. Hence, the present path to peace, as laid out in the peace preliminaries, represented the best option for Britain.

Anne and Oxford agreed that Bolingbroke, in his official capacity as secretary of state, send Ormonde Restraining Orders: Britain's commander in chief must avoid any military action until further notice. To the "great surprise [of the other allied commanders,] Ormonde showed the Orders not to act offensively against the French; he seemed to be very uneasy with these orders but said he must obey them."[10]

The Restraining Orders were not made public at home. But rumors about them "struck us here in England with amazement. [The queen's] ministers would neither confess, nor deny the matter, pretending the Oath of Secrecy."[11] Horrified Whigs protested the sacrifice of their country's honor—Britain could not simply abandon her allies on the field. Self-defense forced Oxford to reveal the secret commercial concessions negotiated with France and Spain as part of the peace preliminaries. Consequently, parliament crushed a Whig motion asking Anne to rescind the Orders. By this time, the country preferred peace with advantage to peace with honor.

Bolingbroke and Oxford subsequently refused to admit any responsibility for the Orders. At his impeachment trial in the next reign, Bolingbroke damned the Orders and denied all culpability for them. He may not have originated the Orders, but at the time Bolingbroke showed neither disinclination nor distress in imparting them to Ormonde. On trial for his life some years later, Oxford put all the blame on Anne. Although devising, let alone issuing, the Orders on her own would have been uncharacteristic of Anne, she did sign them. Hence, the queen and her prime minister must be held accountable for the Restraining Orders.

—⁓—

After its glory years under the Duke of Marlborough's command, the entire allied army received news of the Restraining Orders with shock; the same sentiment gripped the allied ministers assigned to The Hague, to say nothing of the allied diplomats negotiating at Utrecht. Dutch diplomats protested to a senior British delegate; he denied any knowledge of the Orders, but had, two days ago, "received a letter … from the queen, in which she complained that [despite her having approached Holland with a request] to enter with her upon a plan of peace," the Dutch reply had been disappointing. "Therefore, she did now think herself at liberty to enter into separate measures to obtain a peace for her own convenience."

This contravened "all their alliances and treaties, [the Dutch protested]; besides, their deference to Anne] on all occasions, [had earned them] much better usage from her."[12]

The ruckus that the Restraining Orders raised in England, plus Oxford's consequent disclosure of Britain's separate, and thus far secret, peace with France, including details of French and Spanish commercial concessions, failed to stop the prime minister from going one step further. He ordered Ormonde to take his army off the field altogether. In return, King Louis agreed that the French port of Dunkirk, long a haven for pirates plundering British ships, would have its fortifications destroyed under British supervision.

Queen Anne's half-brother, the Pretender Prince James Stuart, meanwhile, realized that the Utrecht negotiations might well determine his fate. So, James sent his sister a letter. It expressed disbelief that Anne really meant to keep him from wearing the crown of their ancestors. Naturally, she must prefer her brother to strangers; naturally, she must want Stuarts to continue to sit on the British throne. Anne should consider what she owed their father, her father, who had never stopped loving her. Ignoring all this could easily cause civil war; for Anne must remember that the House of Hanover constituted only a distant connection. Further, the Hanoverians spoke a different language, had distinct, not necessarily British, interests; in fact, a Hanoverian king would promote Germans at the expense of Britons. Catholic James, on the other hand, would change nothing, not even the Church of England.

If Anne had any reaction to this missive, she kept it to herself.

—m—

The allied powers signed the Peace/Treaty of Utrecht[13] (March 31, 1713) after negotiating for a little over a year. Utrecht gave the contentious European continent seven decades of stability—until the wars of the French Revolution.

Utrecht confirmed the demise of the Dutch Republic as a major European player. Financial heft had raised Holland to great power status in the previous century, but the War of the Spanish Succession depleted the Dutch treasury and exhausted the nation. Hence, having lost its position, Holland acquiesced to a barrier (a string of forts facing France in the Spanish Netherlands) that turned out to be less than originally sought but enough to secure the country from French intrusion. As well, Holland's immediate neighbor, the Spanish Netherlands, became part of the polyglot Hapsburg empire, which would be unlikely to challenge Dutch commercial hegemony in the immediate environs.

This property transfer worked to Britain's advantage as well; for, rather than facing belligerent Spain across the Channel, the island nation faced benign Austria. Besides, Dutch diminution reduced a major commercial and maritime rival.

In exchange for ceding the, by now hopeless, Hapsburg claim to the Spanish throne, the Austrian empire got, in addition to the Spanish Netherlands, Spain's central and southern Italian possessions in exchange. A Hapsburg presence in the Mediterranean weakened Spain to Britain's advantage.

In fact, Queen Anne's country became a Mediterranean power. Because Britain kept her conquests of Gibraltar (to Spain's chagrin—a chagrin that persists until today) and Port Mahon on the island of Minorca.

Utrecht opened north America to British control. Queen Anne's predecessors had established colonies on the continent's eastern seaboard. France now ceded its north American colonies of Newfoundland and Nova Scotia. France also gave Great Britain northern Canada's vast, strategically located Hudson's Bay area, important because Hudson's Bay functioned as not only a center of trade with the interior, but also as jumping-off point for inland exploration—and future conquest.

Britain gained France's former West Indies colony of St. Kitts. Together with current British colonies (including Antigua, Barbados, and Jamaica) St. Kitts enhanced Britain's naval and commercial position in the Caribbean.

King Louis XIV's grandson freely gave up his claim to the French throne, which facilitated, for Queen Anne's subjects, the acceptance of Britain's agreement that Philip keep Spain and its empire. In return, Spain and France granted Britain commercial concessions in the Mediterranean. And Spain allowed Britain trading rights in South America including the lucrative *Asiento*, which gave Britain a thirty-year monopoly to supply African slaves to Spain's American colonies.

Utrecht recognized Queen Anne's right to the British throne as well as the legitimacy of her Protestant Hanoverian successors. And to confirm the end of French insistence that the Catholic Pretender constituted Britain's rightful king, France's Louis promised to expel Prince James from his country.

Utrecht recognized France's reduced prestige and military power. Forced to abandon the principle that united Europe against him in the War of the Spanish Succession, King Louis agreed formally to promise that the thrones of France and Spain would never be united under one monarch.

Great Britain had justified the fears of her allies—that she would benefit most from the Peace of Utrecht. But Britain achieved peace at the expense of good relations with Hanover. Oxford sent a special envoy to persuade the elector to align himself with British policy and, thus, endear himself to his future subjects. But the elector replied that since the queen still had many years ahead of her, and his mother the dowager electress would succeed to the British throne before him, he must think as a German prince and act in the best interests of Hanover. Dowager Electress Sophia told Oxford's envoy that because Utrecht had driven a wedge between Hanover and Britain, parliament should confirm her and her heirs' succession by conferring an official pension on her. Queen Anne did not ask her ministers to make such a motion in parliament.

—⟋⟍⟍—

The queen and two of her ministers achieved the Peace of Utrecht—prime minister Oxford as architect, secretary of state Bolingbroke as negotiator, head of state Anne as facilitator.

She had backed the peace effort from its inception. Against her inclination the queen had agreed to create twelve peers, an action that enabled passage of the peace preliminaries in the house of lords. To obliterate opposition to peace, the queen had reluctantly acquiesced in the dismissal of Marlborough, her friend, her oldest and most trusted counselor. She had agreed to issue the Restraining Orders, which effectively meant deserting her allies on the field of battle, an action that kept Anne's promise to serve her country's interests before all else.

Ever practical, the queen judged her realm to have faced realities: no country could afford to continue fighting forever; No Peace Without Spain proved untenable; Britain must act when France showed itself ready for concessions.

Anne's nation rejoiced over the Peace of Utrecht. British diplomacy had held the Alliance together; English gold had financed the war; British armies had a key role in winning all major battles; and England had given the Allies their greatest general. The country thought it right that Queen Anne and her ministers determine peace terms to the nation's advantage.

She awarded Oxford the Order of the Garter for his role in achieving peace. Anne denied the honor to Bolingbroke; his immoral personal life made him unfit to wear the Garter.

—⟋⟍⟍—

On a late spring morning when clouds resembling blown feathers drifted across a pure azure sky, the ambient air filled with a delicate scent of flowers and promise of warmth to come, Queen Anne's smartly liveried heralds raised their burnished brass trumpets to proclaim peace as official throughout her realm. The queen would drive in state to St. Paul's Cathedral for the magnificent thanksgiving service she had planned down to the last detail, hear the Tower guns thunder their last salute to war, and listen to the *Te Deum et Jubilate* she had commissioned George Frederic Handel to write in celebration of the signing of the peace treaty.

On the preceding day Anne held a formal audience for foreign diplomats. She had been feeling well for some time, but gout prevented the queen from standing during the lengthy ceremony; as well, it tired her. Hence, Dr. Hamilton advised against going to St. Paul's. "However, I think both Houses should go thither and I will perform my devotions at St. James's and be contented without a sermon, [Anne wrote Oxford.] It is really very uneasy for me that I cannot go, which I hope all my friends believe."[14]

But the queen did hear Handel's composition. It so pleased her that Anne added his name to the list of musicians who received an annual royal stipend.

By the time parliament adjourned for its summer recess, the queen's ministry had not only survived the ado over the Restraining Orders but managed to fortify itself. Oxford had smashed Whig opposition to peace by engineering the Duke of Marlborough's fall; the recently revealed commercial concessions pleased a public craving peace and prosperity; and Oxford tackled Britain's immediate war-related financial woes by introducing the South Sea Act into parliament—those holding government obligations would exchange their debts for shares in the new South Sea company, created to trade with Spanish America.

Having "dined at Hampton Court," where she and Prince George used to enjoy sitting in the garden banqueting house beside the river, watching the countless rowing boats and sailing ships go by, to say nothing of the regal white swans, Anne, "next day in the evening [arrived at Windsor Castle for the summer.] She has the use of her limbs more than I have known her for this 5 or 6 years past." Consequently, Anne indulged herself by visiting Ascot for the races, and daily going "out to take the air in her chaise in this forest."[15]

A chilly wind then descended on Windsor. Forty members of the Castle's household staff succumbed to influenza. But not the queen.

She suffered a bout of the gravel (kidney stones).

Having recovered quickly, Anne developed an extremely gouty foot. To facilitate negotiating the stairs, she used the pulley chair custom made one hundred and fifty years ago, to accommodate her ancestor King Henry VIII's lame leg.

Gout persisted. But it failed to stop the queen from opening parliament with a speech delivered in her usual superb manner, if somewhat weaker voice, and presiding over her weekly cabinet meeting. There, to Queen Anne's dismay, bitter words between Oxford, Bolingbroke, and their respective backers peppered the proceedings.

Nineteen

The Last Stuart

"Farewell old year, for thou canst ne'er return,
No more than the great queen for whom we mourn;
Farewell old year, with thee the Stuart race
Its exit made, which long our isle did grace;
Farewell old year, the Church hath lost in thee
The best defender it will ever see."[1]—
Anonymous contemporary verse

Since the day of Anne Stuart's birth, succession to the throne had, to a greater or lesser degree, been a factor in her life. Deteriorating health in the months before Anne's death, cast the question of who should succeed her into sharp focus.

Having recovered from her late summer (1713) gout attack, Anne, by autumn, needed only the help of a cane to stroll through Windsor Castle's gardens and admire the vivid purple verbena, tall, yellow sunflowers, and gleaming orange daisies growing in profusion. Some weeks later the queen walked in the crisp air unaided.

But on Christmas Eve she startled her court with a new illness. Anne fell into a coma. On regaining consciousness after several hours, the queen shivered intensely, then became extremely hot, thirsty, and agitated; as well, Anne's pulse fluttered alarmingly and she complained of a stabbing pain in her right thigh. The queen's physician thought gout had traveled up her leg, but as pain intensified, Anne let her male doctor examine the thigh, which showed an inflammation with pustules. The physician diagnosed what today we know as erysipelas, a streptococcal infection of the skin. The doctor ordered embrocation, and various vile tasting medicines.

Within a few days Anne felt fit enough to receive, in her bedroom, some senior members of her household; but she stayed unwell for weeks. The queen emerged from her sickroom with a discolored face. She disguised this unhappy result of her illness with make-up. Still, Anne's puffy face and slow, breathless speech shocked a Danish visitor, one of her late husband's friends, who had met the queen several times before.

—◊◊◊—

The new year (1714) swept in on a wave of razor-edged northeast winds. They kept Queen Anne at Windsor. Gout returned. London buzzed with speculation—the queen lay on her death-bed, the French were about to invade England on the Pretender's behalf. These rumors prompted Anne to announce her intention of opening parliament. Wearing a warm velvet dress of dark blue, an ermine-lined, high-collared matching velvet cloak, her hands cozily encased in a huge ermine muff, feet resting on a hot brick, the queen, on a freezing February afternoon stepped into her comfortable carriage, its leather curtains drawn and fur rug covering the floor to ward off draughts, and returned to her capital.

Anne addressed the legislature in her customary clear, melodic voice. And despite often feeling unwell, she worshipped regularly at St. James's chapel. Besides, the queen received an address from the Commons, and appeared at a formal drawing room.

Conscious of her role as the unifying force in a nation whose deep Tory-Whig divide affected every aspect of her subjects' lives, the popular queen hid her ill health in order to reassure. Anne "really grows better every day, and since she has come to town has been often publicly seen,"[2] a courtier reported. The queen also continued to Touch for the King's Evil. She asked her keeper of the privy purse to increase the order for pieces of Healing Gold, since Anne meant to Touch as many poor people as possible.

—〰—

Despite the queen's efforts to soothe her subjects, the question of who would succeed her began to consume them. Certainly, parliament had legislated that no Catholic could succeed to the British throne. Certainly, the Act of Settlement (passed in 1701 after the death of Anne's son the Duke of Gloucester) and the Regency Act (passed in 1705 to assure a smooth transition) provided that Anne's Protestant cousin Sophia, Dowager Electress of Hanover, and her progeny would succeed Anne. Certainly, the recently signed Peace of Utrecht (1713) confirmed Queen Anne's legitimacy and the lawful right of the Hanoverian royal family to succeed her. But as certainly, laws could be overturned.

Some Tories had always believed the queen's Catholic half-brother Prince James Stuart, Pretender to his deposed father's throne, held the legitimate right to succeed Anne. Other Tories turned to the Pretender when they saw the Hanoverian court oppose their pet project—the Peace of Utrecht. Jacobites jumped in, using Anne's broad-based popularity to buttress the Pretender's legitimacy. Another faction of the Tory party proved strongly pro–Hanover. More Tory MPs than any of these groups were ready to support the Pretender if he converted to Anglicanism and—if Anne backed him first.

The disciplined Whigs were united. Hanoverians must succeed the queen.

Her policy had consistently combined ambition and principle. After Gloucester's death, Princess Anne supported parliamentary statutes designating Protestant Sophia her successor; for, if her Catholic half-brother had a hereditary right to the crown, it surpassed hers. Queen Anne held to the principle that her Hanoverian heirs must stay in Germany during her reign, since their presence in England would inevitably draw the disgruntled of both parties, thereby adding another discordant element to the toxic political environment. Anne thus excluded Hanoverian and Jacobite while preserving her authority.

—〰—

Two potent women now struggled over the succession. Queen Anne's heir apparent, Sophia, Dowager Electress of Hanover, sought to cap a lifetime of achievement with a crown. Anne continued to be convinced that her successor (or a member of her successor's family) must not reside in England during her reign. In fact, Sophia's special representative in London had already advised the dowager that on this subject "the queen ... is extremely determined and very fierce."[3]

Many saw Anne's refusal to invite either Sophia, her son, or grandson to England as a sign of her dislike for the Hanoverian royal family, even a sign of her intent to restore her Catholic half-brother. Actually, the queen dreaded the effect of Sophia's presence. Since the formidable electress had been meddling in English politics since the day of her designation as heir apparent, she would ipso facto form a rival court thereby not only exacerbating the already acrid rivalry between political factions, but also distracting from Anne's ability to be a unifier, all of which would weaken the nation.

The patriotic queen had proved her point while princess. As senior Protestant royal residing in England during her Catholic father's reign, Anne made every effort to stop herself and her court from developing into the center of political opposition. Likewise, in William and Mary's reign, for Anne's dispute with them had been purely personal.

As for wanting to restore the Pretender, Anne had regularly cast doubt on the legitimacy of his birth, played an active role in the revolution against her father, proceeded forcefully against threats of a Jacobite invasion, supported the Hanoverian succession in her first speech to parliament and throughout her reign, and for nine years, waged a costly war as de facto head of the Protestant coalition against Catholic France. Moreover, a lifetime of piety and devotion to the Anglican church made it ludicrous to imagine Anne considering a Catholic successor.

The queen had never shown the least sign of favoring her brother's restoration. In fact, she had ignored Prince James's several pleas. In his latest, the Pretender appealed to her proverbial good nature, as well as family feeling, at the same time assuring his half-sister that he would never "abandon his just right.... It is for yourself that a work so just and glorious [his restoration] be reserved. The voice of God and nature calls you to it; the promises you made to the king our father enjoin it; the preservation of our family, the preventing of unnatural wars require it; and the public good and welfare of our country recommend it to you."[4]

Prince James promised "to give all the security that can be desired ... to make the law of the land the rule of my government, to preserve every man's right, liberty, and property, equally with the rights of the crown; and to secure and maintain those of the Church of England, in all their just rights and privileges, as by law established; and to grant such a toleration to dissenters as the parliament shall think fit."[5]

The Pretender concluded by declaring himself always "ready to agree to whatever you shall think most convenient for my interest, which, after all, is inseparable from yours."[6]

Anne had an excellent memory. She recalled that, on his ascent to the throne her father, King James II, made similar promises only to break them. Besides, as a constitutional queen who respected statute law, Anne could scarcely be expected to entrust her crown to a Catholic not only after parliament banned Catholics from the throne, but also to a Catholic who had grown up under the autocratic rule of his benefactor French King Louis XIV.

The queen scoffed at rumors of the Pretender's possible return—with her consent— or without it to force her hand. Such reports were baseless; they could never coerce Anne, even for one moment, into the idea of restoring her half-brother.

—❦—

Two potent men wielded the succession as a weapon in their political rivalry. Constrained to rely on fickle rank and file Tory backing to govern, Queen Anne's prime minister, moderate Tory Lord Oxford, refused to give either the Tory party or the nation a clear lead on the succession. Rather, Robin the Trickster flattered the Jacobite court and pardoned returning Jacobites to keep domestic Jacobite Tories on his side; concomitantly, Oxford courted Whigs and assured Hanover's electoral family of his support.

Tory secretary of state Lord Bolingbroke refused to cater to Whigs or cultivate Hanoverians. Focused on his ambition to lead the ministry, Bolingbroke, whose open and incisive style, not to mention captivating oratory, attracted adherents, believed Tories would follow him in backing whichever successor would profit the party; and the recent Tory election victory bolstered Bolingbroke's belief that the ministry must shed Oxford's moderate policy so as to win rank and file Tory support.

Anne's poor health prompted Bolingbroke to initiate contacts with the Pretender. Oxford spoke of his intent to bring James to the throne; but the prime minister opposed Bolingbroke's plan to staff the army's officer corps with High Tories and Jacobites; and Oxford kept Whig and Tory moderates in public office.

Many believed Oxford and Bolingbroke favored the Prince James's return. Others were sure the queen would reinstate him. Indeed, rumor claimed that the silk purse, strung on a silk thread, which Anne always wore around her neck and under her white linen shift, contained secret papers. Should she die suddenly, these papers would empower Tories to restore the Pretender.

—⟶∭⟵—

Oxford had for so long got used to hiding "his true intentions, [to speaking in an] ambiguous and obscure way, [that one could] hardly ever" understand him when he wanted to be understood or believe him when he particularly "desired it."[7] Honed over a lifetime in politics, Oxford's habit of speech grew more pronounced as he maneuvered to protect his position in the next reign.

Signing herself as Oxford's "very affectionate friend," the queen always spoke frankly to him, as she believed friends should do. Hence, when gout in her fingers subsided enough to allow Anne to hold a pen, she "again [asked Oxford to] speak plainly, lay everything open and hide nothing from me or else how is it possible I can judge of anything?"[8]

Anne's exasperation with her prime minister and lord treasurer could hardly be expected to abate when she learned that most of her household staff had not been paid since he took over the treasurer's office. "One of the best mistresses to servants,"[9] Anne several times pressed Oxford to find funds to pay some, at least, of the arrears. His growing forgetfulness and inattention to detail caused the queen often to draw Oxford's attention to overlooked matters of business.

Her prime minister's new habit of lateness further irritated Anne. Oxford then tried to slide his nominee for household treasurer past her by presenting a blank warrant for the queen to sign. Having already promised the position to someone else, "I desire you would not have so ill an opinion of me as to think when I have determined anything in my mind I will alter it, [Anne chided.] "When you come hither bring the warrant with his name."[10]

Oxford now committed a blooper. Having arranged to marry his only son to England's richest heiress, daughter of a duke whose title died with him, Oxford, as part of the marriage settlement, promised to effect a revival of the title in favor of his son. According to Oxford, the queen agreed. So, after the marriage, he asked her to grant the title.

Anne had always protected her right to ennoble. Not long ago she had overcome her aversion to creating new peers because Oxford's request for twelve Tory lords served the national interest—passage of the peace preliminaries. Anne now judged it improper not only further to dilute the nobility but also to grant its highest rank as a personal favor to her prime minister. She refused Oxford's request.

Some weeks later a shattering blow struck Oxford. His dearly loved daughter died. The queen shared his sorrow. Still, the grieving prime minister visited her less often, and when he did, spoke more obscurely than ever. Besides, Oxford drowned his distress in drink to such an extent that his inebriation offended Anne.

All these factors shook the queen's faith in her first minister.

—⚬⚬—

As the fresh spring sun moved in and out of fleecy white clouds scudding across London from the sea, "chilliness, vomiting, a pain in the leg, the pulse very disordered and in every manner as two months ago except [she] did not shiver, [struck the queen.] Chilliness and cold continued twelve hours [followed] by very great heat, thirst and all the symptoms of very high fever which lasted till the next evening."[11] And the queen's physicians feared gangrene from the persistent infection in Anne's thigh.

Two weeks later, the queen and her court celebrated the April anniversary of her accession in customary splendid style. Richly gowned and elaborately made-up, the extremely popular monarch graced a magnificent evening drawing room; entertainment included a professionally performed ballet. Up and down the land, bonfires, illuminations, and other expressions of joy lit the night sky.

Queen Anne continued to connect with her poorer subjects by Touching for the King's Evil twice weekly, a practice Anne's ladies-in-waiting frowned upon. For the pious queen fasted before, and afterwards ate sparingly for several days, which, in her ladies' judgement, "does her hurt."[12]

Nonetheless, "the queen is well and grows better and better every day."[13] She attended her drawing room regularly, conversed fluently with the French ambassador in his native language, and played basset. "She looked mighty well."[14]

—⚬⚬—

Illness returned. It prompted the queen's ministry to replace some military and civil officials with Jacobites. That inspired the pro–Pretender party openly to advocate his return, which caused others to clamor for a member of Hanover's royal family to reside in England.

These rumblings soon reached Dowager Electress Sophia. Ambitious for the crown, the redoubtable octogenarian decided to take matters into her own hands.

On passage of the Regency Act, the queen had created Sophia's grandson the electoral prince, Duke of Cambridge. This title gave him a seat in the house of lords. Every member of that chamber received, from Anne's lord chancellor, an official writ of summons commanding his presence in the upper house.

Consequently, the dowager's large, confident, black-lettered handwriting sloped boldly across the page of the missive she wrote, without her son the elector's knowledge, to Hanover's unofficial envoy in London. Sophia asked Georg von Schütz to inform the queen's lord chancellor "that here we are astonished that no writ has been sent to my grandson the electoral prince to enable him to enter parliament as Duke of Cambridge, for that is due him according to the patent that the queen gave him."[15]

Sophia put herself in the wrong. Diplomatic practice dictated that the dowager approach Anne first, via an official request through proper diplomatic channels. And Sophia should have made her request with the consent of her son the elector since only he, had responsibility for Hanover's relations with foreign powers. The dowager not only broke the rules of diplomacy, but by so doing, also made also a diplomatic mistake.

Schütz compounded it. Instead of consulting the queen and Oxford in private, or referring the question to the elector, Schütz conferred with Whigs. Afraid Anne's frail health and possible imminent death would trigger the Pretender's arrival; hoping to regain popularity lost over Whig opposition to peace, by having the electoral prince in England where he could show his family to be pro–Whig, these men advised that the electoral prince come to England immediately.

Schütz, therefore, formally asked the lord chancellor for the writ of summons. An astounded, not to say embarrassed, silence greeted this request. The chancellor then murmured that he must consult the queen.

Shocked, let alone insulted, by Sophia's action, Anne reacted angrily. She had not received the application for the writ through proper channels, but from a cabinet minister, her servant, and via Hanover's unofficial envoy, no less..

That evening Queen Anne presided over an emergency cabinet meeting. She heatedly declared that Schütz had acted without proper orders from Hanover, had, as well, let himself be manipulated by ruthless elements in London. Furious that her repeated affirmations of friendship for Hanover had been ignored, that Schütz omitted the courtesy of applying directly to her, Anne wanted to reject Sophia's demand. Bolingbroke unctuously backed her. Oxford acknowledged the request for the writ as legitimate—thereby also protecting his position in the next reign, for the prime minister could not then be impeached for breaking the law in what would be seen as the Pretender's interest. Oxford's position earned him the queen's disapproval, but she grudgingly accepted his reasoning.

Schütz got the writ. Anne barred him from court. Sophia and her son the elector were officially informed of the queen's fury; and told that sending the electoral prince to take his seat in the house of lords would be extremely unwise. The elector disavowed the entire business and replaced Schütz.

Soon thereafter, however, the Hanoverian court sent an official memorandum to London. Sophia and her son demanded that the Pretender, currently living in Lorraine, must move to Italy; that parliament should grant the dowager electress an allowance; and that a member of the electoral family must move to England.

—⁂—

Making small comfortable sounds, a brightly burning wood fire in the grate of Anne's private parlor at St. James's Palace, and fresh May sunshine slanting through the windows, illuminated the queen's writing table. Drawing a crackling sheet of paper towards her, Anne dipped her pen into the inkwell of her silver standish, and started to write.

Since the day parliament declared the "right of succession to my kingdom [to belong to] you and your family, [the queen addressed the dowager electress,] disaffected persons [acting in] their own interests [have tried to] establish a prince of your blood to my estates ... whilst I am yet living."[16]

Well aware of Whig encouragement that Sophia apply for the writ to summon the electoral prince to take his seat in the house of lords as Duke of Cambridge, Anne decided, in the best interests of all concerned, to be forthright.

Until now, she had never thought "this project could have gone so far as to have made the least impression [on Sophia. But lately,] industriously spread [rumors affirm that the electoral prince entered] into this sentiment. [The] succession of your family [required the queen to tell her cousin the electress that] such a proceeding will infallibly draw along with it some consequences ... dangerous to that succession. [It would not, in fact, be] secure [unless the ruler] actually wearing the crown maintain her authority and prerogative."[17]

The electoral prince's arrival in England would not only encourage Jacobites to demand the Pretender's presence, but also further pollute an already poisonous political climate, even drive Anne's divided nation into civil war, she pointed out. For very many people "here (such is our misfortune) are seditiously disposed. [The queen left Sophia] to judge what tumults they may be able to raise if they should have a pretext to begin a commotion. [Anne believed Sophia could] never consent that the least thing ... be done that may disturb the repose of me or my subjects."

The queen concluded by encouraging Sophia to be as frank with her as Anne had been, to "propose whatever you think may contribute to the security of the succession. I will come into it with zeal provided it does not derogate from my dignity, which I am resolved to maintain."[18]

Having settled herself more comfortably against the cushions of her padded arm-chair, the queen then tackled her cousin the elector. Growing rumors about the electoral prince's decision to "settle in my lifetime in my dominions, [caused Anne to lose no time in writing to the elector directly,] to communicate to you my sentiments upon a subject of this importance."

The queen could not conceive that a prince with the "knowledge and penetration of your electoral highness, can ever contribute to such an attempt. [Writing as one sovereign to another, Anne believed the elector] too just to allow ... any infringement ... on my sovereignty which you would not choose to be made on your own. [He surely would not permit the] smallest diminution of your authority: I am [the same; and] determined to oppose a project so contrary to my royal authority, however fatal the consequences may be."

The elector must, in justice, agree that Anne had always given "proofs of my desire that your family should succeed to my crowns; which I always recommend to my people as the most solid support of their religion and their laws. [But, the queen pointed out, one cannot] derogate from the dignity and prerogatives of the prince who wears the crown, without making a dangerous breach on the rights of the successor. [Hence, she felt confident that with] your usual wisdom, you will prevent the taking of such a step, and you will give me an opportunity of renewing to you assurance of the most sincere friendship."[19]

Because she respected etiquette, Anne addressed the electoral prince as well. Since the request for the writ of summons "ought to have been first to me, so I expected you would not have given ear to it without knowing my thoughts about it. [Nonetheless, the queen owed her] own dignity, the friendship I have for you and the electoral house to which you belong, and the true desire that it may succeed to my kingdoms, [to tell the prince that] nothing can be more dangerous to the tranquility of my estates, to the right of succession in your line, and consequently more disagreeable to me, than such a proceeding at this juncture."[20]

Sophia reacted "very moaningly to ... the queen's letters.... She was certainly very desirous of having her grandson in England."[21] The electress sent Anne's letter to several courts as well as to the Duke and Duchess of Marlborough, still living in self-imposed exile on the Continent. Sophia wanted the letters published. The duchess did not disappoint her. Sarah leaked the letters to the Whig press.

That gave the dowager electress scant satisfaction. When the weather in Hanover turned balmy and a westering sun bathed the octogenarian dowager's well-tended gardens, Sophia decided to go for one of her vigorous evening walks. As usual, her ladies strove to keep up with their mistress as she strode briskly along the paths flanking borders full of brightly colored spring flowers. Suddenly, Sophia collapsed. She died instantly.

Anne immediately ordered that The Elector of Hanover should replace The Princess Sophia in the relevant section of the Anglican Church's *Book of Common Prayer*. But the brouhaha surrounding the electoral prince's projected residence in England left a disagreeable aftertaste at both the British and Hanoverian courts. Indeed, Hanover blamed the affair for the dowager's death.

—⚭—

Although the queen recovered from the illness that felled her in January, and again in April, she felt far from well as spring days lengthened into summer. Gout continued to plague Anne's weakened body; her quarreling cabinet preyed on the queen's spirit. She had fought the War of the Spanish Succession for nine long years. Her government had brought about the beneficial Peace of Utrecht. Great Britain should now unite and get on with its business. Instead, Anne's ministers "sought for themselves."[22]

Inured to loss—in childhood her grandmother, aunt, and mother; father and children before gaining a throne; then her cherished husband, inseparable, loyal, and irreplaceable life-partner—Anne felt very much alone. Her best friend Sarah had not only destroyed their friendship, but also undermined Anne's faith in the two ministers, Marlborough and Godolphin, she trusted most, saw as the mainstay of her government. The queen's sole remaining friend, Elizabeth, Duchess of Somerset, often left court to be with her family. Anne had never considered her favorite bedchamber woman, Abigail Masham, as a friend; now the queen suspected Abigail of eavesdropping, never mind helping herself to funds from the privy purse. The queen felt unable to trust anyone.

She still valued Oxford's moderation, upright moral character, fiscal probity, and parliamentary skills. But the prime minister's laxity in business matters—like withholding salaries from the queen's household staff and trying to bypass her appointment of household officers, not to mention his opacity and excessive drinking, weakened Anne's faith in her long-time political confidant.

The queen acknowledged Bolingbroke's abilities, but deplored his depraved personal life, especially the way Bolingbroke treated his spouse; nor did Anne appreciate his outright Toryism. Besides, she had never fully trusted Bolingbroke. Having lived her entire life amid sycophants, the queen at once recognized him as one—most recently the secretary had tried to insinuate himself into her good graces by pandering to her aversion at having a Hanoverian royal reside in England while she lived; besides, Bolingbroke tried to influence Anne via staunchly Tory Abigail. (The secretary had succeeded in transferring her loyalty from Oxford to himself.) But since Anne had always refused to discuss politics with Abigail, it is extremely doubtful that Bolingbroke's conquest brought him much benefit.

—⚭—

Bent on protecting his position in the next reign, meanwhile, Oxford sent his cousin on a special mission to Hanover to assure the electoral court of his loyalty to the Hanoverian succession. At the same time, the prime minister negotiated with the Pretender. Oxford asked Prince James to change, or at least hide, his Catholicism via an official declaration. It must proclaim the prince's conversion to Anglicanism; endorse Oxford's moderate administration; and promise never to try to seize the throne by military force (i.e., raise armed rebellion in Scotland). Equally focused on self-protection, Bolingbroke made a separate—and secret—appeal, similar only in that it omitted endorsement of Moderation.

Prince James refused to convert.

That meant a Hanoverian succession. Oxford instantly assured the elector of his eternal devotion. Bolingbroke backed the Protestant succession in parliament but omitted to mention Hanover. Rumor insisted that both men were pro–Pretender.

Out to break his rival, Bolingbroke brought a Schism bill before parliament. The Bill required all teachers at dissenting schools periodically to prove that they took the Anglican sacrament.

Anne favored the Bill, for it would allow Anglicans to monopolize education. Because every Tory backed the Bill, the party coalesced around Bolingbroke. The Bill easily passed in the Tory dominated house of commons. Oxford defanged the Bill in the Lords, hoping thereby to retain his Whig and dissenter backing as well as satisfy the queen by supporting the Bill in its final form; instead, Oxford alienated all three. The prime minister then wooed Whigs by convincing the cabinet to offer a large reward to anyone who caught the Pretender in Britain; and he averred his willingness to let the electoral prince live in England; at the same time, the prime minister assured Anne that only he had enough influence at Hanover to prevent it.

At this juncture the Whig press published Queen Anne's letters to Hanover. That killed Oxford's credibility with Whigs. He could no longer cultivate their support by claiming his desire for the electoral prince to come to England; nor could Oxford any longer position himself as the only person who could assure the Hanoverian succession.

Since Anne's ministers "neither regarded her health, her life, nor her peace,"[23] the exasperated queen commanded Oxford and Bolingbroke to resolve their differences and focus on governing in the country's best interests.

—⁊⁊⁊—

To facilitate the reconciliation, Anne engaged the good offices of someone she knew well. Principled, incapable of deceit, and with considerable diplomatic talent, member of Princess Anne and Prince George's Cockpit Circle, one of the Immortal Seven who had pledged life, honor, and fortune to bring William of Orange to England, the moderate Whig Duke of Shrewsbury had stood by the princess when the joint monarchs banned her from court. He hated party strife, had voluntarily retired from office for several years before joining Anne's current moderate cabinet.

Not feeling well enough to go to Windsor for the summer, unwilling, besides, to leave her capital while the government remained unsettled, the queen decided to escape London's dirt and heat while making it easy for ministers to meet with her. She moved to Kensington Palace.

Shrewsbury failed to settle matters between Anne's two warring ministers. She, therefore, faced a choice—between devious, dilatory, often blotto Oxford and ingratiating, immoral Bolingbroke.

The prime minister "neglected all business ... was seldom to be understood ... when he did explain himself she could not depend upon the truth of what he said ... he never came to her at the time she appointed … often came drunk, [and,] to crown all he behaved himself towards her with ill manner, indecency, & disrespect."[24] The chronically cash-strapped secretary of state had recently been accused of larceny and treason because a major scandal over the financial terms of the Spanish commercial treaty (part of the secret peace preliminaries with France that Bolingbroke negotiated) had brought his dubious financial dealings to light.

—⁂—

The queen decided to dismiss Oxford. But did not appoint Bolingbroke lord treasurer and, thus, de facto prime minister. Because Anne doubted if the secretary could be trusted with a position that Godolphin and Harley had held with such a high degree of probity. True, Bolingbroke had ability, but life-long financial dependence on his family drove the secretary to seek funds from shady characters, even those who had proven themselves adept at pilfering government coffers. Further, the queen recently heard about Boling-broke boasting that, after he bowed himself out of her presence, he got drunk on champagne over dinner, then had two peers of the realm tuck him into bed with the Prettiest Whore in England, all while relying on his wife for cash. Anne could not trust such a man to lead her government.

On a sultry late July afternoon, the clouds hovering over Kensington palace held a hint of thunder as the queen met privately with her prime minister in her private wood-paneled parlor. Since Anne's feelings were less involved than they had been over Godolphin and Marlborough's dismissal, she conveyed her decision in a long and friendly farewell interview. Nonetheless, Oxford unnerved the queen with a piece of unsolicited advice—she should not be cashiering him without appointing a treasury commission to take over his fiscal duties.

That evening, as rain splashed against the window panes, Anne opened the cabinet meeting. To her horror, Oxford's backers reacted to the news of his dismissal with a vicious attack against Bolingbroke, who readily reciprocated.

The queen tried to reconcile her ministers, to rebuild her cabinet. The first order of business consisted of selecting the five treasury commissioners. At two o'clock in the morning, only one commissioner had been agreed on. Feeling extremely unwell, the distraught queen ordered waiting footmen to carry her into her bedchamber. There, Anne wept for a long time. She told the attending physician that she could not bear much more.

—⁂—

Recognizing herself as the unifying force in a country riven between Whig and Tory, between Hanover and Jacobite, the queen wanted a prime minister who practiced Moderation, who stood above party, someone who could direct the knitting together of the nation. And Anne wanted a chief minister who would renew friendly relations with her successor; for, the ado about having the electoral prince reside in England, to say nothing of Hanover's opposition to the Peace of Utrecht, (Hanover signed one year after Britain) had left a sour aftertaste.

Shrewsbury advised the queen to turn to her first and most trusted advisor. Anne still felt personal affection for the Duke of Marlborough, had recently received a Marlborough daughter who came to court to present a letter from him, written after another daughter's death. Anne accepted the letter. She now asked Bolingbroke to open direct negotiations with the duke about forming a ministry; its initial order of business would be to mend fences with Hanover.

Meanwhile, because Merciless Men of both parties had muddied, were still muddying, the succession issue, the queen decided to act. Misunderstandings with Hanover must be resolved forthwith.

She conceived a plan to assure the elector that ministerial change meant neither harm to, nor a decrease in, Anne's friendship for him. The queen chose her physician, David Hamilton, as her envoy. He should send his son, currently studying at Oxford, to a Dutch university, thereby giving the doctor a pretext to ask for the queen's leave to visit him. From Holland, Hamilton could easily travel to Hanover unofficially, to achieve a "sincere friendship [with the elector and remove] all occasions of jealousy [in such a way, as to give Anne] least disquiet."[25]

The queen wanted Hamilton to present his sovereign's hand-written letter assuring the elector of her friendship, a letter written, moreover, "without the knowledge of any of her ministry. [This, plus Hamilton's account of his position at court, would give the elector] confidence to open to me and to write" to Anne frankly, also without the knowledge of his ministers. For so eager had the queen become to prevent civil strife over the succession from damaging her realm, that she proposed to break with her policy of keeping any Hanoverian royal out of her domains. Hence, Hamilton must encourage the elector to ask Anne to let him visit her for a few weeks. To give him "entire satisfaction and she quiet."[26]

—⁂—

Having concluded her conference with Hamilton, the queen, still suffering considerable stress, presided over the cabinet meeting which adjourned after she left it at two o'clock that morning. Ministers continued to disagree over who should lead the treasury. By now visibly ill, Anne's condition worsened. Her cabinet decided to postpone further discussion.

The queen retired to her bedroom where, for the next three days, she suffered headaches, insomnia, appetite loss, and vomiting, her ministers' harsh words all the while reverberating in her head. Strong convulsions then clutched the queen. She rallied but could barely speak. Shaking hands, aching head, high fever, grogginess, and some bleeding from her nose followed. Anne's physicians prescribed cupping and bleeding. Their patient slept.

The queen awoke to bright morning sunshine streaming into her bedroom. Feeling somewhat better, she asked to have her hair combed. Sat up. Suddenly confused and dizzy, Anne found herself unable to read the dial of her handsome, wall-mounted clock. Frightened to see the queen staring fixedly at the clock, Anne's chambermaid called for help.

Diagnosing an apoplectic fit, (today known as a cerebral hemorrhage) the doctor on duty bled Anne. After lying unconscious for an hour, she woke to find her friend and favorite lady-in-waiting Elizabeth, Duchess of Somerset, gently asking how she felt. "Never worse, [the queen replied.] "I am going."[27]

—⁂—

She could not go in peace. The lord treasurer's post remained vacant. Neither Anne nor her cabinet wanted her death to leave the nation without a chief minister during the interregnum.

Ministerial consensus began to build around moderate Whig Shrewsbury, the only man acceptable to Whigs, Tories, and Hanoverians. Making a virtue of necessity, Bolingbroke proposed that Shrewsbury become lord treasurer.

The queen's cabinet, senior clerics, and household staff gathered round the dying woman's bed. Paralyzed, speechless, but still mentally aware, Anne managed, herself, to nudge the lord treasurer's white staff of office into Shrewsbury's hands. She could rest assured that a political moderate and a man of probity would lead the transition government.

Shrewsbury at once called the cabinet, now turned into a privy council including all senior Whigs and Tories, to order. The council sent a special courier galloping post-haste to Hanover with a formal letter signed by each privy councilor; it urged the elector to leave for England at once.[28]

—⟊—

The worn out, barely conscious queen lay in her Kensington Palace bedroom surrounded by the Bishop of London with attendant chaplains, three ladies-in-waiting, and two bedchamber women, but not Abigail Masham who, overcome by a bout of hysterics, sobbed in the anteroom. Elizabeth Somerset spoke to Anne in a "soft courteous way; [her] look and motion of her face in receiving it, tho' so ill, and without sometimes answering a word, [showed] solid inward satisfaction in her friend's presence."[29]

The queen's seven doctors agreed that gout from her knee and foot had affected Anne's nerves and traveled to her brain; they also agreed that anguish over the political situation aggravated her condition. "My dear mistress's days were numbered even in my imagination, and could not exceed certain limits, [said one physician.] But of that small number a great deal was cut off by the last troublesome scene of contention among her servants."[30]

To give the queen some relief, her medical men ordered heated cups applied to the persistent erysipelas on her thigh, and hot irons used to blister her forehead and the soles of her feet. Attendants forced Anne to swallow a vile concoction to induce vomiting, other minions covered her feet with fresh garlic, and, to mitigate the queen's fever, shaved her head clean of her still luxuriant brown hair.

As evening approached, forty-nine-year-old Anne escaped from these horrors, to say nothing of further medical ministrations, by slipping slowly into a coma. Queen Anne died early the following morning (August 1, 1714).

"Sleep was never more welcome to a weary traveler than death to her."[31]

—⟊—

Anne's death revealed that the silk purse she had always worn around her neck and under her shift did, indeed, contain letters. On the topmost paper, the queen had, in her own hand, written orders to burn the letters unread. As they crackled in the flames of her bedroom fire, witnesses observed the letters to be written in French. Since the Pretender always wrote to his half-sister in English, the witnesses concluded that the papers must be Prince George's early letters.

—⟊—

King George I ordered his predecessor's burial to take place before he arrived from Hanover. Hence, three weeks after the queen's death, (to give her ladies time to ready their mourning clothes) "was solemnized, in the collegiate church of this place, [Westminster] the private interment of her late most excellent majesty Queen Anne, of blessed memory."[32]

The queen had specified that her funeral be identical to that which she had arranged for Prince George. So, the day before the ceremony, a "funeral chariot drawn by eight horses caparisoned in purple hoods [carried Anne's purple-draped coffin] from Kensington Palace to Westminster.… A vigil then took place; all the queen's ladies-in-waiting and maids of honor took part, as well as fourteen countesses."[33] Each had received twenty-six yards of black crape to wear as mourning veils.

At ten that evening, "the royal corpse was borne under a canopy of purple velvet, preceded by a great number of her majesty's servants, judges, privy councilors, the lords spiritual and temporal, and the great officers."[34] They walked in serried ranks and solemn procession from the house of lords to Westminster Abbey; twelve yeomen of the guard dressed in purple and black carried the queen's coffin. Six dukes walked behind—but not Marlborough, who, with his duchess, landed in England on the day after Anne's death. One of the Tower's great guns boomed "every minute, until her majesty was interred."[35]

"In the absence of the Duchess of Somerset, who was indisposed," another ducal lady-in-waiting performed the offices of chief mourner. After a brief service the queen was buried in the "same vault with their late majesties King Charles the Second, King William and Queen Mary, and his Royal Highness the Prince of Denmark."[36]

For twelve action-packed years the last Stuart, of strong spirit and kind heart, overcame the confines of her sex and health to impress her views on ambitious men; to protect the English constitution and Anglican church; to give her country security; and to reign in a volatile age that paid her ultimate praise: it adopted her name.

Afterword:
The Age of Anne

"The only married queen that ne'er knew strife,
Controlling monarchs, but submissive wife:
Like angels' sighs her downy passions move,
Tenderly loving and attracting love.
Of every grace and virtue she's possessed—
Was mother, wife, and queen and all the best."[1]
—Anonymous contemporary verse

Anne Stuart's ascent to the throne satisfied her wish to see the "sunshine day [she had awaited] with patience" during the dark night of her predecessor King William's reign. And the twelve-year Age of Anne fulfilled her "hope [that] England will flourish again."[2]

—⁂—

She ruled as a statutory queen during the launch of constitutional monarchy. Two seventeenth century revolutions established the supremacy of parliament over crown to curb royal power; but when Anne became queen, the sovereign still stood at the center of politics and government. No official could afford to ignore the queen. Discussing business daily with ministers, presiding at cabinet meetings, attending house of lords debates, consulting with a spectrum of politicians, and keeping in touch with her subjects empowered Anne to influence political events.

Neither brilliant of intellect nor educated in statecraft, the queen applied common sense to government. She did not challenge the pre-eminence of parliament or of statute law. But Anne did protect crown prerogatives; and as head of the Church of England, the queen guarded her cherished church against political abuse.

—⁂—

The outpouring of patriotism and popularity that greeted Anne's advent as queen, lasted throughout her reign. This, despite the long, costly War of the Spanish Succession, to say nothing of the political partisanship that permeated every aspect of life during the Age of Anne.

Resolved not to serve as a cipher for the Merciless Men of either party, deploring the discord of party warfare because she thought it weakened her nation, Anne sought to preserve the crown's independence by governing via Moderation. She kept a balance between Tories and Whigs so that the crown could stay above party and serve as a unifying and stabilizing force in her divided nation.

The queen's first ministry fused all Tory factions. Anne put Sidney Godolphin, nominally a moderate Tory, actually above party, in charge of the nation's finances; he became, in effect, prime minister. The queen chose John Churchill, Duke of Marlborough, to command her armed forces. Like his best friend Godolphin, and his sovereign, a moderate Tory who loathed party strife, Marlborough, since the War of the Spanish Succession defined foreign policy, also functioned as foreign minister.

By the third year of her reign, Anne's ministry had evolved into her model government—Moderation—a non-party group of ministers loyal to the queen. In the next three years Anne's moderate ministry settled the Protestant succession, won exceptional military victories against France, and achieved the historic union of England and Scotland.

After six years, Whigs outweighed moderates in Anne's ministry. The Duchess of Marlborough's persistent pro–Whig diatribes, meanwhile, as well as her method of delivering them, not only destroyed the close friendship between queen and duchess, but also subverted Marlborough and Godolphin's political position.

The queen hated having to govern with a Whig cabinet, but the death of her beloved husband Prince George of Denmark, the sole surviving comfort of her life, left Anne too grief-stricken to resist Whig domination.

Within two years the queen had rallied. Anne formed a moderate, mostly Tory ministry that, with her backing, negotiated the Peace of Utrecht. (1713) It ended nine years of war, gave the combative European continent seven decades of stability, and brought Great Britain to the brink of global hegemony.

—◊◊—

Queen Anne kept the crown independent and functioned as a unifying force in her fractured nation because she embodied both a Tory dream—a Stuart strictly loyal to the Church of England and a Whig ideal—a constitutional queen who rejected divine right and renounced rigid hereditary succession. Anne's moderate government carried out Whig policies such as extension of financial reforms begun in the prior reign to develop the nation's wealth; focus on land rather than naval warfare in the war against France; the Regency Act which secured the Protestant Succession; and Union with Scotland, which created Great Britain under the rule of a constitutional monarchy. The queen's moderate Tory government solidified Whig war gains via the Peace of Utrecht.

—◊◊—

The War of the Spanish Succession dominated the Age of Anne. She waged war against Europe's superpower, Catholic France, partly to maintain the balance of power, partly to prevent French supremacy in international commerce, partly to protect her right to the throne and the legitimacy of her Protestant successors.

After Utrecht, Anne continued to wage war—against persistent ill health. Nonetheless, she remained at the center of government and politics until her death.

—◊◊—

Of "we four" who must "never part,"[3] Sidney Godolphin predeceased Anne. Marlborough returned from self-imposed exile in time to welcome his former battlefield subordinate, the Elector of Hanover, to England as King George I; but a series of strokes prevented the duke from taking an active part in politics. He died eight years after the queen. Sarah Marlborough lived until her eighty-fourth year. She avoided court, and spent her final days incapacitated by arthritis with only a couple of faithful servants in attendance; for Sarah had fallen out with her only surviving daughter and several grand-children.

Towards the end of her life the duchess commissioned, at significant expense, "a very fine" statue of Queen Anne. "I have a satisfaction in showing this respect to her, because her kindness to me was real."[4]

Queen Anne had a person and appearance very graceful, something of majesty in her look. She was religious without any affectation, and certainly meant to do everything that was just ... her being so easy in letting King William come before her to the crown ... she thought it more for her honor to be easy in it, than to make a dispute who should have the crown first, that was taken from her father. And it was a great trouble to her to be forced to act such a part against him...

> She was never expensive, nor made any foolish buildings, nor bought one jewel in [all of]her reign....
> She always paid the greatest respect imaginable to King William and Queen Mary ... never insisted
> on anything of grandeur more than she had when her family was established by King Charles II;
> though after the Revolution she was in the place of a Prince of Wales...
> She was extremely well-bred and treated her chief ladies and servants as if they had been her
> equals ... never refused to give charity, when there was the least reason for anybody to ask it; and
> likewise paid the salaries of most of her sister's servants, notwithstanding the hardships she had suf-
> fered in King William's reign.[5]

Anne "certainly ... meant well and was not a fool.... She ... would have started at anybody's persuading her to profess a falsehood or to have done anything plainly wrong."[6]

"One thing I will say more, that she was as good as an angel and as wise as Solomon in comparison of some that I have the honor to know."[7]

Since Sarah Marlborough prided herself on "never [having] flattered anybody living.... I cannot be suspected of it now the queen is dead."[8]

Appendix

Full Text of Princess Mary's questions and Princess Anne's answers about the birth of their half-brother the Prince of Wales. From Sir John Dalrymple, Memoirs of Great Britain and Ireland, *vol. ii, pp. 305–306, July 21, 1688, PM to PA; and pp. 307–310, July 24, 1688, PA to PM.*

1. MARY: "Whether the queen desired at any time any of the ladies, in particular the Princess of Denmark, to feel her belly, since she thought herself quick; and who those ladies are; and when that was, whether in the beginning of her being quick, or of late"?

   ANNE: "I have never heard anybody say they felt the child stir; but I am told Lady Sunderland [pro–Catholic] and Madam Mazarin [Catholic] say they felt it at the beginning. Mrs. Dawson [bedchamber woman to Anne Hyde, Mary Beatrice, and later Queen Anne] tells me she has seen it stir, but never felt it."

2. MARY: "Whether the milk that, as it is said, was in the queen's breast, was seen by many, or conducted in a mystery"?

   ANNE: "I never saw any milk; but Mrs. Dawson says she has seen it upon her smock, and that it began to run at the same time it used to do of her other children."

3. MARY: "Whether the astringents, that the queen is said to have taken, were taken by her openly, or if a mystery was made of that"?

   ANNE: "For what they call restringing draughts, I saw her drink two of them; and I don't doubt but she drank them frequently and publicly before her going to Bath." [Mary Beatrice had gone to Bath to bathe in the Roman springs and drink the waters. Several weeks later, rumors of her pregnancy started to circulate.]

4. MARY: "Whether the treating of the queen's breasts for drawing back the milk, and the giving her clean linen, has been managed openly, or mysteriously"?

   ANNE: "Once in discourse, Mrs. Bromley told Mrs. Roberts, [bedchamber women] one day Rogers's daughter came into the room, when Mrs. Mansell [queen] was putting off her clouts, and she was very angry at it, because she did not care to be seen when she was shifting."

5. MARY: "At what hour did the queen's labor begin"?

   ANNE: "She fell in labor about eight o'clock.

6. MARY: "At what hour was the notice of it sent to the king? Whether the king did not lie at St. James's, or with the queen that night; or if he was gone back to Whitehall"?

   ANNE: "She sent for the king at about that time, who had been up a quarter of an hour, having lain with her that night, and was then dressing.

7. MARY: "Whether upon sending to the king, the thing was let fly over St. James's and Whitehall; or if the notice was sent secretly to the king"?

   ANNE: "As soon as the king came, he sent for the queen dowager, [wife of Charles II] and all the council. After that, it was known all over St. James's.

8. MARY: "Whether did the king send for the privy councilors; or if he took those who were by accident at Whitehall"?
ANNE: "Most of the other men, I suppose, that were there, were at the king's rising."

9. MARY: "At what time came the king with the council into the queen's chamber"?
ANNE: They came into the room presently after the queen dowager came, which is about half an hour before she was brought to bed."

10. MARY: "Whether was there a screen at the foot of the bed, between it and the rest of the room, or not"?
ANNE: "There was no screen. She was brought to bed in the bed she lay in all night, and in the great bed-chamber, as she was of her last child."

11. MARY: "Whether did any women, besides the confidents, see the queen's face when she was in labor? And whether she had the looks of a woman in labor? Who was in the room, both men and women? What time they came in, and how near they stood"?
ANNE: "The feet curtains of the bed were drawn, and the two sides were open. When she was in great pain, the king called in haste for my lord chancellor, who came up to the bedside to show he was there; upon which the rest of the privy councilors did the same thing. Then the queen desired the king to hide her face with his head and periwig, which he did, for she said she could not be brought to bed and have so many men look on her; for all the council stood close to the bed's feet, and lord chancellor upon the step." Anne then named most of those present.

12. MARY: "How long was the king talking to the privy councilors, after the child was carried into the next room, before he went to look upon it? and in this, as well as in other questions, relating to the point of time, a critical answer, as near to a minute as it is possible, is desired."
ANNE: "As soon as the child was born the midwife cut the naval-string, because the after-burden did not follow quickly." The "king said to the privy councilors, that they were witness there was a child born."

13. MARY: "What women, of one sort or other, were present? And if no woman was called to hold the queen"?
ANNE: "When the queen dowager first came into the room she went up to the bedside, but after that stood all the while by the clock.... Dawson stood behind the Dutch chair that the midwife sat upon to do her work. All the time the child was parted, I do not hear of anybody that held the queen except the king, and he was upon the bed by her all the while."

14. MARY: "Were no ladies sent for? or who were sent for? and at what time the message was sent to the queen dowager? Also, at what time she came"?
ANNE: "I don't hear that any ladies were sent for but the queen's own and they were called presently after the queen dowager."

15. MARY: "Whether in any former labor the queen was delivered so mysteriously, so suddenly, and so few being called for"?
ANNE: "Her labor never used to be so long."

16. MARY: "If many observed the child's limbs being slender at first, and their appearing all of a sudden to be round and full"?
ANNE: "I never heard what you say of the child's limbs. As for seeing it dressed or undressed, they avoid it as much as they can.... In short, it is not very clear anything they do; and for the servants, from the highest to the lowest, they are all papists."

17. MARY: "Is the queen fond of it"?
ANNE: "The queen forbade [the baby's head nurse] to bring the child to her before any company; but that, they say, she used to do to her other children. I dined there the other day, when it was said it had been very ill of a looseness, and it really looked so; yet, when she came from prayers she went to dinner without seeing it, and after played" cards.

18. MARY: "How Mrs. Dawson, Mrs. Bromley stand with the queen? Which of her bedchamber women are most in favor"?

ANNE: "I believe none of the bedchamber women have any credit with the queen but [one;] they say [another] has an interest with the king."

MARY: "Ad. 12. Who took the child, when it was born? Ad. 13. If the king did not use to be nearer the bed, and hold the queen in former labors? Ad. 16. If everybody is permitted to see the child at all hours, dressed and undressed? Ad. 16. Who is about it, rockers and dry nurse? Ad. 3. What doctors were consulted about the queen, before, and since her being at Bath. Whether Dr. Waldgrave alone, or others with him, knew the particulars of her condition, all along."

Chapter Notes

For clarity and consistency, I have used modern spelling and punctuation in quotes; when the letter-writer uses a number or code-name to disguise a person's true name, I have replaced with the actual name. If no date or other details are indicated, the source does not provide them.

Reference Abbreviations

BL: British Library Board
HMC: Historical Manuscripts Commission
ML&M: Morgan Library & Museum

Preface

1. Coxe, William, *Memoirs of John, Duke of Marlborough*, vol. iii, p. 89, Aug. 9, 1706, John Churchill, Duke of Marlborough to his wife Sarah. (Later JM and SM respectively.)
2. Boyer, Abel, *History of Queen Anne*, vol. 1, pp. 715–716.
3. HMC Portland, vol. iv, pp. 510–511, Nov. 6, 1708, Abigail Masham to Robert Harley (henceforth AM and RH respectively.)

Chapter One

1. Ruth Norrington, ed., *My dearest Minette. Letters Between Charles II and his Sister Henrietta, Duchess d'Orléans*, p. 110, Feb. 9, 1665, Charles to his favorite sister.
2. Boyer, *History*, pp. 715–716.
3. Fiennes, Celia, *The Journeys of Celia Fiennes*, pp. 302–303, 1702.
4. Ewald, W.B., *The Newsmen of Queen Anne*. pp. 26–29, from the *London Gazette*, April 23, 1702.
5. Civil war (1642–1649) pitted parliament and Puritans against monarchy and Anglicans, ending with the beheading of Charles I (1649) who sought to establish absolutism (government without parliament) on the French model embodied in the rule of French King Louis XIV.
6. In the later seventeenth century sexual activity, extra-marital or otherwise, occurred no more or less often than at any other time in human existence. But there were rules. Everyone stigmatized a child born out of wedlock as a bastard, an inferior person who lived with distinct handicaps: bastards had no claim to their fathers' recognition, property, or name.

7. Fea, Allen, *James II and His Wives*, pp. 5–6, quoted from *The Autobiography of Mlle. de Montpensier*.
8. Hamilton, Anthony, Count Grammont, *Memoirs of the Court of Charles the Second*, p. 105.
9. Baillon, Charles, Comte de, *Henriette-Anne d'Angleterre, Duchesse d'Orléans*, p. 401, quoted from *Mémoirs* of Mlle. de Montpensier.
10. Wit meant more than quick repartee; wit also meant vivacity and social graces.
11. Maids of honor came from prominent gentry families and served as companions to court ladies.
12. Henslowe, J.R., *Anne Hyde, Duchess of York*, pp. 28–29, from Clarendon MS., vol. xlix., f. 70.
13. Macpherson, James, *Original Papers Containing the Secret History of Great Britain from the Restoration to the Accession of the House of Hanover*, vol. 1, pp. 22–23.
14. *Calendar of State Papers, Domestic, Anne I*, vol. ii, p. 1, Jan. 1661.
15. Hamilton, *Memoirs*, p. 165.
16. Hamilton, *Memoirs*, p. 165.
17. Burnet, Gilbert, *Bishop Burnet's History of His Own Time*, vol. 1, pp. 286–287.
18. Aulnoy, Marie Catherine, Baronne d' *Memoirs of the Court of England in 1675*, pp. 398–399.
19. *Calendar of State Papers, Domestic, Anne I*, vol. ix, p. 342, Oct. 31, 1668.
20. *Calendar of State Papers, Domestic, Anne I*, vol. iii, p. 248, Nov. 3, 1662 and vol. iv, p. 4, Jan. 5, 1663, respectively.
21. Evelyn, John, *The Life of Mrs. Godolphin*, pp. 11 & 13. Mrs. Godolphin, nee Margaret Blagge, one of Anne Hyde's ladies-in-waiting, attended Anne in her last illness; the quote is from Margaret's memoirs.
22. Clarendon papers, vol. 5, p. 511, Clarendon to Nicholas, Oct. 11, 1665.
23. *Calendar of State Papers, Domestic, Anne I*, vol. v, p. 268, Sept. 12, 1664.
24. Ascribed to frailty of the lachrymal gland. Treatment included washing the eyes with strengtheners like spirit of wine, Hungary water (a herbal astringent) spring water, fennel, or Valerian water. Balsamics and medicines such as essence of amber and decoction of the woods could also be taken internally to prevent catarrhs. (From *A New and Complete Dictionary of Arts and Sciences by the Society of Gentlemen*, London, 1763, vol. ii, p. 1190.)
25. *Burnet's History*, vol. 1, p. 301.
26. Baillon, *Henriette-Anne d'Angleterre*, p. 412.
27. Baillon, *Henriette-Anne d'Angleterre*, p. 412, from a letter of Madame de Sévigné, July 6, 1670.

28. *Burnet's History*, vol. 1, p. 288.

29. *Burnet's History*, vol. 1, p. 288.

30. Sarah, Duchess of Marlborough, *Account of the Conduct of the Dowager Duchess of Marlborough*, pp. 9–10.

31. *Burnet's History*, vol. v, p. 2, Onslow addition to Dartmouth note.

32. Boyer, *History*, pp. 715–716.

33. Lord John Russell, ed., *Letters of Rachel, Lady Russell*, vol. 1, p. 13, Sept. 23, 1673.

34. A hundred years before, Holland and Zeeland led the seven northern Netherlands provinces into a union that declared its independence of Spain. The United Provinces thus became the Dutch Republic, or, reflecting its dominance, Holland. Europe's only republic, Holland upheld religious toleration. The Dutch owned most of northern Europe's shipping; replaced Portuguese colonial power in South Africa, India, and Indonesia; and turned Amsterdam into Europe's financial center. William married Mary to improve his chances of succeeding to his childless uncle's throne, as well as to bring England into the anti-French coalition.

35. *Diary of Dr. Edward Lake Chaplain and Tutor to the Princesses Mary and Anne*, p. 9, Nov. 12, 1677.

36. *Lake Diary*, p. 12, Dec. 3, 1677.

37. *Lake Diary*, p. 11, Nov. 29, 1677.

38. *Lake Diary*, p. 12, Dec. 4, 1677.

39. Brown, Beatrice Curtis, ed., *Letters and Diplomatic Instructions of Queen Anne*, p. 10, July 1683, Princess Anne (hereafter referred to as PA, later QA) to Lady Bathurst.

40. Boyer, *History*, pp. 715–716.

41. *QA Letters*, pp. 5–6, Sept. 20 & Sept. 22, 1679, PA to Frances Apsley.

42. Bathurst, Benj., ed., *Letters of Two Queens*, p. 22, pp. 108–109, Sept. 22, 1679, PA to Frances Apsley.

43. *QA Letters*, pp. 5–6, Sept. 20 & Sept. 22, 1679, PA to Apsley.

44. When Queen Elizabeth died (1603) without an heir, Charles's grandfather and Elizabeth's closest male relative, her cousin James VI of Scotland, became James I of England, thus uniting the two crowns, but not the two countries.

45. Bathurst, *Letters*, pp. 136–137, Sept. 8, 1681, PA to Apsley.

46. Wolseley, J.G., Lord, *Life of John Churchill, Duke of Marlborough*, vol. 1, pp. 183–184, year 1676.

47. *Burnet's History*, vol. 1, pp. 755–756.

48. Sheffield, John, *Works*, vol. I, pp. 205–206.

49. Bathurst, *Letters*, pp. 154–156, Nov. 27, 1862, Princess Mary (henceforth referred to as PM, then QM) to Apsley.

50. Bathurst, *Letters*, pp. 154–156, Nov. 27, 1682, PM to Apsley.

51. Clarke, J.S., ed., *Life of James the Second ... Collected Out of Memoirs Writ of His Own Hand*, vol. 1, p. 745.

52. Macky, John, *Memoirs of the Secret Services of John Macky Esq., During the Reigns of King William, Queen Anne, and King George I*, p. 2.

53. Bathurst, *Letters*, p.167, July 18, 1683, Thomas Clarges.

54. *QA Letters*, p. 6, Sept. 22, 1679, PA to Apsley.

55. *Burnet's History*, vol. ii, pp. 515–516.

56. *Burnet's History*, vol. ii, pp. 515–516.

57. *QA Letters*, pp. 10–11, July 1683, PA to Apsley.

58. Ladies of the bedchamber were aristocrats serving as social companions to the princess or queen. A bedchamber lady also helped her mistress to dress, and accompanied her to court functions.

59. BL Add MS 61414, ff. 3–5, 1683, PA to Sarah Churchill (hereafter SC, later SM.)

60. Wolesley, *Marlborough*, vol. 1, p. 251, PA to SC.

61. Sarah, *Conduct*, p. 10.

62. Sarah, *Conduct*, pp. 11–12.

63. *Memoirs of Sarah, Duchess of Marlborough*, pp. 273–276.

64. Cotteril, C., *The Whole Life and Glorious Actions of Prince George of Denmark*, p. 3.

65. Henry VIII built the stand-alone Cockpit as venue for the popular sport of cock fighting; later it became a theater, then a coveted dwelling.

66. Coxe, *Marlborough*, vol. iv, p. 213, Sept. 27, 1708, John Churchill, later Duke of Marlborough (henceforth JC, later JM) to SC.

67. *Letters of the Earl of Chesterfield*, vol. 1, pp. 291–294, Nov. 18, 1748, Chesterfield to his son.

68. *QA Letters*, p. 28, Apr. 11, 1687, PA to PM.

69. Boyer, *History*, vol. 1, pp. 715–716.

Chapter Two

1. Evelyn, John, *The Diary of John Evelyn*, p. 329, Sept. 17, 1685.

2. Dalrymple, John, *Memoirs of Great Britain and Ireland*, vol. ii, p. 299, March 13, 1687–1688, PA to PM (Princess Mary.)

3. Strickland, A., *Lives of the Queens of England*, vol. 5, pp. 464–465, quoted from a contemporary courtier.

4. BL Add MS 61414, f. 108, Aug. 12, 1686, PA to SC.

5. Strickland, *Lives*, vol. v, pp. 464–465, quoted from a contemporary courtier.

6. Approximately $3,500,000 today.

7. BL Add MS 61426, ff. 9–10, Sarah, Duchess of Marlborough's *Character of Princes*.

8. King Charles had rewarded John Churchill with a barony.

9. BL Add MS 61414 f. 17, 1685, PA to SC.

10. BL Add MS 61414, f. 72, April 1, 1686, PA to SC.

11. BL Add MS 61414, ff. 15–16, 1683–1684, PA to SC.

12. Green, D.B., *Sarah, Duchess of Marlborough*, p. 47, PA to SC.

13. BL Add MS 61414, f. 39, summer 1685, PA to SC.

14. *QA Letters*, p. 12, Sept. 20, 1684, PA to SC.

15. Sarah, *Conduct*, p. 12.

16. Strickland, *Lives*, vol. v, p. 463.

17. BL Add MS 61414, f. 98, July-Aug. 1686, PA to SC.

18. Battle of Sedgemoor, 1685.

19. HMC Rutland, vol. ii, p. 109, June 2, 1686, Howe to Rutland.

20. Kronenberger, Louis, *Marlborough's Duchess— A Study in Worldliness*, p. 14, quote is from the French ambassador.

21. BL Add MS 61426, ff. 9–10, from Sarah's *Character of Princes*.

22. Coxe, *Marlborough*, vol. 1, p. 33, 1686, PA to SC

23. *QA Letters*, p. 17, Aug. 10, 1686, PA to PM.

24. Sarah, *Conduct*, p. 15.

25. *QA Letters*, p. 16, Apr. 29, 1686, PA to PM.

26. *QA Letters*, p. 23, Jan. 31, 1687, PA to PM.

27. Bentinck, M.E. *Lettres et Mémoires de Marie, Reine d'Angleterre, Épouse de Guillaume III*, pp. 24–26, end of Jan. 1687, PA to PM.

28. *Russell Letters*, vol. 1, p. 206, Feb. 9, 1687.
29. *Russell Letters*, vol. 1, p. 212, Feb. 18, 1687.
30. *QA Letters*, pp. 30–32, May 9, 1687, PA to PM.
31. *QA Letters*, p. 33, June 22, 1687, PA to PM.
32. *QA Letters*, pp. 25–27, Mar. 13, 1687, PA to PM.
33. *QA Letters*, pp. 24–27, May 9, 1687, PA to PM.
34. Churchill, W.S., *Marlborough, His Life and Times*, vol. 1, pp. 237–239, Mar. 13, 1687, PA to PM.
35. *QA Letters*, pp. 24–27, May 9, 1687, PA to PM.
36. Dalrymple, *Memoirs*, vol. ii, pp. 298–299, Dec. 29, 1686, PA to PM.
37. Dalrymple, *Memoirs*, vol. ii, pp. 298–299, Dec. 29, 1686, PA to PM.
38. Dalrymple, *Memoirs*, vol. ii, p. 190, May 17, 1687, JC to William of Orange.
39. *QA Letters*, pp. 30–32, May 9, 1687, PA to PM.
40. Ranke, L. von, *A History of England, Principally in the Seventeenth Century*, vol. iv, p. 287, from a diplomat's report.
41. BL Add MS 61414, f. 27, July 1685 PA to SC.
42. *QA Letters*, pp. 30–32, May 9, 1687, PA to PM.

Chapter Three

1. Haile, M., *Mary of Modena, Her Life and Letters*, p. 173, Dec. 22-Jan. 2, 1687/8, Terriesi, Tuscan envoy to London, to his master the Grand Duke of Tuscany.
2. *Burnet's History*, vol. 1, p. 748.
3. *Burnet's History*, vol. 1, p. 749–750.
4. *Burnet's History*, vol. 1, p. 749–750.
5. Pamphlets were an essential method of communicating political opinion.
6. *QA Letters*, p. 35, Mar. 20, 1688, PA to PM.
7. *QA Letters*, p. 34. Mar. 1688, PA to PM.
8. Bentinck, *Lettres et Mémoires de Marie, Reine d'Angleterre*, pp. 26–31, Mar. 13, 1688, PA to PM.
9. *Correspondence of Henry Hyde, Earl of Clarendon and His Brother Lawrence Hyde, Earl of Rochester*, vol. ii, pp. 177–178, June 15, 1688, Clarendon diary.
10. *Clarendon-Rochester Correspondence*, pp. 41–43, June 18, 1688, PA to PM.
11. *Burnet's History*, vol. 1, pp. 751–752.
12. *QA Letters*, p. 37, June 18, 1688, PA to PM.
13. *Clarendon-Rochester Correspondence*, vol. ii, pp. 177–178, June 15, 1688, Clarendon diary.
14. *QA Letters*, p. 38, July 9, 1688, PA to PM.
15. *QA Letters*, p. 42, July 24, 1688, PA to PM.
16. The Immortal Seven were: the Earls of Danby, Devonshire, and Shrewsbury, Bishop Compton (Anne's erstwhile religious tutor and mentor) Henry Sidney, Admiral Edward Russell, and General Henry Lumley.
17. Dalrymple, *Memoirs*, vol. 1, pp. 213–214.
18. Clarendon, Henry Hyde, *State Letters and Diary of Henry Earl of Clarendon*, vol. ii, pp. 76–77, Oct. 22, 1688.
19. Dalrymple, *Memoirs*, vol. 1, pp. 213–214.
20. *Clarendon Letters and Diary*, vol. ii, p. 81, Nov. 1, 1688.
21. Bentinck, *Lettres et Mémoires de Marie, Reine d'Angleterre*, pp. 33–34, Mar. 20, 1688, PA to PM.
22. Dalrymple, *Memoirs*, vol. ii, pp. 333–334, Nov. 18, 1688, PA to Prince William.
23. *Macky Memoirs*, pp. 2–3.
24. *Burnet's History*, vol. 1, p. 447.
25. *Clarendon Letters and Diary*, vol. ii, pp. 65–66, Sept. 23, 1688.
26. *Burnet's History* vol. ii, pp. 68–69, Sept. 27, 1688.

27. *Burnet's History*, vol. 1, p. 447.
28. *Clarendon Letters and Diary*, vol. ii, p. 84, Nov. 9, 1688.
29. Sarah, *Memoirs*, pp. 273–276.
30. WSC, *Marlborough*, vol. 1, p. 300, Nov. 24, 1688, Prince George to King James.
31. Cotteril, *Prince George of Denmark*, p. 5.
32. BL Add MS 61426, f. 11, from Sarah's *Character of Princes*.
33. HMC Dartmouth, p. 214, Nov. 26, 1688, court official Pepys to Dartmouth.
34. HMC Dartmouth, p. 214, Nov. 26, 1688, Pepys to Dartmouth.
35. Bathurst, *Letters*, pp. 215–219, Nov. 26, 1688, Pepys to Dartmouth.
36. HMC Dartmouth, p. 214, Nov. 26, 1688, Pepys to Dartmouth.
37. Macpherson, *Papers*, vol. 1, p. 163, Nov. 26, 1688.
38. Lewis, Jenkin, *Memoirs of Prince William Henry, Duke of Gloucester*, pp. 115–116, Nov. 25, 1688, PA to Queen Mary Beatrice.
39. *QA Letters*, pp. 44–45, Nov. 25, 1688, PA to QMB.
40. Lewis, *Memoirs*, pp. 115–116, Nov. 25, 1688, PA to QMB.
41. Dalrymple, *Memoirs*, vol. 1, p. 230.
42. Ailesbury, *Memoirs of Thomas, Earl of Ailesbury*, vol. 1, p. 233.
43. William sought to avoid any conflict that could plunge the country into civil war and detract from his goal: quickly become king and bring England into the anti-French coalition.
44. Sarah, *Memoirs*, pp. 273–276.
45. Dalrymple, *Memoirs*, vol. 1, p. 230.
46. *Ailesbury Memoirs*, vol. 1, p. 191.
47. Bathurst, *Letters*, p. 220, Dec. 3, 1688, PA to Bathurst.
48. *Clarendon Letters and Diary*, vol. ii, pp. 148–149, Jan. 17, 1689.
49. *Clarendon Letters and Diary*, vol. ii, pp. 148–149, Jan. 17, 1689.
50. A loose silk coat worn indoors, the fashionable manto featured a train pinned up in folds at the back.

Chapter Four

1. Bathurst, *Letters*, p. 222, from a contemporary skit.
2. Doebner, R., ed., *Memoirs of Mary, Queen of England Together with Her Letters*, p. 23, Mary Stuart's Diary, 1690.
3. Although Mary received the news of her betrothal to William with sobs, she soon fell in love; and neither her miscarriages nor his infidelity slackened her adoration of sickly, acerbic, small and bent William.
4. Sarah, *Conduct*, p. 22.
5. Clarendon, *Letters*, vol. ii, p. 168, Mar. 12, 1689.
6. Bathurst, Letters, pp. 222–223, undated but probably end of February 1689, PA to Bathurst.
7. Clarendon, *Letters*, vol. ii, p. 168, Mar. 12, 1689.
8. Doebner, *Mary Memoirs and Letters*, p. 11, Mary Stuart's Diary, 1689.
9. Cowper, William, *Private Diary*, p. 37, Jan. 30, 1706.
10. Dalrymple, *Memoirs*, vol. ii, Appendix part 2, p. 15, from a memorandum attributed to King William's

secretary of state, quoting from an April 9, 1689 letter from King James II to his daughter Mary.

11. *Burnet's History*, vol. 2, p. 246.
12. Boyer, *History*, p.5.
13. Sarah, *Conduct*, p. 25.
14. Sarah, *Conduct*, p. 115.
15. Sarah, *Conduct*, pp. 25–26.
16. Sarah, *Conduct*, pp. 25–26.
17. Dalrymple, *Memoirs*, vol. ii, p. 117, June 21/July 1, 1690, QM to King William III. (hereafter KW.)
18. Sarah, *Conduct*, p. 25.
19. Sarah, *Conduct*, p. 23.
20. *Burnet's History*, vol. ii, pp. 90–92.
21. The government's annual grant to the sovereign to cover expenses associated with official duties.
22. *Burnet's History*, vol. ii, pp. 90–92.
23. £70,000 would be almost $17,000,000 today.
24. Dalrymple, *Memoirs*, vol. 1, pp. 369–370.
25. Sarah, *Conduct*, p. 29.
26. Dalrymple, *Memoirs*, vol. 1, pp. 370–371.
27. William had confirmed Churchill as major general and put him in charge of rebuilding the army. James's Catholic officers, all cashiered, could not sell their commissions; new officers must buy them from Marlborough; and when William expanded the army, John sold yet more commissions.
28. *Burnet's History*, vol. 1, pp. 762–763.
29. *Burnet's History*, vol. 1, pp. 762–763.
30. Dalrymple, *Memoirs*, vol. 1, pp. 405–406.
31. Doebner, *Mary Memoirs and Letters*, pp. 17–18, Diary.
32. Dalrymple, *Memoirs*, vol. ii, p. 94, Dec. 25, 1689, Marquis of Wharton to KW.
33. Dalrymple, *Memoirs*, vol. 1, pp. 405–406.
34. Sarah, *Conduct*, p. 34.
35. Sarah, *Conduct*, p. 36.
36. Dalrymple, *Memoirs*, vol. ii, pp. 127–129, July 4/13, 1690, QM to KW.
37. Clarke, G. (secretary to Prince George) *Autobiography of Dr. George Clarke*, p. 273.
38. Sarah, *Conduct*, p. 38.
39. Sarah, *Conduct*, p. 38.
40. Sarah, *Conduct*, p. 38.
41. Prince George soon became Mr. Morley, John Churchill, Mr. Freeman, and Sidney Godolphin, close friend of both Churchills whom they had introduced into the Cockpit Circle, and who now joined the ranks of Anne's advisors, Mr. Montgomery.
42. Sarah, *Conduct*, p. 14.
43. BL Add MS 61414, ff. 147–9, April 1691, PA to SM.
44. *QA Letters*, p. 52, Aug. 2, 1691, PA to KW.
45. *QA Letters*, pp. 52–53, Dec. 1, 1691 PA to KJ.
46. Dalrymple, *Memoirs*, vol. 1, p. 501.
47. Sarah, *Memoirs*, pp. 32–33, QM to PA.
48. Sarah, *Conduct*, pp. 46–47, Feb. 5, 1692, QM to PA.
49. *QA Letters*, p. 53, Feb. 6, 1692, PA to QM.
50. BL Add MS 61414, f. 161, Feb. 8, 1692, PA to QM.

Chapter Five

1. Lewis, *Memoirs*, p. 13.
2. Sarah, *Conduct*, 78, pp. 102–103.
3. *Burnet's History*, vol. ii, pp. 90–92.
4. Ailesbury, *Memoirs*, vol. 1, pp. 180–181.

5. BL Add MS 61414 f. 166, Feb. 23, 1692, PA to SM.
6. *Macky Memoirs*, pp. 2–3
7. BL Add MS 61414 f. 166, Feb. 23, 1692, PA to SM.
8. Sarah, *Conduct*, p. 88.
9. BL Add MS 61414, f. 79–180, Apr.-May 1692, PA to SM.
10. *QA Letters*, Mar. 19, 1692, PA to SM
11. BL Add MS 61414, f. 178, early April 1692, PA to SM.
12. Lewis, *Memoirs*, p. 19.
13. Lewis, *Memoirs*, p. 76.
14. Sarah, *Conduct*, p. 69, April 17, 1692.
15. Sarah, *Conduct*, p. 70. Sarah tells us that Anne recounted this exchange immediately after the event.
16. *QA Letters*, pp. 55–56, May 1692, PA to SM.
17. *QA Letters*, p. 58, summer 1692, PA to SM.
18. Ailesbury, *Memoirs*, vol. 1, pp. 292–293.
19. Ailesbury, *Memoirs*, vol. 1, pp. 292–293.
20. Ailesbury, *Memoirs*, vol. 1, pp. 296–297.
21. Strickland, *Lives*, vol. vi, pp. 84–85, QM to PA.
22. Sarah, *Memoirs*, p. 101.
23. BL Add MS 61415 f. 14, Aug. 30, 1692, Nottingham to Mayor of Bath.
24. BL Add MS 61415 f. 17, Sept. 6, 1992, PA to SM.
25. Ailesbury, *Memoirs*, vol. 1, p. 308.
26. BL Add MS 75400, summer 1693, PA to SM.
27. BL Add MS 61415, f.37, Feb. 1693, PA to SM.
28. BL Add MS 61415 f. 162, 1692–1693, PA to SM.
29. Sarah, *Conduct*, p. 103.
30. Sarah, *Conduct*, pp. 103–104.
31. Freed from the Tower on bail under Habeas Corpus, Marlborough had, at his subsequent trial, been fully cleared of the treason charge.
32. BL Add MS 61415 f. 39, Mar. 19, 1693, PA to SM.
33. Ranke, *History*, vol. vi, p. 264, Dec. 28, 1694/Jan. 7, 1695, report from a German diplomat.
34. Ranke, *History*, vol. vi, p. 264, Dec. 28, 1694/Jan. 7, 1695, report from a German diplomat.
35. Sarah, *Conduct*, pp. 109–110.
36. Sarah, *Conduct*, p. 110
37. *Burnet's History*, vol. ii, pp. 312–313.
38. Macpherson, *Papers*, vol. 1, p. 246, 1694.
39. Ranke, *History of England*, vol. iv, p. 287, from a diplomat's report.
40. BL Add MS 75400, Oct. 15, 1697, PA to SM.
41. Caused by a build-up of uric acid in the blood that leaves deposits in the joints, gout rarely occurs in females, or before menopause (Anne menstruated at least until forty-five); Anne's gout affected several joints. Modern medicine diagnoses Anne as having had some form of arthritis. In her day, doctors used gout as a catch-all for several sorts of painful swelling not fully understood. No cure then existed.
42. BL Add MS 75400, Oct. 15, 1697, PA to SM.
43. Lewis, *Memoirs*, p. 49.
44. Sarah, *Conduct*, p. 118
45. *QA Letters*, p. 66, 1699, PA to Bathurst.
46. Vernon, J., *Vernon Correspondence*, vol. ii, p. 382, Dec. 9, 1699, Vernon to Shrewsbury.
47. *Vernon Correspondence*, vol. ii, p. 432, Feb. 15, 1700, Vernon to Shrewsbury.
48. BL Add MS 61415 f. 168, Feb. 15, 1700, PA to SM
49. No definitive medical explanation exists for

Anne's futile childbearing, although so many failures were unusual even for that time. Modern medicine posits pelvic inflammatory disease with concomitant infertility, common in Anne's day, as the most probable cause of her stillbirths and miscarriages.

50. BL Add MS 61415, f. 141, Oct. 30, 1697, PA to SM.

51. *Burnet's History,* vol. ii, p. 246.

52. After exhaustive review of the extensive autopsy recorded by the royal physicians, modern medical authorities conclude that Gloucester died from acute bacterial infection of the upper and lower respiratory tracts culminating in pneumonia.

53. *Burnet's History,* vol. ii, p. 246.

54. Lewis, *Memoirs,* pp. 103–104.

55. Lewis, *Memoirs,* pp. 103–104.

56. The Marlboroughs had accepted only half of the handsome dowry Anne gave when their eldest daughter, Henrietta, married, with the understanding that Henrietta's sister would get the other half upon her marriage. But nuptials for her god-daughter Anne brought the princess scant joy for Sarah's second daughter married the son of Lord and Lady Sunderland, whom the princess had distrusted since her father's reign; and this Sunderland son openly advocated republicanism.

57. ML&M, Rulers of England Box XIA, William and Mary, #22, August 4, 1700, KW to PA, author's translation from French.

58. Besides the Philippines and large sections of North and South America, Spain owned territory in Italy and the Netherlands.

59. The treaty of Grand Alliance accepted Louis's grandson as King Philip V of Spain on terms: no union of the French and Spanish possessions; Spain's possessions in the Netherlands and Italy must go to Austria; England and Holland would get commercial concessions; the war effort would focus on Flanders to secure the southern Netherlands as a barrier against French expansion into Holland; the Allies would negotiate jointly with France for peace. France had two months to accept Allied conditions.

60. J.S. Clarke, ed., *Life of James II ... Collected Out of Memoirs Writ of His Own Hand,* vol. ii, p. 602, Sept. 27, 1701, QMB to PA.

61. *QA Letters,* pp. 67–68, Sept. 23, 1701, PA to Sidney Godolphin (henceforth SG).

Chapter Six

1. Winn, J.A., *Queen Anne, Patroness of Arts,* p. 284, from *The Church of England's Joy on the Happy Accession of Her Most Sacred Majesty,* 1702.

2. Boyer, *History,* vol. 1, p. 3.

3. *Burnet's History,* vol. ii, pp. 309–310.

4. Verney, Lady Margaret, ed., *Verney Letters of the Eighteenth Century,* vol. 1, p. 104, Mar. 10, 1702, Lady Gardiner to J. Verney.

5. *Burnet's History,* vol. ii, pp. 309–310.

6. Verney, *Letters,* vol. 1, p. 104, Mar. 10, 1702, Gardiner to Verney.

7. HMC Portland, vol. iv, p. 34, Mar. 8, 1702, SG to Robert Harley (hence forth RH.)

8. HMC Portland, vol. iv, p. 34, Mar. 9, 1702, SG to RH.

9. Elizabeth's nearest male relative, Stuart King James VI of Scotland (Anne's great-grandfather) became King James I of England at Elizabeth's death.

10. *Burnet's History,* vol. ii, pp. 312–313.

11. *QA Letters,* p. 172, July 11, 1702, QA to SG.

12. Moderates were the smallest Tory section.

13. Sarah, *Memoirs,* pp. 236–237.

14. Godolphin's duties also included managing the government; domestic, Scottish, and foreign affairs; and with Marlborough, war planning. All that, plus his role as liaison between queen, cabinet, and parliament made Godolphin de facto, and, Britain's first modern, prime minister.

15. Ranke, *History,* vol. iv, p. 287, from a diplomat's report.

16. Boyer, *History,* vol. I, p. 49.

17. HMC X App. 4, pp. 49–51, Earl Westmoreland MSS.

18. *Burnet's History,* vol. ii, pp. 338–339.

19. *Burnet's History,* vol. ii, pp. 338–339.

20. *Burnet's History,* vol. ii, pp. 338–339.

21. *Burnet's History,* vol. ii, pp. 338–339.

22. BL Add MS 61416, f. 36, Jan. 19, 1703, QA to SM.

23. BL Add MS 61416, f. 53, Feb. 27, 1703, QA to SM.

24. *Burnet's History,* vol. ii, pp. 338–339.

25. Ailesbury, *Memoirs,* vol. ii, pp. 525 & 649 respectively.

26. Fiennes, *Journeys,* pp. 302–303, 1702.

27. Boyer, *History,* pp. 715–716.

28. Fiennes, *Journeys,* pp. 302–303, 1702.

29. Fiennes, *Journeys,* pp. 302–303, 1702.

30. Ewald, W.B., *The Newsmen of Queen Anne,* pp. 26–29, from the *London Gazette,* April 23, 1702.

31. *Verney Letters,* vol. 1, p. 356, May 15, 1714, M. Lovett to Fermanagh.

32. BL Add MS 61415, ff 135–136, Oct. 20, 1697, PA to SM.

33. BL Add MS 61415, ff 135–136, Oct. 20, 1697, PA to SM.

34. The bedchamber woman performed "royal body service." She came on duty "before the queen's prayers, which was before her majesty was dressed. The queen often shifted in the morning ... the bedchamber-*woman* gave the shift to the [bedchamber] lady ... and the lady put it on. Sometimes, likewise, the bedchamber-*woman* gave the fan to the lady."

"When the queen washed her hands, the page of the back-stairs brought and set down upon a side table the basin and ewer; then the bedchamber-*woman* set it before the queen and knelt on the other side of the table over-against the queen" and "poured the water out of the ewer upon the queen's hands." (*Letters to and from Henrietta, Countess of Suffolk,* vol. I, pp. 292–293, J. Arbuthnot to H. Howard, from Abigail Hill's description of a bedchamber-woman's duties.)

35. *QA Letters,* p. 341, Sept. 13, 1711, QA to RH.

36. Pepys, S. *The Diary of Samuel Pepys,* vol. ii, p. 225, 1704.

37. *QA Letters* p. 117, spring 1703, QA to Hedges.

38. West, Richard, *The Life and Strange Surprising Adventures of Daniel Defoe,* p. 208, quoted from Defoe's *An Appeal to Honor and Justice.*

39. *Letters of Sarah, Duchess of Marlborough from the Original Manuscripts at Madresfield Court,* p. 37, May 16, 1713, SM. to Robert Jennens, trusted friend, relative, and business agent.

40. Traditionally someone close to the crown, the ranger is responsible for overseeing the protection and upkeep of the Park's almost five thousand acres of gardens, woods, and grassland.

41. H.L. Snyder, ed., *Marlborough-Godolphin Correspondence*, vol. 1, p. 65–67, May 19, 1702, QA to SM.

42. BL Add MS 61416 f. 93, June 14, 1703, QA to SM.

43. *QA Letters*, pp. 98–99, Oct. 24, 1702, QA to SM.

44. *QA Letters*, pp. 98–99, Oct. 24, 1702, QA to SM.

Chapter Seven

1. Boyer, *History*, vol. 1, p. 49.

2. HMC Bath vol. 1, p. 199, Shrewsbury papers.

3. Reid, Stuart, *John and Sarah, Duke and Duchess of Marlborough*, p. 139, QA to SM

4. Ashton, John, *Social Life in the Reign of Queen Anne*, p. 374.

5. *Vernon Correspondence*, vol. iii, pp. 228–229, Nov. 6, 1702, Vernon to Shrewsbury.

6. *Verney Letters*, vol. 1, p. 112, Aug. 25, 1702, Lady Gardiner to Sir John Verney.

7. The Battle of Vigo Bay resulted in Portugal switching its allegiance from France to the Allies, thus giving England access to Brazilian bullion and the port of Lisbon.

8. Coxe, *Marlborough*, vol. 1, p. 202, Oct. 22, 1702, QA to SM.

9. Coxe, *Marlborough*, vol. 1, pp. 204–205, Nov. 6, 1702, JM to SM.

10. *QA Letters*, p. 103, Dec. 16, 1702, QA to SM.

11. After breaking with Anne eight years later, Sarah helped herself to the accumulated money despite the post office pension already having been made permanent.

12. BL Add MS 61416 f. 50, Feb. 22, 1703, QA to SM.

13. *QA Letters*, p. 116, Feb.-Mar. 1703, QA to SM.

14. BL Add MS 61416, f. 48, Feb. 21, 1703, QA to SM.

15. BL Add MS 61416 f. 100, June 20, 1703, QA to SM.

16. BL Add MS 61416 f. 95, June 1703, QA to SM.

17. BL Add MS 61416 f. 95, June 1703, QA to SM.

18. BL Add MS 61416 f. 64, 1703 [no specifics of date given] QA to SM.

19. BL Add MS 61416 f. 86, June 11, 1703, QA to SM.

20. BL Add MS 61416 f. 97, June 18, 1703, QA to SM.

21. BL Add MS 61416, ff. 122–123, July 9, 1703, QA to SM.

22. BL Add MS 61416 f. 130, Aug. 20, 1703, QA to SM.

23. Fiennes, *Journeys*, p. 18.

24. Fiennes, *Journeys*, p. 18, quote from diarist Samuel Pepys.

25. Fiennes, *Journeys*, pp. 19–20.

26. *QA Letters*, p. 127, Oct. 1703, QA to SM.

27. BL Add MS 61416, f. 139, Oct. 16, 1703, QA to SM.

28. Sarah, *Private Correspondence,* vol. 1, pp. 402–403, Oct. 30, 1710, F. Hare [Marlborough's chaplain] to SM.

29. *M-G Correspondence*, vol. 1, p. 183, May 13, 1703, JM to SM.

30. *QA Letters*, pp. 128–129, Dec. 1703, QA to SM.

31. Queen Anne's Bounty lasted for more than two centuries uniting, in 1947, with other Anglican charities that supported the Church's work.

32. Coxe, *Marlborough*, vol. 1, pp. 273–274, July 1703, QA to SM.

33. Coxe, *Marlborough*, vol. 1, pp. 273–274, July 1703, QA to SM.

Chapter Eight

1. Reverand, C.D., p. 46, Queen Anne and the Arts, Defoe's 'A Hymn to Victory,' 1704.

2. Coxe, *Marlborough,*, vol. 1, p. 319, Apr. 30, 1704, JM to SG.

3. *M-G Correspondence*, vol. 1, p. 277, April 14, 1704, JM to SG.

4. *Sarah, Letters*, vol. 1, p. 411.

5. Lediard, Thomas, *Life of John, Duke of Marlborough*, vol. 1, pp. 285–287.

6. *M-G Correspondence*, vol. 1, p. 285, Apr. 24, 1704, SG to SM.

7. BL Add MS 61416, f. 174, Apr. 1704, QA to SM.

8. BL Add MS 61416 f. 158, May 17, 1704, QA to SM.

9. BL Add MS 61416, Nov. 21, 1704, QA to SM.

10. BL Add MS 61416, f. 162, May 26, 1704, QA to SM.

11. BL Add MS 61416, f. 164, June 9, 1704, QA to SM.

12. Union's failure met with approval from English (Whig) merchants involved in colonial commerce, as well as Tories who refused to recognize the established Presbyterian Church of Scotland to which most Scots belonged. A vocal minority of Scots adhered to the country's disestablished Anglican church. They, and the Catholic highland clans, supported a Jacobite restoration as the means to regain national and religious freedom.

13. Burnet, *History*, vol. ii, p. 405.

14. To hide his march across Europe with forty thousand men, Marlborough built an extremely effective intelligence service (well-placed informants throughout the Continent, as well as the French court). His agents spread false rumors; built fake supply bases; and the duke moved in the pre-dawn dark to disguise his march from the enemy.

15. Coxe, *Marlborough*, vol. 1, p. 366, July 4, 1704, JM to SM.

16. WSC, *Marlborough*, vol. iv, p. 53, July 23, 1704, JM to SM.

17. Coxe, *Marlborough*, vol. 1, pp. 413–414, Aug. 13, 1704, JM to SM.

18. A guinea consisted of one pound and one shilling.

19. *QA Letters*, pp. 149–150, Aug. 21, 1704, QA to JM.

20. BL Add MS 61101, f. 71, Aug. 15, 1704, Prince George to JM.

21. *Diary of John Evelyn*, p. 441, Sept. 7, 1704.

22. Richly ornamented trappings.

23. *Evelyn Diary* p. 441, Sept. 7, 1704.

24. *Evelyn Diary* p. 441, Sept. 7, 1704.

25. Despite her rift with Sarah, Anne also gave the soon-to-be-married youngest Marlborough daughter a generous dowry, created her bridegroom's father a duke, and promised his high court office would descend to his son.

26. Prominent architect, Sir John Vanbrugh received the commission to build Blenheim Palace, *the* great monument of Queen Anne's reign.

27. When Carlos traveled from Vienna to Madrid,

Anne and George received him in state before an English vessel carried Carlos to his new kingdom.

28. Coxe, *Marlborough*, vol. ii, p. 27, Aug. 23, 1704, JM to SG.

29. BL Add MS 61416, f. 177, Aug. 21, 1704, QA to SM.

30. BL Add MS 61416 f. 183, Sept. 1, 1704, QA to SM.

31. *M-G Correspondence*, vol. 1, p. 366, Sept. 1, 1704, SG to SM.

32. *Russell Letters*, vol. ii, p. 169, Nov. 2, 1704.

33. *QA Letters*, p. 153, Nov. 17, 1704, QA to SM.

34. BL Add MS 61416, ff. 197–198, Nov. 20, 1704, SM to QA.

35. *QA Letters*, p. 226, 1704, QA to SM.

Chapter Nine

1. Clerk, John, *Memoirs of the Life of Sir John Clerk of Penicuik*, p. 62, July 1706.

2. *Burnet's History*, vol. 1, p. 448.

3. *Burnet's History*, vol. ii, p. 436.

4. Ashton, *Social Life*, p. 229.

5. Bathurst, *Papers*, pp. 262–263, Oct. 23, 1705, QA to Apsley.

6. *QA Letters*, p. 172, July 11, 1705, QA to SG.

7. *QA Letters*, p. 172, July 11, 1705, QA to SG.

8. *QA Letters*, p. 172, July 11, 1705, QA to SG.

9. Coxe, *Marlborough*, vol. ii, p. 185, Sept. 2, 1705, JM to SM.

10. BL Add MS 61416, f. 210, Sept. 17, 1705, QA to SM.

11. Coxe, *Marlborough*, vol. ii, p. 236, Sept. 29, 1705, JM to QA.

12. ML&M, Rulers of England Box XIB, Anne, #9, Sept. 27, 1705, QA to JM.

13. Coxe, *Marlborough*, vol. ii, p. 132, July 6, 1705, JM to QA.

14. Coxe, *Marlborough*, vol. ii, p. 189, Sept. 17, 1705, QA to JM.

15. Coxe, *Marlborough*, vol. 1, pp. 228–229, June 7, 1703, JM to SM.

16. Coxe, *Marlborough*, vol. iv, pp. 193–194, Aug. 9, 1708, JM to SM.

17. The queen would assign all church livings yielding more than a minimum annual income.

18. Toland, John, *An Account of the Courts of Prussia and Hanover*, pp. 65–69, Sept. 23, 1702.

19. Fricke, Waltraut, "Leibnitz und die Englische Sukzession des Hauses Hanover," p. 64, Mar. 19/30, 1706, Falaiseau (Sophia's representative in London) to Leibnitz (her senior advisor.) Author's translation from German.

20. *Burnet's History*, vol. ii, p. 407.

21. HMC Portland, vol. iv, p. 154, Dec. 1704, SG to RH.

22. HMC Portland, vol. iv, p. 154, Dec. 1704, SG to RH.

23. *Cowper Diary*, p. 13, Nov, 11, 1705.

24. *QA Letters*, p. 176, Nov. 13, 1705, QA to JM

25. *QA Letters*, p. 176, Nov. 13, 1705, QA to JM

26. Coxe, *Marlborough*, vol. ii, p. 61, Nov. 23, 1704, JM to SM.

27. Firmly in support of the Grand Alliance, the elector wanted neither his energetic mother nor his erratic son in England; for, if politicians maneuvered them to oppose the queen, they would become Tory tools used to fracture the Alliance. Conversely, if he declined an invitation, Tories would paint the elector as caring little for England or the succession.

28. Coxe, *Marlborough*, vol. ii, p. 260, Dec. 8, 1705, JM to SG.

29. *Burnet's History*, vol. ii, p. 430.

30. *Burnet's History*, vol. ii, p. 429.

31. Anne's former secretary of state Nottingham, backed Rochester. Nottingham's support of the Hanoverian invitation caused the queen three times to block his return to office—he had insulted her by supporting the motion to invite Sophia to England, especially after previously convincing Anne that whoever proposed bringing her successor to England, intended to depose her.

32. *Burnet's History*, vol. ii, p. 430.

33. Most Tories expected their monarch to obey the law but believed she could sometimes use her royal prerogative to overrule it.

34. Charles Montagu, Earl of Halifax, combined literary talent with financial expertise; having advised King William to cover part of the cost of his continental wars by raising long-term loans on the security of specific taxes, Halifax attracted investors with a parliamentary guarantee of a good interest rate on annuities they would own for life. He thus played a key role in founding the Bank of England and creating the national debt. Partisan and timid, a versatile politician and riveting orator, Halifax craved position, and cultivated the queen's favor.

35. *QA Letters*, p. 177, Nov/Dec. 1705, QA to SM.

Chapter Ten

1. Coxe, *Marlborough*, vol. iii, p. 89, Aug. 9, 1706, JM to SM.

2. *Newsmen of Queen Anne*, p. 43, from the *Post Boy*, February 5–7, 1706.

3. *Newsmen of Queen Anne*, p. 43, from the *Post Boy*, February 5–7, 1706.

4. BL Add MS 61101, May 21, 1706, QA to JM.

5. BL Add MS 61101, f. 94, May 28, 1706, PG to JM.

6. Coxe, *Marlborough*, vol. iii, p.21, Sept. 26, 1706, JM to SM.

7. Coxe, *Marlborough*, vol. iii, pp. p. 101, Oct. 11, 1706, JM to SM.

8. *M-G Correspondence*, vol. ii, p. 843, early July 1706, JM to SM.

9. BL Add MS 61417, f. 9, July 3, 1706, QA to SM.

10. Coxe, *Marlborough*, vol. iii, p.111, Aug. 1706, SM to QA.

11. Coxe, *Marlborough*, vol. iii, p.114, Sept. 1, 1706, SG to SM.

12. BL Add MS 61417, f. 5, summer 1706, QA to SM.

13. Cowper *Diary*, p. 33, Jan. 5, 1706.

14. HMC Portland, vol. iv, p. 536, Mar. 10, 1710, Abigail Hill to Robert Harley—henceforth RH.

15. Lever, Tresham, *Godolphin, His Life and Times*, p. 159, Aug. 31, 1706, SG to QA.

16. *QA Letters*, pp. 196–197, Aug. 30, 1706, QA to SG.

17. *QA Letters*, pp. 196–197, Aug. 30, 1706, QA to SG.

18. *QA Letters*, pp. 196–197, Aug. 30, 1706, QA to SG.

19. Lever, *Godolphin*, Aug. 31, 1706, SG to QA.

20. *QA Letters*, pp. 199–201, Sept. 21, 1706, QA to SG.

21. Coxe, *Marlborough*, vol. iii, pp. 97–98, Sept. 16, 1706, JM to SG.

22. *QA Letters*, pp. 199–201, Sept. 21, 1706, QA to SG.

23. Lever, *Godolphin*, p.160, Sept. 21, 1706, SG to JM.

24. Coxe, *Marlborough*, vol. iii, p. 118, Oct. 24, 1706, JM to QA.

25. *Sarah, Private Correspondence*, vol. 1, p. 73, Oct. 20, 1706, SM to QA.

26. *QA Letters*, pp. 203–204, probably Oct. 30, 1706, QA to SM.

Chapter Eleven

1. Frank Ellis, ed., *Poems on Affairs of State*, vol. vii, p. 68, anon., 1705.

2. For his many years of outstanding service to the nation, Queen Anne had created Sidney Godolphin an earl at the end of 1706.

3. Clerk, J., *Memoirs of the Life of Sir John Clerk of Penicuik*, pp. 60–61, July 1706.

4. Lockhart, George, *Letters of George Lockhart of Carnwath*, p. 34, May 26, 1706.

5. Clerk, *Memoirs*, pp. 60–61, July 1706.

6. Lockhart, George, *Letters of George Lockhart of Carnwath*, p. 34, May 26, 1706.

7. Clerk, *Memoirs*, p. 62, July 1706.

8. M-G Correspondence, vol. 1, p. 65–67, May 19, 1702, QA to SM. (In BL FU file)

9. Ewald, *Newsmen of Queen Anne*, pp. 50–51, *Daily Courant* March 3, 1707.

10. Clerk, *Memoirs*, p. 68, May 1707.

11. *M-G Correspondence*, vol. ii, p. 843, July 7, 1707, JM to QA.

12. ML&M, Rulers of England, Box XIB Anne, #5, July 26, 1703, QA to Richard Hill.

13. *Burnet's History*, vol. ii, pp. 486–487.

14. *Burnet's History*, vol. vi, pp. 36–37, Dartmouth note.

15. *QA Letters*, p. 213, late 1706, QA to SM.

16. *QA Letters*, p. 213, late 1706, QA to SM.

17. BL Add MS 61417, f.129, Mar. 13, 1707, SM to QA.

18. In Anne's day passion referred to any strong feeling.

19. BL Add MS 61417, f. 79, July 18, 1707, QA to SM.

20. *QA Letters*, p. 229, 1707–1708, QA to SM.

21. BL Add MS 61417, f. 65, June 17, 1707, QA to SM.

22. BL Add MS 61417, f. 67, June 18, 1707, QA to SM.

23. BL Add MS 61417, f. 79, July 18, 1707, QA to SM.

24. Coxe, *Marlborough*, vol. iii, pp. 328–329, Aug. 29, 1707, JM to SM.

25. Coxe, *Marlborough*, vol. iii, pp. 325–325, Aug. 22, 1707, JM to SM.

26. A.W. Thibadeau, ed., *Catalogue of the Collection of Autograph Letters and Historical Documents*, vol. iv, p. 148, Oct. 7, 1707, JM to QA.

27. Coxe, *Marlborough*, vol. iii, pp. 371–372, beginning of Sept. 1707, QA to JM.

28. Lever, *Godolphin*, p. 188–189, Sept. 11, 1707, SG to QA.

29. *QA Letters*, pp. 231–232, Sept. 12, 1707, QA to SG.

30. *QA Letters*, pp. 231–232, Sept. 12, 1707, QA to SG.

Chapter Twelve

1. *QA Letters*, p. 196, Aug. 30, 1706, QA to SG.

2. *Burnet's History*, vol. v, pp. 353–354.

3. Coxe, *Marlborough*, vol. iv, p. 24, Jan. 1708, JM to QA.

4. Holmes, G., and Speck, W.A., "The Fall of Harley Reconsidered," pp. 695–696, based on at least two reliable contemporary accounts.

5. *Burnet's History*, vol. v., pp. 354–355.

6. *Burnet's History*, vol. v., pp. 354–355.

7. HMC Westmoreland, X, appendix, part iv, p. 50.

8. *Burnet's History*, vol. v., pp. 354–355.

9. HMC Rutland, vol. ii, p. 188, Mar. 4, 1708, Granby to Rutland.

10. Sarah, *Memoirs*, p. 257.

11. HMC Portland, vol. iv, pp. 495–496, July 21, 1708, Abigail Masham (henceforth AM) to RH.

12. Coxe, *Marlborough*, vol. iv, pp. 194–195, July 22, 1708, QA to JM, Anne's emphases.

13. Coxe, *Marlborough*, vol. iv, p. 45, Mar. 31, 1708, SM to QA.

14. BL Add MS 61417, f. 132, Mar. 31, 1708, SM to QA.

15. BL Add MS 61417, f. 133 Mar. 31, 1708, QA to SM.

16. *QA Letters*, pp. 244–245, late Feb.,1708, QA to JM.

17. BL Add MS 61417, f. 153, July 24, 1708, SM to QA.

18. *Poems on Affairs of State*, vol. vii, p. 309.

19. Boyer, *History*, vol. 1, pp. 715–716.

20. BL Add MS 61417, f. 153, July 26, 1708, SM to QA.

21. BL Add MS 61417, f. 153, July 26, 1708, SM to QA.

22. WSC, Marlborough, vol. v, p. 397, Eugene note, July 1708.

23. *QA Letters*, p. 252, July 17, 1708, QA to JM.

24. Coxe, *Marlborough*, vol. iv, pp. 153–154, July 12, 1708, JM to SM.

25. *QA Letters*, pp. 254–255, July 24, 1708, QA to JM.

26. *QA Letters*, p. 249, June 18, 1708, QA to JM.

27. *QA Letters*, pp. 255–256, mid–August 1708, QA to JM.

28. Coxe, *Marlborough*, vol. iv, pp. 186–188, Aug. 2, 1708, JM to QA.

29. BL Add MS 61417, f. 151, July 7, 1708, QA to SM.

30. Fiennes, *Journeys*, p. 358.

31. Fiennes, *Journeys*, pp. 358–359.

Chapter Thirteen

1. Cotteril, *Prince George of Denmark*, p. 8.

2. BL Add MS 61417, ff. 166–167, Aug. 1708, SM to QA.

3. *QA Letters*, p. 258, Aug. 1708, QA to SM.

4. BL Add MS 61417, f. 170, Aug., 1708, SM to QA.

5. *QA Letters*, pp. 256–258, Aug. 27, 1708, QA to JM.

6. *QA Letters*, pp. 256–257, Aug. 17, 1708, QA to JM.

7. Coxe, *Marlborough*, vol. iv, pp. 202–203, Aug. 27, 1708, QA to JM.

8. BL Add MS 61434, ff. 67–69, Oct. 17, 1708, SG to SM.

9. Facilities to service, provision, and repair the fleet (dry docks, stores, building yards, etc.)

10. *Burnet's History*, vol. ii, pp. 491–492.

11. *Burnet's History*, vol. ii, p. 489.

12. HMC Westmoreland, X, appendix, part iv, p. 50.

13. HMC Westmoreland, X, appendix, part iv, p. 51.

14. *M-G Correspondence*, vol. ii, p. 594, July 1, 1706, JM to SG.

15. Boyer, *History*, p. 357.

16. Burnet's History, vol. ii, p. 515.

17. BL Add MS 61423, ff. 31–34, Sarah's *Account of ... What Passed at the Prince's Death.*

18. Sarah, *Private Correspondence*, vol. 1, pp. 412–414.

19. BL Add MS 61423, ff. 31–34, Sarah's *Account of ... What Passed at the Prince's Death.*

20. Sarah, *Private Correspondence*, vol. 1, pp. 412–414.

21. BL Add MS 61423, ff. 31–34, Sarah's *Account of ... What Passed at the Prince's Death.*

22. Sarah, *Letters*, vol. 1, p. 415.

23. Sarah, *Letters*, vol. 1, pp.415.

24. Sarah, *Letters*, vol. 1, pp.412–416.

25. Sarah, *Letters*, vol. 1, pp.412–416.

26. *QA Letters*, p. 263, Oct. 28, 1708, QA to SM.

27. *Vernon Correspondence*, vol. iii, p. 367, Oct. 30, 1708, Vernon the Shrewsbury.

28. Coxe, *Marlborough*, vol. iv, p. 318, Oct. 29, 1708, SG to JM.

29. Macky, *Memoirs*, pp. 2–3.

30. *Burnet's History*, vol. ii, pp. 515–516.

31. *Letters and Dispatches of John Churchill*, vol. iv, pp. 323–324, Nov. 27, 1708, JM to Secretary of State Henry Boyle.

32. George Murray, ed., *Letters and Dispatches of John Churchill, First Duke of Marlborough*, vol. iv, p. 208, Sept. 7, 1708, JM to Prince George.

33. After their victory at Oudenarde, the duke and Prince Eugene decided to carry out a difficult crossing of the Scheldt river as part of their ultimately successful siege of Lille, France's second largest city.

34. *Letters and Dispatches of John Churchill*, vol. iv, pp. 323–324, Nov. 27, 1708, JM to Secretary of State Henry Boyle.

35. BL Add MSS 61001, f. 94, May 28, 1706, PG to JM.

36. HMC Westmoreland, X, appendix, part iv, pp. 49–50.

37. BL Add MS 17677 CCC, f. 627, Nov. 9, 1708, QA to Holland's States General.

38. HMC Portland, vol. iv, pp. 510–511, Nov. 6, 1708, AM to RH.

39. HMC Portland, vol. iv, pp. 510–511, Nov. 6, 1708, AM to RH.

40. Sarah, *Conduct*, p. 223.

41. BL Add MS 61417, f. 179 Nov./Dec. 1708, QA to SM.

Chapter Fourteen

1. *QA Letters*, pp. 285–6, Oct. 25, 1709 QA to JM.

2. *M-G Correspondence*, vol. ii, pp. 1157–1158, Dec. 3, 1708, JM to SM.

3. *Burnet's History*, vol. ii, p. 525.

4. *Burnet's History*, vol. ii, p. 525.

5. *Burnet's History*, vol. ii, p. 525.

6. BL Add MS 61417, f. 187, Aug. 6, 1709, SM to QA.

7. BL Add MS 61423, ff. 65–66, Dec. 22, 1710, SM

to the queen's physician Dr. David Hamilton (hereafter referred to as DH) in which the duchess quotes Anne's Oct. 26, 1709 letter to her.

8. BL Add MS 61418, f. 106, June 12, 1710, QA to SM.

9. Hamilton, David, *The Diary of Sir David Hamilton*, p. 12, July 10, 1710.

10. *Hamilton Diary*, p. 12, July 10, 1710.

11. Sarah, *Correspondence*, vol. ii, p. 382, Oct. 3, 1709, JM to SM.

12. *M-G Correspondence*, vol. iii, Oct. 3, 1709, JM to SM.

13. The Dutch Barrier consisted of a ring of cities and fortresses that Holland considered crucial for its security against French incursion.

14. BL Add MS 61418, f. 16 et passim, Oct. 16, 1709, SM to QA.

15. HMC Portland, vol. iv, p. 524, Aug. 9, 1709, AM to RH.

16. HMC Portland, vol. iv, p. 525, Sept. 4, 1709, AM to RH.

17. BL Add MS 61418, f. 14, Oct. 27, 1709, QA to SM.

18. BL Add MS 61418, f. 52, Oct. 29, 1709, SM to QA.

19. BL Add MS 61418, f. 68, Nov. 7, 1709, QA to SM.

20. Coxe, Marlborough, vol. v, p. 108, Aug. 19, 1709, JM to SM.

21. Burnet's *History*, vol. v, p. 454, Dartmouth note.

22. Sarah, *Correspondence*, vol. i, pp. 188–189, June 5, 1709, JM to SM.

23. Snyder, "Marlborough's Request of the Captain-Generalcy for Life," Oct. 10, 1709, JM to QA. Excerpted from Marlborough's only surviving letter to Anne on the subject.

24. Snyder, "Marlborough's Request of the Captain-Generalcy for Life," Oct. 10, 1709, JM to QA.

25. Snyder, "Marlborough's Request of the Captain-Generalcy for Life," Oct. 10, 1709, JM to QA.

26. Snyder, "Marlborough's Request of the Captain-Generalcy for Life," Oct. 10, 1709, JM to QA.

27. Snyder, "Marlborough's Request of the Captain-Generalcy for Life," Oct. 10, 1709, JM to QA.

28. BL Add MS 61101, Oct. 29, 1709 QA to JM.

29. *QA Letters*, pp. 285–6, Oct. 29, 1709 QA to JM.

30. *QA Letters*, pp. 285–6, Oct. 29, 1709 QA to JM.

31. BL Add MS 61101, f. 163, Oct. 25, 1709 QA to JM.

32. BL Add MS 61123, f. 76, Sept. 1704, RH to JM.

Chapter Fifteen

1. *QA Letters*, pp. 231–232, Sept. 12, 1707, QA to SG.

2. Those unable to read, gathered round those who could.

3. BL Add MS 61422, f. 49, Jan. 1710, Sarah's *Account.*

4. Sarah, *Conduct*, pp. 124–125.

5. C. Buck and G. Davies, "Letters on Godolphin's Dismissal in 1710, " *Huntington Library Quarterly*, p. 237, Aug. 24, 1710, Bridges (senior treasury official at the center of politics and government) to Drummond.

6. BL Add MS 61422, ff. 51–52, Sarah's *Account.*

7. HMC Portland, vol. iv, p. 532, Feb., 1710, AM to RH.

8. Wilkins, W.W., *Political Ballads of the Seventeenth and Eighteenth Centuries*, vol. ii, p. 83.

9. *Political Ballads* vol. ii, p. 83.

10. *Hamilton Diary*, p. 23, Dec. 28, 1710.

11. BL Add MS 61423, ff. 73–75, Dec. 1710, SM to DH.

12. BL Add MS 61418, f. 81, Sarah's account.

13. *QA Letters*, p. 301, Apr. 3, 1710, QA to SM.

14. *QA Letters*, pp. 301–302, Apr. 6, 1710, QA to SM.

15. *QA Letters*, pp. 301–302, Apr. 6, 1710, QA to SM.

16. BL Add MS 61426, f. 162, undated, Sarah's self-serving *Character of Princes*.

17. BL Add MS 61426, f. 162, Sarah's *Character of Princes*.

18. BL Add MS 61426, f. 162, Sarah's *Character of Princes*.

19. BL Add MS 61426, f. 166, Sarah's *Character of Princes*.

20. Burnet's *History*, vol. v, p. 454, spring 1710, based on the account of a lady-in-waiting sitting in the queen's ante-room.

21. BL Add MS 61426, f. 167, Sarah's *Character of Princes*.

22. Burnet's *History*, vol. v, p. 454, spring 1710, based on the account of a lady-in-waiting sitting in the queen's ante-room.

23. HMC Portland, vol. iv, p. 536, Mar. 10, 1710, AM to RH.

24. HMC Portland, vol. iv, p. 540, Apr. 17, 1710, AM to RH.

25. Influential head of Scotland's Campbell clan, Argyll attracted disgruntled army officers; furious besides, at Marlborough's request that the queen appoint him captain general for life, Argyll, hungering for honors and power, now welcomed working with Harley. Somerset had served the queen as a senior member of her household (master of the horse, which carried cabinet rank) since her accession.

26. Burnet's *History*, vol. ii, pp. 546–547.

27. Coxe, *Marlborough*, vol. v, pp. 243–244, May 29, 1710, SG to JM.

28. Coxe, *Marlborough*, vol. v, p. 260, June 10, 1710, JM to SG—letter to be given to the queen.

29. Coxe, *Marlborough*, vol. v, pp. 263–264, June 13, 1710, QA to SG.

30. Coxe, *Marlborough*, vol. v, pp. 264–265, June 14, 1709, QA to SG.

31. BL Add MS 61418, ff. 88–92, June 7, 1710, SM to QA.

32. BL Add MS 61418, f. 106, June 12, 1710, QA to SM.

33. *Hamilton Diary*, p. 12, July 10, 1710.

34. *Hamilton Diary*, p. 12, July 10, 1710.

35. Uffenbach, Zacharias Conrad von, *London in 1710*.

36. Coxe, *Marlborough*, vol. v, p. 279.

37. *M-G Correspondence*, vol. iii, p. 1549, June 26, 1710, SG to JM.

38. *M-G Correspondence*, vol. iii, p. 1548, n. 4, July 2, 1710, cabinet minute.

39. Godolphin instituted more open and honest management of public funds; pressed tax agencies to improve processes; expedited valuation and collection of the government's major source of revenue—the land tax; and worked to eliminate corruption.

40. Dickinson, William C., *Sidney Godolphin, Lord Treasurer*, p. 238, quoted from Daniel Defoe, propagandist for Harley.

41. *Hamilton Diary*, p. 5, Dec, 23, 1709.

42. *Hamilton Diary*, p. 9, May 11, 1710.

43. Lever, *Godolphin*, p. 225; quote is from Sunderland's Feb. 21, 1710 letter to Marlborough.

44. *Hamilton Diary*, p. 9, May 11, 1710.

45. Sundstrom, R.A., *Sidney Godolphin, Servant of State* pp. 257–258, Aug. 7, 1710, QA to SG.

46. Swift, Jonathan, *The Correspondence of Jonathan Swift*, vol. 1, p. 291, Sept. 9, 1710.

47. Coxe, *Marlborough*, vol. v, p. 322, Aug. 8, 1710, QA to JM.

48. *QA Letters*, p. 10, July 1683, PA to Bathurst.

49. *Burnet's History Of His Own Time*, vol. vi, pp. 143–144, Dartmouth note.

50. *Burnet's History Of His Own Time*, vol. vi, pp. 143–144, Dartmouth note.

51. *Hamilton Diary*, p. 65, July 27, 1714.

52. Wilkins, *Political Ballads*, vol. ii, p. 68, quoted from Boyer, *History*.

Chapter Sixteen

1. MM&L, Rulers of England, Box XIB, Anne, #9, Sept. 27, 1705, QA to JM.

2. Sarah, *Conduct*, pp. 142–143.

3. *Hamilton Diary*, p. 12, July 10, 1710.

4. *Hamilton Diary*, p. 9, July 8, 1710.

5. *Hamilton Diary*, p. 28, Jan. 11, 1711.

6. BL Add MS 61423 ff. 16–17, Nov. 28, 1710, SM to DH.

7. Coxe, *Marlborough*, vol. v, p. 403.

8. *Hamilton Diary*, p. 21, Dec. 11, 1710.

9. Burnet's *History*, vol. vi, p. 33, Dartmouth note.

10. Burnet's *History*, vol. vi, p. 34, Dartmouth note.

11. Cowper, *Diary* p. 49, Oct. 14, 1710.

12. Burnet's *History*, vol. vi, p. 34, Dartmouth note.

13. *Hamilton Diary*, p. 23, Dec. 29, 1710.

14. Coxe, *Marlborough*, vol. v, p. 405.

15. *Hamilton Diary*, p. 23, Dec. 29, 1710.

16. *Hamilton Diary*, pp. 23–24, Dec. 30, 1710.

17. *Hamilton Diary*, pp. 25–26, Jan. 8, 1711.

18. *Hamilton Diary*, p. 25, Jan. 6, 1711.

19. Coxe, *Marlborough*, vol. v, pp. 410–411, Jan. 17, 1711, SM to QA.

20. Coxe, *Marlborough*, vol. v, pp. 410–411, Jan. 17, 1711, SM to QA.

21. Coxe, *Marlborough*, vol. v, p. 411.

22. Coxe, *Marlborough*, vol. v, p. 411.

23. Boyer, *History*, p. 485.

24. *Hamilton Diary*, p. 49, Jan. 12, 1713.

25. *Hamilton Diary*, p. 38, Jan. 24, 1712.

26. Shortly before returning her gold key, Sarah helped herself to a sizeable sum from the privy purse, the accumulated stipend she had refused several years before.

27. *Burnet's History*, 18, vol. ii, p. 579.

28. Ailesbury, *Memoirs*, vol. ii, p. 639.

29. Jacobites were stronger among parliamentary Tories than at any other time in Anne's reign. Harley cultivated their support of his moderation. Hoping Harley would effect his restoration, the Pretender told Jacobites to back him.

30. Older, larger, and less homogeneous than the

cabinet, the privy council met to conduct executive business, but no longer initiated policy.

31. *Burnet's History*, vol. ii, pp. 566–567.

32. Wilkins, *Political Ballads*, vol. ii, pp. 116–119.

33. Stanhope, Earl of, *History of England Comprising the Reign of Queen Anne*, vol. 1, p. 216.

34. *Burnet's History*, vol. ii, pp. 566–567.

35. H.C. Foxcroft, ed., *A Supplement to Burnet's History of My Own Time*.

36. Burnet's History, vol. ii, pp. 566–567.

37. *QA Letters*, p. 340, Aug. 21, 1711, QA to RH.

38. Hervey, John, *Letter Books of John Hervey, first Earl of Bristol*, vol. 1, p. 291.

39. Burnet's History, vol. ii, pp. 566–567.

40. Holmes, *Marlborough*, p. 460, Oct. 8, 1711, JM to RH.

41. *QA Letters*, pp. 340–341, Sept. 1711, QA to RH.

42. Based on Tory naval war strategy, the attack on Quebec, if successful, would have brought the entire American sub-continent under British rule to benefit British trade. While Harley convalesced, St. John rammed the Quebec expedition through the cabinet despite Anne's doubts. A large fleet carried the several thousand troops St. John had removed from Marlborough's command; and St. John earned Abigail Masham's eternal gratitude by putting her brother, Four Bottle Jack Hill, in charge.

43. Henceforth referred to as Oxford and Bolingbroke respectively.

44. *QA Letters*, p. 343, Sept. 20, 1711, QA to RH.

45. HMC, Bath, vol. 1, p. 212, Sept. 24, 1711, QA to RH.

Chapter Seventeen

1. *QA Letters*, p. 232, 1707, QA to SG.

2. *Wentworth Papers*, p. 215, Nov. 27, 1711, Stafford to Wentworth.

3. *Burnet's History*, vol. v, p. 2, Onslow addition to Dartmouth note.

4. Cowper, *Diary*, p. 53, Dec. 1711.

5. *Burnet's History*, vol. ii, pp. 582–583.

6. HMC, Bath, p. 216, Nov. 9, 1711, QA to RH.

7. *Burnet's History*, vol. ii, pp. 582–583.

8. *QA Letters*, p. 393, Nov. 21, 1712, QA to RH.

9. *Burnet's History*, vol. ii, pp. 582–583.

10. *Hamilton Diary*, p. 30, Feb. 15, 1711.

11. Coxe, *Marlborough*, vol. vi, p. 153.

12. BL Add MS 61426, Sarah, *Character of Princes*, f. 204.

13. *Letters of the Earl of Chesterfield*, vol. 1, pp. 291–294, Nov. 18, 1748, Chesterfield to his son.

14. *Burnet's History*, vol. 1, pp. 755–756.

15. BL Add MS 61426, Sarah, *Character of Princes*, f. 198.

16. BL Add MS 61426, Sarah, *Character of Princes*, f. 199.

17. BL Add MS 61426, Sarah, *Character of Princes*, f. 199.

18. Churchill, *Marlborough*, vol. vi, p. 507.

19. HMC Bath, vol. 1, p. 223, Nov. 27, 1712, QA to RH.

20. Swift, Jonathan, *Poetical Works*, p. 97.

21. *Hamilton Diary*, p. 37, Jan. 24, 1712.

22. *Hamilton Diary*, p. 37, Jan. 10, 1712.

23. Parliament authorized Marlborough's successor as commander in chief to charge the same commission for bread contracts and make the same deduction from the payment of foreign troops.

24. *Burnet's History*, vol. vi, p. 95, Dartmouth note.

25. *Burnet's History*, vol. vi, p. 95, Dartmouth note.

26. *Hamilton Diary*, p. 35, Dec. 29, 1711.

27. HMC Bath, vol. 1, p. 236, July 21, 1713, QA to RH.

28. *Burnet's History*, vol. vi, pp. 36–37, Dartmouth note.

29. *Burnet's History*, vol. vi, pp. 36–37, Dartmouth note.

30. *QA Letters*, p. 397, Jan. 3, 1713, QA to RH.

31. Battle of Zenta, 1697.

32. *Wentworth Papers*, pp. 247–248, Feb. 12, 1712, Stafford to Wentworth.

33. *Wentworth Papers*, pp. 247–248, Feb. 12, 1712, Stafford to Wentworth.

34. Coxe, *Marlborough*, vol. vi, p. 221.

35. Cowper, *Diary*, p. 54, Nov. 1712.

Chapter Eighteen

1. *Hamilton Diary*, pp. 45–46, Dec. 19, 1712 and p. 28, July 29, 1714, respectively.

2. HMC Dartmouth, p. v.

3. HMC Dartmouth, p. v.

4. *Hamilton Diary*, p. 48, Dec. 31, 1712.

5. *Hamilton Diary*, p. 46, Dec. 22, 1712.

6. *Hamilton Diary*, p. 48, Dec. 31, 1712.

7. *Hamilton Diary*, pp. 58–59, Sept. 18, 1713.

8. *Hamilton Diary*, pp. 58–59, Sept. 18, 1713.

9. Wentworth Papers, p. 287, Apr. 5, 1712, Stafford to Wentworth.

10. *Burnet's History*, vol. ii, p. 606.

11. *Burnet's History*, vol. ii, p. 606.

12. *Burnet's History*, vol. ii, p. 607.

13. The Dutch Republic, France, and Great Britain signed the Treaty of Utrecht on March 31, 1713. Austria's Hapsburg Emperor and his German allies—including the Elector of Hanover—decided to continue the war to force France to better terms but accepted the treaty a year later.

14. HMC Bath, vol. 1, p. 235, July 5, 1713, QA to RH.

15. Wentworth Papers, p. 292, July 25, 1712, Stafford to Wentworth.

Chapter Nineteen

1. Ellis, *Poems on Affairs of State*, vol. vii, p. 613, Anon.

2. *Wentworth Papers*, p. 358, Mar. 2, 1714, Stafford to Wentworth.

3. Fricke, Waltraut, "Leibnitz und die Englische Sukzession des Hauses Hanover," p. 64, Mar. 19/30, 1706, Falaiseau to Leibnitz.

4. Macpherson, *Original Papers*, vol. ii, pp. 223–225, May 1711, Prince James (hereafter PJ) to QA.

5. Macpherson, *Original Papers*, vol. ii, pp. 223–225, May 1711, PJ to QA.

6. Macpherson, *Original Papers*, vol. ii, p. 295, Mar. 28, 1712, PJ to QA.

7. Sarah, *Conduct*, p. 142.

8. *QA Letters*, p. 403, Dec. 8, 1713, QA to RH.

9. *Hamilton Diary*, p. 28, July 29, 1714.

10. HMC Bath, vol. 1, p. 237, Aug. 21, 1713, QA to RH.

11. Green, *Queen Anne,* p. 300, Apr. 7, 1714, John Shadwell, one of QA's doctors.

12. *Verney Letters*, vol. 1, p. 356, May 15, 1714, M. Lovett to Fermanagh.

13. *Wentworth Papers*, p. 375, Apr. 23, 1714, Stafford to Wentworth.

14. *Wentworth Papers*, p. 375, Apr. 23, 1714, Stafford to Wentworth.

15. Baily, F., *Sophia of Hanover*, pp. 229–230, author's translation from French.

16. *QA Letters*, p. 413, May 19, 1714, QA to Electress Sophia, hereafter ES.

17. *QA Letters*, p. 413, May 19, 1714, QA to ES.

18. *QA Letters*, p. 413, May 19, 1714, QA to Dowager Electress Sophia.

19. *QA Letters*, pp. 413–414, May 19, 1714, QA to Elector of Hanover.

20. *QA Letters*, pp. 414–415, on or about May 19, 1714, QA to Electoral Prince of Hanover.

21. Sarah, *Letters,* p. 110, July 2, 1714, SM to R. Jennens.

22. *Hamilton Diary*, p. 66, July 27, 1714.

23. *Hamilton Diary*, p. 66, July 27, 1714.

24. Swift, *Correspondence*, vol. ii, p. 31, July 27, 1714, Lewis to Swift.

25. *Hamilton Diary, Diary,* p. 66, July 27, 1714.

26. *Hamilton Diary*, p. 66, July 27, 1714.

27. Green, *Queen Anne*, p. 320.

28. The council also voted unanimously to allow seizure of arms and horses belonging to Roman Catholics; surveillance of suspected persons; regiments moved towards London; British regiments stationed abroad brought back to England if needed; and closure of all ports. Britain asked her Dutch ally for aid in pro-tecting the Hanoverian settlement; and sent a squadron to the Dutch coast to escort the elector to England.

29. *Hamilton Diary*, p. 46, Dec. 22, 1714.

30. Beattie, L., *John Arbuthnot*, p. 26, Arbuthnot to Swift.

31. Beattie, L., *John Arbuthnot*, p. 26, Arbuthnot to Swift.

32. Ewald, *The Newsman of Queen Anne,* pp. 88–89, from the *London Gazette* August 24–28, 1714.

33. Ewald, *The Newsman of Queen Anne,* pp. 88–89, from the *London Gazette* August 24–28, 1714

34. Ewald, *The Newsman of Queen Anne,* pp. 88–89, from the *London Gazette* August 24–28, 1714

35. Ewald, *The Newsman of Queen Anne,* pp. 88–89, from the *London Gazette* August 24–28, 1714.

36. Ewald, *The Newsman of Queen Anne,* pp. 88–89, from the *London Gazette* August 24–28, 1714.

Afterword

1. Strickland, *Lives of the Queens of England*, vol. vi, p. 303, contemporary verse.

2. *QA Letters*, Mar. 19, 1692, PA to SM

3. Coxe, *Marlborough*, vol. 1, pp. 273–274, July 1703, QA to SM.

4. Thomson, G.S., *Letters of a Grandmother*, p. 152, June 24, 1735, SM to her favorite granddaughter Lady Diana Spencer.

5. Sarah, *Memoirs*, pp. 273–276.

6. Sarah, *Memoirs*, pp. 255–6.

7. BL Add MS 61462 f. 171, late 1730s, SM to Lady Hardwicke.

8. Sarah, *Memoirs*, p. 276.

Bibliography

Archives

British Library, London: Althorp, Blenheim, Godolphin, Marlborough Papers.
Morgan Library & Museum, New York: Rulers of England, William and Mary; Anne.

Primary Sources

Ailesbury, Thomas Bruce, 2nd earl of, *Memoirs of Thomas, Earl of Ailesbury,* Nichols and Sons, London, 1890.

Anonymous, *The Lives of the Two Illustrious Generals,* London, 1713.

Aulnoy, Marie Catherine, Baronne d' *Memoirs of the Court of England in 1675,* Mrs. William Henry Arthur, trans., George David Gilbert, ed., John Lane, London, 1913.

Bathurst, Benjamin, ed., *Letters of Two Queens,* Robert Holder & Co., Ltd., London, 1924.

Bentinck, Mechtild Emma von Waldeck-Pyrmont Grafin, *Lettres et Mémoires de Marie, Reine d'Angleterre, Épouse de Guillaume III,* Martinus Nijhoff, The Hague, 1880.

Boyer, Abel. *The History of Queen Anne,* T. Woodward, London, 1735.

_____. *History of the Reign of Queen Anne digested into Annals,* A. Roper and F. Coggan, London, 1703–1715.

Brown, Beatrice Curtis, ed., *The Letters and Diplomatic Instructions of Queen Anne,* Cassell and Company Ltd., London 1935.

Burnet, Gilbert, *Bishop Burnet's History of His Own Time (with the suppressed passages of the first volume and notes by the earls of Dartmouth and Hardwick, and speaker Onslow, hitherto unpublished to which are added the cursory remarks of Swift and other observations.)* Clarendon Press, Oxford, UK, 1823.

Calendar of State Papers, Domestic, Anne I, 1702–1713, Robert Petland, ed., Kraus Reprint, Leichtenstein, 1968.

Calendar of the Clarendon State Papers, F.J. Routledge, ed., Oxford University Press, London, 1970.

Chesterfield, Earl of, *Letters of the Earl of Chesterfield,* Charles Strachey, ed., G.P. Putnam's Sons, New York, 1901.

Clarendon, Henry Hyde, Earl of, *Correspondence of Henry Hyde, Earl of Clarendon and His Brother Lawrence Hyde, Earl of Rochester,* Singer, Samuel Weller, ed., Henry Colburn, London, 1828.

_____. *The State Letters of Henry Earl of Clarendon during the Reign of James the Second and His Lordship's Diary for the Years 1687–1690,* Clarendon Press, Oxford, 1763.

Clarke, George, "Autobiography of Dr. George Clarke," *Historical Manuscripts Commission, Reports of Manuscripts of F.E. Leybourne-Popham, Esq.,* Her Majesty's Stationery Office, Norwich, UK, 1899.

Clarke, J.S., ed., *The Life of James the Second ... Collected Out of Memoirs Writ of His Own Hand,* Longman, Hurst, Rees, Orme, and Brown, London, 1816.

Clerk, Sir John, *Memoirs of the Life of Sir John Clerk of Penicuik,* Scottish Historical Society, vol. xiii, University Press, Edinburgh, 1892.

Cotteril, Sir Charles, *The Whole Life and Glorious Actions of Prince George of Denmark,* A. Hinde, London, 1708.

Cowper, Countess Mary, *Diary of Mary, Countess Cowper,* Hon. Spencer Cowper, ed., John Murray, London, 1865.

Cowper, William, Earl, *Private Diary of William, First Earl Cowper,* Edward Craven Hawtry, ed., E. Williams, Eton, 1833.

Dalrymple, Sir John, *Memoirs of Great Britain and Ireland, from the Dissolution of the Last Parliament of Charles II till the Capture of the French and Spanish Fleets at Vigo,* Strahan and Cadell, London, 1771–1773.

Doebner, Richard, ed., *Memoirs of Mary, Queen of England (1689–1694) Together with Her Letters and Those of James II and William III to the Electress Sophia of Hanover,* David Nutt, London, 1886.

Ellis, Frank H., ed., Ellis, *Poems on Affairs of State; Augustan Satirical Verse, 1660–1714,* Yale University Press, New Haven, CT, 1975.

Evelyn, John, *The Diary of John Evelyn,* Guy de la Bédogère, ed., The Dorset Press, UK, 1933.

_____. *The Life of Mrs. Godolphin,* London, William Pickering, London, 1847.

Fiennes, Celia. *The Journeys of Celia Fiennes,* Christopher Morris, ed., Cresset Press, London, 1949.

Foxcroft, H.C., ed. *The Life and Letters of Sir George*

Saville ... First Marquis of Halifax, Longmans, Green and Co. London, 1898.

_____. *A Supplement to Burnet's History of My Own Time. Derived from His Original Memoirs, His Autobiography, His Letters to Admiral Herbert, and His Private Meditations.* Clarendon Press, Oxford, 1902.

Hamilton, Anthony (Count Grammont) *Memoirs of the Court of Charles the Second,* Sir Walter Scott, ed., Henry G. Bohn, Ltd., London, 1864.

Hamilton, Sir David, *Hamilton Diary: The Diary of Sir David Hamilton, 1709–1714,* Philip Roberts, ed., The Clarendon Press, Oxford, 1975.

Hervey, John, First Earl of Bristol, *Letter Books of John Hervey, First Earl of Bristol,* Ernest Jackson, Wells, UK, 1894.

Historical Manuscripts Commission:

Bath, Marquis of, Mackie & Co. Ltd., London, 1904.

Dartmouth, Earl of, Eyre and Spottiswoode, London, 1887.

Downshire, Marquess of, His Majesty's Stationery Office, London, 1924.

Portland, Duke of, Eyre and Spottiswoode, London, 1891.

Rutland, Duke of, Eyre and Spottiswoode, London, 1888/9.

Westmoreland, Earl of, Eyre and Spottiswoode, London, 1885/5.

Jesse, John Heneage, *Memoirs of the Court of England During the Reign of the Stuarts,* Richard Bentley, London, 1840.

Lake, Dr. Edward, *Diary of Dr. Edward Lake Chaplain and Tutor to the Princesses Mary and Anne in the Years 1677–78,* George Percy Elliott, ed., Camden Society, London, 1866.

Lewis, Jenkin, *Memoirs of Prince William Henry, Duke of Gloucester,* P. Hayes, ed., Payne and Murray, London, 1789.

Lockhart, George, *Letters of George Lockhart of Carnwath,* Daniel Szechi, ed., Pillans & Wilson, Edinburgh, 1989.

Macky, John, *Memoirs of the Secret Services of John Macky Esq., During the Reigns of King William, Queen Anne, and King George I,* printed in London, 1733.

Macpherson, James, *Original Papers Containing the Secret History of Great Britain from the Restoration to the Accession of the House of Hanover, to Which Are Prefixed Extracts from the Life of James II as Written by Himself,* W. Strachan and T. Cadell, London, 1775.

Marlborough, *Letters and Dispatches of John Churchill, First Duke of Marlborough,* Sir George Murray, ed., John Murray, London, 1845.

Marlborough, Sarah, Duchess of, *Account of the Conduct of the Dowager Duchess of Marlborough from Her First Coming to Court to the Year 1710,* James Bettenham, London, 1742.

_____. *Letters of Sarah Duchess of Marlborough from the Original Manuscripts at Madresfield Court,* John Murray, London, 1875.

_____. *Memoirs of Sarah, Duchess of Marlborough Together with Her Characters of Her Contemporaries and Her Opinions,* William King, ed., George Routledge & Sons/Kraus Reprint, New York, 1969.

_____. *Opinions of Sarah, Duchess-Dowager of Marlborough: Published from the Original Manuscripts,* Lord Hailes, ed., London, 1788.

_____. *Private Correspondence of Sarah, Duchess of Marlborough,* Henry Colburn, London, 1838, Kraus Reprint New York, 1972.

Marlborough-Godolphin Correspondence, Henry L. Snyder, ed., The Clarendon Press, Oxford, 1975.

Norrington, R., ed., *My dearest Minette. The Letters Between Charles II and His Sister Henrietta, Duchess d'Orléans,* Peter Owen Publishers, London, 1996.

Pepys, Samuel, *The Diary of Samuel Pepys,* Robert Latham and William Matthews, eds., University of California Press, Berkeley, 1970.

Russell, Lord John, ed., *Letters of Rachel, Lady Russell,* Longman, Brown, Green & Longmans, London, 1853.

Sanders, Francis, *An Abridgement of the Life of James II ... Extracted from an English Manuscript of the Reverend Father Francis Sanders, of the Society of Jesus and Confessor to His Late Majesty ... Done out of the French from the Paris Edition,* R. Wilson, London, 1704.

Sheffield, John (Duke of Buckinghamshire and Normanby) *Works,* John Barber, London, 1723.

Somers, Lord, *A Collection of Scarce and Valuable Tracts,* T. Cadell et al., London, 1814.

Suffolk, Henrietta Countess of, *Letters to and from Henrietta, Countess of Suffolk,* J.W. Croker, ed., John Murray, London, 1824.

Swift, Jonathan, *Journal to Stella,* Herbert Davis, ed., Oxford, 1948.

_____. *Swift Correspondence: The Correspondence of Jonathan Swift,* David Woolley, ed., Peter Lang, Frankfurt, Germany, 1999.

_____. *Swift Poetical Works,* Herbert Davis, ed., Oxford University Press, London, 1967.

Thibadeau, A.W., ed., *Catalogue of the Collection of Autograph Letters and Historical Documents Formed ... by Alfred Morrison,* Strangeways & Sons, London, 1890.

Toland, John, *An Account of the Courts of Prussia and Hanover,* John Darby, London, 1705.

Verney, Lady Margaret, ed., *Verney Letters of the Eighteenth Century,* Ernest Benn Ltd., London, 1930.

Vernon, James, *Vernon Correspondence: Letters Illustrative of the Reign of William III 1696 to 1708 ... by James Vernon, Secretary of State,* G.P.R. James, ed., Henry Colburn, London, 1841.

Wentworth, Thomas, *The Wentworth Papers, 1705–1739, Selected from the Private and Family Correspondence of Thomas Wentworth, Lord Raby, Created in 1711 Earl of Stafford,* J.J. Cartwright, ed., Wyman & Sons, London, 1883.

Secondary Sources

Amusson, S., *An Ordered Society—Gender and Class in Early Modern England,* T.J. Press, Ltd., Cornwall, UK, 1988.

Arbuthnot, P. S-M., *Memories of the Arbuthnots of Kincairdineshire and Aberdeenshire,* George Allen & Unwin Ltd., London, 1920.

Ashley, Maurice, *England in the Seventeenth Century,* Hutchinson & Co., London 1952

_____. *The Stuarts in Love; With Some Reflections on Love and Marriage in the Sixteenth and Seventeenth Centuries,* Macmillan Company, New York, 1964.

Ashton, John, *Social Life in the Reign of Queen Anne,* Charles Scribner's Sons, New York, 1937.

Baillon, Charles, Comte de, *Henriette-Anne d'Angleterre, Duchesse d'Orléans; Sa Vie et Sa Correspondence avec Son Frère Charles II,* Perrin et Cie, Paris, 1887.

Baily, F.E., *Sophia of Hanover and Her Times,* Hutchinson & Co., London, 1936.

Barnett, Corelli, *Marlborough,* Eyre Methuen, London, 1974.

Baxter, Stephen, *William III and the Defense of European Liberty,* Harcourt, Brace & World, Inc., New York, 1966.

Beattie, Lester, M., *John Arbuthnot: Mathematician and Satirist,* Harvard University Press, Cambridge, MA, 1935.

Beatty, Michael A, *The English Royal Family of America,* McFarland, NC, USA, 2003.

Beem, Charles, *The Lioness Roared: The Problems of Female Rule in English History (Queenship and Power),* Palgrave Macmillan, New York, 2006.

Black, Jeremy, *The English Press in the Eighteenth Century,* Croom Helm, London, 1987.

_____. *Trade, Empire and British Foreign Policy 1689–1815,* Routledge, New York, 2007.

Bowen, Marjorie, *The Third Mary Stuart,* John Lane the Bodley Head, London, 1929.

Bowers, Toni, *The Politics of Motherhood: British Writing and Culture, 1680–1760,* Cambridge University Press, UK, 1996.

Brewer, John, *The Sinews of Power: War, Money, and the English State 1688–1783,* Unwin Hyman Ltd., London, 1989.

Brown, Irene Q., "Domesticity, Feminism, and Friendship: Female Aristocratic Culture and Marriage in England (1660–1760)," *Journal of Family History,* vol. vii, no. 4, pp. 406–424, National Council on Family Relations, Minneapolis, MN, USA, 1982.

Bryant, Arthur, *King Charles II,* Collins, London, 1955.

Bucholz, Robert O., *The Augustan Court; Queen Anne and the Decline of Court Culture,* Stanford University Press, Stanford, CA, 1993.

_____. "Nothing but Ceremony: Queen Anne and the Limitations of Royal Ritual," *Journal of British Studies,* vol. 30, #3 (1991) pp. 288–323, University of Chicago Press, Chicago, ILL.

Buck, Clara, and Davies Godfrey, "Letters on Godolphin's Dismissal in 1710," *Huntington Library Quarterly,* vol. iii, no. 2, pp. 25–242, Henry E. Huntington Library and Art Gallery, San Marino CA, 1940.

Burton, Ivor, *The Captain-General: The Career of John Churchill Duke of Marlborough from 1702–1711,* Constable & Co., London, 1968.

Butler, Iris, *Rule of Three, Sarah, Duchess of Marlborough, and Her Companions in Power,* Hodder and Stoughton, London, 1967

Callow, John, *The Making of King James II: The Form-ative Years of a Fallen King,* Sutton Publishing Limited, Gloucestershire, UK, 2000.

Chancellor, Frank, *Sarah Churchill,* Philip Allan, London, 1932.

Chapman, Hester W. *Mary II, Queen of England,* Jonathan Cape, London, 1953.

_____. *Queen Anne's Son; a Memoir of William Henry, Duke of Gloucester,* Andre Deutsch, Limited, London, 1954.

Churchill, Winston S., *Marlborough, His Life and Times,* Charles Scribner's Sons, New York, 1933.

Clark, J.C.D., *English Society, 1688–1832,* Cambridge University Press, Cambridge, UK, 2000.

Clark, Sir George N., *The Later Stuarts,* Oxford University Press, London, 1961.

Colley, Linda, *Britons: Forging the Nation, 1707–1837,* Yale University Press, New Haven CT, 2005.

Colville, Mrs. Arthur, *Duchess Sarah, Being the Social History of the Times of Sarah Jennings Duchess of Marlborough,* Longmans, Green, And Co, London, 1904.

Connell, Neville, *Anne, the Last Stuart Monarch,* Thornton Butterworth Ltd., London, 1936.

Courtenay, Thomas P., ed., *Memoirs of the Life, Works, and Correspondence of Sir William Temple,* Longman & Longman, London, 1836.

Coward, Barry, *The Stuart Age: England, 1658–1714,* Pearson Education Limited, UK, 2003.

Cowles, Virginia, *The Great Marlborough and His Duchess,* George Weidenfeld & Nicholson Limited, London, 1983.

Coxe, William, *Memoirs of John, Duke of Marlborough,* Longman, Hurst, Rees, Orme, and Brown, London, 1820.

_____. *The Private and Original Correspondence of Charles Talbot, Duke of Shrewsbury,* Longman, et. al., London, 1821.

Cruikshanks, Eveline, ed., *By Force or by Default? The Glorious Revolution of 1688–1689,* John Donald Publishers Ltd., Edinburgh, 1989.

Cumming, Valerie, *Royal Dress,* B.T. Batsford Ltd, London, 1989.

Cunnington, C.W. & P., *Handbook of English Costume in the Seventeenth Century,* Faber & Faber Limited, London, 1963.

Curtis, Gila, *The Life and Times of Queen Anne,* Weidenfeld and Nicholson, London, 1972.

Dickinson, H.T., *Bolingbroke,* Constable & Company Ltd., London, 1970.

Dickinson, William C., *Sidney Godolphin, Lord Treasurer, 1702–1710,* Edward Mellen Press, Lewiston, NY, 1990.

Dobrée, Bonamy, ed. *As Their Friends Saw Them,* Jonathan Cape, London, 1933.

_____. *Six Brilliant English Women,* Gerald Howe, London, 1930.

_____. *Three Eighteenth Century Figures,* Oxford University Press, London, 1962.

Donoghue, Emma, *Passions Between Women: British Lesbian Culture 1668–1801,* Scarlet Press, London,

Duggan, J.N., *Sophia of Hanover, from Winter Princess to Heiress of Great Britain,* Peter Owen Publishers, London, 2010.

Dutton, Ralph, *English Court Life from Henry VII to George II,* B.T. Batsford Ltd., London, 1963.

Emson, H.E. and Rolls, Roger, "For Want of an Heir: The Obstetrical History of Queen Anne," *British Medical Journal,* CCCIV, no. 6841, pp. 66–67, British Medical Association, London, 1992.

Ewald, W.B., *The Newsmen of Queen Anne,* Riverside Press, Cambridge, 1956.

Faderman, Lillian, *Surpassing the Love of Men,* William Morrow and Company, Inc., New York 1981.

Faulkner, Thomas, *History and Antiquities of Kensington,* D. Jaques, London, 1820.

Fea, Allen, *James II and His Wives,* Methuen and Co., London, 1908.

Field, Ophelia, *The Favorite; Sarah Churchill, Duchess of Marlborough,* Hodder and Stoughton, London, 2003.

Foot, Michael, *The Pen and the Sword,* MacGibbon and Kee, London, 1957.

Fricke, Waltraut, "Leibnitz Und Die Englische Sukzession Des Hauses Hanover," *Quellen Und Darstellungen Zur Geschichte Niedersachsens,* No. 56, August Lax Buchdruckerei, Hildesheim, 1957.

Furdell, Elizabeth Lane, *The Royal Doctors, 1485–1714,* University of Rochester Press, 2001.

Green, David Bronte. *Blenheim,* 1974, Collins, London, 1974.

_____. *Gardener to Queen Anne,* Oxford University Press, London, 1956.

_____. *Queen Anne,* William Collins Sons & Co. Ltd., 1970.

_____. *Sarah, Duchess of Marlborough,* Collins, London, 1967.

Gregg, Edward. *Queen Anne,* Yale University Press, London, 2001.

_____. "Was Queen Anne a Jacobite?," *History* vol. LVII, pp. 358–375, The Historical Society, October 1972.

Grier, Barbara, and Reid, Coletta (eds.,) *Lesbian Lives,* Diana Press, Inc., Oakland, CA, 1976.

Haile, Martin, *Mary of Modena, Her Life and Letters,* J.M. Dent & Co., London, 1905.

Hamilton, Lady Elizabeth. *The Backstairs Dragon: A Life of Robert Harley, Earl of Oxford,* Hamish Hamilton, London, 1969.

_____. *William's Mary,* Hamish Hamilton Ltd., London, 1972.

Harris, Frances, "Accounts of the Conduct of Sarah Duchess of Marlborough," *British Library Journal,* vol. viii, no. 1, The British Library, London, 1982.

_____. *A Passion for Government: The Life of Sarah Duchess of Marlborough,* Clarendon Press, Oxford, 1991.

Harris, Tim, *Politics Under the Later Stuarts,* Longman, London, 1993.

Hart, A & North, S., *Fashion in Detail,* Rizzoli International Publishers, Inc., New York, 1998.

Hedley, Olwen, *Windsor Castle,* St. Edmundsbury Press Ltd., Great Britain, 1994.

Henslowe, J.R., *Anne Hyde, Duchess of York,* T. Werner Laurie Ltd., London, 1915.

Hibbert, Christopher, *The Marlboroughs,* Viking Press, London, 2001.

Hill, Brian W., *Robert Harley: Speaker, Secretary of State and Prime Minister,* Yale University Press, New Haven CT, 1988.

Holmes, Frederick, *The Sickly Stuarts. the Medical Downfall of a Dynasty,* Sutton Publishing, Gloucestershire, UK, 2003.

Holmes, Geoffrey, and Speck, W A, ed. *The Divided Society: Parties and Politics in England 1694–1716,* Edward Arnold, London, 1967.

_____. "The Fall of Harley in 1708 Reconsidered," *English Historical Review* vol. LXXX, pp. 673–698, Longmans, Green and Co Ltd., London, 1965.

Holmes, Geoffrey, ed. *Britain After the Glorious Revolution, 1689–1714,* 1969.

_____. *British Politics in the Age of Anne,* The Hambledon Press, London, 1987.

_____. *The Making of a Great Power,* 1993.

_____. *The Trial of Dr. Sacheverell,* Eyre Methuen, London, 1973.

Holmes, Richard, *Marlborough: England's Fragile Genius,* 2008. Harper Press London, 2008.

Hopkinson, M.R., *Anne of England,* Constable & Co Ltd, London, 1934.

Hopkirk, Mary, *Queen Over the Water; Mary Beatrice of Modena, Queen of James II,* Murray, London, 1953.

Impey, Edward, *Kensington Palace: The Official Illustrated History,* Merrell, London, 2012.

Israel, Jonathan, ed., *The Anglo-Dutch Moment: Essays on the Glorious Revolution and Its World Impact,* Cambridge University Press, UK, 1991.

Jones, J R. *Country and Court: England 1658–1714,* Harvard University Press, Cambridge, MA, 1978.

_____. *The Revolution of 1688 in England,* W.W. Norton & Company Inc., New York, 1972.

Kellaway, G.R., ed., *The Hot Springs of Bath,* Bath City Council, 1991.

Kemble, James (M.D.) *Idols and Invalids,* Methuen & Co. Ltd., London, 1933.

Kishlansky, Mark, *A Monarchy Transformed,* The Penguin Press, England, 1996.

Kroll, M., ed. & trans., *Letters from Liselotte, Elizabeth Charlotte, Princess Palatine and Duchess of Orléans, "Madame," 1652–1722,* Victor Gollancz Ltd., London, 1970.

Kronenberger, Louis, *Marlborough's Duchess—A Study in Worldliness,* Alfred A. Knopf, New York, 1958.

Law, Ernest, *Kensington Palace,* London, 1899.

Lediard, Thomas, *The Life of John, Duke of Marlborough,* Wilcox, London, 1736.

Lever, Sir Tresham, *Godolphin, His Life and Times,* John Murray, London, 1952.

Locke, A. Audrey, *The Seymour Family,* London, 1911. Houghton Mifflin Company, New York, 1914.

MacArthur, W.P., "The Cause of the Death of William, Duke of Gloucester, Son of Queen Anne in 1700," *British Medical Journal,* Mar. 24, 1928, pp. 502–503, British Medical Association, London.

MacKinnon, James, *Union of England and Scotland,* Longmans, Green, and Co., London, 1896.

McInnes, Angus, *Robert Harley, Puritan Politician,* Victor Gollancz Ltd., London, 1970.

McKay, Derek, *Prince Eugene of Savoy,* Thames and Hudson Ltd., London, 1977.

Miller, John, "James II and Toleration," *By Force or by Default? The Revolution of 1688–1689,* Eveline Cruikshanks, ed., Edinburgh, 1989.

Nenner, Howard, *The Right to Be King: The Succession to the Crown of England 1603-1714,* Macmillan, London, 1995.

Nicholson, T.C., and Turberville, A.S., *Charles Talbot, Duke of Shrewsbury,* Cambridge, The University Press, 1930.

Oman, Carola, *Mary of Modena,* Hodder and Stoughton, Ltd., London, 1962.

Oxford Dictionary of National Biography, Oxford University Press, New York, 2004.

Plumb, J.H., *The Growth of Political Stability in England 1675-1725,* Macmillan, London, 1967.

Prior, Mary, ed., *Women in English Society 1500-1800,* Methuen & Co., London, 1985.

Ranke, Leopold von, *A History of England, Principally in the Seventeenth Century,* AMS Press, Inc., New York, 1966.

Reid, Stuart J., *John and Sarah, Duke and Duchess of Marlborough 1660-1744,* Charles Scribner's Sons, New York, 1914.

Reverand, Cedric D., *Queen Anne and the Arts,* Bucknell University Press, Lewisburg, PA, 2015.

Reynolds, Anna, *In Fine Style,* Royal Collection Trust, London, 2013.

Ribeiro, Aileen, *Fashion and Fiction,* Yale University Press, London, 2005.

Richardson, Mrs. Aubrey, *Famous Ladies of the English Court,* Herbert Stone & Company, New York, 1899.

Schulte, Regina, ed., *The Body of the Queen,* Berghahn Books, New York, 2006.

Sichel, W., *Bolingbroke and His Times,* 2 vols., 1901-1902.

Snyder, Henry. L. "The Duke of Marlborough's Request of the Captain-Generalcy for Life," *Journal of the Society for Army Historical Research,* XLV, pp. 67-83. Gale & Polden Ltd., London, 1967.

_____. "The Last Days of Queen Anne: The Account of Sir John Evelyn Examined," *Huntington Library Quarterly,* vol. XXXIV, #3, pp. 261-276, Henry E. Huntington Library and Art Gallery, California 1971.

Somerset, Anne, *Queen Anne: The Politics of Passion,* Random House, New York, 2014.

Somerville, Dorothy H., *The King of Hearts: Charles Talbot, Duke of Shrewsbury,* George Allen & Unwin Ltd., London, 1962.

Southorn, J., *Mary of Modena, Queen Consort of James II and VII,* The Royal Stuart Society, London, 1992.

Speck, W.A., *The Birth of Britain: A New Nation, 1700-1710,* Blackwell Publishers, Oxford, UK, 1994.

Stanhope, Philip Henry, Earl of Stanhope, *History of England, Comprising the Reign of Queen Anne Until the Peace of Utrecht,* Bernhard Tauchnitz, Leipzig, 1870.

Stone, Lawrence, *Family, Sex, and Marriage in England, 1500-1800,* Weidenfeld and Nicolson, London, 1977.

Strickland, Agnes, *Lives of the Queens of England Since the Norman Conquest,* Bell & Daldy, London, 1873.

Sundstrom, Roy A., *Sidney Godolphin, Servant of State,* Associated University Presses, Cranbury, NJ, 1992.

Sutherland, James, *Background for Queen Anne,* Methuen & Co., Ltd., London, 1939.

Taylor, F., *The Wars of Marlborough,* G.W. Taylor, ed., Blackwell, Oxford, 1921.

Thomson, A.T., *Memoirs of Sarah, Duchess of Marlborough,* Henry Colburn, Publisher, London, 1839.

Thomson, Gladys Scott, ed., *Letters of a Grandmother,* Jonathan Cape, London, 1943.

Toynbee, Margaret, "Princess Anne (Afterwards Queen) as a Patroness of Painters," *Burlington Magazine,* vol. 112, no. 804, pp. 149-153, March 1970, The Burlington Magazine Publications Ltd., UK.

Trevelyan, George M., *England Under Queen Anne,* Longmans, Green and Co., New York, 1930

_____. *England Under the Stuarts; The Political, Constitutional, and Social History of England in the Seventeenth Century,* Pelican Books, England, 1960.

Turner, F.C., *James II,* Eyre & Spottiswoode, London, 1948.

Uffenbach, Zacharias Conrad von, *London in 1710: From the Travels of Zacharias Conrad Von Uffenbach,* W.H. Quarrell and M. Mare, trans. & ed., Faber & Faber, London, 1934.

van der Zee, Henri, and Barbara, *William and Mary,* Macmillan, London, 1973.

Waller, Maureen. *1700: Scenes from London Life,* Four Wells Eight Windows, New York, 2000.

_____. *Ungrateful Daughters, the Stuart Princesses Who Stole Their Father's Crown,* St. Martin's Press New York, 2002.

Ward, A.W., *The Electress Sophia and the Hanoverian Succession,* Ward, Goupil & Co., London, 1903.

Warner, R., *The History of Bath,* 1801.

Waterson, Nellie M., *Mary II Queen of England, 1689-1694,* Duke University Press, Durham, NC, 1928.

Way, Thomas R., and Chapman, F., *Ancient Royal Palaces in and Near London,* John Lane, London, 1892.

Weill, Rachel, *Political Passions: Gender, the Family, and Political Argument in England, 1680-1714,* Manchester University Press, Manchester, 1999.

West, Richard, *The Life and Strange Surprising Adventures of Daniel Defoe,* HarperCollins Publishers, London, 1997

Wilkins, W. Walker, *Political Ballads of the Seventeenth and Eighteenth Centuries,* Longmans, Green, Longmans, and Roberts, London, 1860.

Winn, J.A. *Queen Anne, Patroness of Arts,* Oxford University Press, New York, 2014.

Wolseley, Joseph Garnet, Lord, *The Life of John Churchill, Duke of Marlborough,* Richard Bentley and Son, London, 1894.

Index

Numbers in **_bold italics_** indicate pages with illustrations

Ailesbury, Elizabeth, countess 56
Ailesbury, Thomas Bruce, earl 56–57
Alien Act 124
Alliance *see* Grand Alliance
Allies *see* Grand Alliance
Almanza, battle of 129, 134–136
Americas 196, 203, 205, 217–219
Anglican *see* Church of England
Anne, princess, later queen *see* Stuart, Anne, princess, later queen
Antigua 217
Apsley, Frances, later Lady Bathurst 9, 12–13, 19, 103
Ascot 198, 219
Asiento 64, 200, 218
Austria/Austrian Empire 64–65, 71, 89–91, 94–95, 98, 114, 123, 160, 165, 190, 196, 200, 205, 209, 217

Barbados 217
Barrier Treaty 165, 196, 200
Bath 31–32, 57, 80–81, 86
Bathurst, Benjamin, sir 19
Bavaria 89–90, 95, 128
Berkeley, John, colonel 19
Berkeley House 57, 59–60
Berlin 109
Berwick, James Fitzjames, duke of 129
Bill of Rights 40
Blandford, John Churchill, marquess 83–84, 155
Blenheim, 98–99, 105; battle *see* Marlborough, John Churchill, duke of; palace 97, 131, 137, 194–195, 204, 210; significance 96–97, 112, 114, 120, 123–124, 128, 160
Bolingbroke *see* St. John, Henry, Viscount Bolingbroke
Bothmer, baron 205
Bourbon, house of *see* Louis, (Bourbon) King of France; Philip, Duc d'Anjou, (Bourbon) King Philip V of Spain

Boyne, battle of the 47–48
Breda 4, 6
Brihuega, battle of 195–196
Bristol 81
Britain *see* Great Britain
Brussels 12, 14–15, 28
Burnet, Gilbert, Bishop of Salisbury 202–205

Cadiz 82
Cambridge 83–84, 103
Canada 217
Canterbury, archbishop of 79
Caribbean, sea 141, 217
Carlos (Charles) III, (Hapsburg) King of Spain 98, 114, 160–161, 165, 196
Channel 25, 27, 89, 94, 96, 159, 163, 191
Charles I, king *see* Stuart, Charles I, king
Charles II, king *see* Stuart, Charles II, king
Church of England 2–3, 6, 8–10, 24–25, 31–32, 43, 46, 64, 74, 77, 87–88, 102, 175, 208, 217, 221–222, 227–228, 232–234
Churchill, Arabella 129
Churchill, George, admiral 116, 151–152, 155–156, 167
Churchill, John *see* Marlborough, John Churchill, duke of
Churchill, Sarah *see* Marlborough, Sarah Churchill née Jennings, duchess of
the City 138, 172, 183–184, 192
Clarendon, Henry Hyde, second earl 18, 32, 34–35, 38, 41
Cockpit 19, 21, 14, 27, 36, 38, 42, 45, 51–52, 125, 157, 180, 228
Commons, house of 13, 45–46, 61, 71–73, 87, 97–99, 102, 126, 130, 135–136, 138–139, 151, 164, 170, 174, 176, 204–206, 208, 210, 212, 221, 228
Compton, Henry, bishop 9–10, 37–38

the Continent 46–47, 55, 70, 78–79, 83–*85*, 95, 106, 119, 124, 127–128, 138, 144, 150, 168, 182, 198, 210–211, 215, 217, 227, 234
Cornwallis, Katherine 15
Cowper, William, sir, later earl 104–105, 107, 114, 124, 168–169, 174, 181, 189, 195, 202, 204, 208, 211

Danube river 94–95
Dartmouth, William Legge, earl 182, 186, 189, 200, 212, 214–215
Defoe, Daniel 76, 90
Denmark 17, 27, 44, 62, 64, 95, 151, 156
Denmark, King Christian V of 17, 27, 42, 58
Denmark, Prince George of 2, *16*–21, 26–28, 34–36, 38, 40–41, 43–44, 47–49, 51–55, 57–60, 62–63, 65–67, 71, 74, 115, 118, 126, 131, 159, 162, 166–167, 170, 188, 194, 198, 219, 231–232; health 26, 80–81, 112–113, 117, 125, 146–147, 152–154; interest in science 103, 139, 155–157; lord high admiral 72–73, 106, 108, 116, 137–138, 150–151, 189; political influence 72, 138, 152, 156, 158, 182
Denmarks, prince and princess of 20, 23, 26, 34, 41–42, 49, 52, 54, 57, 60–61, 228
Dieppe 7
Dijkvelt, Everard 28–29
Dunkirk 138, 160, 200, 216
Dutch *see* Holland

Edict of Nantes 25
Edinburgh 13–14, 124
Elizabeth I, queen 67
England 1, 9, 13, 17, 23, 27–28, 36, 38–42, 44, 46, 48–50, 64–65, 67, 69–72, 79, 90, 92–94, 96, 99, 101–102, 108–109, 111, 115, 122, 124–127, 133, 137, 140, 151, 161, 188, 196, 209–211, 216, 218, 220–221, 224–227, 231–234

Europe 31, 33, 36–37, 64–65, 68–69, 71, 82, 94, 96, 121, 133, 150, 159–160, 163, 196, 203–205, 215
Exclusion crisis 12–13

France 1, 24, 33, 36, 38, 44, 46–50, 59, 63–65, 69–71, 77–79, 84, 89–90, 92–96, 101, 105–106, 112–114, 119, 121, 123–124, 128–129, 136, 143–144, 149, 151, 153, 160–161, 163–164, 171, 173, 181, 195–196, 198–205, 207, 209–211, 216–218, 222, 234
Frankfurt 106

Gaultier, abbé 196
Germany 64–65, 90, 94, 96, 105–106, 109, 113, 123, 129, 161, 211
Gibraltar 98, 217
Gloucester, Prince William Henry, duke of 42–43, 54, 57, 58, 59, 61–63, 68, 84, 110, 158, 202, 221
Godolphin, Sidney, baron, later earl 19, 21, 53, 59, 62, 65, 67, 227; allies with Whigs 103–104, 106, 111, 115–116, 135, 140, 149, 152, 165–166, 171; dismissal see Stuart Anne, princess, later queen; lord treasurer and prime minister 70–71, 76, 79–84, 86–92, 94, 98–99, 102, 109–110, 114, 118, 121–122, 124–125, 128, 132–133, 136, 138–139, 145, 153, 155–156, 159, 164, 168, 173–176, 178–180, 189–192, 198, 206; offers resignation 119–120, 134, 137, 150, 181, 183
Grand Alliance 1, 64–65, 67, 69–71, 79, 82, 90, 95–96, 98, 109, 112, 114, 121, 128–129, 138, 149, 152, 160–161, 164, 168, 172, 190–192, 195–196, 199–200, 202, 204–205, 209–211, 215–216, 218
Great Britain 106–107, 126, 132, 134, 136, 143, 159–161, 164–165, 168, 172–173, 180–181, 191, 195–196, 199–202, 204–205, 209–211, 216–219, 228–229, 234
Greg, William 136, 138
Guiscard, Louis, marquis 196–197

Hague, The 4, 12, 24, 29, 69, 71, 86, 90, 113, 133, 140, 160, 174, 194, 216
Halifax, Charles Montagu, earl 111, 125
Hamilton, David, sir 163, 182–184, 188–192, 195, 204, 208, 214–215, 219, 230
Hampton Court Palace 42, 219
Handel, George Frederick 194, 210, 219
Hanover, electorate of 63–64, 67, 72, 94–95, 107–110, 196, 227, 230–231
Hanover, George, elector of, later King George I 13, 72, 109, 190, 194, 204–207, 218, 224–228, 230–231, 234

Hanover, George, electoral prince of, Duke of Cambridge 108–109, 111, 140, 224–226, 229
Hanover, Sophia, electress, later dowager electress of 13, 63–64, 76, 92, 107–109, 111, 140, 149, 204, 218, 221–222, 224–227
Hanoverian Succession 93, 104, 107–108, 110–111, 123, 125–6, 149, 175, 200, 210, 218, 223, 226–229, 234
Hapsburg, empire/house of see Austria/Austrian Empire
Harley, Robert, later Earl of Oxford and Mortimer 61, 65, 67, 71, 82, 102, 109, 118, 120–122, 125, 130–133, 139–140, 145, 149, 152, 157–158, 184; attempt to assassinate 197–199; coup attempt 135–138; dismissal see Stuart, Anne, princess, later queen, disillusion with Harley, Robert, Earl of Oxford and Mortimer; prime minister 185–186, 189–190, 195–196, 200, 202–207, 209–216, 218–219, 225, 228–229; schemes to become prime minister 166, 168–169, 172–173, 181–182
Heinsius, Anthonie, grand pensionary of Holland 82, 94, 160, 184, 192
Henrietta Maria, Dowager Queen of England 3, 4, 5, 7–8, 100
Hesse 94–95
Hill, Abigail see Masham, Abigail née Hill, later baroness
Hill, Alice 167, 209
Hill, Jack 173–174, 181
Holland 12, 16, 27, 31, 33, 41, 44, 53, 63–65, 69, 71–73, 82, 89–92, 94–95, 105–106, 119, 120, 133, 137, 153, 157, 160–161, 164, 173, 181–182, 184, 190, 196, 200, 203, 205, 215–217, 230
Hudson's Bay 217
Huguenots 24, 25, 33
Hungary 115
Hyde, Anne, Duchess of York 4, 5, 6, 7, 8, 15, 20, 21, 75
Hyde, Edward, sir, later first earl Clarendon 4, 5, 100
Hyde, Henry see Clarendon, Henry Hyde, second earl
Hyde, Laurence see Rochester, Laurence Hyde, earl
Hyde Park 22, 210

Immortal Seven 33, 37, 45, 170, 180, 228
Ireland 18, 33, 41–42, 46–48, 61–62, 70, 79, 156, 208
Italy 67, 94, 96, 105–106, 112–114, 123, 128, 217, 225

Jacobite 43–44, 46, 50, 55–56, 68, 76, 78, 86, 91–94, 96, 99, 101, 108, 131–132, 139, 167, 175, 182, 196, 204, 210–211, 221, 223–224, 226, 229

Jeffries, John, chief justice 24
Jennings, Sarah see Marlborough, Sarah Churchill née Jennings, duchess of
Jersey, Edward Villiers, earl of 196, 199
Junto 104, 110, 114–116, 118–120, 122, 125, 128, 136, 138–141, 148–153, 159, 171, 176, 180, 186, 189

Kensington Palace 57, 92, 125–127, 137, 152–154, 165, 178, 185, 228–229, 231–232

La Hogue 56, 170
London 3, 5, 8, 13, 23, 27–28, 31–32, 34–39, 47, 52, 70, 79–81, 89, 92, 97, 108–109, 117, 126, 134–135, 139, 147, 151–152, 166, 175, 177, 180, 182–183, 191–192, 196, 203, 205, 208–209, 220, 224, 228
Lords, house of 13, 46, 67, 71–73, 93, 99, 102, 126, 135, 139, 176–177, 201, 205, 207–210, 218, 224–225, 232–233
Louis XIV (Bourbon) King of France 3, 12, 16, 24–26, 33, 41, 46, 55, 62, 64–65, 89–90, 93–94, 96, 99, 110, 113, 119–120, 129, 138, 160–161, 163–164, 174, 196, 199–200, 203, 212, 215–218, 222

Malaga 98
Malplaquet, battle of see Marlborough, John Churchill, duke of; significance of 165, 169, 171–172
Marlborough, John Churchill, duke of 2, 14–15, 17–19, 23, 28–29, 34–37, 41, 43, 45–46, 48–50, 53, 55, 59–62, 64–65, 85–88, 94, 115, 118–119, 122, 128, 131, 157–158, 172, 184, 191, 193, 226–227, 229, 232, 235; Blenheim, battle of 95–96, 112, 116, 145, 164, 182, 209; Bouchain, fortress 199, 203; captain general 69–72, 76, 78–80, 82, 84, 89–93, 98–99, 102, 104–111, 114, 120–121, 124–125, 129, 132–133, 135–141, 143, 148–153, 159–162, 166, 173–174, 180–181, 183, 190, 192, 195, 198, 216, 219; death of Denmark, Prince George of 156; dismissal see Stuart, Anne, princess, later queen, dismisses Marlborough, John Churchill, duke of; exile 210–211, 215; lifetime captain generalcy 168–171, 206; Lines of Brabant 105; Malplaquet, battle of 163–164, 209; opposes peace 201, 203–205, 208; Oudenarde, battle of 144–145, 147, 209; Ramillies, battle of 113, 116, 145, 164
Marlborough, Sarah Churchill, née Jennings, duchess of 2, 9, 14–15, 18, 22–23, 25, 28–29, 34, 36, 38, 41–43, 45–50, 52–58, 60, 62, 66,

69, 71, 73, **100**, 115, 125, 128, 137, 168–169, 175, 208, 214, 226–227; accuses the queen of lesbianism 141–143, 154, 165, 167, 174, 191; clashes with the queen 85–86, 91–92, 94, 98–101, 105, 107, 117, 121–122, 129–133, 136, 140, 145, 147–149, 153, 157, 162–163, 177–179, 181–182, 193, 195, 206, 210; dismissal *see* Stuart, Anne, princess, later queen, dismisses Marlborough, Sarah Churchill, née Jennings, duchess of; epitaph for the queen 235; influence over Godolphin, Sidney, baron later earl 98–99, 104, 116, 120, 150, 152, 178, 184; offices (groom of the stole, mistress of the robes, keeper of the privy purse, first lady of the bedchamber, ranger of Windsor great park) 76–77, 91, 104, 149, 176, 193; political ambition 77–78, 84, 88, 99, 102, 114, 116–117, 121, 159, 171, 203; view of Masham, Abigail née Hill, later baroness 75, 118–119, 129–130, 132, 136, 155, 158, 170, 187

Mary Beatrice d'Este of Modena, Duchess of York 11–14, 16, 18, 21, 26–32; queen 33–34, 36–37, 39, 43, 65, 94

Masham Abigail, née Hill, later baroness 75, 117–118, 121, 129–131, 133, 140–143, 145, 147–149, 153, 157–159, 165–166, 169, 180, 184, 188, 214, 227, 231; *see also* Marlborough, Sarah Churchill, née Jennings, duchess of; Stuart, Anne, princess, later queen

Masham, Samuel, colonel, later baron 131, 209

Maynwaring, Arthur, sir 141–143, 166, 168, 174, 178, 210–211

Mediterranean, sea 151, 217–218

Mesnager, Nicholas 199–200

Minorca 200, 217

Monmouth, James Scott, duke of 13, 23–24, 76

Mons 163

Montaigne, Michel de 22–23

Moselle, river 90–91, 105

Mulgrave, John Sheffield, earl 15–16

Netherlands *see* Spanish Netherlands

Newfoundland 217

Newmarket 103, 180, 198

Newton, Isaac, sir 103, 139

Nottingham 38

Nottingham, Daniel Finch, earl 70, 80, 88, 102, 106, 108, 115

Nova Scotia 217

Oates, Titus *see* Popish Plot

Occasional Conformity 87–89, 139

On the Conduct of the Allies 204–205; *see also* Swift, Jonathan

Orange, William, prince of *see* William of Orange, King William III

Orangery 126–128

Orford, Edward Russell, earl 162, 165, 170–172

Orléans, duchess of 8

Ormonde, James Butler, duke of 215–216

Oudenarde, battle of *see* Marlborough, John Churchill, duke of; significance of 144, 149, 160

Oxford 38, 230

Oxford, earl *see* Harley, Robert, later Earl of Oxford and Mortimer

Paris 4, 7, 94, 110, 160, 199, 203, 209, 213, 215

Parke, Dan, colonel 95–96

Parliament 12–13, 24–26, 40, 44, 50, 52–53, 60–62, 64, 79–80, 87, 89, 97, 109, 119–120, 156, 176, 187, 200–201, 216, 219–220, 233

peace preliminaries 200–205, 207, 210, 212, 215, 224

Philip, Duc d'Anjou (Bourbon) King Philip V of Spain 64, 110, 114, 160–161, 217

Pope/Papacy 11, 26, 39

Popish Plot 12

Port Mahon *see* Minorca

Pretender *see* Stuart, James Francis Edward, Prince of Wales, the Pretender

print media 68, 88–89, 173, 190, 205

Prior, Matthew 199

Prussia 64, 94–95, 190

Purcell, Henry 19, 25, 118

Quebec expedition 199

Queen Anne's Bounty 88

Ramillies battle of *see* Marlborough, John Churchill, duke of; significance of 114, 119–120, 123–124, 128, 134

Regency Act 110–111, 123, 125, 134, 139, 149, 156, 221, 224, 234

Restraining Order 216, 218–219

Rhine, river 129

Richmond Palace 8, 9, 11, 27, 43

Rochester, Laurence Hyde, earl 17–18, 21, 32, 48, 54, 59, 69–71, 78–80, 83, 102, 106, 115, 174, 189, 199

Rome 71, 157, 180

Ryswick, Treaty of 62, 64–65

Sacheverell, Henry 175–177, 179, 181, 186–187, 204

St. Albans 22, 55, 57–58, 75, 84, 137

St. James's Palace 6, 11, 13, 19, 39, 60, 65, 74, 91, 97, 126, 144, 147–148, 152, 154, 157–159, 177, 191, 195, 208, 219, 225

St. James's park 11, 12, 19, 53, 94, 97, 99, 112, 119, 198

St. John, Henry, later Viscount Bolingbroke 135–136, 138, 189, 190, 196–197, 199–200, 203–205, 209–211, 213–216, 218; attempts to be prime minister 223, 225, 227–230

St. Kitts 217

St. Paul's Cathedral 41, 82, 97, 113, 127, 146–148, 175, 219

Savoy, Prince Eugene of 94–95, 105–106, 113–114, 129, 144, 163–164, 184, 190, 192, 209–210

Schism Act 228

Schütz, Georg von 224–225

Scotland 13–14, 92–94, 110, 124–126, 134, 138–139, 149, 170, 228, 234

Seine, river 94, 159

Settlement, Act of 64, 92, 221

Shrewsbury, Charles Talbot, duke of 45, 57, 60–61, 71, 157, 180–182, 184, 189, 192, 195–196, 200, 228–231

Shrewsbury, duchess of 157, 180

Somers, John, baron 125, 139–140, 144–145, 148–150, 152–153, 155, 169, 172, 174, 181, 189, 195

Somerset, Charles Seymour, duke of 26, 52, 75, 137–138, 180, 194, 207–208

Somerset, Elizabeth Seymour, duchess of 52, 73, 75, 176, 194–195, 205, 207–209, 213–215, 227, 230–232

Sophia of Hanover *see* Hanover, Sophia, electress, later dowager electress of

Sorbonne 7

South Sea Act 219

Spain 24, 64, 98, 129, 135, 160–161, 196, 199, 203, 205, 209–210, 215–218

Spanish Empire 64, 110, 196, 210, 217

Spanish Netherlands 12, 46, 48, 55, 64, 82, 87, 89–90, 94, 96, 105, 112–114, 119, 123, 128, 160, 163–165, 181, 190, 196, 211, 217

Spanish Succession, War of 65, 69–70, 72, 79–80, 95, 112, 135, 160, 172, 191, 195, 201, 212, 217–218, 227, 233–234

Stuart, Anne, princess, later queen; adolescence 11–15; appearance 7, 15, 66–67, 73; cabinet formation 70–72, 156, 180–181, 189, 229; childhood 1–2, 4–**8**, 9–10; coronation 3, 73–74; creates peers 208–209, 218, 224; diligence 76, 79, 81, 86, 107, 109, 112, 127, 147, 155, 230–231, 234; disillusion with Harley, Robert, later Earl of Oxford and Mortimer 223–224, 227–229; dismisses Godolphin, Sidney, baron, later earl 184–186, 206, 229; dismisses Marlborough, John Churchill, duke of 205–207, 211, 218, 229; dismisses

Marlborough, Sarah Churchill, née Jennings, duchess of 183, 188–189, 192–194; domestic policy 85–90, 93–94, 97, 99, 106–107, 119–121, 132, 134, 145, 166; finances 19, 21, 44–46, 53, 76, 88, 131, 144; flight 36–38; friendship 22–23, 26, 29, 53–58, 62, 73, 77, 80, 83–86, 88–89, 91, 98, 104–105, 117, 119, 122, 130–132, 140–142, 145, 149, 186, 195, 198, 208, 211, 214, 223, 231; gardens 91, 125, 127, 147, 152; health 7–8, 11, 58, 60–62, 67, 73–74, 80–81, 85–87, 92, 97, 99, 103, 145, 153, 157, 159, 170, 178, 197, 199, 202, 212–213, 219–220, 224, 230–231, 234; horse racing 103; household 18, 65, 75, 136, 143, 147, 167; hunting 10, 13, 61, 115, *146*–147; marriage 2, 16–20, 72–73, 81, 84, 96, 143, 150, 153–154; Moderation 68, 77–78, 80, 102–104, 106, 111, 114–115, 118, 123, 125, 134–136, 149, 168, 172, 180–181, 187, 213, 229, 233–234; motherhood 20, 23–24, 26–27, 29, 42–43, 48, 54, 57–59, 61, 63, 74; music 10, 19, 25, 54, 83, 97, 112, *127*–128, 194; patriotism 2, 36, 39, 41, 44, 66–69, 75, 115–116, 122, 144, 149, 215; peace policy 114, 161, 165, 170, 172–173, 179, 191, 196, 199–200, 203, 205, 216, 218; popularity 66–68, 73–75, 97, 103, *213*, 221, 233; presence at Lords debates 93–94, 102, 109–111, 126; Princess of Denmark 20–22, 24–25, 27–28, 32–34, 39, 42–43, 47, 49, *58*, 60; quarrel with Stuart, Mary, princess, later queen 46, 48, 50–57, 59; relations with Masham, Abigail, née Hill, later baroness 118, 129–132, 136, 143, 173–174, 180, 194–195, 209, 215, 215, 231; religion 1, 10, 21, 24–31, 35–39, 41, 44, 47, 63, 65–66, 68–69, 74, 77–78, 83–84, 96, 99, 128, 141, 143, 146, 158, 177, 198, 203, 222, 235; royal prerogative 79–80, 95, 102, 104, 115, 122, 128, 132–134, 138–140, 150–152, 168–169, 171, 173, 207, 209, 233; royal progress 80, 103, 105; royal ritual 25, 50, 66–67, 74, 112–13, 126, 183, 194, 210; speech 10, 67–68, 126, 187, 202; speeches from the throne 67, 126, 134, 138, 171, 219, 221; split with Marlborough, Sarah née Jennings, duchess of *85*–86, 88, 92, 98, 100–101, 106–107, 116–117, 121–122, 128, 130–

132, 141–142, 145, 148, 163, 178–179, 183, 191; succession 40–41, 44, 63, 65, 108–109, 110–111, 218, 220, 222, 225–226, 230; Touching for the King's Evil 74–75, 198, 221, 224; Union (with Scotland) policy124–127; war policy 80, 82, 90–91, 94, 96, 98, 106, 113–114, 129, 192, 196; widow154–160, 162, 166
Stuart, Charles I, king 3–4, 10–11, 100, 121
Stuart, Charles II, king 1, 3–17, 19–20, 23, 34, 68, 70, 83, 103, 144, 156, 232, 235
Stuart, Isabella, princess 12–13
Stuart, James, Duke of York 1, 3–*6*-17, 72; King James II 20–21, 23–25, 27–28, 30–31, 33–38, 40–44, 46, 49, 50, 121, 129, 131, 222, 235
Stuart, James Francis Edward, Prince of Wales, the Pretender 42, 49, 59, 63, 65, 68, 70, 74, 77–78, 85, 93–94, 107–108, 110, 138, 160–161, 170, 181, 196, 200, 203–204, 213, 218, 221, 223, 225–226, 228, 231; birth 32–34, 237–239; letters to Stuart, Anne, princess, later queen 217, 222
Stuart, Mary, Princess Royal of England and Princess of Orange 4–5, 11
Stuart, Mary, princess 7–11; Princess of Orange 12, 14, 16–17, 20–21, 24–28, 30, 31, 33, 40–41; queen 42–43, 45–47, 50–54, *55*, 56–60, 66, 74, 79, 101, 107–108, 146, 157, 222, 232, 235
Succession, Act of *see* Settlement, Act of
Sunderland, Charles Spencer, third earl 73, 114–116, 118–120, 122, 124, 128, 134–135, 139, 152, 158, 168, 172, 174, 176–177, 181–183, 185–186, 189, 206
Sunderland, Robert Spencer, second earl 27, 28, 73
Sweden 17, 44, 49, 62, 64
Swift, Jonathan 190, 198, 204–205, 207–208
Syon House 52–55, 73, 77, 176, 207

Tack 73, 99, 102–103
Test Acts 25, 26, 31, 178
Thames, river 5, 8, 22, 27, 41, 126, 159, 171, 196
The Hague *see under* H
Torcy, Jean-Baptiste Colbert, marquis 199
Tory party 1, 2, 45–46, 68–69, 77–78, 80, 82–83, 85, 89, 91, 97–100,

102–104, 106, 108–110, 118, 121–122, 128, 130, 132, 134–136, 139, 150, 152, 166–168, 173, 175, 177, 183–184, 186–187, 194–195, 206–208, 210–213, 221–223, 228–231, 234
Toulon 129, 134
Tournai 163
Tunbridge Wells 23, 32
Turin 114, 123, 128, 134
Turkey 104

Union *see* Scotland
Utrecht, Peace/Treaty of 2, 217–218, 221, 217, 229, 234; city of 201, 208–210, 213, 215–216

Versailles 159–160
Vienna 71, 89, 94–96, 115
Vigo Bay, battle of 82
Villars, Claude, duke of and marshal 163–164
Villiers, Barbara 9, 12, 19
Villiers, Frances, lady 9

West Indies *see* Americas
Westminster Abbey 3, 42, 60, 63, 73–74, 126, 154, 232
Westminster Hall 73–74, 176–177, 208, 231–232
Westmoreland, Thomas Fane, earl 152, 157
Wharton, Thomas, marquis, 110, 125, 153, 156, 158, 172
Whig party 1, 12–13, 46, 68–69, 71, 73, 77–78, 85–86, 89, 91, 94, 100, 102–104, 106–110, 114–116, 118–122, 128, 132, 134–136, 149–152, 168, 173–175, 194–195, 201, 206–211, 213, 216, 221, 223, 225, 229–231, 234; ascendancy 138–139, 153, 155, 158, 161, 164, 170–172, 177, 180, 182–183, 187
Whitehall Palace 6, 18, 24, 41–43, 70, 177
William, Prince of Orange 1, 11, 13, 16–7, 21, 23–25, 27–29, 31–34, 36–41; King William III 42–47, 49–53, 55–56, 59–65, 66–70, 74, 82, 92, 103, 157, 166, 174, 176, 180, 206, 222, 232–233, 235
Winchester 105, 128, 220, 228
Windsor 15, 28, 65, 94, 96, 115, 146, 152, 162, 174, 198
Woodstock 97
Wren, Christopher, sir 126

York, Anne *see* Hyde, Anne, duchess
York, James *see* Stuart, James, Duke of York, later King James II